Violence against Women
in Kentucky

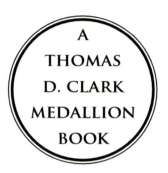

A
THOMAS
D. CLARK
MEDALLION
BOOK

The Thomas D. Clark Medallion was established to honor the memory and contributions of Dr. Thomas Dionysius Clark (1903–2005). A beloved teacher, prolific author, resolute activist, and an enthusiastic advocate of publications about Kentucky and the region, Dr. Clark helped establish the University of Kentucky Press in 1943, which was reorganized in 1969 as the University Press of Kentucky, the state-mandated scholarly publisher for the Commonwealth. The Clark Medallion is awarded annually to one University Press of Kentucky publication that achieves Dr. Clark's high standards of excellence and addresses his wide breadth of interests about the state. Winners of the Thomas D. Clark Medallion are selected by the Board of Directors of the Thomas D. Clark Foundation Inc., a private nonprofit organization established in 1994 to provide financial support for the publication of vital books about Kentucky and the region.

VIOLENCE AGAINST WOMEN IN KENTUCKY

A History of U.S. and State Legislative Reform

CAROL E. JORDAN

UNIVERSITY PRESS OF KENTUCKY

Scholarly publisher for the Commonwealth,
serving Bellarmine University, Berea College, Centre College of Kentucky,
Eastern Kentucky University, The Filson Historical Society, Georgetown College,
Kentucky Historical Society, Kentucky State University, Morehead State
University, Murray State University, Northern Kentucky University, Transylvania
University, University of Kentucky, University of Louisville, and Western
Kentucky University.
All rights reserved.

Editorial and Sales Offices: The University Press of Kentucky
663 South Limestone Street, Lexington, Kentucky 40508-4008
www.kentuckypress.com

Figures by Richard Gilbreath, University of Kentucky Cartography Lab.

Library of Congress Cataloging-in-Publication Data

Jordan, Carol E., author.
  Violence against women in Kentucky : a history of U.S. and state legislative
reform / Carol E. Jordan.
     pages cm
  Includes bibliographical references and index.
  ISBN 978-0-8131-4491-7 (hardcover : alk. paper) —
  ISBN 978-0-8131-4493-1 (pdf) — ISBN 978-0-8131-4494-8 (epub)
  1. Women—Crimes against—Kentucky—History. 2. Family violence—
Kentucky—History. 3. Rape—Kentucky.—History. 4. Law reform—Kentucky—
History. I. Title.
  KFK1767.W53J67 2014
  345.769'02555—dc23   2014003072

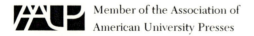

A special thank you to our generous sponsors:

Sue Cumbee Badgett
Mark B. Davis Jr.
Lawrence and Sherry Jelsma
Melanie J. Kilpatrick
Stan MacDonald
Mark and Kate Neikirk
Alice Stevens Sparks
Myra Leigh Tobin
Orme Wilson

To women around the globe who have faced violence and who are so deserving of justice, and to the advocates who steadfastly took on the fight to achieve freedom for and with them.

To my advocate sisters who championed legislative reforms with me, and to the sense of humor we somehow kept despite the craziness of those days pushing our cause in the halls of the state capitol.

To the Kentucky General Assembly and its select brave members who, year after year, took on our cause as their own.

À Ma Famille

À mon pére, plus profondément et toujours.

Et à ma mère qui était présent pour chaque instant de ma vie.

À Michel et Bradley, personne d'autre ne peut être aussi bien passé et l'avenir de mon cœur que vous êtes.

Aux trois enfants qui sont venus au monde, vous êtes la source d'une joie sans fin et, si vos parents le croient ou non, la perfection absolue.

Contents

Preface

If an author must identify the moment when she decided to write a book, for me, it was when I was speaking to a group of women's advocates and they were astonished by the stories I told of the legislative reforms we had made over the past decades. They knew nothing of them. And it was the moment when I noticed that the phone was not ringing as often with people calling to ask me when we had passed a particular piece of legislation addressing rape, domestic violence, or stalking. I took the absence of the ringing phone to mean that this generation of advocates and practitioners was beginning to take reforms for granted, that they did not understand that the protections and services they count on daily were not always available. And it was the moment when a supportive legislator asked me why we advocates were less visible in the halls of the state capitol. And it was certainly the moment when a favorite colleague asked me to write our history. Admittedly, that is four moments, but sometimes it takes repeated encouragement to undertake an awesome task.

This book is a history, a chronicle of legislative reforms related to domestic violence,* rape, and stalking. In addition to articulating what a book offers, it is important for an author to be clear about what a book cannot achieve. This book, for example, cannot provide a total history of women in Kentucky. To provide context, there are snippets of women's history in Kentucky, but the complete story will not be found here. Nor is this book a comprehensive look at the violence against women movement in Kentucky; it is much more narrowly focused on the legislative reforms we have achieved. As this book goes to print, there are still more stories to be told about our movement, more of a history to be written about the development of

---

* Throughout the book, I use the term *domestic violence* to refer to violence between adult intimate partners. Although advocates and scholars are trending toward the term *intimate partner violence*, I retain the older term here because it has been used in most statutes over the years, including in Kentucky. See chapter 2 for a discussion of the different terms of art used in our field and their significance.

domestic violence programs, rape crisis centers, adult protective services reforms, innovative policies, and more. I encourage my readers to make sure those stories are written. This book is a selective look at legislation—just over 100 bills—that I believe impacted the violence against women movement in Kentucky. Arguably, other advocates could point out important bills that should have been included and perhaps some that should have been left on the cutting room floor.

The book is a history of Kentucky, to be sure, but it also covers national reforms, and its guidance for legislative strategies can be applied to any state. The stories of how Kentucky advocates worked to win passage of controversial reforms will resonate with advocates across the country. In this sense, the book is a case study of one state's experience reforming the law on behalf of battered women and rape survivors.

The latter part of the book contains the legislative chronicle. These chapters tell the tales of reforms that sought to restore justice to those from whom it had been stolen and reforms intended to increase the protection of women and children. These legislative accomplishments took several forms. First, and perhaps most visibly, they amended the criminal law by strengthening existing statutes and creating new ones; they amended civil statutes to adapt to the unique needs of rape, domestic violence, and stalking victims; they created and improved protective and other services for women; they articulated special rights for all crime victims; and, finally, they appropriated funding for the critical network of service providers across the state.

The chronology focuses heavily on legislation proposed and drafted by advocates in the anti-rape and domestic violence communities, but it would not be complete without the inclusion of significant reforms made by the General Assembly on its own or with other interest groups. Inclusion of these bills ensures that rape and domestic violence reforms are placed in the context of the criminal justice system of the Commonwealth and other systems of care and protection. The chronicle, particularly for the decade of the 1970s, also notes key legislative reforms related to the legal status of women, including the Equal Rights Amendment and the state codification of Title IX.

The narratives describing each decade in chapters 6–9 consist of four sections. First, I set the stage by describing the climate of the decade and what celebrations, disasters, and events were commanding the attention of Kentuckians. The second section turns to the political landscape, recounting elections and changes in power in the capitol and describing the primary policy and budgetary concerns being addressed by the General Assembly. The third section provides the chronology of bills passed. Finally, for select bills, I include the "colorful" stories behind their passage. The importance of these stories cannot be overstated; they not only enlighten readers about what occurred during a certain legislative session but also provide insight into legislators' and advocates' working environment—whether that included compelling moments in Kentucky history or mundane fights for political power and influence that either ensured a bill's passage or led to its demise.

Compiling a history of legislative reforms is no small task. I relied on the resources of the University of Kentucky College of Law Library to secure copies of the legislative records from 1970 to 2012; the Kentucky house and senate journals; and the bound versions of introduced, amended, and final versions of legislation. I also benefited from my own records of legislation passed each session since the beginning of my career in this field—spreadsheets covering 1982 to 2012. Finally, my files also included records from each of the task forces and councils on which I served (or that I staffed), which proposed a significant number of the bills described herein.

Another invaluable source of memories, facts, stories, and opinions was the almost forty interviews I conducted in the course of writing this book. I interviewed advocates who led the legislative reform movement. (I only wish I could have interviewed everyone who contributed in this way.) I interviewed legislators who honorably acted as sponsors and shepherds for our legislation. (I finally got to ask them why they were willing to take on such controversial legislation.) I interviewed governors whose administrations saw the passage of seminal legislation, as well as one very special Kentucky First Lady. Attorneys and legislative staff also offered unique insights. Finally, I am grateful to the family members of women lost to violence and to the women who survived it for their insightful and emotional interviews. Their perspectives enrich this book and remind us why it had to be written.

Storytelling involves some risk for those who undertake it, for it relies on well-intended but fallible memories—memories that were once clear but may have faded with time. I am indebted to all my colleagues and the survivors and family members who shared their memories to bolster my own and to ensure that the tales told here are true reflections of events occurring in the halls of the General Assembly. Any inaccuracies or omissions are entirely unintended and terribly regretted, even before I know what they are. There is one more caution for readers: This book is intended to be a history and a tool of learning; it is not intended to reflect the current state of any particular statute. For that, advocates should always turn to the statutes and court rules themselves, which are updated annually.

Acknowledgments

When one person decides to write a book, 200 should duck, because it takes at least that many to make the pages come to life. For this book, there may have been a single author, but I would not have been able to complete the project without the help of many others.

To Pat and John Byron, Paul Doyle, Burniece Whitaker Minix, Lisa Murray, Holly Dunn Pendleton, and Diana Ross, who allowed their stories and those of their daughters and mother to be used in this book.

To the almost forty people who shared their memories and stories in interviews with me, making this book as much theirs as mine.

A special thanks to Steve Wrinn, director of the University Press of Kentucky, whose encouragement and guidance proved priceless. All authors should be as lucky as I was to find a publisher like him.

A grateful nod to Sherry Currens for her invaluable input on draft versions of the book, and to the incredible anonymous colleagues inside of Kentucky and out who reviewed and critiqued the book before it was finalized. And a second nod to Eileen Recktenwald, whose encouragement for me to write this book was among the loudest.

For helping me find historical photographs, I am indebted to John Perkins, Office of the Governor; Lisa Thompson, Kentucky Department of Libraries and Archives; Charlotte Land and Tonya Capito, Legislative Research Commission; Ron Garrison, *Lexington Herald-Leader*; Jaime M. Bradley, Special Collections and Archives at Berea College; Delinda Stephens Buie, Special Collections at the University of Louisville; Jason Flahardy and Deirdre Scaggs, Special

Collections at the University of Kentucky; and Nancy Sherbert, Kansas State Historical Society.

For aiding me with the hours and hours of research the book required, my thanks to Laurie Depuy and Emily Lane, Center for Research on Violence Against Women at the University of Kentucky; Tina M. Brooks, College of Law at the University of Kentucky; Gerald Smith, College of Arts and Sciences at the University of Kentucky; Jamie Lucke, *Lexington Herald-Leader*; Eleanor Jordan, Kentucky Commission on Women; Tim Tingle, Kentucky Department of Libraries and Archives; and Dudley Cotton and Stuart Weatherford, Legislative Research Commission.

Introduction

The Commonwealth's history is rich with dramatic stories—sometimes glorious and sometimes violent—of coalfields, conflicts, horses, sports legends, and bourbon. These stories not only tell the history of Kentucky but also tie its past to its future, as the lessons of history still inform Kentucky's present. These stories also humorously depict Kentucky as being famous for its fast horses, bourbon, and beautiful women. This characterization would suggest that women are part of the documented annals of Kentucky, but a more serious read of history shows they are not. Historians have been all too silent when it comes to telling the stories of Kentucky women and their experiences.

A vibrant story exists under that silence. And an important part of that narrative involves more than a century of fighting for women's rights. Women have fought for the right to vote, the right to own property, the right to have a job and control their wages, the right to obtain custody of their children, and more. And, with their lives at stake, women have fought to be free from violence. Lost in the silence surrounding women's history in Kentucky are cries that reverberate across generations from women whose lives have been marred by men's violence—unwelcome, unwanted, terrifying violence.

This book's primary aim is to give voice to the stories of Kentucky women who have faced rape, domestic violence, and stalking and to the stories of Kentucky women and their legislative allies who have changed the law on their behalf. There are many ways to recount such a history. This book uses the vehicle of storytelling to share the tales of those who waged the legislative fight for suffrage and other legal rights; those who took up that newfound freedom and devoted themselves to public service; those who undertook the legislative effort to protect women from domestic violence, rape, and stalking; and those who served as the inspiration for these reforms by bravely telling their personal stories of the harshest kind of human cruelty.

1

The stories of these women were, and are, powerfully interwoven, merging the personal and the political and, in so doing, shaping the women's reform movements of the past century and the law of today.

While the legislative reforms that are central to this book began in the 1970s, the story begins in the nineteenth century, when women first fought for the rights on which we would build our reform efforts a century later (see chapter 1). In the 1900s women's advocates across the country adopted the mantles of the suffrage movement and the temperance movement. Suffrage and temperance issues were aligned because both movements had the mission of freeing women—from legal and social powerlessness and from violence and mistreatment. Reforms achieved in the 1900s brought economic freedom and increased legal standing, and they gave women a voice in the electoral process and a place in public service. After these priority reforms were secured in the 1920s, the women's reform movement seemed less urgent. It became less visible, and the progress in securing women's freedoms slowed for more than forty years.

It was not until the late 1960s that a second reform movement reignited the battle for women's rights. This second wave of the women's movement gave rise to the anti-rape and domestic violence movements, which began in earnest across the nation in the 1970s and combined activism; the development of grassroots, woman-run services for rape victims and battered women; and legislative efforts to reform the criminal and civil justice systems. Prior to these reforms, all too often the U.S. criminal and civil justice systems, rather than alleviating suffering, only extended the trauma experienced by rape survivors and battered women. Many of these women found the justice system a harsh and even punitive place where fairness and protection were lacking. In Kentucky, women who were raped were subjected to a hot and unforgiving spotlight as their rapists' trials began, questioned about their own private sexual histories and asked whether they had really wanted to stop the rape. Others never made it to court, their cases rejected because they did not fight off the rapist with sufficient force or did not report the offense within a certain period of time. Women raped by their spouses learned that the law did not even consider their egregious assaults a crime. Victims of domestic violence found themselves similarly situated, asked by reluctant police officers what they had done to provoke their violent husbands or told there was nothing the law could do. Stalking victims had neither a name nor a law that acknowledged their experience, much less a remedy. Whether Kentucky women sought justice from the courts or simply protection from future violence, more often than not, they encountered a justice system unable or unwilling to come to their aid. And though it may be startling to today's advocates, prior to the women-led reforms of the 1970s, victims and survivors had to face their ordeals alone, as rape crisis centers and battered women's shelters, which are the bedrock of services today, did not yet exist on the landscape. Women's experiences and the definitions and prevalence of violence are discussed in chapter 2.

The first two decades of the domestic violence and anti-rape movements resulted in more legal reforms for women than the previous three centuries combined. These successes did not come easily, as they were often based on legal treatises and theories that were centuries old. Nonetheless, reform was achieved because of advocates' strong will and insistence that women's lives should be violence free. Chapters 3 and 4 provide an overview of the rape, domestic violence, and stalking legislative reforms taking place across the nation from the 1970s through the 2000s, setting the tone for reforms that would follow in the Commonwealth. Chapter 5 turns from what was accomplished to how it was done, discussing the legislative strategies used and how tomorrow's advocates can continue the reforms of previous generations.

As advocacy grew in communities across the Commonwealth and at the state level, Kentucky women found believers in the General Assembly, legislators in both chambers and from both sides of the political aisle who came together to protect women and improve their lives. Chapters 6–9 provide a decade-by-decade account of the laws specifically related to rape, domestic violence, and stalking that were passed by the Kentucky General Assembly from the 1970s through 2012. Some of the bills found easy passage, while others were so controversial that they seemed to set the capitol on fire. Some were initiated by the legislators themselves, others came from coalitions of advocates, and still others were proposed by executive and legislative branch task forces and councils. Kentucky's first anti-rape legislation passed in 1976, establishing a rape shield law in criminal cases. The first domestic violence laws, passed two years later, created a uniform reporting form for law enforcement agencies and added spouses to the mandatory reporting laws in Kentucky. These earliest bills hint at what is revealed by a forty-year analysis of

Kentucky's legislative reforms: the majority of rape-related reforms over the years have involved changes in the criminal law and in the forensic medical responses to rape, while domestic violence reforms have focused on expanding civil protections and instituting policy and practice reforms directed at law enforcement and prosecutors.

In addition to the legislation specifically targeting violence against women, an equal number of bills with a broader focus have had a dramatic impact on battered women, rape survivors, and stalking victims. These include the Kentucky Penal Code, the Kentucky Rules of Evidence, family court legislation, and others. In combination, the 100-plus laws covered in this book are representative of Kentucky's legislative reforms specifically addressing or dramatically impacting violence against women. Chapter 10 summarizes and analyzes the past four decades of reforms related to domestic violence, rape, and stalking and reflects on how to move forward.

The primary purpose of this book is to use the vehicle of storytelling to chronicle Kentucky's legislative response to rape, domestic violence, and stalking from 1970 to 2012. It tells the stories of bills passed and a few that failed; the stories of brave advocates and those who were successful because they just acted like they were brave; the stories of honorable legislative champions and others whose roles in our legislative history would earn them stellar reputations in the anti-rape and domestic violence communities. And throughout this chronicle, there are stories of survivors and their families who helped shaped legislative ideals and inspired their passage.

Beyond giving a colorful recitation of individual bills and their passage, this book reminds us that when the Constitution of the Commonwealth was adopted in the nineteenth century and when the state's first penal code was written, the laws that now protect battered women and rape survivors did not exist. Each law that now shields a woman from harm or ensures her justice after experiencing violence resulted from the efforts of advocates who, year after year and session after session, made their presence known in the state capitol and insisted that changes be made. The fact that the strength of our current laws is the result of long-fought battles should never be forgotten by today's advocates. The new generation of women's advocates who inhabit the halls of state capitols and staff crisis programs is part of a profoundly important and successful movement of reformers who began their work decades ago.

This book is also intended to remind readers that what has been hard won is not necessarily permanently held. Passage of a bill is never the end of a legislative effort. As noted in the 1980s, "The most important part of any legislation is how decision makers put the provisions of the statutes into practice; unfortunately, once legislation is passed, it is mistakenly credited with solving the problem" (Stanko, 1985, p. 165). Clearly, we ignore the implementation of legislative reforms at our peril. As so aptly put by Susan Schechter, "it is necessary to save what we have won" (Schechter, 1982, p. 4). As legislative reforms are put into practice, the need for additional changes in the law is always revealed. And as the needs of women change, laws must evolve to keep pace. The next generation must be ready to respond to the new wave of legislative reform (see chapter 5).

As every great legislative reform was accomplished, we made a steadfast commitment to the next generation of women that we would devote ourselves to ensuring that their lives would be violence free. To hold steadfast to that promise, we must now affirm anew, this time to the advocates of the next generation, that we will share all we achieved, teach all we learned, and inspire them to achieve even more for Kentucky's women than did we.

1

Kentucky Women
and the Advocates
Who Fought for Them

Kentucky women are not idiots—even though they are closely
related to Kentucky men.
                    —Madeline McDowell Breckinridge, 1915
                              (quoted in Irvin, 2009)

One gets a sense of Kentucky from its mountains in the east and
its fields stretching across the Mississippi plains in the west; from
its high buildings and urban face to its rural green landscapes;
and, collectively, from its boundaries with seven other states.
Kentuckians' connection to the land has been captured by state
historian James Klotter: "For many Kentuckians the land continues to provide their roots, giving generation after generation a
sense of place, a tie that binds them to those who have walked the
ground before them, a bridge from past to present" (Appleton,
Hay, Klotter, & Stephens, 1998, p. 11). Kentucky's land informs
its identity and its name. The latter reflects the Commonwealth's
conflicting reputations in its early years. The name *Kentucky* is of
Native American origin and has been attributed to several different Indian languages with several different meanings, including
the Iroquois word *Ken-tah-ten*, which means "land of tomorrow,"
and a second translation that means "dark and bloody ground."
For the first century of Kentucky's statehood, the latter seemed a
more apt description.

A HISTORY OF VIOLENCE

In the nineteenth century, Kentucky's homicide rate was more than twice what it is today (Ireland, 2000). As noted by one writer, "While nineteenth century Kentucky produced fine horses, hemp and whiskey, she excelled most in crime" (Ireland, 1983, p. 134). In fact, Kentucky held the distinction of having one of the highest crime rates in the nation in those years (Wall, 2010). One of the primary causes of this rampant aggression was a code of honor rooted in the sacredness of men's reputations. Any affront or embarrassment, no matter how trivial, often led to a duel and the attendant loss of life. For this reason, most homicides in the nineteenth century involved the killing of men by men (Ireland, 2000). Women sometimes found themselves drawn into the violence when it entailed acts of individual retribution, such as when one man killed another for having sex with his wife. In one such case reported by Harrison and Klotter (1997), in April 1883 Congressman Philip B. Thompson Jr. of Harrodsburg killed a man who had allegedly "debauched" his wife. He was acquitted by a Kentucky jury. In another case from the 1890s, an irate husband in Louisville caught his wife in an intimate position with the son of former governor John Young Brown; he shot and killed them both but was found not guilty. (John Young Brown served as governor from 1891 to 1895; he is not related to Governor John Y. Brown Jr., who served from 1979 to 1983.)

The end of the Civil War and Reconstruction brought another kind of violence to Kentucky: racial killings and lynchings. Fully one-third of these acts occurred in the counties of the Commonwealth between 1865 and 1874 (Wright, 1990). Kentucky had been a border state in the Civil War, yet its severe and brutal treatment of African Americans in the years after the war rivaled that of the Deep South. Ironically, Kentucky's loyalty to the North during the war meant that its citizens were allowed to rule their own affairs during Reconstruction, unlike those in the former Confederate states; this laissez-faire approach meant that federal officials often turned a blind eye as freed slaves suffered under the rope and by the whip of hostile whites who had supported the Union cause and resented the racial equality intended by emancipation (Wright, 1990).

Assassinations also accounted for some homicide cases, as election days in the nineteenth century were often followed by violent arguments between political parties and the killing of candidates or elected officials. The most famous assassination occurred in 1900 when newly elected governor William Goebel was shot and killed as he neared the state's capitol (Powell, 2001). Violence and homicide in the nineteenth century can also be attributed to family feuds that originated in conflicts over the Civil War, tobacco, and coal, exacerbated by growing rates of alcoholism and perhaps even the lax justice system that prevailed at the time (Klotter, 2003; Wall, 2010).

In her book on the impact of violence on the reputation of Kentucky's horse industry, Maryjean Wall describes how violence and lawlessness influenced horsemen to choose horse farms in the Northeast rather than exposing themselves to the brutality in the hills of the Commonwealth. She shares a quote from the *New York Times* that reflects Kentucky's violent reputation: "So long as these midnight assassins continue to ply their trade within the shadow of the state capitol, Kentucky has no claim to be considered a civilized state" (Wall, 2010, p. 93).

The beginning of the twentieth century saw a decline in the homicide rate in Kentucky, largely because some of its primary causes (the honor code, lynchings, and family feuds) began to decline. Importantly, however, a tradition of violence would persist. As noted by one historian, "murderous violence within families continues to be a problem, as do occasional outbursts of violence during the labor disputes in the coalfields. One has to wonder whether Kentucky residents today are safer from violence than the Kentuckians who lived a hundred years ago" (Ireland, 2000, p. 170). Despite the trend toward lower homicide rates, the settings in which killings occurred suggested that, for women, this did not mean an improvement in their safety.

THE HISTORY OF KENTUCKY WOMEN

The archives of Kentucky's history are strangely silent on the experience of women. Historians note that before 1900, women experienced the same hardships as men, but they were almost invisible in any written records and other documentation (Harrison & Klotter, 1997; Potter, 1997). "Too few pre–Civil War Kentucky women left accounts of their lives, and so they remain somewhat vague figures in the background of the period. They were indispensable to the development of the state, although they seldom appear in its public records" (Harrison & Klotter, 1997, p. 148). The inadequacy of written history belies the fact that women lived with the same challenges as their male counterparts, but they did so without the legal rights afforded men. And, as the next chapter attests, they lived with significant exposure to, and little relief from, violence.

Throughout the first century of Kentucky's statehood (secured in April 1792), women had few legal rights. Women could not vote, make a will, own property, control their own wages, or obtain custody of their children (Crowe-Carraco, 2000). When a woman married, both she and any property she may have inherited became the property of her new husband (Harrison & Klotter, 1997). If a woman married an intolerable, cruel, or violent man, she had few options. Although divorce was legal in the years after statehood, the burden of proof was on the woman, who had the difficult task of complaining about her husband's cruelty while living under society's rule that she must endure and obey (Harrison & Klotter, 1997). There were few pathways for women to escape their plight, in part because they had little opportunity to go to school past the lowest grades. Any advanced education was likely to be a finishing school that prepared upper-class girls for life as "genteel ladies" (Harrison & Klotter, 1997).

At the turn of the twentieth century, working women were most often employed by Kentucky industry, the higher (or so-called white-collar) professions being closed to them. In fact, almost 45,000 females over ten years of age were employed in Louisville factories in the early 1900s (Irvin, 2009). Mirroring the decades that would follow, women were paid less than men and, for the most part, were excluded from unions (Irvin, 2009). The latter left them powerless in the face of twelve- to fourteen-hour days, even as men successfully pushed for eight-hour workdays.

Thus, for much of its early history, the Commonwealth trailed other states in affording women legal protections. The antebellum women's rights movement that had gained attention in other parts of the country had not yet attracted the attention or interest of women in Kentucky (Harrison & Klotter, 1997). And when the national Seneca Falls Convention launched the first women's movement in America in July 1848, Kentucky seemed oblivious.

THE HISTORY OF WOMEN'S ADVOCATES IN KENTUCKY

While the vast majority of Kentuckians in the 1800s and 1900s seemed content to ignore the national women's movement, a small

Laura Clay, August 1917. (Courtesy of Special Collections, University of Louisville)

group of women began to make waves, seeking to improve the status of Kentucky women. They faced a daunting task. Kentucky was among the most backward states when it came to women's rights, as it had not adopted the progressive reforms embraced by other states. Because it had not seceded from the Union during the Civil War, it had not experienced the postwar constitutional revisions that improved the status of women in the former Confederate states (Irvin, 2009). Among the early reformers who joined the national fight were Laura Clay, Madeline "Madge" McDowell Breckinridge, Mary E. Britton, Josephine Henry, Lida Calvert Obenchain, Linda Neville, Cora Wilson Stewart, Mary Breckinridge, and Eliza Calvert Hall (Crowe-Carraco, 2000; Fuller, 1992; Hay, 2009; Niedermeier, 2007). These women lived in eastern, western, and central Kentucky, but they fought for women across the Commonwealth.

Laura Clay was born in 1849, less than a year after the eruption of the first women's movement at the Seneca Falls Convention.

For her, the struggle for women's rights was deeply personal as well as political (Fuller, 1992; Irvin, 2009). During Clay's childhood, her father, Cassius Clay, served as ambassador to Russia and lived in Europe, away from his family, for nine years. While he was away (first in Russia and later on exploits to Mexico and while campaigning for anti-slavery political candidates), Clay's mother, Mary Jane Warfield Clay, made extensive improvements to the family's estate, which became a profitable farm under her watchful eye and hard-working hands. She devoted her time, hard work, family money, and ingenuity to the farm. She also oversaw vast renovations to the family home, White Hall, and succeeded in repaying her husband's debt when his bank failed.

Cassius Clay eventually returned to Kentucky, bringing with him a Russian boy whose paternity he did not deny. That affront was the breaking point in what had become a very difficult marriage. Mary Jane Clay left and took her daughters Laura and Annie, the only two children still living at home, to her family's residence in Lexington. Mrs. Clay charged her husband with breach of the marriage contract, but he ultimately filed for divorce against her, ironically charging that she had deserted him for five years (as required by Kentucky's divorce law at the time). Mary Jane Clay was fortunate that her wealthy family saved her from the poverty that otherwise would have been her lot. After the divorce, she lost all access to and possession of White Hall, its properties, and its resources. Some have speculated that Laura Clay became such a fervent activist for women's rights because of her firsthand knowledge of the challenges encountered by women who lived without the benefit of legal rights (Fuller, 1992). In Laura Clay, the women's rights movement in Kentucky found a champion. She founded the Kentucky Woman Suffrage Association (KWSA) and the Kentucky Equal Rights Association (KERA) and left a lasting mark on the Commonwealth.

Madeline "Madge" McDowell Breckinridge, a descendant of Henry Clay, was born in 1872. Like Laura Clay, her personal history may well have influenced her choice to participate in social movements on behalf of those in need. Her early years were marred by health problems, family conflicts, and marital infidelities. She suffered from tuberculosis of the bone in her right foot, requiring her to wear a formidable boot with sturdy braces on each side. She endured multiple surgeries, and at age twenty-four, her right foot was amputated. By then, the tubercle bacilli had invaded her body and left her susceptible to the disease for the rest of her life (Hay, 2009). Breckinridge's reaction to the amputation was a marvel. Many young women of her day would have withdrawn from social life after losing a foot, but she did exactly the opposite. According to her biographer, "for Madge the coming years would prove that adversity only invigorated her, while physical suffering increased her empathy for the poor, the sick, and the downtrodden. . . . Instead of retreating from the world, Madge began to focus on reforming it. . . . Her belief in women's rights had begun to emerge" (Hay, 2009, p. 46).

Breckinridge enrolled in college (at what would later become the University of Kentucky), attending on a part-time basis from 1890 to 1894. She used her writing skills to publish articles in the *Lexington Herald* on the causes in which she so fervently believed. Her gift with words made her one of the most quotable women's activists in Kentucky and across the nation, and she was known for electrifying her suffrage audiences (Tice, 1997). Her activism led her to become president of the Kentucky Equal Rights Association and vice president of the National American Woman Suffrage Association. In the latter role, she lobbied for Kentucky's ratification of the Nineteenth Amendment, which gave women the right to vote in 1920. Her lifetime of work provided a lasting benefit to the women of the Commonwealth and beyond. In 1914 Madeline Breckinridge and Laura Clay became the first women to address a joint session of the Kentucky legislature, bravely blazing a path for the women's advocates who would follow them.

Communicating to the General Assembly, in this case through written commentary, also became a regular practice for another Lexington woman in the late 1800s. In 1892 Mary E. Britton wrote a highly critical article published in the *Kentucky Leader* explicating why the legislature should not pass a law that required blacks and whites to ride in separate railway coaches (Smith, 2002). While her articulate opinion piece did not stop passage of the law, it was an exemplar of the advocacy that would become part of Mary Britton's everyday life. She was born in Lexington in 1855, the daughter of a free black couple. She grew up in an era when little black girls were not expected to strive for careers of any kind, and certainly not the career path the outspoken and accomplished Britton would pursue (Eblen, 2012). At age sixteen, she enrolled in Berea College (the first college or university in Kentucky to admit African Americans), where she learned to connect teaching with social activism. After

Madeline McDowell Breckinridge, circa 1900. (Courtesy of Special Collections, University of Kentucky)

Dr. Mary E. Britton, circa 1900. (Courtesy of Special Collections and Archives, Berea College)

five years in Berea, Britton returned to Lexington, where she taught in the segregated schools of that era. It was during this time that she wrote the *Kentucky Leader* commentary. Britton's social activism for educational and civil rights was soon joined by a desire to improve health care in the African American community. To address this need directly, Britton went to Chicago and graduated with a medical degree from the American Missionary College. In 1902 she became the first black woman in Lexington to obtain a medical license, and for two decades she practiced medicine from her home, a practice heavily influenced by her conversion to the Seventh Day Adventist Church (Wilkinson, 2000). In addition to her busy medical career, Britton remained active as a fighter for civil rights and women's rights. She died in Lexington in 1925.

Laura Clay, Madge Breckinridge, Mary Britton, and other reformers in the nineteenth and twentieth centuries fought for a wide range of women's rights. Suffrage, the right to express their views and to influence the political sphere, was a prominent part of their platform. Legal reforms, such as the right to own property, secure custody of their children, and control their wages, also gained the attention of the reform movement, as did health care, maternal and child care, and the needs of the poor. Slowly, their efforts in Kentucky paid off: in 1894, laws were passed allowing women to own property and to make wills; female physicians were permitted to work in women's wards in hospitals in 1898; in 1900, women were given the right to keep their own earnings; and in 1910, women won the right to seek custody of their children, and the age at which Kentucky girls could legally marry was raised from twelve to sixteen (Crowe-Carraco, 2000; Irvin, 2009).

The advancement of women's education was also exceedingly important. Once they were admitted to institutions of higher education, these educated and empowered women were in a better position to advocate on behalf of their gender. The University of Kentucky (initially called the Agricultural and Mechanical College of Kentucky) was established in 1865, and the first women were admitted in 1880. These first female students were allowed to earn only certificates, not degrees; it would be 1888 before the first woman broke the barrier and graduated with a degree from the university. Parenthetically, while the University of Kentucky is well known for its men's basketball program, the first basketball team at the university was the women's team (University of Kentucky, 2010). Transylvania University opened its doors to women in 1889, and Georgetown did so in 1892; Berea had admitted women from its founding (Crowe-Carraco, 2000). The modern University of Louisville and the normal (teacher training) schools in western and eastern Kentucky were established in the early twentieth century and admitted women from their inception. A century later, women accounted for more than half the undergraduate (54 percent) and graduate (60 percent) student populations (Sugarman, 1999).

As suffragists campaigned for the vote and other social and legal reforms, the temperance movement addressed what many viewed as the evils of "intoxicating spirits." In Kentucky, the suffrage and temperance movements were often aligned. At a practical level, the older temperance movement (led in Kentucky by Madison County native Frances Beauchamp from 1895 until her death in 1923) was helpful to the suffragists, in that it tended to be more well organized (Irvin, 2009). Opponents of the two movements also bonded; many of the business interests that opposed the temperance movement also opposed suffrage, fearing that if women were given the right to vote, then they would vote for prohibition (Kee, Frost, Albu, Lindberg, & Robert, 1998). Temperance and suffrage issues were also aligned because the social ills targeted by the temperance movement disproportionately impacted women. In that sense, both movements had the mission of freeing women—from legal powerlessness and from violence and mistreatment. The work of the temperance movements across the nation ultimately resulted in the Eighteenth Amendment, banning the manufacture, sale, and transportation of alcohol and signaling the beginning of Prohibition.[1] Kentucky ratified the Eighteenth Amendment in 1919, the same year it became law.

Among the most visible and controversial leaders of the national temperance movement was Carry A. Nation, born Carry Amelia Moore on November 25, 1846, on a farm in Garrard County, Kentucky.[2] At the time of her birth, Garrard County was a "hotbed of religious fervor" that included the strict order of the Shakers and the enthusiastic revivals held at Cane Ridge (Grace, 2001). Her own family members were devout Protestants. The marriage of Nation's parents was a second union for both, each having been widowed. Nation's father, George Moore, had been financially successful in the years before the Civil War, but because he depended heavily on slave labor, he lost his economic stability with emancipation. Nation had a close but rather conflicted relationship with her father; though their bond was deep and affectionate, he could be harsh and occasionally violent (Grace, 2001). Nation's relationship with her mother was distant, likely owing to Mary Moore's emotional instability, which some have depicted as severe mental illness (or, in the nomenclature of the day, insanity). Mary's first husband and two sons had died in close succession before she was even twenty years old. Her second husband, George Moore, was significantly older than Mary and had four children from his first marriage. According to some stories, insanity ran in Mary's family, and she supposedly had delusions with a paranoid quality, believing herself to be Queen Victoria and expressing concerns about being killed. When her delusions became unmanageable, she was ultimately hospitalized in an insane asylum (Grace, 2001; Irvin, 2009).

Carry Nation's first husband was a physician named Charles Gloyd, but his alcoholism led her to leave him shortly after the marriage. From this experience, she acquired both a personal distaste for alcohol and one child, Charlien, who was infirm from birth and spent part of her adult years in an insane asylum (like her grand-mother). Her second husband, whom she married in 1877, was David Nation, a minister who shared her fervent religious faith. His career as a traveling preacher took the young couple to Texas and then to a Christian church in Medicine Lodge, Kansas, in 1889. It was there that she helped establish a local chapter of the Women's Christian Temperance Union, which became her vehicle for speaking out against alcohol and two other "evils": tobacco and women's immodest dress.

In Kansas, residents had voted for prohibition, but the law was rarely enforced until Nation took action. At first, beginning in 1890, she merely knelt in prayer in front of saloons. By 1900, however, she had adopted a more violent and confrontational approach, using rocks and bricks until she finally settled on the instrument that would make her famous: the hatchet.

In 1901 Nation met with Kansas governor William Stanley to appeal for enforcement of the state's laws. When the governor gave her no assurances, she pointed to a black eye she had received during a demonstration in Enterprise, Kansas, and accused the governor of giving her that black eye. A rattled Governor Stanley told her that women had to know their place; they should not be raising the kind of disturbance that came so naturally to Nation (Grace, 2001; Nation, 1909).

In the end, Carry Nation led a movement with no followers and fought her battle alone. She may have been the most visible figure associated with the temperance movement, but her hatchet-wielding ways were not endorsed by the national Women's Christian Temperance Union. Although she fought for women's rights (supporting suffrage because she viewed women's votes as votes in favor of prohibition), feminists were not comfortable with her intensely religious dogma; likewise, the religious community distanced itself from her because she was a staunchly independent woman who had "deserted" her husband (Grace, 2001). That she became somewhat of a caricature should not obscure her historical importance. As noted by one of her biographers: "Yet many people were oddly compelled by her. She galvanized thousands of followers to pursue a radical form of activism. . . . Carry Nation's emergence as a reformer underscores the power of tragedy in formation of a crusading identity" (Grace, 2001, p. 281).

Among the temperance activists in Kentucky was an African

Carry Nation, circa 1901–1911. (Courtesy of Kansas State Historical Society)

American woman named Elizabeth B. "Lizzie" Fouse. She was already well known for her work with the National Association of Colored Women (serving as its president), her founding of the Phyllis Wheatley branch of the YWCA in Lexington, and her strong advocacy for the education of young women of color. When the first state convention of the Kentucky Women's Christian Temperance Union (KWCTU) was held in Lexington in 1881, however, she was not involved: membership was not open to African American women. In the early 1900s the KWCTU began to organize auxiliary unions that African American women could join. Ultimately, all the auxiliary branches broke away from the KWCTU and created the Kentucky Sojourner Truth Woman's Christian Temperance Union, with Fouse as president (Notable Kentucky African Americans Database, 2011). Fouse died in October 1952. Her tombstone in Cove Haven Cemetery reads: "To Live in Hearts We Leave Behind Is Not to Die" (Smith, 2002).

WOMEN AND SUFFRAGE

As noted above, suffrage was central to the fight for women's rights in the early twentieth century. But it was an extremely difficult goal to obtain, as the opposition was strong. Opponents of women's suffrage argued against what they saw as a "social revolution" and "a loss of sexual identity" (Thébaud, 1997). Henry Watterson, editor of the *Louisville Courier-Journal*, called the suffragists "silly-sallies," "crazy Janes," and "red-nosed angels" (Irvin, 2009). J. W. Porter, editor of the *Kentucky Baptist* newspaper, wrote that the National Suffrage Association had originated "out of the brain of a semi-masculine Minerva. . . . Its ultimate ideal is to de-womanize the woman and make of her a female man. . . . The feminine demons, knowingly or otherwise, are pointing womankind to the path that leads to harlotry and to hell" (Morgan, 2003, p. 22). Those naysayers were ultimately drowned out when Congress passed the Nineteenth Amendment in 1919 and when it was ratified by thirty-six states in 1920 (including Kentucky on January 6, 1920).

Ironically, women in Kentucky had been given the right to vote in 1838, making it the first state in the country to do so (Crowe-Carraco, 2000). That right was something of a trompe l'oeil, however. It was limited to only one situation: widows with school-age children who lived in rural school districts were allowed to vote for

Elizabeth "Lizzie" Fouse, circa 1880s. (Courtesy of Special Collections, University of Kentucky)

members of the school board. In 1902 even that right was rescinded because people claimed it allowed too many illiterate black women to vote (Crowe-Carraco, 2000). Thus, in addition to being the first state to give women the vote, Kentucky had the distinction of being one of only two states to rescind that right.

Despite the centrality of suffrage to the women's movement, not all activists took the same approach. In fact, a major split occurred in the final stretch before suffrage was secured in August 1920. In the end, suffrage was won not via state laws but through a federal constitutional amendment. A staunch states' rights advocate, Laura Clay fought the federal amendment, arguing that voting rights were a state matter. What lay behind the states' rights argument, in the view of many, was actually the issue of race. Though a formidable and highly successful women's activist, Clay was also a white supremacist, as were many others at the time (Irvin, 2009). The argument for state-level decision making became an argument over whether black women should be given the right to vote. Clay urged that an education requirement be implemented for women voters. Although not specifically referring to race, the practical effect of such a requirement would be to disqualify black women from voting because of their limited educational opportunities. Sadly, as women were finally winning the right to vote, suffragists in Kentucky were split. Laura Clay had appointed Madge Breckinridge to follow her as president of the KERA, but in the end, their ideologies were far apart.

Kentucky Women and Public Office

Oddly, more than two decades before women won legal suffrage in 1920, they were being elected to public office in the Commonwealth.[3] At first, women won some local elections in Kentucky (even though they could not vote for themselves), but in 1923, things changed. Once suffrage passed, the question became not just what women would do with the vote but also what impact their votes would have on the election of women to public office. That spring, those questions led Democratic Party officials to discuss the idea of placing a woman on the statewide ticket. Emma Guy Cromwell was serving as state librarian for the Kentucky legislature when she heard rumors of those discussions and rumors that she was being considered. In fact, the party asked Cromwell to run for secretary of state—an invitation she accepted. In winning, Cromwell became Kentucky's first

Emma Guy Cromwell, circa 1925–1936. (*Herald-Post* Collection, courtesy of Special Collections, University of Louisville)

woman to hold an elected statewide office. As she mused on the night of her election, "It was a question of whether Kentucky women had upheld a woman candidate, and whether men had carried their traditional Kentucky gallantry and chivalry to the polls to do justice to womanhood. . . . Those questions were settled when the vote was counted" (Cromwell, 1996, p. 51). In her role as secretary of state, Cromwell also became the first woman to serve as acting governor (when the governor and lieutenant governor were both out of state while attending the Democratic National Convention). After serving as secretary of state for one term, Cromwell went on to be elected state treasurer in 1927 and then failed in an effort to recapture the secretary of state position.

Thirty years later, another Kentucky woman would use the post of secretary of state as a springboard to higher office. After serving three terms in the house, Thelma Stovall set her sights on a state-level post and won election as secretary of state in 1956. In the political equivalent of musical chairs, Stovall and two other perennial candidates traded off terms in the posts of secretary of state and state treasurer. (At the time, Kentucky law did not allow successive terms in those offices.) Stovall won a term as secretary state (1956), followed by a term as state treasurer (1960), then secretary of state (1964), state treasurer (1968), and secretary of state (1972). While serving as secretary of state, Stovall assumed the role of acting governor when both the governor and the lieutenant governor were out of state, doing so to take the controversial step of pardoning three convicted offenders. This would not be Stovall's last provocative act while serving in the capacity of acting governor.

In 1975 Stovall became the first woman in Kentucky to achieve a higher statewide office when she was elected lieutenant governor. At one point in 1978, when Governor Julian Carroll traveled out of state, Stovall invoked her powers as acting governor to call the Kentucky General Assembly into special session and, quite famously, vetoed the General Assembly's repeal of its earlier ratification of the Equal Rights Amendment (ERA). Kentucky had passed the ERA in 1972 but later repealed it, becoming one of five states to do so. (The other states were Idaho, Nebraska, Tennessee, and South Dakota.) As quoted in a newspaper story at the time, Stovall asked the legislators, "How is it going to look for Kentucky with a woman lieutenant governor, to take this slap at women?" (Associated Press, 1978, p. 3).[4]

Stovall ran for governor in 1979 but lost to John Y. Brown Jr. The

Thelma Stovall (far left) during her tenure as Kentucky secretary of state, circa 1960s. (Courtesy of the Public Records Division–Kentucky Department for Libraries and Archives)

next woman to serve as lieutenant governor, Martha Layne Collins, would succeed where Stovall could not. After receiving a bachelor's degree from the University of Kentucky, Collins taught school in both Louisville and Versailles. It was in Versailles that her interest in politics began to emerge. She worked her way through the ranks of the Democratic Party, helping on multiple campaigns, and in 1971 she was appointed central Kentucky coordinator of women's activities for Wendell Ford's gubernatorial campaign. After Ford's election, he named her Democratic national committeewoman from Kentucky. Collins's commitment to public service eventually led her to seek elective office herself. In 1975 she decided to run for clerk of the Court of Appeals, won the Democratic nomination in a five-way primary, and defeated Republican Joseph E. Lambert (who, some years later, would become chief justice of the Kentucky Supreme Court). In her first campaign, Collins adopted a style that would serve her well. She believed that for women to win elections, they

Lieutenant Governor Martha Layne Collins presiding in the senate, circa 1980.
(Courtesy of the Public Records Division–Kentucky Department for Libraries and
Archives)

had to work harder, know more, and be more credible than men of equal stature. During her campaign, she traveled to all 120 counties of the Commonwealth, rather than limiting herself to the roughly forty media markets in Kentucky, as many candidates did (Collins, 2013).

During her tenure as clerk, a constitutional amendment restructured the court system of the Commonwealth (see chapter 7), turning the Court of Appeals into the Kentucky Supreme Court. Collins was subsequently named to the appointed position of clerk of the Kentucky Supreme Court and played a substantive role in educating the citizenry about the court's new structure and role. Collins thus became the last person to hold the office of clerk of the Court of Appeals and the first to hold the office of clerk of the Kentucky Supreme Court (Ryan & Fraas, 2004). Collins approached her role in the judicial branch with an eye toward educating the Commonwealth's citizens and making the court more accessible to them. She created booklets explaining the history of the court and showing photographs of judges and distributed them to schoolteachers across Kentucky, with the goal of making the judicial system less intimidating to children; she moved aside the secret veil of the court and allowed the citizens of the Commonwealth to look in (Collins, 2013). Her time in the judicial branch was a learning experience, to be sure, but it was also extremely beneficial on a practical level, as attorneys from around the state encouraged her to take the next step and seek higher office.

After her service in the judicial branch, Martha Layne Collins became Kentucky's second female lieutenant governor in 1979 (after besting six candidates in the primary and Republican Hal Rogers in the general election), serving under Governor John Y. Brown Jr. (Harrison, 1993; Harrison & Klotter, 1997). During Brown's four-year term, Collins served as acting governor for more than 500 days when the governor traveled out of state, and she visited all 120 counties of the Commonwealth (Ryan & Fraas, 2004). During her tenure as lieutenant governor, she announced her intention to run for the office of governor.

In 1983 Martha Layne Collins became the Commonwealth's first woman governor, closely edging out Harvey Sloane and Grady Stumbo in a tough primary (Stumbo had been endorsed by Governor Brown) and then Jim Bunning in the general election. At her swearing in, she stood with her hand on her grandmother's Bible, and in her inaugural address, Collins said, "True, the governor of Kentucky is a woman. And, if I am a symbol, then let it signify the kind of individual freedom and opportunity precious to typical Kentuckians from whom I come and with whom I remain. With a deep awareness of the responsibilities conferred by your trust, I vow that this 'first' for Kentucky will be ever dedicated to putting Kentucky first" (Johnson, 2012, p. 112). Collins's governorship would be known for its blended focus on education and economic development (see chapter 7).

With her election as governor, Collins also became the highest ranking Democratic woman in the United States at the time (Powell, 2001). In the 1980s Governor Collins was very active in national politics and was seriously considered by several presidential candidates as a running mate. She was interviewed for the position by Walter Mondale, who ultimately selected Geraldine Ferraro (Ryan & Fraas, 2004).

WOMEN IN THE KENTUCKY GENERAL ASSEMBLY

Kentucky women broke the electoral glass ceiling in the state legislature in 1921 when Democrat Mary Elliott Flanery of Catlettsburg, in Boyd County, won a seat in the Kentucky house representing the Eighty-Ninth District. A native of eastern Kentucky, Flanery was born in April 1867 and, after graduating from the University of Kentucky, became a teacher. When Flanery took her seat in January 1922, she was not only the first female member of the Kentucky General Assembly but also the first female legislator elected south of the Mason-Dixon Line (Kleber, 1992). An advocate for women's rights, Flanery was part of the Equal Rights Association and worked for the amendment's passage. She served just one term in the house because she decided to run for secretary of state (at the time, no woman had yet held statewide office). That pitted her against Emma Guy Cromwell, who, as noted above, was the first woman elected to that post. Cromwell said of her opponent during the campaign: "May I say now that here was a real opponent, a charming and intellectual woman who would be in earnest in her efforts to be nominated. . . . I will say that she and I kept on being good friends . . . we often met and had lunch together. Each kept her own secrets, if she had any, and we closed the heated campaign with no mudslinging and none of the inevitable regrets that follow such a course . . .

Mary Elliott
Flanery, circa
1921. (Courtesy
of Special
Collections,
University of
Kentucky)

we ever remained good friends and co-workers" (Cromwell, 1996, p. 30).

It would take another forty years for the gender and color barriers to be broken simultaneously.[5] That would be accomplished by two African American women from Louisville: Republican Amelia M. Tucker in 1961 and Democrat Mae Street Kidd in 1968. Kidd had been in the insurance business and had never expected to seek public office when she was approached by representatives from the local Democratic Party, who asked her to run in the primary. Reluctant at first, Kidd ultimately embraced politics with vigor and won eight straight elections in what became a seventeen-year legislative career (until she was beaten in 1984 by Democrat Tom Riner).

Representative Mae Street Kidd speaking with Governor John Y. Brown Jr., circa 1980. (Courtesy of the Public Records Division–Kentucky Department for Libraries and Archives)

Kidd was best known for her advocacy of open housing and low-income housing, and in fact, a housing bill named after her created the Kentucky Housing Corporation in 1972. (Governor Louie Nunn had vetoed the bill in prior sessions.) When asked to identify her proudest achievement, however, Kidd chose her resolution ratifying the Thirteenth, Fourteenth, and Fifteenth Amendments to the U.S. Constitution (Hall, 1997).

• • •

"It's not easy to get a bill passed, especially a controversial one that plows new ground. You've got to convince a lot of people to vote for it. Some of the legislators said, 'If we don't vote for her bill, Mrs. Kidd will choke us with our neckties.' I didn't exactly say that, but I didn't care what they said I said as long as they voted for the bill."
— Mae Street Kidd talking about the 1970 legislative session
(quoted in Hall, 1997, p. 117)

• • •

On the senate side of the General Assembly, the glass ceiling was breached when Democrat Carolyn Conn Moore of Franklin, in Simpson County, became the first female senator in 1950, serving out the remaining year of her deceased husband's term. Pauline Burton Davis also followed her husband in the state senate, although she was elected in her own right in 1958, becoming the first Republican woman elected to the senate. It would be 1968 before Kentuckians elected a female state senator who was not replacing her husband in that office. That occurred when Georgia Davis Powers took her civil rights career to the senate. Senator Powers chose a seat on the senate floor in the second row, purposely avoiding the back row and the humiliating symbolism of the back of a bus (Powers, 1995). She would not be able to avoid all signs of discrimination, however, for even as an elected official, her skin color meant that she could not rent a hotel or motel room in Frankfort. That experience fueled her interest in legislation to outlaw housing discrimination, which became a major focus during her time in Frankfort. By the second year of her twenty-year legislative career, Senator Powers had been named chair of the Health and Welfare Committee, where she championed civil rights, child protection, education, mental health, and women's issues. In 2010 Senator Powers began a close collaboration with the Center for Research on Violence Against Women at the University of Kentucky and publicly shared her own experience of being victimized at age thirteen by a male friend of the family. Through her visible partnership with the center, Senator Powers has proved herself to be a powerful and vocal advocate for justice and legal reform, well deserving of an endowed chair in her name.

While women have served in the Kentucky General Assembly since the 1920s, even today they remain significantly underrepresented in both the house and the senate (see table 1.1). The Commonwealth ranks forty-second in the nation in the percentage of female legislators and is among only eleven states (Kentucky, Tennessee, Virginia, West Virginia, Pennsylvania, Mississippi, North Dakota, Alabama, Oklahoma, Louisiana, and South Carolina) where less than 20 percent of state legislators are women (National Council of State Legislatures, 2012c). Only nineteen women have ever served in the Kentucky senate, and only seventy have served in the house; four of the female senators began their legislative careers in the Kentucky house.[6]

The first five women to become Kentucky state senators (beginning in 1950) followed their husbands in office, either filling their

Senator Georgia Davis Powers standing at her desk in the senate chamber, circa 1968. (Courtesy of Georgia Davis Powers)

unexpired terms or in separate elections. They served short terms of less than three years each, and often just one year. As noted above, Georgia Powers was the first woman elected without riding her husband's coattails, and her twenty years in office still stand as the longest term of any woman in the Kentucky senate. Patty Weaver and Helen Garrett each served for more than a decade in the 1970s and 1980s, and since 1995, it has become more common for female senators to serve for a decade or longer.

Table 1.1. Kentucky General Assembly by Year, Party Affiliation, and Gender

Year	Democrat	Republican	Independent	Percentage of Women
1970	95	43	0	4
1990	100	37	0	5
2012	81	56	1	18

Likewise, in the Kentucky house of representatives, the first female legislators served short terms, most commonly two years. After forty years, that changed in 1968 with the election of Mae Street Kidd, who went on to serve for seventeen years. Two Kentucky representatives have had legislative careers lasting more than two decades: Ruth Ann Palumbo, a Democrat from Lexington who was first elected in 1991; and Dorothy "Dottie" Priddy, a Democrat from Louisville who served from 1970 to 1991.

Dottie Priddy was a flamboyant legislator, easily identifiable by her bright jewelry and hats but perhaps even better known for the .38-caliber revolver she was said to wear strapped to her ankle. Her constituents in Louisville knew her to be a staunch opponent of court-ordered busing to integrate schools. Although Priddy was the only female legislator to vote against the Equal Rights Amendment in 1972, almost two decades later she would make remarkable comments about the rights of women from the floor of the house to influence passage of a bill outlawing marital rape.

Ruth Ann Palumbo continues to be one of the most liberal members of the General Assembly and is one of the few women to serve as a committee chair. In the 2000s Palumbo became part of a liberal caucus of women legislators that included Joni Jenkins, Susan Johns, Eleanor Jordan, Mary Lou Marzian, Kathy Stein, and others. When they recognized that their collective voice was more powerful than their singular opinions, they began to caucus together, each assuming responsibility for tracking legislation in her respective area of expertise. They tracked legislation addressing women's health, domestic violence and rape, women's representation on state boards and commissions, fairness bills, and more, and together they organized support for or opposition to legislation impacting women. They gained early, visible notoriety by building statewide opposition to a bill that, before their organized effort, likely would have gone unnoticed and passed easily. That bill would have removed the requirement that educational institutions offer women's softball in addition to men's baseball, violating the spirit if not the letter of Title IX (Stein, 2013).

The number of women in the Kentucky legislature has been and continues to be small, but for nearly a hundred years, they have shown themselves to be substantial in voice. The earliest reformers who took their seats in the Kentucky General Assembly saw what contemporary women's advocates still see: the strongest sustainable reforms on behalf of women are secured in the halls of the Kentucky legislature.

A WOMEN'S MOVEMENT TO END VIOLENCE IN AMERICA

The legal and political reforms of the early twentieth century changed women's lives substantially. They provided economic freedom, gave women legal standing as individuals, and gave them a voice in the electoral process. After the vote was secured in the 1920s, however, the women's reform effort seemed less urgent and became less visible in communities across America. Many women's advocates had considered suffrage their sole goal and felt their job was over with passage of the Nineteenth Amendment. This limited view and episodic attention slowed the progress of women's rights and was a pattern that would be repeated in years to come.

In the 1960s a second wave of reform began in the United States. The women's movement that blossomed in the late 1960s and 1970s was part of an international groundswell whereby women sought both civil and national rights. Within this overall movement, there were two specific campaigns to address violence against women: the anti-rape movement and the domestic violence movement. As social movements, both shared a broad goal: to end violence against women in all its forms. Advocates engaged in collective action guided by the idea of justice, a pattern consistent with long-standing theories of social movements (Touraine, 1981).

Like other movements, the anti-rape and domestic violence movements sought to implement change at multiple levels with a combination of services and activism: the local organization of women-run services (such as rape crisis centers and battered women's shelters); efforts to reform the legal, criminal justice, and service systems; and bipartisan political pressure to advance the cause of women (Bergen & Maier, 2011; Stark, 2007). These early efforts created an important connection between advocacy to build services and improve protection and political activism to change laws. They involved women telling their own personal stories, which, in the hands of advocates, became a political force. "Through the thread of these stories, women came to understand that the personal was indeed political. Women's stories and women's experiences have shaped the development of the field of women and the law" (Schneider & Wildman, 2011, p. 1).

The presence of anti-rape and domestic violence advocates was felt first in local communities, where grassroots shelters and crisis services were built outside the standard service system. In fact, "activists perceived violence against women as integrally linked to gender inequality and viewed the political and legal establishment with suspicion, maintaining that it perpetuated institutional forms of sexism. This perception led the domestic violence movement to focus initially outside of the governmental sphere . . . on the establishment of shelters, empowerment groups, and community education workshops" (Epstein, 1999, p. 128).

Similarly, in the anti-rape movement, volunteer advocates often believed that women would be best served not in collaboration with professionals in the legal system but in spite of them. This approach reflected a learned distrust of law enforcement and other professionals and a belief that women were revictimized by the legal process. Although the provision of direct services was and always will be the bedrock of the domestic violence and anti-rape movements, advocates were increasingly seen in the halls of statehouses and state offices, where they tried to change state law and policy. While victim services remained a priority, as these movements grew, advocates realized they could make changes at the macrolevel as well. In addition to responding to individual women who had been victimized by an intimate and then unsupported by the criminal justice system, they sought to change the system that had inflicted the wrong. And they urgently sought to reform a culture that perpetuated disempowering views of women as property and victimizing views of women's culpability when they were raped or battered (i.e., it must have been her fault). Survivors themselves were involved at every level: individual advocacy, systemic advocacy, and cultural change. The stories they told in the early days of the anti-rape and domestic violence movements gave an immediate face to the issue of violence against women (Polletta, 2006). Their stories were compelling and grabbed the attention of all who heard them. Stories told by women who had experienced rape or domestic violence emphasized the victims' ability to recover (Dunn, 2005; Loseke, 2000) and painted a portrait of survivors as strong and resilient rather than passive, weak, or deserving of pity. And they depicted survivors as "just like me" to audiences, countering the tendency to blame the victim and attribute her plight to some failing of her own, rather than the force used against her.

One Lofty Mission with Two Paths

The anti-rape and domestic violence movements enabled the legislative changes achieved on behalf of women over the past four decades. But the relationship between the two movements—one fighting against sexual violence and the other seeking to protect battered women—has at times been an uneasy and ambivalent alliance. The two movements never battled each other in any direct sense, and certainly they were both fueled by the desire to stand up for women. However, the dearth of financial resources, limits on political capital, and constant sense of having to fight outsiders created tension and moments of competition between the two movements. For instance, some bemoaned the reduction in attention to rape when feminists seemed to become more concerned about domestic violence (Caringella, 2009). But feminists do not always think alike or approach problems in the same way. As such, ideological differences and practical pressures have separated the two movements historically and continue to do so at times today.

The bifurcation between rape and domestic violence seen at the birth of the two movements was not just an artifact of the era, for even today, service providers often define themselves as serving rape victims *or* domestic violence victims. In the academic community, scholars tend to specialize in studying rape or domestic violence or stalking, rather than all forms of violence against women (Jordan, 2009a); researchers seek a marriage between a hard science approach that advances rigorous empiricism and a social justice approach that advances the end of violence against women (Campbell, 2009; Jordan, 2009a, 2009b).

Within the contemporary movement to end violence against women, distinct anti-rape and domestic violence movements can still be found, although in some states, the separation has become less apparent. At the national level, coalitions of rape and domestic violence advocates have marched together on Washington, D.C., and on Congress (most recently in support of the federal Violence Against Women Act), and state advocates have found that there is power in numbers, leading to combined efforts to secure funding for both domestic violence and rape programs. In a number of states, combined programs now provide services to battered women and rape survivors. Arguably, however, a scratch of the proverbial surface often reveals that the old separations persist. There may be one lofty mission, but perhaps, here and there, we find two paths to reach it.

The Movement Evolves

As described above, early efforts against rape and domestic violence involved a marked connection between advocacy to build services and political activism to change laws. Political advocacy, however, became off-limits or more complicated to engage in when domestic violence and anti-rape programs began to accept government, corporate, and foundation funding that specifically prohibits the use of those funds to support lobbying efforts. While struggling philosophically with the pressures to shift away from pure grassroots organizing and activism, advocates have continued their legal reform work.

The collection of activists pushing for legal reforms has also expanded its reach. Some advocates who began their careers in battered women's shelters and rape crisis centers have moved into positions in the government, providing a voice for women from within the executive and legislative branches. Others have moved into the private sphere, adding a voice from foundations. Still others have joined universities, where research can be used as a tool of advocacy.

Within the past decade, another group of victim advocates has appeared with a criminal justice perspective (e.g., prosecutor-based advocates, Mothers against Drunk Drivers, Parents of Murdered Children) that has not always been congruent with that of the more traditional anti-rape and domestic violence advocates. Disparate points of view have emerged around issues such as the death penalty, with criminal justice advocates advancing a pro–death penalty viewpoint and anti-rape and domestic violence advocates, with their more liberal grassroots histories, taking the opposite view. Fetal homicide is another issue that has caused a split between many in the domestic violence and anti-rape movements and other advocates who have a more conservative point of view about legal reforms in this area.

The voices of anti-rape and domestic violence advocates catalyzed the legal and legislative reforms of the past four decades. This same voice, in some cases handed down to the next generation of advocates, continues to speak for women across the nation in the halls of state capitols. But have these advocates succeeded? Some forty years later, it can be argued that survivors and advocates have both succeeded and failed. As noted by Dobash and Dobash (1992, p. 1):

> For the women who have been physically abused in the home by the men with whom they live, the past two decades have seen both radical change and no change at all. The lives of some have been touched by an ever expanding, worldwide movement to support women who have been battered and to challenge male violence. Some legal and social institutions have begun to respond, while others remain in a nexus of traditional tolerance of male violence and indifference to those who suffer from such violence. This is a time marked by social change and resistance to change, by innovation and reassertion of tradition. Both the new and the old responses are used, challenged and defended by those with differing views about the nature of this problem and how best to confront it. The arena of change and challenge is alive with ideas and activity.

While this perspective may be realistic, one cannot discount the extraordinary difference that advocates have made. In fact, the early results of the movement are quantifiable. The first battered women's shelter was opened as early as 1967 (Lemon, 2009), and in 1978 the growing number of shelters across the United States came together to form the National Coalition against Domestic Violence (Fulkerson & Patterson, 2006). In the latter part of the 1970s, there were barely two dozen emergency shelters for battered women, but a decade later, approximately 1,200 shelters were housing 300,000 annually (Stark, 2007). By 1985, legislators in more than half the states had listened to advocates and passed statutes funding domestic violence shelters (Buzawa & Buzawa, 1990, 1992). By 1994, when the first federal Violence Against Women Act was signed, U.S. shelters were serving more than 1 million women annually (Stark, 2007). Services for rape victims have also expanded, growing to more than 1,200 organizations by 2010 (Bergen & Maier, 2011).

The presence of the movement was just that: a physical presence. Advocates' combined voices made some communities think that the rape and battering of women had suddenly worsened, but in fact, these crimes were finally piercing the consciousness of Americans. In this process, words became all-important. Domestic violence advocates created and doggedly held on to terms such as *woman battering* and *wife abuse* to accurately characterize this type of violence as a gendered phenomenon.[7] The anti-rape movement, similarly, worked hard to use the word *rape* publicly. By naming rape and wife battering, the movement gained power from the public's growing awareness.

A WOMEN'S MOVEMENT TO END VIOLENCE IN KENTUCKY

As the national movements to end rape and domestic violence took root in the 1970s, reforms also began to emerge in the Commonwealth. Not unlike the national anti-rape and domestic violence movements, the first responses in Kentucky took shape in local communities, where services for rape survivors and battered women sprouted. Volunteers staffed crisis hotlines for rape survivors, and communities found beds for women who were fleeing violent homes. These informal grassroots efforts led to the creation of formal advocacy organizations and statewide networks of services, collaborations with other Kentucky practitioners, and enormous legislative reforms. Just as the national movements linked advocacy for victims with political activism, so did reforms in the Commonwealth.

In a symbolic way, a call to a telephone hotline in the late hours of the night launched the anti-rape movement in Kentucky. In 1971 a volunteer staffing a hotline in Lexington answered a call from a woman who had been raped. Shortly thereafter, the first rape crisis center was opened in Kentucky, called the Lexington Rape Crisis Center (now operating as the Bluegrass Rape Crisis Center). In 1975 the Rape Relief Center (now the Center for Women and Families) became Kentucky's second such center, operating under the auspices of the YWCA in Jefferson County. This was followed in 1976 by the Rape Crisis Center of Northern Kentucky (now the Women's Crisis Center of Northern Kentucky) and in 1982 by Rape Victim

Services Program in Owensboro (now called New Beginnings). Over the fifteen-year period between 1971 and 1986, these four centers were the only funded programs of their kind operating in Kentucky.[8] Notably, the majority of these programs began as grassroots, volunteer efforts; as they began to receive local and state funding, additional volunteer programs sprang up around the Commonwealth. At present, there are thirteen rape crisis centers, divided regionally to serve each county in the state.

The earliest funding from the state government was a pass-through of federal preventive health and health services (PHHS) block grant funding. The state's Department for Public Health (now part of the Cabinet for Health and Family Services) served as the administering agency. The PHHS block grant was originally split among the first three rape crisis centers in Kentucky, but in the 1980s, in an expression of solidarity, those three programs asked that the limited funding be split four ways to help support the new center in Owensboro. In 1985 the Kentucky Department for Mental Health and Mental Retardation Services assumed responsibility for administering the PHHS block grant, a move that coincided with the department's creation of a Sexual and Domestic Violence Services Program for victims of rape, domestic violence, and child abuse administered by the state's network of community mental health centers.[9] As the department assumed responsibility for the administration of funding for Kentucky's rape crisis centers, it also prioritized the expansion of these programs statewide. This led to the first state general funds for rape crisis centers in 1986 (an accomplishment covered in more detail in chapter 7).

As the department began to coordinate the growth of rape crisis centers, the centers' directors had the opportunity to meet on a regular basis. Growing in number each year, these directors strengthened the individual services provided through their programs, and they organized a formal statewide coalition. In 1990 the Kentucky Rape Crisis Center Association was created as an independent advocacy organization unattached to the government; it later changed its name to the Kentucky Association of Sexual Assault Programs (KASAP).[10]

Meanwhile, in 1977 the first spouse abuse shelter (as it was then called) opened in Louisville. Like the Rape Relief Center, this program was operated under the auspices of the YWCA, although its rape and domestic violence services were initially administered independently.[11] In 1978 the YWCA also opened a spouse abuse shelter in Lexington (now called the Bluegrass Domestic Violence Program).[12] The Barren River Area Safe Space opened in 1980,[13] and soon thereafter the Women's Crisis Center in Northern Kentucky expanded its scope to include victims of domestic violence as well as rape survivors, adopting a model that blended those services.[14] Shelters in Paducah and Barbourville followed.

By 1981, there were six shelter programs serving battered women and their children across the Commonwealth. That year, those six programs formed a statewide coalition, the Kentucky Domestic Violence Association (KDVA), whose membership included all domestic violence programs in the state.[15] An early goal of the KDVA was to increase the number of programs so that each area development district in the Commonwealth was served, a goal it reached in 1985. Among the KDVA's earliest successes was obtaining state funding for domestic violence programs, accomplished during the administration of Governor John Y. Brown.[16] This came at a crucial time, as key federal funding had been slashed, and directors struggled to provide crisis services for battered women while dealing with a 50 percent cut in funding (Van Houten, 2013). Additionally, the General Assembly passed legislation in 1982 to expand funding, establishing the spouse abuse shelter fund (now called the domestic violence fund) under the Adult Protection Act (see chapter 7).

• • •

"We shall someday be heeded, and when we shall have our amendment to the Constitution of the United States, everybody will think it was always so, just exactly as many young people believe that all the privileges, all the freedom, all the enjoyments which woman now possesses always were hers. They have no idea of how every single inch of ground that she stands upon today has been gained by the hard work of some little handful of women of the past."

—Susan B. Anthony, 1894 (quoted in Sherr, 1995, p. xi)

• • •

The founding of rape crisis centers and domestic violence programs and the creation of state-level associations to address sexual assault and domestic violence formed the bedrock for Kentucky's legislative reforms. These outspoken and visionary activists joined with other women's advocates in the state government and local grassroots organizations (e.g., the Kentucky Coalition against Rape and Sexual Assault) to advance the protection of women and children by legislative reform. Their stories, which are told in detail in later chapters, gave women a visible role in Kentucky's history. While revealing the destructiveness of rape and domestic violence, they showed the true strength and resiliency of women, and they changed the face of the Commonwealth for generations to come.

2

The Prevalence of Violence and the Stories of Women Who Lived It

Among the greatest hardships faced by women from every generation across time and in every state across the country are those posed by domestic violence, rape, and stalking. These insidious violations are not just crimes against the few; they are crimes against the many. In the United States, one of the earliest nationally representative studies on the prevalence of violence against women, the National Family Violence Survey, reported that fully one-fourth of American couples experience at least one episode of violence at some point during their relationship (Straus, Gelles, & Steinmetz, 1980; Straus & Gelles, 1990). A second study found that one in five couples in America experience at least one incident of domestic violence in a year (Schafer, Caetano, & Clark, 1998). More than 1 million cases of intimate partner violence occur every year in the United States (Rennison & Welchans, 2000).

. . .

Prevalence is defined as the total number of people in a population who are impacted by a condition at any given time. It is used to estimate how common a condition is within a population. In the context of violence against women, prevalence helps answer the question, how many women? In contrast, *incidence* reflects the total number of times a condition occurs. In the context of violence against women, incidence helps answer the question, how often?

. . .

In 2011 the Centers for Disease Control and Prevention released the most recent national study on the prevalence of violence against women (Black et al., 2011). The National Intimate Partner and Sexual Violence Survey (NIPSVS) was conducted through interviews with 9,086 women, and it included several types of violence that had not previously been measured in national population-based surveys, including sexual violence other than rape, psychological aggression and coercive control, and control of reproductive or sexual health. The study also used improved, behavior-specific definitions to assess the presence of victimization among the women surveyed. One of the key findings of the NIPSVS was that more than one in three women (35.6 percent) in the United States have experienced rape, physical violence, and/or stalking by an intimate partner in their lifetime.

Defining the Problem: What's in a Name?

Since the time of Shakespeare's star-crossed lovers Romeo and Juliet, the question "what's in a name?" has had significant and symbolic meaning. So it is in the field of violence against women. When violence against women first emerged as an issue of concern to Americans in the 1970s, it was thrust into the public consciousness by women who had seen themselves and their sisters trapped in violent marital relationships. This experience and this understanding of violence informed the name it was given: *wife battering*. Early advocates and the early research literature used this term to explain the context in which women experience egregious acts of violence. Notably, the term also had an aggressive and even political flavor, which was intentional on the part of advocates. Over time, the field's understanding of violence against women matured, and the labels it was given changed (Jordan, 2009a, 2009b). Trends in the use of terms can be measured, for as the field's descriptors of violence evolved, the scientific literature generally followed. For example, in the scientific literature, the early term *wife battering* gave way to terms such as *spouse abuse* in the 1980s, and *interpersonal violence* was a popular term for a short time in the 1990s. Beginning in the late 1980s, *domestic violence* became the term of choice, and it continues to be used in the scientific literature to describe the intimate assault of a woman. Over the past thirty years, it has often been used in statutory definitions of violence against women. In the 2000s, the term *intimate partner violence* gained acceptance, and today it is second only to *domestic violence* as the most frequently used term in the literature. This evolution of terms has communicated something important. As *wife battering* and *spouse abuse* were replaced by *domestic violence*, for example, that change reflected the reality that victims of violence are not just wives but also girlfriends and women cohabiting with a partner. The term *intimate partner violence* signals the recognition that violence can occur between both women and men in any of these relationships, as well as in same-sex relationships.

Similar trends have occurred in the terms used to describe sexual violence. The earliest published work in the broad field of violence against women involved rape (Jordan, 2009a, 2009b). While still the most commonly used word in the literature with respect to sex crimes, *rape* is now often replaced by the terms *sexual assault*, *sexual violence*, and *sexual abuse*, again reflecting a broader understanding of the type of victimization experienced by women. The term *sexual harassment* is also found in the literature, most often in legal scholarship and articles about civil remedies and lawsuits.

The terms *psychological abuse* and *stalking* began to appear in the scientific literature in the late 1990s. In the case of stalking, the name of the crime originated from the creation of a statute (Beatty, 2003; Tjaden & Thoennes, 1998). In the case of psychological aggression, there has been a push among scientists to measure a previously misunderstood and amorphous construct (Maiuro, 2001).

So, what's in a name? Nothing short of how the field understands violence against women.

THE LOOK AND FEEL OF VIOLENCE: TYPES OF VICTIMIZATION

As the field matured, violence against women came to be understood not as a singular act or form of abuse but as the aggregate of physically, sexually, and psychologically abusive behaviors experienced by a women (Jordan, Nietzel, Walker, & Logan, 2004). It is also empirically understood that violence against women is predominantly a phenomenon of male aggression (Tjaden & Thoennes, 1998). For example, in the National Violence Against Women Survey, all the women (aged eighteen and older) who were raped were raped by a male, most (91.9 percent) of the women who were physically assaulted were assaulted by a male, and nearly all (97.2 percent) the women who were stalked were stalked by a male offender (Tjaden & Thoennes, 1998). These findings were replicated in the more recent NIPSVS, in which, across all types of violence, the majority of female victims reported that their perpetrators were male (Black et al., 2011).

Violence against women has also come to be understood as primarily a crime committed by intimate partners. In the National Violence Against Women Survey, for example, fully two-thirds of the women who reported being raped, physically assaulted, and/or stalked were victimized by a current or former husband, cohabiting partner, boyfriend, or date (Tjaden & Thoennes, 1998). The survey also found that women who were raped or physically assaulted by a current or former spouse, cohabiting partner, boyfriend, or date were significantly more likely than women who were raped or physically assaulted by other types of perpetrators to report being injured during that incident (Tjaden & Thoennes, 1998).

The fact that violence most often occurs in intimate relationships makes it challenging to address legislatively, because historically, there has been a reluctance to intrude into the marital relationship. Doing so would require entering the home, in violation of a cultural belief that a man's home is his castle and that what occurs there is not for public consumption. There is also an assumption that if violence happens between intimate couples, the blame resides with both partners or perhaps with just the woman for "provoking" violence from her mate. Those who question the latter assumption should review some early court cases in which either a male offender was found not guilty or the charge was reduced from murder to manslaughter based on the so-called provocative behavior of the female victim to whom he was married (e.g., Nourse, 1997).

The abusive behaviors most often seen in cases of violence against women can be divided into four specific types, described below.

Physical Violence: When Hands Hurt

Women living with abusive partners know that physical violence comes in many forms. Some offenders strike out in anger: pushing, shoving, slapping, hitting, hitting with objects, kicking, choking, threatening, or using weapons. The effects are bruises, marks, burns, scratches, abrasions, swollen faces, permanent scars, and even disability. Some offenders are more sociopathic and instrumental in their use of violence: they make sure to leave bruises and marks only where clothing can hide them, or they pull out hair so that a head covering can mask the harm. In the NIPSVS, approximately one in four women (24.3 percent) had experienced severe physical violence by an intimate partner at some point in their lifetime (Black et al., 2011). Specifically, 17.2 percent of women had been slammed against something by a partner, 14.2 percent had been hit with a fist or something hard, and 11.2 percent reported being been beaten by an intimate partner (Black et al., 2011).

· · ·

When Lisa Murray first met him, he was like no man she had ever known. He was European and spoke five languages. He was attentive and thought-ful—always doing little things to impress her. His family was accomplished, creative, and professional, and when she was with them, she felt like she was part of something important. What she didn't know about him seemed dark and mysterious and attractive. Three years after they met, they married, and subtle signs began to emerge—so subtle that she recognizes them only in hindsight: his strange behavior when they were with a group of people, his criticisms and rude statements, his tendency to put her down in front of others, his withdrawal of intimacy. Most disturbing was his lack of empa-thy. When she was thrown from a horse and hospitalized, he showed no concern. When his friend died in an automobile accident, he seemed not to care. Another warning sign was that Lisa's daughter, Jeren, disliked him so much that mother and daughter were estranged for more than five years.

Over time, his verbal abuse grew. He screamed at Lisa, accused her of stealing his belongings and ruining his life. He broke glass objects and threw things at her. One night in September 2011, his verbal and emotional assaults peaked, and Lisa had finally had enough. She turned around and, with all the confidence she could muster, told him never to say those things to her again. She then turned to walk away and never heard him coming. He grabbed her, threw her down, beat her with his fists, and repeatedly slammed her head against the wooden floor until she lost consciousness. When she awoke, still lying on the floor, she knew she had to flee. She mustered her strength and ran to a nearby gas station, where she collapsed. Police were called, and she was taken to the hospital, confused, frightened, and injured.

These days, Lisa feels like she can breathe freely again. She and Jeren once again share each other's lives. But even in the silence she revels in, the fear is there. As she says, "I'm always looking over my shoulder."

· · ·

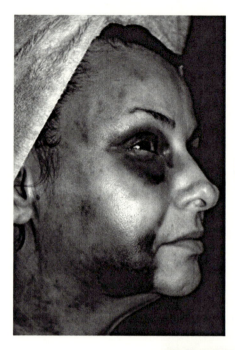

Lisa Murray following the assault by her husband, September 2011. (Courtesy of Lisa Murray)

Lisa Murray with her daughter Jeren, September 2012. (Courtesy of Lisa Murray)

Notwithstanding these findings, in recent years, a number of men's advocacy groups and a limited number of scholars (e.g., Straus, 2011) have contended that women are as physically violent as men. This claim originates largely from the findings of two National Family Violence Surveys conducted by Murray Straus and Richard Gelles. The first, conducted in 1975, derived data from a nationally representative sample of 2,113 married and cohabiting couples; the second, conducted in 1985, surveyed 6,002 couples. In both surveys, the rate of female-to-male assault was slightly higher than the rate of male-to-female assault (Straus & Gelles, 1986, 1990). A different picture emerges from the National Violence Against Women Survey (including 8,000 women and 8,005 men), which found that women experience more intimate partner violence than men do (22.1 percent of surveyed women, compared with 7.4 percent of surveyed men). This means that, each year, approximately 1.3 million women and 835,000 men are physically assaulted by an intimate partner in the United States (Tjaden & Thoennes, 2000a). National crime data also provide evidence that most victims of domestic violence are women. Specifically, women experience violence at the hands of an intimate partner at a rate five to eight times greater than men (Bachman & Saltzman, 1995; Federal Bureau of Investigation, 1992; US Department of Justice, 2000); approximately 85 percent of victims of intimate partner violence are women (Rennison & Welchans, 2000).

One could argue that using the data from the National Family Violence Surveys to contend that "women are as violent as men" is an overly simplistic interpretation (Edleson, 1998). These surveys capture only the number of incidents of assault; they do not reflect the context of the violence, the degree of injury sustained, or the intent of the violence. A significant number of studies have revealed how important these factors are in fully understanding domestic violence. For instance, studies have found that there are key gender differences. Specifically, women tend to suffer more injuries from domestic violence than do men (Logan, Walker, Jordan, & Leukefeld, 2006). The National Violence Against Women Survey reported, for example, that fully 40 percent of women suffer injuries, compared with 25 percent of men (Tjaden & Thoennes, 2000a). Even the primary proponent of the gender symmetry argument acknowledged that his review found that, compared with men, women inflict fewer injuries and sustain greater injuries from domestic violence (Straus, 2011). Also relevant is the tendency for men to underreport their perpetration of assaults (Dutton, 1988; Stets & Straus, 1990).

Also missing from many studies is an analysis of the intent of violent partners. Why is violence used, and to what end? If a man assaults a woman and she hits back in self-defense, does that fairly or accurately define them as equally violent? Even the law would not use that characterization. Recent scholarship has aimed to define intent by describing three different types of domestic violence (M. P. Johnson, 2008). First, *intimate terrorism* involves physical and sexual violence combined with nonviolent control tactics such

as psychological aggression or economic abuse. It is most often perpetrated by men and represents the type of domestic violence advocates have responded to for more than four decades. The second type
is *violent resistance*, in which victims respond to intimate terrorism
with self-protective violence. Third, *situational couple violence* generally starts as an argument that turns aggressive; it often involves
violence perpetrated by both parties. In responding to contentions
that women are as violent as men, Johnson points out, "Because intimate terrorism and violent resistance have low base rates to begin
with, and because perpetrators and victims of intimate terrorism are
highly likely to refuse to respond to surveys—perpetrators because
they do not wish to implicate themselves, victims because they fear
reprisals from their partner—the violence in general surveys is heavily dominated by situational couple violence" (M. P. Johnson, 2011,
p. 290).

Controversies, both statistical and political, are common in the
fields of domestic violence and rape. To grasp the true nature of
violence against women, it is necessary to absorb its complexity. It
is true that women use violence against men in intimate relationships, and they are sometimes the primary aggressor. But women's
violence is much more often an act of self-defense born out of fear
for themselves and their children. To ignore the complexity of wom-
en's actions is to misunderstand the phenomenon.

Sexual Assault: When Hands and Bodies Invade

The term *rape* is used not only in the popular media and in prevalence studies but also in state, federal, and tribal statutes. Although
the specific wording varies, for many years the term *rape* has referred
to an act of penile penetration of the vagina committed with some
degree of force or the threat of force (Berger, Searles, & Neuman,
1988). *Sexual assault*, in contrast, reflects a broader range of behaviors, typically referring to acts of sexual penetration or touch that are
committed through force or the threat of force or when the victim is
incapacitated or otherwise unable to consent.

A review of prevalence studies assessing rape and sexual assault
finds that approximately 15 to 33 percent of women have experienced these forms of violence in their adult lifetimes (Bachar &
Koss, 2001). In the NIPSVS, nearly one in five women (18.3 percent) reported being raped at some time in their lives, a finding that

translates to almost 22 million women across the United States. The most common form of rape experienced by survey respondents was completed forced penetration, with about 5 percent of women experiencing attempted forced penetration and 8 percent experiencing alcohol- or drug-facilitated completed forced penetration (Black et al., 2011). When a broader range of behaviors was considered, a startling 45 percent of women had experienced sexual violence victimization (Black et al., 2011).

Notably, studies have found that violence against women is often preceded by an experience (or multiple experiences) of childhood or adolescent victimization. The National Violence Against Women Survey found that the female population at greatest risk is teenaged and younger. Of the 18 percent of respondents who said they had been the victim of a completed or attempted rape at some time in their lives, more than 20 percent were younger than twelve when they were first raped, and more than 30 percent were aged twelve to seventeen. As noted by the survey authors, "more than half (54%) of the female rape victims identified by the survey were younger than age 18 when they experienced their first attempted or completed rape" (Tjaden & Thoennes, 1998, p. iv). In addition to identifying the risk for teenage girls, this finding has implications for adult women, as there is a relationship between victimization as a minor and victimization as an adult. In the National Violence Against Women Survey, women who reported being raped before age eighteen were twice as likely to report being raped in adulthood. The serious implications of childhood victimization also apply to other forms of adult victimization. Women who were physically assaulted as children or teenagers were twice as likely to report being physically assaulted in adulthood, and women who were stalked before age eighteen were seven times more likely to report being stalked as adults (Tjaden & Thoennes, 1998).

Women participating in the NIPSVS who reported a rape experience were asked who perpetrated that assault. More than half (51.1 percent) reported that at least one perpetrator was a current or former intimate partner, 40.8 percent reported being raped by an acquaintance, 13.8 percent reported being raped by a stranger, 12.5 percent reported being raped by a family member, and just over 2 percent reported being raped by a person in a position of authority (Black et al., 2011). Based on responses in the NIPSVS regarding the perpetrators of rape and sexual assault, the authors concluded that nearly one in ten women in the United States (9.4 percent) has been raped by an intimate partner in her lifetime, and an estimated 17 percent of women have experienced sexual violence other than rape by an intimate partner (Black et al., 2011).

These findings mirror the earliest studies on marital rape, which found that 10 to 14 percent of married women will be raped by their partners (Bergen, 1996; Finkelhor & Yllo, 1985; Russell, 1990), usually multiple times (Koss, Dinero, Seibel, & Cox, 1988; Mahoney, 1999; Russell, 1990). In fact, one study found that about 20 percent of women who had been sexually assaulted by their intimate partners reported more than ten separate rapes in a six-month period (Mahoney, 1999). While these data have always been available to the public, only recently have women opened up about their experiences of marital or intimate partner rape. As the violence against women movement grew, more women found the strength to show their bruises and cuts, but they could not find the words to describe the sexual violence they endured at the hands of their partners. The shame they felt was often a barrier to their disclosure, and they kept silent about what humiliated them the most. Early scholars began to create sound in that void of silence by documenting the size of the problem and communicating that no woman suffers rape alone.

In addition to shame, embarrassment, and fear, another significant barrier that has kept women from seeking help is a cultural one. It is the belief, held even by women themselves, that a husband cannot legally rape his wife. From biblical writings to early legal treatises, women have been considered the property of their husbands and, as such, have no legal standing to charge a spouse with sexual assault. (The evolution of the law related to women is discussed in chapters 3 and 4.) Deep-seated cultural beliefs are slow to change. They are found not only among the general population but also in legislative bodies, making the passage of laws against marital rape a challenge. Even today, some women do not see forced sex by an intimate partner as a crime; to them, it is just an extension of the abuse they experience at their partner's hand. These women do not tell, which leaves them to suffer in silence. Their stories are not forgotten, however, and are chronicled in this book.

For about one in seven women, however, sexual violation occurs at the hands of a stranger. Research has identified several different types of stranger rape, most often informed by the offender's psychological makeup, his deviant sexual behavior and modus operandi (the method by which he makes his attack), or the type of victim he selects. The Rape, Abuse, & Incest National Network has identified three types of stranger rape using the modus operandi approach: In blitz sexual assault, the perpetrator rapidly and brutally assaults the victim with no prior contact. Blitz assaults usually occur at night and in a public place. In contact sexual assault, the offender contacts the victim and tries to gain her or his trust and confidence before the assault. Contact perpetrators might select their victims in bars, lure them into their cars, or otherwise try to coerce their victims into situations conducive to sexual assault. Finally, in home invasion sexual assault, the perpetrator breaks into the victim's home to commit the rape (Rape, Abuse, & Incest National Network, 2009).

Psychological Aggression: When the Bruises Are Emotional

While psychological aggression has yet to be criminalized,[1] no discussion of women's experience of violence would be complete without mentioning this form of abuse. It is difficult to define, as it leaves no visible marks; there are no physical parameters to define when a behavior is violent. National prevalence rates of psychological maltreatment are not readily available, but there is evidence that psychological abuse routinely co-occurs with physical and sexual violence (Jordan, Campbell, & Follingstad, 2010).

In the first national prevalence study to measure psychological aggression, the NIPSVS found that nearly half of all women in the United States (48.4 percent) had experienced at least one form of psychological aggression by an intimate partner during their lifetimes (Black et al., 2011). To highlight the serious effects of psychological aggression, Maiuro (2001) described four impacts that the abusive actions would be designed to accomplish: denigrating damage to partner's self-image or esteem; passive-aggressive withholding of emotional support and nurturance; threatening behavior, either explicit or implicit; and restricting personal territory and freedom.

· · ·

When he arrived home unexpectedly, she looked like someone who had spent hours scrubbing and cleaning (which she had): a bit sweaty, no makeup, dowdy clothes. Without any apparent anger or malice, he told her how terrible she looked, but he didn't stop there. He found fault with the messy house, criticized her ability to parent the children, and claimed she had never made him happy. He then turned and walked away, in no hurry, leaving her to wonder why. Concluding that he was reacting to the way she looked, and wanting to please him, she showered, dressed nicely, put on makeup, and did her hair the way he liked—anticipating that these changes would be rewarded. But instead, he spat in her face and accused her of planning to go out to meet another man. He shoved her onto the floor and walked away again, leaving her shattered. This taught her that her own behavior could not influence the outcome of her life. Only he could. Psychological abuse felt just the way he intended.

• • •

Stalking: When Following Became a Crime

Until the 1990s, when a woman was followed, when someone left notes on her car or excessive messages on her answering machine, when an abusive partner waited for her in the parking lot as she left work, she had no words to articulate what was happening to her. Law enforcement officers had no civil or criminal remedies to stop these forms of harassment, and researchers had yet to operationalize women's experiences or to document their prevalence. All this changed in 1990 when California enacted the first state law criminalizing stalking (Beatty, 2003).

California's stalking law had been prompted by several high-profile cases. On March 15, 1982, Theresa Saldana was stabbed in the torso ten times, nearly killing her. Her attacker, forty-six-year-old Arthur Jackson, had been stalking her since seeing her performance in the 1980 film *Defiance*. He hired a private investigator to find the Saldana family's address. Jackson then called Saldana's mother and identified himself as a famous movie director's assistant, claiming that he needed her daughter's home address so that he could contact her about a film role. Innocently, she gave him the address. Jackson approached Saldana in front of her home, in broad daylight, and stabbed her repeatedly with a five-inch knife, attacking her so viciously that he bent the blade. Jackson served a fourteen-year prison term for the assault and was then extradited to England in 1996 to be tried for a 1966 murder. Jackson died of heart failure in a British mental hospital in 2004 at age sixty-eight.

In 1984 Richard Farley began to stalk his coworker, twenty-three-year-old Laura Black. The two first met in April of that year at a company function. When Black rebuffed his advances, Farley began to leave cards and gifts on her desk—the start of what became a four-year ordeal. Black obtained a temporary restraining order against Farley on February 2, 1988, and had a February 17 court date to make the order permanent. But on February 16, Farley shot and killed seven people and wounded four others at the company where they both worked. Black was among the wounded. Farley was convicted of seven counts of first-degree murder and is currently on death row at San Quentin State Prison.

On July 18, 1989, actress Rebecca Schaeffer was murdered by Robert John Bardo, an obsessed fan who had been stalking her for three years. In 1987 Bardo traveled to Los Angeles and attempted to see Schaeffer on the set of her television program *My Sister Sam*, but he was turned away by security. Angered, he tried again a month later, this time armed with a knife, but was again turned away. Initially, Bardo was motivated by a delusional love for the actress, but this turned to hate in 1989 when he saw a movie in which she was in bed with a male actor. For Bardo, this triggered an obsessive belief that Schaeffer should die. Bardo had read about the attack of Theresa Saldana several years earlier and knew that her stalker had obtained her address through a private investigator. Bardo used the same means to locate Schaeffer's residence. He approached her apartment and rang the bell, and when Schaeffer answered the door, he showed her a letter and an autograph her agent had previously sent him. Schaeffer spoke to him briefly and then asked him not to return to her home. An hour later, angry and armed with a shotgun, Bardo returned to Schaeffer's apartment, and when she answered the door, he shot her in the chest. Paramedics rushed her to the hospital, but some thirty minutes later, Schaeffer was pronounced dead. The following day, Bardo was arrested in Tucson and immediately confessed. He was convicted of capital murder and sentenced to life in prison without the possibility of parole.

That same year, four other women would be murdered in Orange County, California. In each case, the offender was a former husband or boyfriend of the victim. Patricia Kastle, a former Olympic skier, was fatally shot in the head and back by her ex-husband, Lee Strumer. Manijeh Bolour, a nurse, had been tormented for ten years by her former boyfriend Hossein Ghaffari, until he intentionally drove his car into hers, causing an explosion that took her life.

Brenda Thurman had recently left her boyfriend, Rodney Cornegay, who hired a private detective to find her and gunned her down three weeks later. Nineteen-year-old Tammy Davis and her twenty-one-month-old child had previously been assaulted by her ex-boyfriend Brian Framstead, causing them both to be hospitalized. In the weeks before Framstead shot her to death, Davis had desperately questioned the police's inability to act before she was harmed again. "What does he have to do," she cried, "shoot me?" (quoted in Schaum & Parrish, 1995, p. 10).

These cases forced stalking into the awareness of Americans in a brutal and graphic way. It would take almost a decade for the research literature to catch up with legislative reforms, but its findings merely confirmed the importance of enacting stalking laws to protect victims, particularly victims of intimate partner violence. Using a narrow, legalistic definition of stalking, the National Violence Against Women Survey was the first nationally representative study to assess the prevalence of stalking, finding that one in a hundred women in the United States were stalked each year (equal to 8.1 percent of all U.S. women), and nearly one in twelve experienced stalking at some point in their lifetimes (Tjaden & Thoennes, 2000a). With a broader, more informed definition, the more recent NIPSVS found that one in six women (16.2 percent) will experience stalking in her lifetime (Black et al., 2011). A meta-analysis (a systematic review of data from existing studies) revealed that stalking rates reached approximately 24 percent among U.S. women (Spitzberg, Nicastro, & Cousins, 1998). Like other forms of violence against women, stalking is most often perpetrated by males against their female partners. Specifically, in the majority of cases (59 to 66.2 percent), when women are stalked, it is by an intimate partner (Black et al., 2011; Tjaden & Thoennes, 2000a). There are significant and dangerous links between stalking and domestic violence. Studies show that intimate partner stalkers are more violent than other stalkers who are not in an intimate relationship with the victim (Mohandie, Meloy, McGowan, & Williams, 2006).

Subsequent research has found that many stalkers have criminal histories, particularly arrests for alcohol- and drug-related crimes (Harmon, Rosner, & Owens, 1995; Jordan, Logan, Walker, & Nigoff, 2003). Again reflecting the close connection between domestic violence and stalking, studies have found that 18 percent of stalking victims are physically assaulted by the stalker, and more than a third are raped by him (Tjaden & Thoennes, 1998). Studies have also found that almost half of all stalking occurs at the point of a couple's separation, and physical assault accompanies stalking 86 percent of the time (Brewster, 2000). Finally, a majority of the women murdered by an intimate were stalked by him in the year preceding their deaths (McFarlane et al., 1999).

HOMICIDE: THE ULTIMATE VIOLENT ACT

Homicide is the leading cause of death among African American women aged fifteen to forty-five and the seventh leading cause of premature death among women overall (Campbell et al., 2003). Death is the most severe outcome of intimate partner violence, and it may lead to the simultaneous death of children in the home and the suicide of the offender.

Intimate Partner Homicide

Women are far more likely than men to be killed by an intimate partner, while men are more likely to die at the hands of a stranger or an unidentified assailant. In fact, among murder victims of all ages, females are much more likely than males to have been murdered by an intimate (Cooper & Eaves, 1996; Fox & Zawitz, 2007). This is not a new trend; between 1976 and 2005, intimate partner homicide accounted for 30 percent of female victims but only 5 percent of male victims (Fox & Zawitz, 2007). Similarly, according to the U.S. Department of Justice (2000), intimate homicides account for approximately 33 percent of all female murders but only 6 percent of murders involving male victims; of the individuals murdered by their spouses between the 1970s and the 1990s, about six in ten were women. Historically, studies have found that women are killed by their intimate partners at a rate eight times that of men (Craven, 1997). In 2006 more than 3,600 women in the United States lost their lives to homicide (Snyder, Finnegan, & Kang, 2007). According to the National Violent Death Reporting System, which analyzes homicides in sixteen reporting states, the homicide rate for females in the United States is 2.6 per 1,000 (Karch et al., 2008).

Importantly, studies show that the murder of intimate partners is not limited to adult couples; it touches the lives of very young women. The Washington State Domestic Violence Fatality Review, for example, found that 40 percent of victims were younger than eighteen years at the time of their deaths (Starr, Hobart, & Fawcett, 2004).

• • •

Kelly Doyle was smart, hardworking, and well organized; she was warm, social, and well loved. According to her father Paul, a social worker, when Kelly lost her mother to cancer at age nine, she seemed to take that grief and channel it into the pursuit of life. She was on the honor roll in high school and received a bachelor's degree in communications in four years, even while working thirty-two hours a week. She often talked of starting her own business. Kelly loved baking and was particularly fond of trying out new recipes on friends and family.

Kelly's greatest joy came with the birth of her son, Cian, a name from Irish mythology that means legendary and amazing. As she reveled in her son's new life, however, the child's father became more violent and controlling. When Cian was six months old, Kelly moved out and sought a protective order against her boyfriend, telling the court that he had shaken her in the past, had harmed their pet, and was stalking her.

Christmas 2009 was a wonderful time, as Kelly and her family gathered to celebrate. Kelly spent New Year's Day with Cian and a friend at home in her new apartment. At 3:15 AM her ex-boyfriend arrived at the apartment, hit and stabbed Kelly's friend, and then chased him outside. The friend ran next door and called for help. Meanwhile, the ex-boyfriend went back to Kelly's home, where he brutally strangled her and stabbed her sixty times. Cian slept in the next room as his mother was murdered.

During the trial, the ex-boyfriend's attorney explained that his client had murdered Kelly because he did not want their relationship to end and was jealous of other men. In August 2010 the ex-boyfriend was convicted of murder and assault and sentenced to fifty-five years in prison.

Cian now lives with Kelly's father, who describes his grandson as the spitting image of his mother.

• • •

Although shocking when they occur, most intimate partner homicides do not come out of the blue; they are usually preceded by the presence and escalation of physical violence against the female partner (Langford, Isaac, & Kabat, 1998; Mercy & Saltzman, 1989). Clearly, not all cases of domestic violence end in homicide, but

Kelly Doyle with her son, Cian, on Christmas Eve 2009, eight days before her murder. (Courtesy of Paul Doyle)

research suggests that there are specific risk factors for a deadly outcome, including the presence of firearms in the home and illicit drug use (Bailey et al., 1997; Campbell, 2004). This powerful connection among domestic violence, guns, and drugs is a life-threatening one for women. Other risk factors include the separation of a couple that has been living together, or the victim asking the offender to leave;

the presence of a child in the home, particularly if the child is not the offender's biological offspring; and the offender being unemployed (Bailey et al., 1997). Additionally, there is a fivefold increase in the homicide risk when the victim has left the offender for another partner or the offender's violence was triggered by jealousy (Bailey et al., 1997).

One of the largest studies of femicide (the homicide of women) was that reported by Jacquelyn Campbell and her colleagues (2003). With the goal of identifying risk factors for femicide, they conducted an eleven-city study involving 220 femicide cases and a comparison group of 343 abused (but not murdered) women. Their findings were striking and reinforced what the literature had suggested. Of the women killed by their partners, 81 percent had been physically abused by the offender in the year prior to the femicide, 23 percent were beaten while pregnant, and 72 percent had reported harassment and stalking (Sharps et al., 2001). Other identified risk factors included the offender's access to a gun and previous threats with a weapon; the presence of a stepchild (i.e., not the offender's biological child) in the home; and estrangement of the couple, especially from an extremely controlling male partner. The point of separation was even more dangerous if the victim left her partner for another man. Other significant risk factors included stalking, forced sex, and abuse during pregnancy. The authors also identified factors that made femicide less likely, such as the victim never having lived with the offender and the offender being arrested for his violent conduct (Campbell et al., 2003).

Intimate partner homicides have been on the decline in recent decades in each gender and racial category. There has been an 81 percent decline in homicides committed against black men by a partner, a 56 percent decline in homicides against white men, and a 49 percent decline in the murder of black women. For white women, however, the reduction in the rate of dying by homicide is less striking, at only 9 percent (Fox & Zawitz, 2004). A reasonable explanation for the decline in homicides against white men may be that, over these same decades, white women have had access to local resources such as battered women's shelters, legal advocacy services, protective orders, and other remedies that make violence unnecessary. When given a safe option to flee or stop the violence against them, the data may be suggesting that women most often choose not to strike out violently.

Sexual Homicide

It is now well known that the physical and psychological effects of sexual violence can be severe and long lasting. At the extreme of the sexual violence continuum are those cases resulting in the death of the victim. Sexual homicide represents approximately 1.7 percent of homicide cases reported to law enforcement in the United States (US Department of Commerce, 2012). It has been defined in the literature as homicide in which a sexual element or sexual activity underlies the sequence of acts leading to the victim's death (Douglas, Burgess, Burgess, & Ressler, 1992). In these murders, the sexual behavior might occur before, during, or after the victim's death; the perpetrator's sexual behavior can involve fantasy, physiological arousal, masturbation, or actual penetration (oral, anal, or vaginal) of the victim with a variety of animate or inanimate objects (Meloy, 2000). Sexual fantasies are often sadistic in nature, and these offenders may act them out to achieve psychosexual gratification through the torture of another individual (Chan & Heide, 2009). The sexualization of the homicide may also be expressed in a graphically symbolic way, such as through mutilation of the victim's genitals before or after death. When a perpetrator commits multiple or serial sexual homicides, some of these acts may be a feature of every crime, serving as the offender's "signature." The offender's signature "infers the ritual or symbolic component of the sexual homicide that gratifies fantasy and remains psychosexually arousing" (Meloy, 2000, p. 10). For these offenders, there is a lethal pairing of sexual arousal and extreme violence.

The majority of perpetrators of sexual homicide are men younger than thirty (Meloy, 2000); their female victims are most often complete strangers or casual acquaintances (Dietz, Hazelwood, & Warren, 1990; Meloy, 2000; Myers & Blashfield, 1997). The strategic selection of strangers as victims can assist in preserving the perpetrator's anonymity or may serve his fantasy of grotesquely categorizing some women (his mother or his wife) as pure and others (his victims) as deserving of torture and violent death.

A number of taxonomies or classification schemes have been used to explain the personalities and behaviors of sexual homicide offenders. One based solely on those who kill adult women identifies two distinct profiles: sadistic offenders and anger offenders (Beauregard & Proulx, 2007). A sadistic sexual murderer is one who carefully premeditates his attack. He uses physical restraints and psychological or verbal abuse to dominate, control, and humiliate his victims. The crime leading up to the homicide usually lasts longer than thirty minutes, with body mutilation being a key feature. After killing the victim, the perpetrator moves her body to a different site, a method used to evade apprehension and delay identification of the victim. In contrast, an anger offender commits crimes of opportunity without careful planning. Violence is a strong theme in this type of murder, and physical restraints and mutilation are common tools of death. The crime takes less time than a sadistic killing, often less than thirty minutes. The profile suggests that angry sexual killers tend to leave the victim's body undisturbed at the crime scene rather than transporting her to another location in an attempt to hide her and delay identification.

Sexual homicide is the one type of violence against women in which the perpetrators and victims are usually strangers rather than intimate partners. When women are asked what type of crime they most fear, sexual violence by a stranger is the most common answer. Though these types of crimes are statistically rare and significantly less common than partner violence, the names Ted Bundy (1974–1978), the Night Stalker (1985–1989), the Green River Killer (1982–2000), the Dark Strangler (1926–1927), the Freeway Killer (1979–1980), the Bayou Killer (1997–2006), and the Railroad Killer (1986–1999; see story below) give women nightmares.

Women Who Murder

Women represent a relatively small percentage of violent offenders, so discussions of intimate partner homicide typically focus on men. There are, however, cases in which women use lethal violence, and when they do, it is usually against an intimate. Specifically, studies have found that when women commit homicide, 42 to 44 percent of the time they kill their male intimate partners (Greenfeld & Snell, 1999; Gauthier & Bankston, 1997; Starr, Hobart, & Fawcett, 2004). Men are much more likely to kill acquaintances or strangers; only 7 percent of their victims are female intimate partners (Gauthier & Bankston, 1997; Greenfeld & Snell, 1999).

One cannot gain an understanding of women's use of violence by analyzing men's violence, as there are significant gender differences in intimate partner homicide (Jordan, Clark, Pritchard,

& Charnigo, 2012). One of the major differences is the offender's motivation or intent at the time of the murder. Research studies reveal that men's reasons for killing their female partners are related primarily to jealousy and a need to control (Block, 2000; Block & Christakos, 1995; Wilson, Daly, & Daniele, 1995). Men are more likely to kill their female partners after an escalation of violence, and often when a woman attempts to escape his violence (Kellermann & Heron, 1999; McFarlane et al., 1999). Women's motives are quite different. Studies show that women's use of violence is usually a response to violence by their male partners (Campbell, 1995; Kellermann & Mercy, 1992; Mann, 1998), a phenomenon some have described as "victim-precipitated homicide." In short, men kill their intimate partners when the woman attempts to flee, and women kill their partners in self-defense or when they see no other alternative (Dugan, Nagin, & Rosenfeld, 1999; Gagne, 1998; Jones, 1996; Jurik & Winn, 1990; Maguigan, 1991; Steffensmeier & Allan, 1996).

Homicide-Suicide: 'Til Death Us Do Part

People who kill others rarely take their own lives afterward. The exception seems to be offenders who have killed their intimate partners (Dawson, 2005). When the view narrows to consider only fatalities from domestic violence, studies show that fully one-third of men who kill their intimate partners also commit suicide (Bossarte, Simon, & Barker, 2006). The rate of homicide-suicide in the United States (and, in fact, around the world) has remained stable over the past forty years (Eliason, 2009).

Understanding this specific subset of homicide is somewhat challenging, as homicide-suicides are relatively rare, and not all states collect specific data on these cases. Studies have found that homicide-suicides in the general population account for 1,000 to 1,500 deaths a year in the United States, or 20 to 30 a week (Marzuk, Tardiff, & Hirsch, 1992). Research on the national and international rates of homicide-suicide has estimated that Kentucky has a homicide rate of 5 per 100,000 population and a homicide-suicide rate of 0.3 per 100,000 (Milroy, 1995).

Who commits homicide and then kills themselves? Studies show that the majority of homicide-suicide offenders are male, with a mean age of forty to fifty years (Bossarte, Simon, & Barker, 2006;

Eliason, 2009; Travis, Johnson, & Milroy, 2007). They usually have a fairly low rate of criminal offending in their backgrounds (Eliason, 2009); among those who have committed crimes in the past, their offenses are often related to domestic violence. Approximately 70 to 88 percent of the homicide victims in homicide-suicide incidents are female (Campanelli & Gilson, 2002; Logan et al., 2008).

The homicide-suicides that attract the most media attention are those that involve strangers or youths. The April 1999 massacre at Columbine High School massacre is a startling example. In that case, two seniors, Eric Harris and Dylan Klebold, shot and killed twelve students and one teacher and then committed suicide. While these sensational events with multiple victims get the most publicity, the majority of homicide-suicides involve just two people, and the homicide victim is usually the current or former spouse or girlfriend of the perpetrator (Aderibigbe, 1997; Bossarte, Simon, & Barker, 2006; Campanelli & Gilson, 2002; Harper & Voigt, 2007; Logan et al., 2008; Marzuk, Tardiff, & Hirsch, 1992). In a cluster of homicide-suicide events that occurred in Kentucky between 1985 and 1990, 70 percent of the offenders were husbands, former husbands, or boyfriends (Centers for Disease Control and Prevention, 1991). In a study of firearm-related intimate partner homicides in Kentucky from 1998 to 2000, 54 percent included the suicide of the offender (Walsh & Hemenway, 2005). Notably, although most cases are associated with a history of domestic violence, a small number of spousal homicide-suicides involve the declining health of an aged female partner and an act of "mercy killing" by a caretaking spouse, who then kills himself (Comstock et al., 2005).

While the majority of homicide-suicide offenders are not mentally ill, depression appears to be more common among those who commit suicide after a murder compared with those who commit homicide alone (Banks, Crandall, Sklar, & Bauer, 2008; Marzuk, Tardiff, & Hirsch, 1992). Depression is often a reaction to the breakup of the offender's relationship.

One of the most significant risk factors for homicide-suicide involving intimate partners is the estrangement associated with divorce or breakup or real or perceived infidelity (Aderibigbe, 1997; Malphurs & Cohen, 2002; Marzuk, Tardiff, & Hirsch, 1992; Comstock et al., 2005). Research suggests that the offender is more likely to kill himself when the motive for murdering his intimate partner is related to possessiveness and jealousy (Bossarte, Simon, & Barker,

2006). Studies have found that in 30 percent of relationships that ended with a homicide-suicide, divorce was pending (Comstock et al., 2005), and among young couples, more than half had separated (Cohen, Llorente, & Eisdorfer, 1998). Other studies have found that only 30 percent of homicide-suicide victims and offenders were cohabiting at the time of the killings (Campanelli & Gilson, 2002), adding to the evidence that the point of separation or estrangement is a particularly dangerous time.

In homicide-suicides, the overwhelming weapon of choice is a firearm (Bossarte, Simon, & Barker, 2006; Hannah, Turf, & Fierro, 1998; Hanzlick & Koponen, 1994; Malphurs & Cohen, 2002). Firearms are also exceedingly common in intimate partner homicides. In one study examining 1,860 homicides, gun ownership was most strongly associated with homicide at the hands of an intimate partner (Kellermann et al., 1993). Another study found that homicide without suicide is often associated with a desire to punish, harm, injure, or seek retaliation, leading to choking, stabbing, or beating and causing multiple and severe injuries (Banks, Crandall, Sklar, & Bauer, 2008).

• • •

Sixteen-year-old Myrtle Whitaker married Allen Whitaker Jr. in June 1973. Although Allen had been good to her in the early days, there was a dramatic change after they married, when he became very controlling. Five months after the wedding, Myrtle gave birth to their first son, Kermitt; daughter Burniece followed one year later, and another son, Darvin, in 1983. Violence and abuse became the norm for this family living in a ramshackle house in a remote hollow of eastern Kentucky, a mile from the nearest road. In 1981 Myrtle and her children took that road, fleeing to her parents' home in another hollow in the area. Days later, Allen, armed with a gun, came to retrieve Myrtle and the children. Her mother said, "He didn't allow them to talk to nobody . . . just whoever he wanted them to speak to. He wouldn't let her speak to nobody" (*Lexington Herald-Leader*, December 30, 1990). Family members recalled that Allen would use a horse whip to control his family. He kept loaded guns in the house and used to tell Myrtle that they'd all be better off dead. Myrtle fled her abusive husband again on January 19, 1990. The rest of the story is best told by her daughter:

"We lived up a hollow called Bear Branch, the only house that was up there; about three-quarters to a mile up the hollow. We had to drive through the creek to get to the house. We didn't have any running water or indoor plumbing; the house was so old that we could see the outside through the cracks in the corner of the walls in one of the bedrooms; we heated it with coal and a woodstove.

"The night we left my dad, we went to our neighbor's house at the mouth of the hollow to use the phone to call my mom's dad. Then we hid in an old school bus building up the road from the neighbors. There we waited for my papaw to come and get us. He took us to an old mining road up behind his house, and he went to call the police. The police came and took us to a domestic violence shelter for abused children and women. My aunts then helped us move into an apartment in Salyersville and helped my mom buy a car so we would have transportation.

"My dad lived in an old shack at the local pay pond [fishing pond]. He had visitation to the boys. They would go and stay all night and go fishing with him.

"Mom and Dad's hearing for their divorce was scheduled for the twenty-first of December. Mom didn't know Dad knew; he always said he would never be divorced from her. So, on December 15, 1990, Kermitt decided he wasn't going to stay with Dad, he was going to go out with Mom that night. Mom had fixed a big dinner that day, she fixed a couple plates of food for Dad and Darvin so she would know they had food to eat that night. She always fixed Dad a plate of food because she worried about him and didn't want the boys to worry about their daddy going hungry.

"But that evening as we pulled up beside his car, he was standing beside it and as we pulled up Kermitt rolled the passenger window down and started handing Dad his and Darvin's food. He took a hold of the food, set it on the car, and said he had a better idea and reached into the car, pointing a gun at my mom. The gun was about an inch away from Kermitt's face. Kermitt pushed the gun and jumped out of the car and started fighting with Dad. Mom got out of the car and started running toward the gas station, and I jumped out and started to run back towards the apartments. Just as I jumped out I heard a shot and felt something hit my shoulder. But I continued to run past Kermitt and Dad. Just as I passed them, Dad shot Kermitt. I continued running, scared he was going to shoot me. Mom remembered the baby [Darvin] in the car and knew that he couldn't run for his life 'cause at seven years of age he was a chunky little boy weighing 136 pounds, so she turned around and ran back to the car and just as she put the car in drive, Dad reached through the passenger window and shot her in her right arm. The bullet traveled through and nicked her spinal cord and lodged in the left side of her neck, paralyzing her. As she became paralyzed her foot hit the gas and [the car] drove over into the culvert; she fell out and the car drove

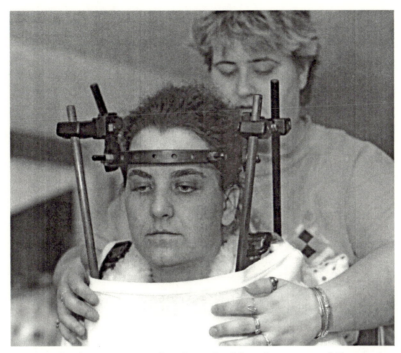

Myrtle Whitaker is supported in her wheelchair by a niece, following her shooting in 1990. (Courtesy of the *Lexington Herald-Leader*)

up on her hip. Her face was down in the dirt and her long black hair covered over her face. He came to the passenger side of the car and Darvin was in the back seat. Darvin began to beg for his life, saying, 'Please Daddy, I'll do anything, go anywhere, please don't hurt me.' Then he shot him twice. He then came and stood over Mom, thinking he had killed her 'cause he couldn't see her breathing 'cause of her hair over her face. She prayed for God not to let her die by his hands. He then went back and shot Kermitt a second time. After doing that, he went into a run and started screaming and shot himself between the eyes.

"Mom lived ten and one-half years paralyzed; she passed away June 3, 2001. The autopsy report ruled her death a homicide. After all those years, she still died at his hands.

"My name is Burniece Whitaker Minix. I'm the only surviving child of Myrtle Whitaker. People ask me all the time how I have lived with what has happened to my family. I just tell them I decided a long time ago that I had two choices in life: to let what happened take me down or use what happened to make me stronger. I chose to use it to make me stronger. I'm a mother of three beautiful kids and a grandmother (Nannie) to a very special little boy. I've been a wife to the same man for twenty years come March third. After twenty-two years I've decided to go back to school, and also have a part-time job. Life for me isn't easy. I have my bad days when I miss my family so bad that I feel I can't go on, but I have my mom in me, one of the strongest women I've ever known. Because of her I live, and because of her I strive to be better every day."

• • •

VIOLENCE IN THE IVORY TOWER

Since the nineteenth century, the term *ivory tower* has been used to designate a world where intellectuals engage in pursuits that are disconnected from the practical concerns of everyday life—far removed from ordinary, pedestrian troubles and certainly not touched by crime. This image belies what many women experience on college and university campuses in the United States, where rates of violence are high. In fact, studies show that college women may be at greater objective risk of certain forms of criminal victimization compared with their similarly aged, non-college-attending counterparts (Baum & Klaus, 2005; Fisher & Cullen, 2000; Fisher, Cullen, & Turner, 2000; Fisher, Sloan, Cullen, & Lu, 1998). College women are at greatest risk for rape, physical assault, and stalking.

In an early, groundbreaking study assessing the prevalence of rape among college women, Mary Koss and her colleagues found that almost one in ten female students (9.3 percent) had experienced an attempted or completed rape in the twelve months preceding the study (Koss, Gidycz, & Wisniewski, 1987). A number of other more recent studies have replicated these findings or documented even higher percentages (12.7 percent in Combs-Lane & Smith, 2002; 21.9 percent in Crawford, Wright, & Birchmeier, 2008; 23 percent in Marx, Calhoun, Wilson, & Meyerson, 2001; 35.3 percent in Fisher, Cullen, & Turner, 2000; and 36.5 percent in Wilcox, Jordan, & Pritchard, 2007).

Physical assault also affects college women. White and Koss (1991) found that over one-third of the women in their study had experienced physical dating violence in their adolescent and college years. Overall, studies have found that between 15 and 40 percent of adolescents and adults have experienced physical dating violence (Avery-Leaf, Cascardi, O'Leary, & Cano, 1997; Foshee, Linder,

MacDougall, & Bangdiwala, 2001; Jackson, 1999; Leonard, Quigley, & Collins, 2002; Lewis & Fremouw, 2001).

As noted earlier, stalking was first defined and became a crime in the 1990s. Stalking is particularly relevant to a discussion of college women, as more than half of stalking victims are between eighteen and twenty-nine years of age (Tjaden & Thoennes, 1998); the average age at which college women experience stalking for the first time is twenty (Nobles, Fox, Piquero, & Piquero, 2009). Prevalence studies on university campuses have found that 6 to 41 percent of college students have been stalked (Coleman, 1997; Fisher, Cullen, & Turner, 2002; Jordan, Wilcox, & Pritchard, 2007; Levitt, Silver, & Franco, 1996; Logan, Leukefeld, & Walker, 2000; McCreedy & Dennis, 1996; Mustaine & Tewksbury, 1999; Spitzberg & Rhea, 1999; Tjaden & Thoennes, 1998). The wide variability in prevalence rates results from differences in the way stalking is defined in each study, the length of time measured, and other research artifacts (Jordan, Wilcox, & Pritchard, 2007). The high rate of stalking victimization, the fact that the majority of stalking victims are women, evidence that twenty is the average age at which college women first experience stalking, and the fact that stalking typically lasts for almost two years (Tjaden & Thoennes, 1998) all reinforce how important it is for universities to implement prevention programs, interdiction, stringent consequences for offenders, and strong academic and emotional support for victims.

In addition to a woman's objective risk of victimization—that is, the rate at which women are raped, assaulted, or stalked—there is her so-called subjective experience of victimization—or a woman's perception of her own safety. This can have a profound effect on how safe women feel in the ivory tower. As noted earlier, although many studies have found that the most likely perpetrator of rape against a woman is her intimate partner, women are most afraid of sexual assault committed by a stranger. This is true for both college-aged and older women (Wilcox, Jordan, & Pritchard, 2006). Women also tend to be more afraid of being victimized by crime than men are (Ferraro, 1995). This fear of crime is a paradox, given that women actually experience lower levels of victimization for most (nonintimate) crimes than men do. Researchers in the field call this paradox the "shadow of rape" (Ferraro, 1995, 1996; May, 2001; Warr, 1984, 1985). They hypothesize that women's inordinate fear of crime is attributable to their intense fear of the specific crime of rape, which is the only index offense with predominantly female victims (Wilcox, Jordan, & Pritchard, 2006). As expressed by Mary Koss and her colleagues (1999) in a chapter heading: "uniting all women: the fear of rape."

While rates of domestic violence, rape, and stalking against college women are startlingly high, campus crimes have historically received little public scrutiny (Hudge, 2000; Nicklin, 2000; Wilcox, Jordan, & Pritchard, 2007). Public awareness of campus crime has been slow in coming because universities have drawn a protective veil of secrecy around their borders. Worried about parents' concerns and a drop in student applications, colleges and universities engaged in a pattern of denial of campus crime. A reform movement finally began to chip away at this practice—a movement strengthened after a young woman named Jeanne Clery lost her life on a college campus. Jeanne's story and the federal law that resulted from her murder are detailed in chapter 3.

• • •

On August 29, 1997, Holly Dunn's life changed forever. She and her boyfriend, Christopher Maier, both students at the University of Kentucky, had just left a party and decided to go for a walk along the railroad tracks. There, they encountered Ángel Maturino Reséndiz, the so-called Railroad Killer. Wielding a sharp instrument, he tied and gagged the young couple, and Holly watched helplessly as Reséndiz bludgeoned her boyfriend to death

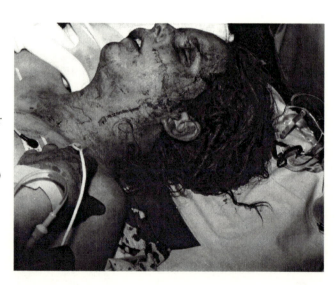

Holly Dunn after being assaulted, August 29, 1997. (Courtesy of Holly Pendleton)

Holly Dunn Pendleton,
January 2012. (Courtesy of
Holly Pendleton)

with a fifty-pound rock. Reséndiz then turned his rage on Holly, raping and stabbing her, beating her on the head with a railroad tie, and leaving her for dead. But Holly didn't die. She became the only known survivor of an attack by Reséndiz and testified at his trial in Texas for murders committed in that state. In June 2007 Reséndiz was put to death for his crimes.

Holly graduated from the University of Kentucky in 2000. In 2006 she helped found Holly's House, a child and adult advocacy center in Evansville, Indiana. That same year, Holly traveled to Washington, D.C., to accept the Jacqueline Kennedy Onassis Award for public service to local communities. Holly now works full time as a speaker, trainer, and advocate for victims' rights. Appearing on *48 Hours Mystery* in 2010, Holly described her recovery this way: "I definitely feel like I have another opportunity at life. I want to live it to the fullest. I can't explain how this changes you. I am a stronger person because of it. I'm—my whole life focus changed because of it. I'm—I'm a dif-ferent person today because this happened. I knew that I had to heal physi-cally first. And then I had to deal with Chris dying. I had to deal with myself almost dying. And then I had to deal with being raped. Your brain works in amazing ways and it kind of sort of let me deal with each thing as I could."

• • •

STUDYING THE PREVALENCE AND INCIDENCE
OF DOMESTIC VIOLENCE IN KENTUCKY

One of the nation's first statewide studies on the prevalence of domestic violence was conducted in the Commonwealth of Kentucky in 1979. The survey was the brainchild of the Kentucky Commission on Women and included 1,793 women who were married to or living with male partners at the time of the study (Schulman, 1979). The survey was conducted by Louis Harris and Associates, and its findings were startling. They forced Kentuckians to acknowledge that intimate partner violence was not a rare phenomenon or one that impacted only large urban centers in other states. It was as commonplace in 1979 as it had been in Kentucky's earliest days, when the Commonwealth earned the moniker "dark and bloody ground." In this case, that dark ground was found inside the homes of the Commonwealth.

The Harris survey first asked the women whether they had been abused by their partners in the past year. One in ten women answered yes to that question—at the time, representing more than 80,000 women. In today's population, considering only women over the age of eighteen, that 10 percent figure represents the experience of 168,968 Kentucky women. The women were then asked whether they had *ever* been abused, and 21 percent said they had been. In today's population, that represents more than 350,000 women in Kentucky. By using the earliest version of the Conflict Tactics Scale (Straus, 1979), the survey was able to document not just the prevalence and incidence of violence but also the severity of the violence reported. The survey found that almost 9 percent of the victims had experienced "severe violence" (defined as being beaten up, threatened with a knife or a gun, or hurt by a knife or a gun). Further, when Kentucky women were asked how their parents and grandparents had resolved disagreements, those who remembered their fathers using violence against their mothers were also most likely to report violence in their own intimate relationships. Specifically, women who had witnessed violence between their parents or had been physically abused themselves were one-third more likely to experience violence in their adult relationships than women who had not (Schulman, 1979).[2] Kentuckians value the stories passed down through the generations and told around the dinner table. But for many of the women participating in the Harris survey, those stories were punctuated by memories of violence.

In 1999 Kentucky had a second opportunity to objectively measure the presence of domestic violence when the University of Kentucky was awarded a $200,000 a year grant from the Centers for Disease Control and Prevention to create an Intimate Partner Violence Surveillance System.[3] The main objective of the project was to monitor the incidence and prevalence of intimate partner violence in Kentucky. From 2000 to 2003, the University of Kentucky Survey Research Center conducted an annual telephone survey on domestic violence, using a random sample of 2,000 adult women from across Kentucky. The 2002 survey found that 755 of the 2,018 women surveyed (37 percent) had been threatened, physically or sexually abused, or stalked by an intimate partner. Of the 755 women who experienced some form of victimization:

- 75 percent suffered multiple forms of violence from an intimate partner.
- 74 percent of physically or sexually abused women were injured, and 68.8 percent of them sustained more than one type of injury.
- 44 percent reported that their children were present during abuse.
- 20 percent reported abuse during pregnancy.
- 15 percent said an intimate partner had threatened a pet, and 5 percent said he had killed a pet.

When asked whether a doctor or nurse had ever screened them for domestic or intimate partner violence, less than 13 percent of the women interviewed said yes. Of the women who had never been screened by a health care professional, 50 percent said they had experienced victimization.

In the fall of 2002 the University of Kentucky's Center for Research on Violence Against Women[4] and the Governor's Office of Child Abuse and Domestic Violence Services[5] requested assistance from the National Violence Against Women Prevention Research Center in estimating the prevalence of rape among adult women in Kentucky. The resulting report found that approximately 11.1 percent of adult women in Kentucky had been victims of one or more completed forcible rapes during their lifetimes (Kilpatrick

& Ruggiero, 2003). Based on that figure, the estimated number of adult women in Kentucky who have ever been forcibly raped exceeds 175,000. That number does not include victims of other forms of sexual assault (including attempted rape and drug-facilitated rape) or rape victims younger than eighteen. As noted by the researchers who prepared the report, "Kentucky has a substantial rape problem as reflected by our conservative estimate that approximately one of every nine adult women . . . has been the victim of forcible rape sometime in her lifetime" (Kilpatrick & Ruggiero, 2003, p. 2).

Based on a belief that women at the University of Kentucky (UK) could be better protected by securing institution-specific data on the prevalence of domestic violence, rape, and stalking, in the spring semester of 2004, the UK Center for Research on Violence Against Women conducted the Women's Safety Study, an extensive study on victimization experiences and fear of crime among female UK students. (The initial study was replicated three years later.)[6] The study included a randomized sample of 1,010 female graduate and undergraduate students who responded to an anonymous telephone survey conducted over a four-week period. The survey was divided into three sections: the first addressed fear of crime among all female students, the second focused on victimization prevalence, and the third gathered specific details about the context of assaults and was administered only to women whose victimization experiences had occurred during their time at UK.

The study found that most female UK students feel safe on campus. In fact, only 15 percent of women reported feeling afraid. Although this appears to be a positive finding, this perception of safety among female students raises concerns, given their actual risk of victimization. Women were also asked about the type of offender they most fear, and the vast majority reported greater fear of assault by a stranger than by a known offender. This finding illustrates a need for education: whereas almost three-fourths of the women reported being more afraid of strangers, the study found that in almost 83 percent of cases, the female students assaulted at UK knew their assailants.

As for the rate of victimization, the Women's Safety Study found that well over one-third (36.5 percent) of female UK students had experienced at least one type of victimization while at UK (see table 2.1). More than 20 percent experienced sexual victimization, 18 percent were stalked, and 10.4 percent were physically victimized. In

Table 2.1. Victimization of Female University of Kentucky (UK) Students by Type

Victimization Type	Percentage of Female UK Students
All victimization types	36.5
Sexual victimization	20.8
Stalking victimization	18.0
Physical victimization	10.4

the replication study, that overall percentage had dropped to 34.1 percent, and rates of specific types of violence decreased as well (19 percent sexual victimization, 15.1 percent stalking victimization, and 10.3 percent physical victimization). The vast majority of women were harmed by someone they knew, such as a friend, an acquaintance, or an intimate partner; in fact, in the case of forcible rape, almost 95 percent of the offenders were known to the women. Notably, the most common type of offender was another UK student (51 percent of sex offenders, 32.3 percent of stalkers, 49 percent of physical assault offenders). Almost three-fourths of sexual victimization incidents and well over three-fourths of physical assaults occurred off campus. Cases occurring on campus occurred most often in dormitories or fraternity houses. Stalking cases showed a different pattern: just over half of stalking events occurred on campus.

One troubling finding was that only 1.5 percent of female victims of all types of sexual offenses reported their experience to the police, whereas 22.8 percent of physical assaults and 18.7 percent of stalking cases were reported to a law enforcement agency. Among cases that were reported, more than 80 percent of all types of offenses were reported within twenty-four hours of the incident, suggesting that victims either report offenses immediately or not at all. There was a significant association between violence and alcohol use for both victims and offenders.

The University of Kentucky's willingness to collect and then make public data on the victimization experiences of its students is atypical among U.S. colleges and universities. The Women's Safety Study was made possible because the university turned away from the old approach of suppressing any information that might be considered negative. The university responded to the study's findings by allocating significant funding for women's safety and supporting educational and prevention programs for its students.

3

Rape and Sexual Violence

A Nation's Reform

> By the time we are women, fear is as familiar to us as air; it is our
> element. We live in it, we inhale it, we exhale it, and most of the
> time we do not even notice it. Instead of "I am afraid," we say, "I
> don't want to," or "I don't know how," or "I can't."
> —Andrea Dworkin (Lewis, 2011)

The first two decades of the domestic violence and anti-rape movements achieved more legal reforms for women than the previous
three centuries combined. The voices of advocates were joined by
those of early researchers, who documented violence against women
and evaluated the police response, and attorneys, who helped survivors sue for equal protection. For anti-rape advocates, the first target was the repeal of unique provisions in sexual offense statutes that
had a harmful effect on rape survivors.

RAPE LAWS

To fully understand the challenges facing advocates in the 1970s,
one must examine the earliest U.S. laws addressing rape. These early
laws dramatically impacted the treatment of domestic violence and
rape victims for centuries, not only because law is based on prece-
dent but also because the attitudes toward women reflected in these
laws became embedded in the nation's culture, not just in its courts.

The first rape laws in the United States were not designed to
punish offenders who victimized women; instead, they were crafted

to punish those who damaged a man's property—that is, his woman (Bohmer, 1991). In blatant legal terms, women were the property of men (first a father and then a husband). It is a sad but ironic truth that early rape statutes made rape an offense against a man rather than against the woman who sustained the assault. This view of women as men's property, coupled with the perception of women as untruthful manipulators, directly impacted the penal codes of all states. Therefore, the first major legislative efforts were directed at changing those attitudes and the effect they had on state laws. Advocates targeted their energies toward repealing statutory provisions that were unfair in their design and harmful to rape victims in their application.

Early reforms were as much about reducing the persecution of rape victims as about increasing the prosecution of rapists. They focused on ensuring that rape victims received the same treatment as other victims of violent crimes and that these women were treated fairly, instead of being viewed with suspicion through the victim-blaming lens that was so prevalent at the time. One goal was to remove statutory roadblocks so that sexual assault became less difficult for victims to report. Another was to make rape cases easier for attorneys to prosecute and for judges and jurors to believe. Overall, advocates strove to reduce the skepticism with which the criminal justice system viewed rape cases (Spohn & Horney, 1992). As noted by one early author, reformers focused on the certainty of punishment rather than its severity (Estrich, 1987).

The inequities of the legal system and its harsh treatment of rape victims presented a very real challenge. Early reformers advocated not only with anecdotes but also with objective evidence of the legal system's failure to provide justice to women. That evidence included the low percentage of rape cases entering the criminal justice system and the high rate of attrition among those that did. For example, rape was (and is) one of the most unreported violent crimes in the nation (Gartner & Doob, 1994; Koss, 1992); only 16 percent of all rapes are reported (Kilpatrick, Edmunds, & Seymour, 1992). The National Violence Against Women Survey found that less than one-fifth (17.2 percent) of the women raped by an intimate had reported it to a law enforcement agency (Tjaden & Thoennes, 2000a). Other studies showed that between 50 and 90 percent of reported rape cases were filtered out of the criminal justice system rather than being fully prosecuted (Caringella, 2009; Frazier & Haney, 1996; Jordan, 2004). The legal system's treatment of rape survivors has been termed "secondary victimization" by scholars (Campbell & Raja, 1999, 2005; Campbell et al., 2001).

Why the particularly harsh and disparate treatment of rape victims? The answer can be found in unique statutory criteria, applied only to the crime of rape, that existed in state penal codes across the country in the 1960s, 1970s, 1980s, and beyond. In particular, advocates strove to rescind statutory language that allowed only a narrow window of time for reporting an assault, required corroboration of the rape victim's testimony, provided for special juror instructions in rape cases, required victims to physically fight off offenders, allowed irrelevant evidence of a woman's past sexual history to be disclosed at trial, and excluded spouses from culpability for rape. These injustices produced a flurry of advocacy, with thirty-six state rape statutes being revised between 1976 and 1978 (Field & Bienen, 1980).

· · ·

"Officer, I've been robbed," the distraught woman told the police officer. "Someone has stolen my wallet."

"OK," said the officer, "let me ask you a few questions about this alleged crime. First, is there someone else who can corroborate what you're saying? Your word alone isn't enough to charge someone with a serious offense like robbery. And second, you have to show some evidence that you tried to keep the robbery from happening. Did you try to fight off the robber? Where are your bruises? You see, under the law, just saying 'no' to him isn't enough; I have to have some physical evidence. And did you report this crime in a timely manner? We can't have you engaging in a nice conversation with this alleged robber one day and then getting mad at him and later claiming that he stole something from you. And you're not married to this man, are you? Because, obviously, your husband can't rob you. And here's an important point: have you ever been robbed before? Do you have a history of being robbed by a lot of different men? And, just so you know, if this case ever gets to trial, the judge will have to tell the jurors that it's easy to allege robbery and awfully difficult for someone to defend himself against that allegation."

· · ·

Reporting Timelines: Now or Never

A number of state rape statutes required so-called prompt reporting, which meant that rape victims had to report the crime to law enforcement within a specified period. The effect of such laws was to place a statute of limitations on rape cases, and in some states, that reporting requirement did not apply to any other felony. In Kentucky, for example, marital rape cases uniquely had a reporting deadline of one year.

Statutes of limitations are a part of common law. They mandate that legal action must commence within a specific time frame following a criminal event. When applied across the board of criminal offenses, their primary purpose is to protect defendants because evidence, memories of witnesses, and other details of a crime might be compromised over time. When applied in rape cases, however, the justification for a statute of limitations was more punitive; it reflected a belief that women might falsely allege rape to gain the upper hand in divorce or custody proceedings or that women might maliciously make false accusations to harm an intimate. That stereotype is embedded in historic court opinions and legal treatises authored by Sir Matthew Hale, whose words heavily influenced not just British common law but also American attitudes and statutes. Lord Hale served as the chief justice of England from 1671 to 1676. His *Historia Placitorum Coronæ* (The History of the Pleas of the Crown) was an influential treatise on English criminal law and served as a model for William Blackstone's commentaries. His writings on rape and the status of women as property continued to impact English law until 1991, heavily influenced American law, and were cited in U.S. courts as recently as 1993. With respect to a statute of limitations on rape cases, Hale wrote, "long delay of prosecution in such case of rape always carries a presumption of a malicious prosecution" (Hale, 1736, p. 633).

During the 1980s and 1990s, a number of states eliminated statutes of limitations in rape cases. At the time of the writing of this book, seventeen states had done so. Most recently, New York eliminated the statute of limitations on rape in 2006 (Goodman, 2006), and Kansas did so in 2013 (Wistrom, 2013). In a more recent trend, a number of states have extended or eliminated statutes of limitations if DNA later becomes available in a rape case.

Corroboration: Her Word Isn't Good Enough

"Women lie." At least, this has been the message communicated by an incredulous court system. The crime of rape has long been characterized as a "he said, she said" phenomenon, with a good deal of skepticism attached to the "she said" part. Fear of false allegations has attached itself to rape like no other crime. These attitudes were codified in early rape statutes, which stipulated that a claim of rape had to be corroborated by another person or other evidence; a victim's testimony was not sufficient. This placed an undue burden on prosecutors, who had to find corroborating evidence for such essential elements of the crime as who raped the victim, whether the sex was consensual, and whether the rapist penetrated her during the act. This requirement clearly gave the advantage to rapists, who most often committed their offenses in private, with no witnesses present. The anti-rape movement was successful in getting states to remove this statutory provision by either legislation or appellate decision. By 1984, only eight states still required corroboration, and two of them limited the requirement to statutory rape cases (Williams, 1984).[1]

Although the statutes have been revised, the controversy over false allegations still permeates the prosecution of rape cases. Fortunately, the ubiquitous myth that women "cry rape" can be addressed with objective data. In a recent review of sexual assault cases reported over a ten-year period, one group of investigators found a false allegation rate of 2 to 10 percent (Lisak, Gardinier, Nicksa, & Cote, 2010)— hardly rising to the level charged by skeptics.

Special Juror Instructions: The Poor Man Can't Defend Himself

In the 1960s and 1970s, many states were still using the so-called Hale's instruction to jurors. In his words, "It is true rape is a most detestable crime, and therefore ought severely and impartially to be punished with death; but it must be remembered, that it is an accusation easily to be made and hard to be prove, and harder to be defended by the party accused, tho never so innocent" (Hale, 1736, p. 635). In practice, judges would admonish juries to be cautious in their deliberations because it was, after all, quite easy for a woman to allege rape and very difficult for a man to defend himself against that charge (Goodmark, 2011).

Resistance by Victims: Does No Mean No?

As originally designed, state rape laws required that victims "earnestly resist" the assault against them; that is, for a sexual act to be considered rape, it had to be perpetrated by force. Said another way, the definition of *force* had essentially two elements: the offender's forcible action, and the victim's earnest attempt to stop him. Proponents of such language argued that because the act of sexual intercourse can, in fact, be engaged in quite happily by two consenting parties, the element of force was needed to differentiate between rape and a romantic or passionate encounter. That provision, however, placed a burden on rape victims that was not required of other crime victims. For example, one did not have to "earnestly resist" a robber for that experience to be legally defined as robbery. In fact, robbery statutes include the use of force by the offender, but they do not require the victim to fight back against the forcible taking.

The qualifier "earnestly" took the requirement one step further: not only did a rape victim have to forcibly fight off her rapist; she had to really mean it. For instance, the Wisconsin Supreme Court reversed a rape conviction on the grounds that the victim, who had screamed and struggled against the rapist, did not resist vociferously enough. The court opined: "there must be the most vehement exercise of every physical means or faculty within the woman's power to resist the penetration of her person, and this must be shown to persist until the offense is consummated" (*Brown v. State*, 1906).

Efforts to repeal force requirements have been modestly successful. Although the majority of states have amended their statutes and softened the definition of force (or forcible compulsion), "earnest resistance" language still exists in many state laws (Schulhofer, 2001). Some states compromised by specifying what constitutes force on the part of the offender, such as using or displaying a weapon, committing another crime at the same time as the rape, and injuring the victim (Spohn & Horney, 1992). By the 1980s, a number of states had completely removed the earnest resistance requirement (de jure removal), including Michigan, Alaska, Iowa, Minnesota, New Jersey, Ohio, Pennsylvania, and Vermont (National Organization for Women Legal Defense and Education Fund, 1987). As detailed in later chapters, Kentucky addressed forcible compulsion in several legislative sessions and was ultimately successful in amending its rape statute so that resistance on the part of the victim is no longer necessary.

Changes in the meaning of force in the context of rape and in the definition of forcible compulsion reflected changing social norms with regard to the sexual behavior of men and women and a growing understanding of the power dynamics in sexual offense cases. In the past, a woman had to forcibly push a man away for an assault to meet the legal standard. Anything short of that was an unfortunate misunderstanding between the parties, perhaps, but not a crime. An appellate case from the early 1980s exemplified the cultural upheaval as social norms changed.

It was the fall of 1977 when twenty-one-year-old Pat attended an alumnae event at the Catholic girls' high school from which she had graduated.[2] After the event, she and her friend Terry decided to drive in their respective cars to Fells Point, Maryland, to have a few drinks. On the way, Pat stopped to telephone her mother, who was caring for Pat's two-year-old son, and inform her of her plans. Pat and Terry visited three different bars that night, and each woman had two to three drinks, although, as police would later testify, Pat remained sober. In the third bar, Pat met a man named Eddie Rusk, whom Terry knew. During their conversation, Pat and Rusk learned that they shared the experience of being separated from their respective spouses and having a child. When Pat told Rusk she had to leave because it was a weeknight and she had to be up early the next morning, Rusk asked her to drive him home, and Pat agreed. According to Pat, on the way, she cautioned Rusk that she was just giving him a ride and there was nothing else to it, to which Rusk assented. After a twenty-minute drive, they arrived at Rusk's apartment, and Pat found herself in a totally unfamiliar neighborhood. As she pulled to the curb, Rusk asked Pat to go upstairs with him, but she refused. He invited her a second time, but she again declined, mentioning that her estranged husband might have hired a detective to watch her. The two disagreed about what happened next, but Pat later testified that even though Rusk was fully aware she did not want to go to his room, and despite her repeated refusals, he reached over, turned off the car's ignition, and took her car keys. He got out of the car, walked over to her side, opened the door, and said, "Now, will you come up?" At that moment, Pat testified, she feared Rusk would rape her. "It was," she said, "the way he looked at me" (*State v. Rusk*, 1981, p. 234).

By then, it was about 1:00 AM. Pat accompanied Rusk across the street into a totally dark house and followed him up two flights of stairs. She neither saw nor heard anyone else in the building. Rusk talked to her in his room for a few minutes and then left her alone for one to five minutes. While he was gone, Pat remained seated in the chair. She made no noise and did not attempt to leave. She said she did not notice a telephone in the room. When Rusk returned, he turned off the light and sat down on the bed. Pat asked if she could leave and told him she wanted to go home. Rusk, who was still in possession of her car keys, said he wanted her to stay. Rusk then asked Pat to get on the bed with him, and he pulled her to the bed by the arms. He then began to undress her, removing her blouse and bra. He unzipped her slacks, and she took them off when he told her to do so. Pat removed the rest of her clothing and then removed Rusk's pants because, she said, "He asked me to do it." After they were both undressed, Rusk started to kiss Pat as she was lying on her back. Pat explained what happened next:

> I was still begging him to please let, you know, let me leave. I said, "you can get a lot of other girls down there, for what you want," and he just kept saying, "no"; and then I was really scared, because I can't describe, you know, what was said. It was more the look in his eyes; and I said, at that point—I didn't know what to say; and I said, "If I do what you want, will you let me go without killing me?" Because I didn't know, at that point, what he was going to do; and I started to cry; and when I did, he put his hands on my throat, and started lightly to choke me; and I said, "If I do what you want, will you let me go?" And he said, yes, and at that time, I proceeded to do what he wanted me to. (*State v. Rusk*, 1981, p. 235)

Pat testified that Rusk made her perform oral sex followed by vaginal intercourse. Immediately afterward, Pat asked if she could leave. When Rusk said yes, she got up and got dressed. Rusk returned her car keys. She asked him for directions out of the neighborhood and left. On her way home, Pat went to a police station and reported what had happened to her.

In the criminal case that followed, Rusk was found guilty of second-degree rape. Under Maryland law, "A person is guilty of rape in the second degree if the person engages in vaginal intercourse with another person by force or threat of force against the will and without consent of the other person" (Maryland Code Art. 27, § 463(a)(1)). On appeal, the conviction was reversed by the Special Court of Appeals because Pat's testimony did not indicate any physical resistance or fear that would have prevented her attempt to resist or escape (*Rusk v. State*, 1979). Specifically, "we find the evidence legally insufficient to warrant a conclusion that appellant's words or actions created in the mind of the victim a reasonable fear that if she resisted, he would have harmed her" (*State v. Rusk*, 1981, p. 235). The Court of Appeals of Maryland subsequently overturned that reversal, affirming Rusk's conviction. At issue for the Court of Appeals was whether the reasonableness of a rape victim's apprehension or fear is a question of law or a question of fact. It was the court's opinion that the reasonableness of a rape victim's apprehension is a question of fact for the jury to determine; further, threats of force need not be made in any particular manner to put a person in fear of bodily harm.

The final appellate decision in *Rusk* was applauded by feminist legal scholars, as it trended away from requiring rape victims to forcibly fight off offenders, a central aspect of the anti-rape movement's reforms (Brownmiller, 1975). In traditional legal circles, however, the court's opinion was not widely accepted. Those negative sentiments were articulated in the rather robust dissent written by Justice J. J. Cole:

> While courts no longer require a female to resist to the utmost or to resist where resistance would be foolhardy, they do require her acquiescence in the act of intercourse to stem from fear generated by something of substance. She may not simply say, "I was really scared," and thereby transform consent or mere unwillingness into submission by force. These words do not transform a seducer into a rapist. She must follow the natural instinct of every proud female to resist, by more than mere words, the violation of her person by a stranger or an unwelcomed friend; she must make it plain that she regards such sexual acts as abhorrent and repugnant to her natural sense of pride. (*State v. Rusk*, 1981, p. 256)

Past Sexual History: She's Done It Before

Historically, rape cases were filled with testimony intended to impugn a woman's reputation and impeach her credibility as a witness. As noted in a case from the early 1900s, "In a prosecution for carnal knowledge, the inducement to perjury and revenge is so great that it is of the highest importance that the motive and character of the prosecutrix should be rigidly investigated, and to that end wide latitude should be permitted in the admission of testimony throwing light upon these points" (*Kidwell v. U.S.*, 1912). A defendant's goal was to convince the judge and jurors that a woman's allegation of rape was not credible because she had willingly had intercourse with lots of men. A woman who had had sex once would most certainly do so again. In addition, the message in courtrooms of old was that if a woman had consented to sex outside of marriage, she was "unchaste," and it was obvious to everyone that unchaste women were liars.

These evidentiary rules and statutory provisions explain why so many rape victims found *themselves* on trial, when the judge's and jurors' attention should have been focused on the offender's behavior and lack of credibility. The anti-rape movement remedied the unreasonable introduction of a victim's past sexual history through so-called rape shield laws. These laws and court rules were intended to protect victims by differentiating between past conduct that has a direct bearing on the crime before the court and past conduct that is brought up solely to impugn the victim's reputation. As noted in *Doe v. United States* (1981), the constitutional justification for excluding reputation and opinion rests on a dual premise: first, an accused is not constitutionally entitled to present irrelevant evidence; and second, reputation and opinion about a victim's past sexual behavior are not relevant indicators of either her likelihood to consent to a specific sexual act or her truthfulness. By the mid-1980s, almost all states and the federal government had adopted rape shield laws (Haxton, 1985).

The *Doe* decision (which held that victims do have standing to challenge adverse rulings at rape shield hearings) raised an interesting point. In that case, the defendant wanted to introduce evidence about the victim's sexual history not just to malign her character but also to show that his state of mind had been influenced by it. The defendant's argument was that, given the victim's past behavior with men, he had naturally assumed she wanted to have sex with him. In *Doe*, the question was whether "evidence of the defendant's state of mind as a result of what he knew of [the victim's] reputation" was admissible under Federal Rule of Evidence 412(a). The court concluded, "There is no indication . . . that this evidence was intended to be excluded when offered solely to show the accused's state of mind" (*Doe v. United States*, 1981).

As rape shield laws were enacted across the country, differences became apparent. Some were fairly weak in implementation, allowing testimony about a victim's sexual history following a showing of relevance. Others were much more restrictive, prohibiting all such evidence with a few specific exceptions, such as evidence showing prior sexual contact with the defendant in the case; evidence showing the source of semen, pregnancy, or a sexually transmitted disease; evidence rebutting sexual contact evidence presented by the prosecution; evidence showing that the victim had a motive to fabricate the allegation; and evidence of prior consensual sexual relations with other men that are substantially similar to the allegations underlying the current case (Spohn & Horney, 1992).

Some states chose not just to identify points of exception but also to differentiate between types of evidence. Therefore, evidence of past sexual contact to prove consent was differentiated from evidence intended to impeach the victim's credibility. In the 1980s, as reforms were progressing, states managed this differentiation in varying ways: California, for example, provided that evidence relating to consent was inadmissible but evidence relating to credibility was admissible. Just the opposite was true in other states, including Washington and Nevada.

As states were designing their laws and court rules, they had to strike a difficult balance between the rights of victims and the rights of defendants. The difficulty of doing so made rape shield laws one of the most controversial reforms pushed by the anti-rape movement. Fundamental legal principles and constitutional rights—such as a defendant's right to confront an accuser, a defendant's right to present evidence, a victim's right to privacy, and a victim's right to equal protection under the law—clashed. While the controversy continues, so far, appellate courts have upheld the constitutionality of rape shield laws (Berry, 2002; Spohn & Horney, 1992).

In 1975 Congress enacted the Federal Rules of Evidence governing the admission of facts in criminal and civil cases. Three years later, Congress enacted Rule 412, the federal rape shield law. Under this rule, any evidence offered to prove that a victim engaged in other sexual behavior or to prove a victim's sexual predisposition is generally inadmissible in any civil or criminal proceeding involving alleged sexual misconduct. Specifically, Federal Rule of Evidence 412 provides:

Rule 412 Sex Offense Cases; Relevance of Alleged Victim's Past Sexual Behavior or Alleged Sexual Predisposition

(a) Evidence Generally Inadmissible.—The following evidence is not admissible in any civil or criminal proceeding involving alleged sexual misconduct except as provided in subdivisions (b) and (c):

(1) Evidence offered to prove that any alleged victim engaged in other sexual behavior.

(2) Evidence offered to prove any alleged victim's sexual predisposition.

(b) Exceptions.

(1) In a criminal case, the following evidence is admissible, if otherwise admissible under these rules:

(A) evidence of specific instances of sexual behavior by the alleged victim offered to prove that a person other than the accused was the source of semen, injury or other physical evidence;

(B) evidence of specific instances of sexual behavior by the alleged victim with respect to the person accused of the sexual misconduct offered by the accused to prove consent or by the prosecution; and

(C) evidence the exclusion of which would violate the constitutional rights of the defendant.

(2) In a civil case, evidence offered to prove the sexual behavior or sexual predisposition of any alleged victim is admissible if it is otherwise admissible under these rules and its probative value substantially outweighs the danger of harm to any victim and of unfair prejudice to any party. Evidence of an alleged victim's reputation is admissible only if it has been placed in controversy by the alleged victim.

Kentucky's rape shield law, implemented in 1976, struck out language that existed in prior Kentucky law, specifically, that "evidence of the victim's prior sexual conduct was admissible to support the proposition that if she consented to have relations with one or more other persons then she consented to the relations with the defendant" (*Smith v. Commonwealth*, 1978). The most recent major amendment to the Commonwealth's rape shield law occurred in 2003 and was initiated by advocates working in partnership with prosecutors. That revision made Kentucky's law analogous to Federal Rule of Evidence 412 and extended the protection to civil cases (Jordan, Hughes, & Gleason, 2005).

Spousal Exclusion: Why Husbands Can't Rape

The earliest scholarly writings on marital rape found that 10 to 14 percent of married women are raped by their partners (Bergen, 1996; Finkelhor & Yllo, 1985; Russell, 1990). These crimes marred the lives of a startling number of women, and studies also showed that the vast majority of marital rape victims are assaulted multiple times (Koss, Dinero, Seibel, & Cox, 1988; Mahoney, 1999; Russell, 1990). These realities fueled the legislative advocacy work of the anti-rape movement. As some of the best-known feminist writers on marital rape have pointed out, the idea of women as men's property underlies the history of sexual assault and the laws that address it (Brownmiller, 1975; Russell, 1990). In the earliest days, sexual activity was defined as criminal not based on force or consent but based on the state of marriage. Sex within the confines of marriage was legal, and extramarital sex was not; force or consent was not especially relevant. From its biblical origins, this notion influenced later laws, making it unthinkable that a husband could rape his wife—his own legal property. Again, Sir Matthew Hale's *Historia* played a significant role. In short, his view was that wives could not charge their husbands with rape because they had no legal right to do so, having given up that right when they married. He believed in the concept of irrevocable consent: once married, consent was assumed as fact. Specifically, "the husband cannot be guilty of a rape committed by himself upon his lawful wife, for by their mutual matrimonial consent and contract the wife hath given up herself in this kind unto the husband which she cannot retract" (Hale, 1736, p. 629).

That concept was officially incorporated into the American legal system in 1857 in *Commonwealth v. Fogerty* (Glasgow, 1980). In that case, the court specifically held that a man (in this case, Patrick Fogerty) had a valid defense to the charge of rape if he could prove that he was the husband of the victim. In what was apparently the first reported decision to apply the preexisting marriage defense to a prosecution for forcible rape, a Texas court held that because of the implied consent doctrine, a husband could not be guilty of raping his wife (*State v. Frazier*, 1945). In the 1970s the tide began to turn. In New Jersey, Daniel Morrison was found guilty of raping his estranged wife in 1978. Six months later in Oregon, John Rideout became the first husband charged with rape while living with his wife (Bennice & Resick, 2003; X, 1999). Even though the Oregon court found Rideout not guilty, it was an important milestone. In 1981 *Commonwealth v. Chretien* resulted in the first marital rape conviction in the United States. In that case, James Chretien broke into his estranged wife's home and physically and sexually assaulted her. He was convicted in 1979 and appealed the verdict. The Massachusetts Supreme Judicial Court, on its own initiative, ordered direct appellate review and affirmed the conviction.

As judicial decisions began to evolve, advocates worked in parallel. Their first success came in 1975, when South Dakota amended its statute to abolish the spousal exemption. In 1975 marital rape was legal in every state, but by July 1993, every state had criminalized marital rape in at least some situations (Bennice & Resick, 2003; X, 1999), with North Carolina being the last state to do so. However, it is important to note that less than half the states have completely abolished the marital rape exemption from their criminal codes (X, 1999; Zorza, 2002). For example, in some states, the victim must have filed for divorce and be legally separated from the offender or must be living apart from him (Caringella, 2009). As discussed in later chapters, Kentucky has a colorful history of amending its penal code to address the spousal exclusion. The effort began in the late 1980s, but complete removal of the spousal exemption would fail. The 1990 Kentucky General Assembly finally passed marital rape legislation, but doing so required some unfortunate compromises.

Rape Is Redefined

During the years of reform, many states moved away from the term *rape* and its definition of "carnal knowledge" and replaced it with *sexual assault*. Roughly half the states enacted statutes that established degrees of severity for sexual assault or criminal sexual conduct, based on objective characteristics of the crime (e.g., use of a weapon, age and incapacitation of the victim, injury to the victim); this allowed punishment to be commensurate with the severity of the crime (Caringella-McDonald, 2000; Marsh, Geist, & Caplan,

1982). An additional modification in some states was to emphasize that rape is violence, not sex, and to bring sex crimes more in line with other types of violent assault (Searles & Berger, 1987). Reformers also sought to broaden the definition of rape to include penetration by objects other than a man's penis (so-called foreign object rape), an amendment accomplished by Kentucky in 1992.

Forensic Rape Examinations

Advocates in the anti-rape movement could not limit their legislative efforts to changing the justice system. They had to address the needs of rape victims as well. Following a sexual assault, the victim needs legal services to ensure her protection; medical services to ensure her physical health or to treat injuries; and, if desired, evidence collection to prosecute the rapist. As advocates escorted women to hospitals, police stations, and courthouses, too often they saw that the services available were inadequate at best; at worst, they subjected women to a veritable second victimization (Campbell et al., 2001). Stories abounded of women sitting for hours in busy, very public emergency rooms, waiting for a physician to perform a rape examination, only to leave with bills they were expected to pay; of women talking to police officers without the support of an advocate; or of cases falling through the justice system's proverbial cracks. The anti-rape movement addressed these weaknesses through legislation to authorize government payment for forensic rape examinations, certification of the medical professionals who perform these examinations, and development of protocols to guide multidisciplinary team responses to rape cases.

To anti-rape advocates, requiring a victim to pay for collection of the forensic evidence necessary to prosecute her case made no practical sense. A victim of breaking and entering would not expect to receive a bill from the police for dusting her home for fingerprints. Although some states banned the billing of rape victims, it was the federal Violence Against Women Act (VAWA, 1994) that effectively stopped the practice. VAWA required states, Indian tribes, and local governmental agencies to assume responsibility for the "full out-of-pocket cost of forensic medical exams" in order to qualify for grants provided under the act. Specifically, to receive the federal funds, states were required to certify that rape victims were not responsible for such costs and to designate a specific entity to pay for the exams (e.g., the state crime victims compensation board, a law enforcement agency, the prosecutor's office, victim services agencies, the health department). In some states (including Kentucky) the law was amended to specifically prohibit the practice of billing victims for rape examinations; this was one of the earliest reforms made by the anti-rape movement in Kentucky in the mid-1980s.

It was critical for the legal and medical systems to be reformed in tandem, because rape victims' experience of the two systems is often inextricably intertwined. Studies have shown that adult victims who report a rape to police are nine times more likely to receive medical care than those who do not (Resnick et al., 2000). Additionally, rape victims who have the assistance of an advocate immediately after the assault are significantly more likely to have police reports taken and less likely to report being treated negatively by police officers; these women also report less distress after their contact with the legal system (Campbell, 2006). Similarly, the presence of an advocate in the emergency department leads to the provision of more medical services to victims (including emergency contraception and sexually transmitted disease prophylaxis), significantly fewer negative interpersonal interactions with health care personnel, and less distress from their medical experiences (Campbell, 2006).

To increase effectiveness, standardize the performance of forensic rape exams, and ensure the linkage of medical, legal, and advocacy services, the anti-rape movement and its allies in the health and criminal justice systems created sexual assault nurse examiner (SANE) programs and sexual assault response teams (SARTs). SANE programs were first developed through voluntary protocols, followed later by the passage of state laws to establish certification credentials for SANEs. The SANE credential was formalized by the International Association of Forensic Nurses (IAFN) in 1996. The first SART program started in Memphis, Tennessee, in 1976, followed by programs in Minneapolis, Minnesota, in 1977 and Amarillo, Texas, in 1979 (Office for Victims of Crime, 2011). Kentucky has taken several steps to provide a coordinated response to rape victims: amending hospital licensure laws to require hospitals with twenty-four-hour emergency departments to maintain the capacity to perform rape exams, at no cost to victims; amending the nursing licensure law to create a SANE certification; creating a SART Advisory Committee; and codifying the existence of rape crisis programs. (All these reforms are described in later chapters.)

Since the implementation of SANE programs and SARTs, a number of efficacy studies have been conducted. Each has shown that this model provides better access to medical care for victims and aids in the prosecution process (Campbell, Patterson, & Lichty, 2005; Hazelwood & Burgess, 2009; McLaren, Henson, & Stone, 2009).

The Special Case of College Women

While reforms were being made on behalf of women in communities across the country in the 1970s, progress in the ivory tower would take longer. In April 1986 Jeanne Clery was a nineteen-year-old freshman at Lehigh University, a private four-year college in Bethlehem, Pennsylvania, when she was raped and murdered by another student in her campus residence hall. Jeanne's parents later learned that almost forty violent crimes had been perpetrated on the Lehigh campus in the three years before her murder. They added their voices to those of other advocates and called for reforms to protect college women. The result was the passage of federal legislation in 1990: the Jeanne Clery Disclosure of Campus Security Policy and Campus Crime Statistics Act (20 USC § 1092(f), with implementing regulations at 34 CFR 668.46). The Clery Act amended the Higher Education Act of 1965 and required all colleges and universities that participate in federal financial aid programs to collect and make public information about crimes that occur on and near their campuses.

The Clery Act was amended in 1992 to ensure that victims of campus sexual assault are afforded certain basic rights. It was amended again in 1998 to expand the reporting requirements and to formally name the law after Jeanne Clery. Subsequent amendments in 2000 and 2008 added provisions dealing with registered sex offender notification, campus emergency response, and protection of crime victims from retaliation. Today the Clery Act impacts approximately 7,500 universities, 4,000 of which are four-year public and private institutions. The law is enforced by the U.S. Department of Education, and failure to implement its provisions can result in a civil fine of $35,000 per violation and the university's suspension from federal student financial aid programs (Ward & Mann, 2011).

A number of states have codified the federal reporting requirements in state law, although this has not been done consistently.

For example, in the majority of states (California, Kentucky, Massachusetts, Oklahoma, Pennsylvania, Texas, Virginia, Washington, West Virginia, and Wisconsin), the reporting requirements apply to both public and private colleges and universities, whereas in others (Connecticut, Florida, Louisiana, and New York), only public institutions are included. Delaware's campus security laws pertain only to schools that receive federal financial aid funding, while Georgia, Minnesota, and Tennessee require only criminal justice agencies or universities with police or security departments to comply (Karjane, Fisher, & Cullen, 2002).

The Clery Act has brought crime on college campuses to national attention, but some argue that the law has not lived up to its intended purpose. For example, there have been charges that the reports generated under the Clery Act dramatically underreport the actual number of crimes. A review of state compliance funded by the U.S. Department of Justice found that only 36.5 percent of schools reported crime statistics in a manner that was fully consistent with the Clery Act (Karjane, Fisher, & Cullen, 2002). Some university representatives claim that the underreporting of campus crime is due to jurisdictional confusion, organizational inefficiencies, and concerns about student confidentiality (Gregory, 2001; Hardy & Barrows, 2001; Nicklin, 1999). In terms of violence against women, Clery reporting is primarily associated with incidents that have been reported to law enforcement, and as already noted, the rates of reporting are extremely low for rape and domestic violence (Fisher, Hartman, Cullen, & Turner, 2002). While some argue that full enforcement of Clery would mean reporting all such cases to campus police, many advocacy and counseling programs provide services to women who do not wish to report the crimes against them. Notwithstanding the ability to report while maintaining the victims' anonymity, many advocates are reluctant to engage in Clery reporting. These limitations of the federal law do not mean that it has been ineffective; at the very least, it has focused attention on a problem that was once hidden in the shadows of the ivory tower. In addition to the Clery Act, the introduction of federal funds through the Grants to Reduce Domestic Violence, Dating Violence, Sexual Assault, and Stalking on Campus Program has significantly expanded the ability of colleges and universities to adopt comprehensive, coordinated responses to these crimes.

PORNOGRAPHY LAWS

Pornography is often seen as a victimless crime, but the faces of the women and girls participating in these photographed and videoed acts suggest that these offenses should be included in a historical review of violence against women. As noted by Andrea Dworkin, one of the most significant early reformers, the anti-pornography movement did not see itself as isolated or separate from movements against the exploitation of women (Wilson, 1982).

Pornography grew from a largely underground business to an enormous exploitive powerhouse in the late 1950s (Bridges & Jensen, 2011) and became a major entertainment industry worth an estimated $10 billion annually (Lane, 2000). Prior to the women's movement, debates around pornography were generally centered on morality questions, with liberal and conservative protagonists waging the battle. With the beginning of the anti-rape movement, advocates began to emphasize how pornography eroticized the domination and subordination of women. They espoused a feminist critique that viewed the production of pornography as misogyny and a way for the patriarchy to exploit women. As noted by Bridges and Jensen (2011, p. 137), "while not denying the ability of women in the industry to make choices, the feminist anti-pornography movement focuses on the economic, social, and cultural factors that influence women's choices to perform, such as histories of sexual abuse in childhood, the violence of pimps, and the control of boyfriends and other men." Some scholar-advocates saw an association between pornography and rape: "Pornography is used in rape—to plan it, to execute it, to choreograph it, to engender the excitement to commit the act" (Dworkin, 1986).

Within this framework, early activists fought for legislation that eschewed traditional criminal obscenity laws in favor of a civil rights approach that allowed women to pursue civil damages against the producers of pornography. These efforts were confronted with arguments about free speech, as noted by Catharine MacKinnon (1984):

> Central to the institutionalization of male dominance, pornography cannot be reformed or suppressed or banned. It can only be changed. The legal doctrine of obscenity . . . has made the First Amendment into a barrier to this process. This is partly because the pornographers' lawyers have persuasively

presented First Amendment absolutism, their advocacy position, as a legal fact, which it never has been. But they have gotten away with this (to the extent they have) in part because the abstractness of obscenity as a concept, situated within an equally abstract approach to freedom of speech embodied in First Amendment doctrine, has made the indistinguishability of the pornographers' speech from everyone else's speech, their freedom from our freedom, appear credible, appealing, necessary, nearly inevitable, principled.

These legal advocacy efforts were ultimately unsuccessful and, in fact, were not supported by all feminists. Although some women activists agreed that pornography represented misogyny, the fear of censorship led them away from that legal strategy. They also feared an unintended consequence: that women would lose the right to choose what they did to and with their own bodies. This latter point of view became more widespread in the 1990s and 2000s, with the belief that women's autonomy and freedom are paramount and cannot be risked even to address the harm of pornography (Bridges & Jensen, 2011).

Within the legislative efforts against pornography are two extremely important lessons about the movements to end violence against women. First, these issues are terribly complex and do not lend themselves to a simple or singular solution. Second, advocates in the anti-rape and domestic violence movements often fought side by side for the same ultimate outcome (freedom from violence), but they did not always speak with one voice.

Reforms against Rape: What Have They Wrought?

As with any complex social and legal reform movement, the anti-rape movement's efforts are ongoing. The routine sexual victimization of women is still present in every state. Although this precludes any grand statement about success, the improvements achieved by the movement have touched the lives of hundreds of thousands of women. More crisis hotlines, counseling services, medical and legal advocacy, and other services have been funded and are available to the women who seek them. The criminal and civil justice systems are more responsive, and the health care system—the physicians, nurses, and therapists who staff hospitals, clinics, and offices—are better prepared to aid victims. Perhaps the best example of effective reform is the introduction of sexual assault nurse examiners working in the context of sexual assault response teams, leading to improved victim services and increased prosecution of offenders.

One of the desired outcomes of legislative reform was that more women victimized by rape would feel comfortable enough to reach out for help from the justice system. If reforms accomplished that, advocates believed, then they would see an increase in the reporting of sex crimes to the police. Results have not met expectations. Early research in Michigan, which implemented some of the nation's earliest and most comprehensive reforms, found no change in the number of rapes reported to law enforcement (Marsh, Geist, & Caplan, 1982). Research on the effectiveness of reforms in six jurisdictions found an increase in reporting rates in some cities but not in others (Spohn & Horney, 1992). Interestingly, the researchers believed the rate increases were more attributable to the publicity surrounding the legal reforms than to their substantive content. In a review of 1,985 reforms in forty-eight states, Berger, Neuman, and Searles (1994) reported that legislative reforms did not appreciably affect reporting rates; however, those reforms that extended who was protected under the rape statutes did have a positive impact. Analysis of data from the National Crime Victimization Survey found that rape victims were slightly more likely to report their victimizations after statutory reforms were in place (Bachman 1991). Finally, research studies have found that a rape occurring in the modern reform era (1990–1996) was significantly more likely to be reported than one that occurred in the pre-reform era (before 1975) (Clay-Warner & Burt, 2005).

Perhaps the most challenging place to find positive change is on the criminal side of the legislative reform effort. There, success is measured by metrics such as rates of arrest and prosecution and percentage of cases resulting in conviction and incarceration, all of which have remained fairly constant (Seidman & Vickers, 2005). In other words, evidence suggests that reforms have not increased the likelihood that offenders will be arrested, prosecuted, and incarcerated. Additionally, in the courtroom, attorneys are still arguing the same points of contention: the meaning of consent, degrees of force, the victim's role as an active or passive participant in the event, and the victim's right to privacy (Bryden & Lengnick, 1997). These lackluster results can be blamed not so much on the way language was codified or policies written but rather on the major extralegal factor affecting victims' experiences in the justice system: the attitudes of relevant decision makers. As noted, these attitudes have not kept pace with statutory reforms (Seidman & Vickers, 2005). De jure reform (i.e., changes in the law) has not translated into de facto reform (i.e., changes in practice) in every jurisdiction. This failure highlights the critical role of rape crisis advocates in escorting women through the criminal justice process. It also underscores the need to redouble efforts to create multidisciplinary teams and to train criminal justice professionals.

There is evidence that the rape shield laws have had a positive effect, but not equally across all kinds of rape cases. In the review of reforms in six jurisdictions cited earlier, the benefits associated with rape shield laws accrued primarily to victims of stranger rape (Spohn & Horney, 1992). In those cases, a victim's sexual history is less likely to be an issue, unless it is considered unusual or extreme (e.g., the victim engaged in prostitution). When consent is the primary point of contention, particularly if the victim had sexual relations with the defendant on prior occasions, the victim's past sexual conduct is still likely to be considered relevant, even in states with strong rape shield laws. This has calmed some of the fears of critics who argued that rape shield laws would prevent the introduction of probative (or relevant) information (Spohn & Horney, 1992).

In their totality, studies suggest that rape reporting rates have been positively impacted by reforms to the justice system, that quality advocacy services are available and make a difference, and that certain reforms have extended legal protections. However, the hoped-for outcome of higher rates of prosecution and conviction has not yet been achieved.

4

Domestic Violence and Stalking

A Nation's Reform

The push to reform the laws pertaining to rape, domestic violence, and stalking did not begin with the judges who interpreted the law, the police who enforced it, or the attorneys who prosecuted violators of it. Rather, it began in the women's movement of the 1970s. Women's rights advocates declared that what happened behind closed doors between husbands and wives was not private but deeply political, setting the stage for the anti-rape and domestic violence movements that followed (Schechter, 1982). While the early courts opined on laws that, in effect, gave abusive men immunity and permitted a veil of secrecy to shield family violence, feminist advocates challenged the concept of family privacy, pierced the veil, and forced the issue of violence against women into the nation's collective consciousness (Schneider, 2000; Siegel, 1996).

• • •

"The movement has . . . challenged the idea that the family is always a safe haven from a brutal world. . . . The seemingly private sphere of the family and the public sphere of social and worklife will never be quite so separate again."
—Susan Schechter (1982, p. 31)

• • •

DOMESTIC VIOLENCE LAWS

Centuries ago, Roman law treated women as the property of their husbands, who were empowered to control, beat, divorce, or even murder their wives if they committed offenses that jeopardized their husbands' reputations or property rights (Schneider, 2000). Almost 2,800 years ago, during the reign of Romulus, wife abuse was accepted and condoned under the "laws of chastisement," which gave husbands the absolute right to discipline their wives physically for various unspecified offenses (Smith, 1988).

Under English common law, which serves as the basis for American jurisprudence, the feudal doctrine of coverture applied, whereby women lost their legal identities when they married. Williams Blackstone confirmed that "by marriage the husband and wife are one person in law; that is, the very being or legal existence of the woman is suspended in marriage" (Blackstone, 1966, p. 442). Early writers in the domestic violence movement observed that this law effectively removed married women's legal status and disempowered them to such an extent that they had no legal protections (Dobash & Dobash, 1979). In practice, this also meant that a husband could legally batter his wife, as long as minimal marks were left. This notion of a permissive level of violence left women without a legal system to turn to for protection. Interestingly, this same thinking still applies to the discipline of children in many cultures where spanking is permissible, but leaving marks is not.

In the seventeenth century, laws were enacted that criminalized physical violence against women. In 1641 the Puritans' Massachusetts Body of Laws and Liberties provided that "every married woman shall be free from bodily correction or stripes (lashing) by her husband, unless it be in his own defense upon her assault" (Pleck, 1987, p. 21). Unfortunately, in practice, these laws were fairly meaningless. The Puritan culture was ruled by religious laws that gave the family patriarch the responsibility of enforcing rules of conduct among family members; thus, a husband had tacit permission to "physically discipline," or batter, his wife (Buzawa & Buzawa, 1996). Evidence of the Massachusetts law's lack of authority is the fact that, between 1633 and 1802, only twelve cases of wife abuse were brought to court in Plymouth Colony (Pleck, 1987).

In the nineteenth century, courts upheld a husband's right to discipline his wife. In 1824 the Mississippi Supreme Court ruled in *Bradley v. State* that a husband could use "moderate chastisement" in cases of emergency. *Bradley* was overturned by *Harris v. State* in 1894, but by then, most states had adopted laws that followed the so-called moderate chastisement standard. At least one court opinion, coming from North Carolina, declared that the defendant had a right to strike his wife as long as he used a switch no longer than his thumb. Specifically, the court ruled: "We find that the defendant struck Elizabeth Rhodes, his wife, three licks, with a switch about the size of one of his fingers (but not as large as a man's thumb), without any provocation except some words uttered by her and not recollected by the witness. . . . The laws of this State do not recognize the right of the husband to whip his wife, but our courts will not interfere to punish him for moderate correction of her, even if there had been no provocation for it" (*State v. Rhodes*, 1868, p. 1). Though never a widely accepted legal principle, for many years, the so-called rule of thumb communicated that a modest amount of violence against a wife was acceptable.

• • •

"Family broils and dissensions cannot be investigated before the tribunals of the country, without casting a shade over the character of those who are unfortunately engaged in the controversy. To screen from public reproach those who may be thus unhappy situated, let the husband be permitted to exercise the right of moderate chastisement, in cases of great emergency, and use salutary restraints in every case of misbehavior, without being subjected to vexatious prosecutions, resulting in the mutual discredit and shame of all parties concerned."

—*Bradley v. State* (1824, p. 157)

• • •

In 1873 the North Carolina Supreme Court issued an opinion that appeared to be a victory for women. The court opined that a husband did not have a right to chastise his wife under any circumstances; however, "if no permanent injury has been inflicted, nor malice, cruelty nor dangerous violence shown by the husband, it is better to draw the curtain, shut out the public gaze, and leave the parties to forget and forgive" (*State v. Oliver*, 1873, p. 89). This approach led to a number of court cases in which a husband's violence toward his wife was upheld as legal and a private matter, unless the violence was particularly egregious or resulted in permanent injury (Dobash & Dobash, 1979; Worden, 2000). The husband's behavior had to reflect a pattern of violence, not just "an occasional incident due to the normal stress of marriage" (Sonkin, 1987, p. 9).

By the end of the nineteenth century, the era of "chastisement" as a defense to wife battering was in decline. In a landmark case in 1871, the Alabama Supreme Court upheld the conviction of George Fulgham for physically abusing his wife, Matilda. In the court's opinion, a husband did not have the right to physically abuse his wife even moderately or with restraint, as previous courts had held. In *Fulgham v. State*, a court finally ruled that a married woman deserved protection under the law.

The same year, the Massachusetts Supreme Court rejected a husband's defense that he had a right to hit his wife because she was drunk (*Commonwealth v. McAfee*, 1871). Hugh McAfee had struck his wife Margaret in the face and on the head. She fell from the momentum of the blows, hit her head on a chair, and died. The court opined that "beating or striking a wife violently with the open hand is not one of the rights conferred on a husband by the marriage, even if the wife be drunk or insolent" (quoted in Siegel, 1996, p. 2131).

In addition to changes in court rulings, in the late nineteenth century, state legislatures began to adopt laws that imposed more severe consequences for wife beating, including Delaware in 1881, Maryland in 1882, and Oregon in 1886. Arguably, one reason for the change was the growing presence of the temperance movement and the suffrage movement. In the nineteenth century, the temperance movement decried the social ills that accompanied alcohol, including the battering of women by alcoholic husbands. In the twentieth century, the women's suffrage movement influenced the domestic violence movement that would follow some fifty years later.

At an 1848 convention held in Seneca Falls, New York, delegates produced a *Declaration of Sentiments* in which women first denounced the common-law doctrine on marital status. "Woman's rights advocates protested the hierarchical structure of marriage; and, as they did so, they attacked the chastisement prerogative as a practical and symbolic embodiment of the husband's authority over his wife" (Siegel, 1996, p. 2128). Despite improving court opinions that gave women legal recourse against their violent husbands, by the late 1960s, convictions, punishment, and true legal reforms were still elusive. Rather than offering protection to battered women, jurisdictions across the United States still largely ignored their cries for help. Both statutes and court opinions had a significant impact on women's legal remedies following an assault. Historically, the courts had defined women as property and lowered a veil of privacy over domestic violence. Even as that veil was being lifted through political activism, the laws were still not protecting women. More would have to be done. Women's advocates believed that legislative reform was imperative.

Reform of the Criminal Justice System

Based on the adage that "the personal is political," the domestic violence movement took the experiences of women and used them in the fight for legislative reforms. In this sense, they created an interrelationship between law and social movement, between rights and politics, between consciousness and social change. Advocates also sought changes in criminal statutes for symbolic reasons: "as the primary institutional mechanism for both limiting and exerting government authority over citizens, the law has become a symbolic marker in the United States of which topics and events should be treated as public and which should be respected as private" (Kelly, 2003, p. 60). Finally, changes had to address what women experienced as either inaction or inappropriate action by law enforcement and prosecutors when they sought legal protection.

• • •

"Past research shows that police did not arrest men who battered their wives, even when victims were in serious danger and directly asked officers to arrest. Activists in the battered women's movement saw failure to arrest as tacit support for battering, contributing to the inability of women to escape violent relationships and in the escalation of abuse to domestic homicides."

—K. Ferraro (1989, p. 1)

• • •

The first generation of domestic violence–related legal reforms focused heavily on ensuring that police and prosecutors would use existing laws to protect victims and hold offenders accountable for their crimes. For decades, research had shown that even when legal remedies were available, they would not be utilized when women sought help. For example, police were often not arresting the offenders when responding to domestic violence calls (Baker, Cahn, & Sands, 1989; Berk & Loseke, 1980; Brown, 1984; Ferraro, 1989). In a sample of sheltered women, Coulter and Chez (1997) found that more than half had contacted police, but less than one-fourth of the offenders had been arrested. Some domestic violence–related reforms were accomplished through legislative changes to penal codes across the nation, and some were achieved through civil lawsuits that charged police with failure to protect and inequitable application of the law.

One of those civil cases put Torrington, Connecticut, on the map. Tracey Thurman lived in Torrington with her son. She had left her husband, Charles (who went by the name Buck), but his abuse continued unabated. Between early October 1982 and June 10, 1983, Tracey and her family members had repeatedly called the police because of Buck's threats against her life and the life of her son, but the Torrington police did nothing to help. Tracey was granted a civil protective order from the court, but the police failed to enforce it when her estranged husband violated its provisions. Early on the afternoon of June 10, 1983, Buck appeared at Tracey's residence and demanded to speak to her. She stayed inside and called the police, informing them that Buck was making threats and violating the protective order and asking the police to come to her house. After waiting more than fifteen minutes for help to arrive, she gave up on the police and went outside to speak to her estranged husband, hoping to persuade him not to harm or take their son. Instead, Buck stabbed Tracey repeatedly in the chest, neck, and throat. Approximately twenty-five minutes after her call to the Torrington police, a single officer arrived on the scene. Buck dropped the bloody knife and, in the presence of the officer, kicked Tracey in the head. He then ran inside the house, emerged from the residence holding his son, dropped the child on his wounded mother, and kicked her in the head a second time. Soon thereafter, two additional officers arrived on the scene, but they still permitted Buck to wander around and continue to threaten his estranged wife. Finally, when he approached Tracey again as she was lying on a stretcher, Buck was arrested and taken into custody. Tracey Thurman defied the odds and survived the attack, although she lost some body functions and motor skills. Her lawsuit against the city and the police department that had failed her resulted in a $2.3 million award and set the tone for "failure to protect" cases across the nation.

In 1999 in Colorado, another wife and mother felt the sting of the law's failure to protect. As told by Fenton (2011), Jessica Gonzales's husband had abused her on repeated occasions and had attempted suicide several times. When she filed for divorce, Jessica obtained a civil order of protection that required her husband to vacate their shared premises and restricted his visitation of their three children—ten-year-old Rebecca, eight-year-old Katheryn, and seven-year-old Leslie—to alternate weekends. On June 22, 1999, in violation of the protective order, Simon Gonzales came to their home at approximately 5:15 PM and kidnapped the three girls from the front yard, where they were playing. Jessica contacted the Castle Rock police to report her children missing but was told to wait to see if they returned. Jessica began to call her estranged husband's cell phone, hoping to learn the whereabouts of her daughters. At 8:30 she finally reached him and ascertained his location. She immediately passed this information along to the police, asking them to retrieve her girls and arrest her husband. Again, the police told her to wait. She called the police at 10:00 and again at midnight (her fifth call for help), but still the police did not take action. At 1:00 AM Jessica arrived at the police station in person to file a criminal complaint, but the officer only took a report; her complaint resulted in no action by the department. At 3:20 AM Simon Gonzales arrived at the Castle Rock police station and opened fire with a semiautomatic handgun he had purchased earlier that evening. The police returned fire, killing him. Inside the cab of his pickup truck, police found the bodies of the three little girls. Jessica was told initially that her estranged husband had shot and killed the girls earlier in the evening, but exactly how and when her daughters were murdered has never been confirmed.

Jessica Gonzales sued in the U.S. District Court for the District of Colorado (under Rev. Stat. § 1979, 42 USC § 1983), claiming that the town of Castle Rock had violated the Constitution's due process clause because its police department had "an official policy or custom of failing to respond properly to complaints of restraining order violations" and "tolerate[d] the nonenforcement of restraining orders by its police officers" (*Castle Rock v. Gonzales*, 2005, p. 754). Her case was dismissed, but on appeal, the Tenth Circuit Court of Appeals found that she had a procedural due process claim. In 2005 the U.S. Supreme Court reversed the Tenth Circuit's decision, reinstating the district court's order of dismissal. In a seven-to-two opinion written by Justice Antonin Scalia, the Court held that a town and its police department could not be sued under 42 USC § 1983 for failing to enforce a restraining order and that, for purposes of the due process clause, Jessica Gonzales did not have a property interest in police enforcement of the restraining order against her

husband. In part, the Court's finding centered around the definition of the word *shall* in the Colorado law and whether it was suffi-
ciently strong to make enforcement mandatory. In the Court's view,
a true mandate of police action would require a decidedly stronger
indication from the Colorado legislature than the law's language that
an officer "shall use every reasonable means to enforce a restraining order" (Colo. Rev. Stat. § 13-14-103). In making its finding, the
Court cited the well-established tradition of police discretion in the
enforcement of such orders. Women's advocates complained bitterly
that the Court's opinion "effectively gives law enforcement a green
light to ignore restraining orders, and will cause tremendous harm to
abuse victims who attempt to leave violent life-threatening environ-
ments" (National Organization for Women, 2011).

Jessica Gonzales's fight for justice did not end with the Supreme
Court of the United States, although she was "devastated" by that
opinion (Fenton, 2011, p. 408). In a unique step, the American Civil
Liberties Union (ACLU) petitioned the Inter-American Commission on Human Rights on her behalf. For the first time, the commission would be asked to consider the affirmative obligations of the
United States to protect its female citizens from domestic violence
(Fenton, 2011). The commission found that the state had failed to
act with due diligence to protect Jessica Gonzales and her children
from domestic violence, which violated the state's obligation not to
discriminate and to provide equal protection under the law. The
commission opined that the state had "failed to undertake reasonable measures to protect the life of Leslie, Katheryn and Rebecca
Gonzales in violation of their right to life" (*Jessica Lenahan [Gonza-
les] et al. v. United States*, 2011, p. 2). The commission offered several recommendations to the United States, among them, to "adopt
multifaceted legislation at the federal and state levels, or to reform
existing legislation, making mandatory the enforcement of protection orders and other precautionary measures to protect women
from imminent acts of violence, and to create effective implementation mechanisms. These measures should be accompanied by adequate resources destined to foster their implementation; regulations
to ensure their enforcement; training programs for the law enforcement and justice system officials who will participate in their execution; and the design of model protocols and directives that can be
followed by police departments throughout the country" (ibid., p.
56). Though nothing could compensate for her overwhelming loss,

the commission's ruling was a great victory for Jessica Gonzales (who remarried and became Jessica Lenahan) and for all battered women in the United States. Her case defined domestic violence as a human rights issue and demonstrated that international tribunals can be venues for women's rights litigation in domestic violence cases. It shined a light on existing imperfections in the U.S. justice system and brought international attention to the need to reduce gender violence (Fenton, 2011).

Law Enforcement Response and Mandatory Arrest. Prior to the success of cases such as Tracey Thurman's and, ultimately, Jessica (Gonzales) Lenahan's, domestic violence was most often treated as a private family matter. This reflected a belief that intervening in families was not the job of law enforcement; this type of "hand-holding" was more appropriately performed by social workers. Police officers did not earn professional recognition or rewards by responding to domestic violence calls, which in those days, rarely resulted in an arrest. Instead, the glory came from arrests in criminal cases, such as burglary, trafficking, and murder. Individual officers felt this way, and this point of view was embedded in police policy, which instructed officers to mediate or use the "walk around the block to cool off" rule, rather than making on-scene arrests for domestic violence–related assaults. Additionally, for many years, police officers viewed domestic disturbances as the most dangerous calls to respond to; they were thought to be associated with a higher risk of serious injury or death to the responding officer than other types of calls (R. R. Johnson, 2011). Although recent research has shown that belief to be false (e.g., MacDonald, Manz, Alpert, & Dunham, 2003), the perceived potential for danger elevated officers' negative views of domestic violence cases. Still, domestic violence scenes are far from safe. Data from the FBI reveal that while the survival rate for officers assaulted in the United States has been steadily increasing, that is not the case for assaults at domestic violence–related scenes (R. R. Johnson, 2008).

Between 1974 and 1994, advocates in the domestic violence movement worked to implement policies that toughened the police response and guided the actions of law enforcement personnel during domestic violence calls (Miller, Iovanni, & Kelly, 2011). Another factor that heavily influenced police policy in domestic violence cases was a 1984 study by Lawrence Sherman and Richard Berk that examined domestic violence calls in Minneapolis, Minnesota. These researchers rocked the practice field when they reported their findings that arrest was associated with lower recidivism compared with other options, such as mediation or separation of the couple. What happened next was an unprecedented, swift application of behavioral science research to the practice field (Jordan, 2004). Within five years of Sherman and Berk's study, and before its findings had been empirically replicated by subsequent research, 84 percent of major police departments in jurisdictions serving populations of 100,000 or more had adopted policies that encouraged on-scene arrests (McFarlane, Willson, Lemmey, & Malecha, 2000). Following the Minneapolis study, five replication studies were conducted and then a meta-analysis by the National Institute of Justice (Maxwell, Garner, & Fagan, 2001). The findings of these studies suggested that the arrest of domestic violence offenders would not live up to the "deterrence hype" of Sherman and Berk's initial work. Although arrest was related to lower recidivism, this was not always statistically significant and did not apply to all offenders. For example, the deterrent effects of arrest were found to be less strong among men with criminal histories. Arrest appeared to work better when the offender had "something to lose" by the arrest. Specifically, employed men who were arrested were less likely to reoffend than unemployed offenders (Sherman et al., 1992).

Despite these equivocal findings, preferred- and mandatory-arrest policies became standard practice in most states, and law enforcement officers were instructed to arrest offenders if probable cause existed, regardless of whether the officer had witnessed the assault. Preferred and mandatory arrest also became a fundamental part of the reforms championed by domestic violence advocates. By 2000, all states had authorized the warrantless arrest of domestic violence offenders based on probable cause that an assault had occurred (the probable cause standard carries a lower burden of proof than criminal cases typically require) (N. Miller, 2004). Twenty-four states had also adopted statutes requiring peace officers to determine the identity of the so-called primary aggressor, to avoid arresting victims for self-defensive actions (Hirschel et al., 2007). While the discussion here relates primarily to criminal cases, it is worth noting that thirty-three states have also applied mandatory arrest to violators of civil protective orders (Hirschel et al., 2007).

On the surface, the implementation of preferred- and

mandatory-arrest policies seemed to be successful. In the 1970s and 1980s arrest rates in domestic violence cases were often in the single digits, while more recent research shows that arrest occurs in up to three-fourths of domestic violence cases (Hirschel et al., 2007). Today, when a victim of domestic violence contacts law enforcement seeking protection, the odds are greater that the offender will be held accountable for his violence. Within these higher arrest rates, however, is a serious unintended consequence: there has been a disproportionate increase in the number of women being arrested. In an analysis of domestic violence arrest data in California between 1987 and 2000, for example, DeLeon-Granados and his colleagues (2006) found that women accounted for 5 percent of all arrests in 1987 and 18 percent in 2000. This increase is not a reflection of women's escalating use of violence, as data do not show a corresponding increase in victimization rates for men (Chesney-Lind, 2002). Instead, mandatory-arrest policies appear to be responsible. These policies do not differentiate between the use of violence to harm or terrorize a partner and the use of violence to self-protect. As a result, a battered woman who calls police for help may find herself in handcuffs for striking back at an offender to protect herself or her children. This partial failure of preferred- or mandatory-arrest policies and the resulting arrest of battered women—either as sole perpetrators or as participants in mutual violence—is now well documented (DeLeon-Granados, Wells, & Binsbacher, 2006; Feder & Henning, 2005; Miller, 2005; Muftic, Bouffard, & Bouffard, 2007).

Another unintended effect of mandatory-arrest policies is the disempowerment of peace officers. They cannot make an arrest based on their discretion and professional judgment as to what took place. Instead, they must comply with departmental policies and law and act to avoid any civil liability associated with not making an arrest. The irony is obvious: Advocates once bemoaned officer discretion because it often meant that offenders were not punished and women were not protected. Now, with better training for peace officers and other reforms that have improved officer response, it is tempting to regret the absence of discretion when it results in the arrest of a victim. What is clear is that neither extreme (failing to arrest offenders or arresting everyone involved) is an effective response from the criminal justice system. Another party who is disempowered by mandatory-arrest policies is the victim; she can no longer express her wishes as to arrest of her partner to an officer on the scene. Victims are uniquely positioned to know the impact of an offender's arrest, including the likelihood that he will retaliate with even more severe violence if he is arrested.

Prosecuting Offenders and Getting Justice. Advocates who accompany victims of domestic violence to court have seen the restorative effect that can occur when a woman feels justice. Even two decades ago, researchers were reporting that victims felt more secure and in control of their lives when their cases were prosecuted (Ford & Regoli, 1992). The prosecution of domestic violence cases has multiple positive effects: upon conviction, it punishes the offender and has the potential to increase victim safety if the offender is incarcerated. But whether the case results in a conviction or not, the act of prosecution makes a clear public statement that violence against women is a crime and is not condoned by the community.

The challenge faced by victims in the 1970s and 1980s, however, was an extremely low rate of prosecution, estimated at less than 10 percent of cases (Fagan, 1989; Sherman, 1992). Early research suggested that prosecutors were reluctant to pursue domestic violence cases because they anticipated that the victim would ultimately ask that the charges be dropped, and prosecutors considered domestic violence to be less serious than other crimes. For example, Davis and Smith (1982) showed that assaults or other crimes occurring in the context of an intimate relationship led to less serious case assessments by prosecutors, even after controlling for victim injury and weapon use. As a result, domestic violence cases had a higher dismissal rate at the prosecution stage (Davis & Smith, 1982).

When domestic violence cases do proceed through the criminal justice system, there is mixed evidence with regard to the impact of conviction on recidivism. For example, Wooldredge (2007) found that convicted offenders (those sentenced to probation, jail, or prison) were seven times less likely to be recharged with intimate partner assault than those whose cases were dismissed. Other studies have not found a significant difference between offenders who were convicted and those who were not (Frantzen, San Miguel, & Kwak, 2011; Garner & Maxwell, 2008). While recidivism is an important factor when reviewing the effectiveness of prosecution, it is not the only measure of success. Even if there were no impact on recidivism, prosecution would still be appropriate in cases in which evidence exists that the law was violated. Approaching it any other way would be like not prosecuting persons who commit robbery because research had found that robbers have a high rearrest rate (see Langan & Levin, 2002).

Another complexity related to the decision whether to prosecute is that, very often, the victim's goals may differ from those of the prosecutor (Jordan, 2004). For example, a victim may be seeking protection from the offender or his mandatory treatment, while a prosecutor is focused on punishing a lawbreaker. Both are appropriate perspectives, but when the victim's needs are not met by the court process, she may withdraw her participation in the case, leaving prosecutors frustrated by high dropout rates. For example, a victim who learns that the offender will not be held in jail pending trial or that convictions often result in probation may feel vulnerable to retaliation by the offender and ask the prosecutor to drop the charges.

To toughen prosecutorial responses and address the complexities in play, advocates and criminal justice professionals pushed for the enactment of statutes and the adoption of consistent prosecution policies. Among the first such policies to be implemented around the country was the "no-drop" prosecution policy, intended to hold victims blameless for the prosecution of their abusers and thereby reduce retribution from angered offenders (Ford, 2003). In implementation, no-drop policies have had mixed success. They have increased the number of cases prosecuted but do not necessarily result in a higher percentage of convictions, particularly when cases must be prosecuted without a participating witness (Goodmark, 2011). Additionally, some studies have found negative outcomes associated with no-drop policies, including more time for cases to be prosecuted, decreased satisfaction among victims, and an increase in pretrial crimes against victims (Davis, Smith, & Taylor, 2003). When poorly applied, no-drop policies can result in women being pressured to participate in court actions that may increase the risk to themselves. This may be the primary factor associated with reports that no-drop policies increase the number of victims who recant their testimony (Goodmark, 2011).

The story of prosecution is not limited to a narrative in which victims want to prosecute and the courts have difficulty meeting their needs. Some victims do not want their abusers to be prosecuted at all. Many see the court system as an unfriendly place, adversarial by nature. Court proceedings leave victims with little control and expose them to offenders they may wish to escape. In addition, victims are "asked to recount a violent episode, not in the supportive or safe environment of a therapy session, but rather to a defense attorney whose role it is to question their credibility, dispute their memory, or even to challenge whether they are telling the truth" (Jordan, Nietzel, Walker, & Logan, 2004, p. 135). And given that the victim and offender were intimates, the offender and his attorney know about her background and perhaps her weaknesses, providing them with more "ammunition" to use against her (Hartley, 2003). Fear of retaliation from the offender is also a significant factor in victims' disinterest in prosecution. Threats are not abstract pronouncements when they come from an offender who has been violent in the past; they are forceful and impactful.

Closely related to no-drop policies, "victimless prosecution" policies have been instituted in some states, allowing prosecutors to move forward when victims are reluctant or refuse to participate in a trial. Also known as evidenced-based prosecution, these cases do not rely primarily on a victim's description of the criminal act; they rely heavily on physical evidence (e.g., photographs of injuries, damaged property, bloody clothing) and the testimony of third parties to support the charges against the defendant (Fulkerson & Patterson, 2006). Investigations in support of evidence-based prosecution operate much like homicide investigations, in that there is no assumption that the victim will testify (Ellison, 2002).

When presented with the option of victimless prosecution, some victims who initially rejected the idea of prosecution have changed their minds. Like no-drop policies, however, this approach involves challenges and controversy. For prosecutors, the biggest challenge is the need to rely on statements made by the victim to law enforcement personnel on the scene, for example, since she will not be testifying in court. As a general rule, out-of-court statements are not allowed, as they fall under the category of hearsay evidence, which is inadmissible by court rule (Federal Rule of Evidence 801). However, there are exceptions to the inadmissibility of hearsay evidence, three of which are heavily relied on in victimless prosecutions (Fulkerson & Patterson, 2006). These three exceptions are "excited utterances" under Rule 803(2), present sense impressions under Rule 803(3), and statements made to medical personnel under Rule 803(4) (Byrom, 2005). Defense counsel often attempts to block the admission of this hearsay testimony, based on the Sixth Amendment of the U.S. Constitution, which gives criminal defendants the right to confront witnesses against them. Another controversial aspect of victimless prosecution is that battered women cannot stop or otherwise influence the prosecution process. The disempowerment of victims appears to be a consistent, unintended consequence when criminal justice processes are mandated or when they proceed without the victim's influence.

After forty years of reform, prosecutors are now seen more as partners of and, in their own way, advocates for victims of domestic violence. In Kentucky, in addition to pursuing specific cases in their respective jurisdictions, prosecutors have been involved at the state level in amending the laws related to domestic violence and rape.

Victim Advocates and Community Responses. As discussed in chapter 1, the first advocacy for victims of domestic violence and rape was provided by grassroots shelters and crisis services built outside the standard service system. Although these services remain separate from formal, state-run programs, the older model of self-sufficiency has evolved as shelters developed a broader array of services (shelter, advocacy, counseling, children's services, education, housing, and more) and began to receive state funding. Some states, including Kentucky, have codified the existence of domestic violence programs that receive state funding. Strategies for funding such programs vary by state and include different sources of funds. In California, for example, $23 of each fee collected for the issuance of a marriage license is deposited into a special fund for use by domestic violence shelter programs (§ 26840). Similarly, Kentucky established a spouse abuse fund in 1982, financed by a $10 fee associated with the issuance of marriage licenses (Kentucky Revised Statute [KRS] 209.160).

In addition, reforms have included the placement of victim advocates in key locations within the justice system process. Advocates had been available through battered women's shelters since the 1960s, but by the 1990s, advocates were also appearing in prosecutors' offices and law enforcement agencies. The roles of these two types of advocates are qualitatively different. Those based in grassroots domestic violence programs address a broad range of victim needs, whereas those based in the justice system focus on facilitating the victim's progress through that system. One key difference between these types of advocates is the applicability of confidentiality or privileged communication, which is cherished by grassroots advocates but is not entirely feasible for criminal justice–based advocates, who are bound by court policies and rules regarding evidence. To address this issue, the Commonwealth of Kentucky passed legislation in 1996 that amended the crime victims' bill of rights to define victim advocates and set parameters for their training and to allow prosecutors to hire advocates to work in their offices (KRS 421.570). Concurrently, the Kentucky Rules of Evidence were amended to extend the counselor-client privilege to these new statutorily defined victim advocates, with the exception of prosecutor-based advocates (Kentucky Rule of Evidence 506(a)(1)(g)).

Finally, the prosecution of domestic violence cases has been strengthened through coordinated community responses that formally bring together victim advocates from grassroots domestic violence programs, law enforcement officers, prosecutors, health care providers, educators, and other key members of the service system (Allen, 2006; Shepard & Pence, 1999). Coordinating councils created through these collaborative efforts provide a structured way to ensure communication among all the critical responders to domestic violence cases (Allen, Larsen, & Walden, 2011).

Judicial Response: Protection and Justice from the Bench. Reform of the U.S. court system was necessitated in part by the increase in domestic violence cases appearing on court dockets as a result of the changes in police and prosecution policies described above. In a ten-year review, one study found a 178 percent increase in the number of domestic violence cases entering the state court systems across the country (Keilitz, 2000). To manage this increase and to ensure that domestic violence cases are handled by well-trained judges, some advocates have pushed for specialized dockets or courts with both criminal and civil jurisdictions to deal with domestic violence cases (Buzawa & Buzawa, 1992). Domestic violence courts are considered "problem-solving" courts that focus on improving the judicial response to domestic violence by linking criminal justice and social services agencies, addressing the unique needs of victims, and implementing court-ordered conditions or mandated treatment services that hold offenders accountable (Gover, 2009). According to the National Center for State Courts, key elements of these courts include case coordination, tailored intake units, specialized court calendars, special judges, and consistent measures for monitoring and enforcing court-ordered treatment for offenders (Keilitz, 2000). There are now between 200 and 300 domestic violence courts across the United States, with California and New York accounting for almost half of them (Keilitz, 2000; Labriola et al., 2009). Preliminary evaluations suggest that domestic violence courts are an effective model for intervention (Gover, MacDonald, & Alpert, 2003), but more research is needed to assess whether expansion of this model is warranted.

In Kentucky, some advocates and judges at the county level have expressed interest in the idea of a domestic violence court, but the state legislature has not addressed the establishment of such courts. This may be the case, in part, because Kentucky has a strong history of advancing the use of family courts. The 1996 General Assembly permitted the formation of a pilot family court within a circuit court, and the 2003 General Assembly passed a constitutional amendment to allow the creation of a statewide family court system (see chapters 8 and 9). Family courts issue domestic violence protective orders and handle other domestic relations cases; however, they typically do not have jurisdiction over criminal cases.

Domestic Violence as a Specific Criminal Offense. While most of the preceding reforms have impacted the criminal justice process, there have also been efforts to substantively change the law itself by creating a specific crime of domestic violence. These efforts are not without controversy. Some advocates argue that domestic violence can be prosecuted under existing criminal laws that apply regardless of the relationship between the offender and the victim; others believe that a specific statute is a better strategy. The argument for the latter is based on the fact that domestic violence is a crime of pattern and recidivism, while statutes almost always target a discrete act without regard for the actor's motivation or other culpable acts (Burke, 2007). As described by one legal scholar, "Premised on a transactional model of crime that isolates and decontextualizes violence, the law applied to domestic abuse conceals that reality of an ongoing pattern of conduct occurring within a relationship characterized by power and control" (Tuerkheimer, 2004, pp. 960–961). Effective July 1, 2000, Alabama became the twenty-sixth state to make domestic violence a separate crime in its criminal code. Missouri, Oregon, Florida, Indiana, and Minnesota also have special domestic violence assault statutes. Although Kentucky has not established domestic violence as a specific crime, it has elevated misdemeanor assaults in domestic violence cases to felonies if they reoccur within a five-year period (KRS 508.032).

Mandatory Reporting of Spouse Abuse. As advocates began their work in the 1970s, domestic violence was a crime that occurred behind closed doors, both literally and figuratively. Individuals and communities chose to remain oblivious to the plight of battered women, preferring to be neither informed nor involved. Women themselves often kept their experiences secret, fearful of retribution from a violent spouse, loss of that spouse to arrest or divorce, or ostracism by unsupportive family and friends. Professionals, including physicians, nurses, and therapists, also played ignorant, choosing not to ask questions that fell outside the scope of their professional roles. The challenge for advocates was how to reach women who were subjected to violence and provide them with services and protection. For some advocates, the answer was to require action by communities and professionals through mandatory reporting laws. The concept of mandatory reporting was not a new one. It had already been enacted in all states to require the reporting of abuse of children or vulnerable adults (the elderly or persons with disabilities). The idea of mandatory reporting when the victim was a legally competent adult was new and controversial. Proponents believed it would allow women to seek protection without having to make the report themselves; it would send a signal to offenders that violent behavior violated a community standard and would not be tolerated; and it afforded states an opportunity to collect data on the extent of the problem of spouse abuse within their borders. In Colorado, for example, advocates of the mandatory reporting law believed that requiring health care workers to report patients' injuries would protect women from potential retaliation if they reported the abuse themselves (Koziol-McLain & Campbell, 2001).

Today the vast majority of states have some form of reporting law, but almost all these laws apply to only certain types of injuries, not certain types of relationships. The broad purpose of such laws is a public safety one; they enable states to identify circumstances in which injuries result from certain crimes or certain weapons. As a result, the burden to report is usually limited to health care professionals, and reports are mandated based on the type of injury sustained (e.g., gunshot wound, knife wound, burns over a certain percentage of the body) and the context in which the injury occurred (e.g., during the commission of a crime, through violence or some other nonaccidental means).

Six states specifically address the reporting of domestic violence (Durborow, Lizdas, O'Flaherty, & Marjavi, 2010; Hyman, 1997; Hyman, Schillinger, & Lo, 1995; Kratochvil, 2010), but most of them (California, Colorado, North Dakota, and Tennessee) simply include domestic violence (or sexual offenses) on the list of crimes that have to be reported. Oklahoma requires the reporting of domestic violence only if the victim requests it. Some states *require* reporting for cases involving incapacitated adults and *permit* reporting in cases of competent domestic violence victims (e.g., New Mexico Statute § 27-7-30). Kentucky is the only state in the nation that requires the reporting of domestic violence (specifically, spouse abuse) without having a broader mandate to report injuries resulting from crimes. States with mandatory reporting typically require that reports be made to law enforcement agencies, but Kentucky requires direct reports to a protective services agency; that agency must then forward the report of spouse abuse to law enforcement (KRS Chapter 209A), so for victims, the effect is essentially the same.

Notably, there are two states that specifically prohibit the reporting of domestic violence, preferring to allow the victim to choose whether a report is made. Under Pennsylvania's statute, failure to report bodily injury is not an offense if the victim is an adult, the injury was inflicted by the victim's current or former spouse or sexual or intimate partner, the victim has been living as a spouse or shares biological parenthood with the offender, the victim has been informed of the physician's duty to report and that such a report cannot be made without the victim's consent, and the victim has been provided with a referral to the appropriate victim services agency. New Hampshire's statute exempts reporting if the victim is more than eighteen years of age, objects to the report, or has been the victim of a sexual assault (the exception does not apply if the victim is also being treated for a gunshot wound or other serious bodily injury) (Durborow et al., 2010).

Mandatory reporting laws have been controversial since their inception. Proponents believe that mandatory reporting increases women's access to protective services. Vocal opposition has been just as strong, however, based on the belief that mandatory reporting encroaches on a victim's autonomy, right to confidentiality, and right to choose whether she wants the state's protection. Some critics are concerned that mandatory reporting might inflict a second kind of victimization on women: "although the policy is intended to enable abused women to be cared for more effectively, advocates and abused women believe that the provider and state actually are imposing the same form of power and control over the woman as her abuser" (Glass & Campbell, 1998, p. 281). It is noteworthy that some of the most vocal critics of mandatory reporting laws are domestic violence advocates and their coalitions (Currens, 2002; Daire, 2000).

A number of research studies and surveys have attempted to gauge the effectiveness of mandatory reporting laws, but their findings are conflicted and somewhat complicated. First, a number of studies have reported that a majority of women support mandatory reporting laws (up to 80 percent in both Caralis & Musialowski, 1997, and Coulter & Chez, 1997; 55.7 percent in Rodriguez, McLoughlin, Nah, & Campbell, 2001). Importantly, however, there is a difference between abused and nonabused women. In a survey of patients in an internal medicine clinic, one research team found that less than half of abused women supported mandatory reporting, while over two-thirds of nonabused women did (Feddock et al., 2009). Similarly, in an emergency room study, 55.7 percent of abused women supported mandatory reporting and 44.3 percent opposed it, while 70.7 percent of nonabused women supported mandatory reporting and 29.3 percent opposed it (Rodriguez et al., 2001). These findings may not be representative of all battered women, however, as the study sample included only those who had already reached out for services. Additionally, when women who were supportive of mandatory reporting were asked about its application to their own cases, they were less supportive (Coulter & Chez, 1997).

The comments offered by women in these and other studies are troubling. A significant number of battered women believe that reporting would make the offender angrier (49 percent), would make life more difficult (40 percent), and would result in additional violence (31 percent) (Coulter & Chez, 1997). Some women believe that such laws could be life threatening for them (Rodriguez, Quiroga, & Bauer, 1996). In one study, almost half (45 percent) the abused women reported that they would be at greater risk for violence from their partners if they were subject to a mandatory reporting law (Malecha et al., 2000). In another study, the women most likely to oppose mandatory reporting were those currently dating or living with abusive partners, non-English speakers, and those who had experienced physical or sexual abuse within the past year (Rodriguez et al., 2001).

Another significant finding from the literature is that more than one-third of women (39 percent) in one study said they would not disclose violence to their health care providers if they knew a mandatory reporting law existed (Hayden, Barton, & Hayden, 1997). Similar findings were reported in a study of more than 400 women: two-thirds thought women would be less likely to tell their health care providers about abuse if there were a mandatory reporting policy (Gielen et al., 2000).

The lesson from the debate over mandatory reporting laws is similar to that learned from mandatory arrest and mandatory prosecution policies. All were conceptualized as methods to compel a reluctant health care or criminal justice system to respond more effectively to abused women and, in some cases, to reach out to women who were not seeking help for themselves. In practice, however, an unfortunate by-product of these laws has been to remove professionals' discretion and to take away choice from victims of domestic violence. As the evaluation of such laws and policies continues, these unintended consequences must be considered.

Reform of the Civil Justice System

Some of the most widespread reforms achieved by the domestic violence movement have come on the civil side of the justice system. Although many aspects of the criminal justice system are separate and distinct from civil law, domestic violence is unique, in that the law includes a combination of civil and criminal remedies (Jordan, 2004). Early on, advocates found that the criminal justice system was less than effective because it was designed solely to punish behaviors after the fact, not to address the ongoing threat to the victims of domestic violence. Domestic violence offenders have information about their victims that a stranger would not know, such as where she lives and works, where the children go to school, where her family lives, and who her friends are. Many women were reluctant to have their husbands arrested (they just wanted the violence to stop, not to punish him), and those husbands who were arrested were usually released from jail only hours later, angry and seeking revenge.

In the middle of the night, a victim might call law enforcement to report her abuser's presence on their property, but officers had little recourse when, on the face of it, he had committed no additional offense. A remedy was needed that women felt comfortable using and that addressed the ongoing threat inherent in domestic violence cases. That remedy was the creation of domestic violence protective orders.

Civil protective orders addressed many of the concerns that kept women from reaching out to the criminal justice system. Orders of protection did not automatically result in arrest (unless the order was violated); instead, they were directed at ending the violence. These orders were designed to allow courts to set conditions on the offender's behavior that included not only a cessation of violence but also mandatory treatment for violence, alcohol abuse, or both; they could also address child custody, support, and visitation (Moracco et al., 2011). The speed of the court's response was also critical for women facing the acute crisis of domestic violence, with the immediate issuance of ex parte orders and hearings set within a fairly short time frame. Studies have confirmed that the entire process of securing civil protection is shorter than a criminal trial (Moracco et al., 2011). The fact that victims can obtain protective orders without the help of attorneys also means that the process is less costly. Civil protective orders require a lower standard of proof than that applied to the prosecution of criminal cases (preponderance of the evidence versus beyond a reasonable doubt), which is important, given that many of these offenses occur behind closed doors, intentionally away from the public's view or witnesses' eyes (Ballou et al., 2007).

When protective orders were first created, their issuance did not result in the offender's loss of employment. That advantage became more complex with passage of the Brady Handgun Violence Prevention Act (1994), which, in an effort to strengthen protections for women, prohibits the possession of a firearm by respondents to a protective order. Therefore, for abusive partners whose jobs require gun possession (e.g., police officers, security guards, gun store owners), issuance of a protective order can, in fact, result in the loss of employment. An unintended and, perhaps, sadly ironic consequence of the Brady Act is that some courts are now reluctant to issue protective orders precisely because offenders would lose the right to possess firearms.

Every jurisdiction has now enacted some form of civil protective order legislation (Eigenberg, McGuffee, Berry, & Hall, 2003; US Department of Justice, 2002), and the vast majority of these statutes provide the essential relief necessary for women, including ex parte relief during the most volatile period when a woman first seeks protection and post-hearing relief, which may include temporary child custody and child support orders (Lemon, 2001). Because there is no federal standard, the provisions of protective orders differ markedly from one jurisdiction to another and can encompass threats, harassment, stalking, and emotional abuse. More than one-third of the states have adopted criminal contempt laws to enforce protective orders, and forty-five jurisdictions have made violating an order of protection a criminal offense (Epstein, 1999; Hirschel et al., 2007; Lemon, 2001). Many states, including Kentucky, statutorily limit a court's ability to issue protective orders that apply conditions to both parties (i.e., mutual protective orders) (N. Miller, 2004). Advocates in Kentucky proposed the Domestic Violence and Abuse Act in 1984 and have successfully lobbied for many amendments to the law over the years; as of this writing, that effort and that struggle continue.

The effectiveness of protective orders has been widely studied. One review of the literature showed that there are three ways to evaluate the effectiveness of protective orders: victims' perception of their helpfulness, the degree to which they influence future violence, and the rate of protective order violation (Logan, Shannon, Walker, & Faragher, 2006). Research suggests that victims find protective orders useful; they report improved quality of life, feeling better about themselves, and feeling safer after securing a protective order (Holt, Kernic, Wolf, & Rivara, 2003; Keilitz, Hannaford, & Efkeman, 1997; Logan & Walker, 2009).

A number of studies have explored rates of reabuse or violation of protective orders. However, before reviewing those data, it is important to note that victims do not always report violations of protective orders or episodes of reabuse to law enforcement; in fact, one study found that only about half of protective order violations were reported to police (Hotaling & Buzawa, 2003). There is also evidence of low arrest rates in response to violations of orders of protection, ranging from 20 to 44 percent (Harrell & Smith, 1996; Kane, 2000; Klein, 1996). Studies often use criminal behavior following the issuance of a protective order as the measure of effectiveness (often an offense associated with violation of the order), and they show mixed results. On the positive side, a number of studies found low rates of protective order violations. For example, in Kaci's (1994) study, up to 92 percent of victims reported that the violence stopped after the protective order was issued; Holt, Kernic, Lumley, and Wolf (2002) found that the existence of a permanent protective order was associated with an 80 percent reduction in police-reported physical violence in the twelve months following the initial incident; Carlson, Harris, and Holden (1999) reported a 66 percent decrease in violence two years after the issuance of an order; and Logan and Walker (2010a) found that during a six-month follow-up period, half the women experienced no violation of their protective orders. In a study of Kentucky women, of those whose abusers did violate protective orders, there was a significant reduction in the amount of abuse and violence they experienced (Logan & Walker, 2010a). Another study from Kentucky also found that offending decreased after the issuance of a protective order, but only for about eighteen months; after that, higher rates of reoffending occurred (Jordan, Pritchard, Duckett, & Charnigo, 2010). Hence, at least in that study, the deterrent effect of protective orders appeared to weaken over time.

Although protective orders actually do protect many women, just as the law intended, not all the findings are positive. Research shows that in up to 70 percent of cases, protective orders are violated (Harrell & Smith, 1996; Keilitz, Hannaford, & Efkeman, 1997; McFarlane et al., 2004; Spitzberg, 2002; Tjaden & Thoennes, 2000a). In the National Violence Against Women Survey, the reported rate of recidivism differed by the type of abuse. For example, 69.7 percent of victims who were stalked, 67.6 percent of victims who were sexually assaulted, and 50.2 percent of those who were physically assaulted by a partner reported a violation of the order (Tjaden & Thoennes, 2000a).

One significant challenge associated with reducing recidivism is that this population of offenders is known to commit repeat offenses. In fact, most respondents to protective orders have encountered the criminal justice system before, and their past criminal conduct is not limited to intimate partner violence; it often includes other misdemeanor and felony arrests (Jordan, 2004). The criminal histories of respondents to protective orders have been widely documented (Jordan, Pritchard, Wilcox, & Duckett-Pritchard, 2008; Keilitz, Hannaford, & Efkeman, 1997; Kethineni & Falcone, 2001). These findings are important because research suggests that offenders with criminal histories are more likely to reabuse their victims (Buzawa,

Hotaling, & Klein, 1998; Kethineni & Beichner, 2009). Patterned and ongoing violence by respondents to protective orders is consistent with research on criminal justice responses. One or more prior arrests for any offense against any victim are consistently associated with new incidents of abuse; in fact, "suspects with prior arrests for any offense are from 250 percent to 330 percent more likely to commit new acts of intimate partner violence" (Maxwell, Garner, & Fagan, 2001, p. 73).

The close association between criminal offending and the issuance and violation of protective orders was studied in Kentucky (Jordan, Pritchard, Duckett, & Charnigo, 2010). That study revealed several important characteristics of the relationship between prior criminal offending and the issuance of a protective order that were identified as risk markers for victims. First, the likelihood of a protective order being granted increased by 30.7 percent with each previous violation of a protective order. In other words, and intuitively, the more times an offender had violated a past protective order, the more likely the court was to issue the one being requested. This finding reflects the cyclical and recurring pattern of domestic violence and speaks to the importance of courts having access to offenders' criminal histories and being empowered to renew orders of protection. In Kentucky and elsewhere, protective orders initially had definitive end points, but since 1996, Kentucky courts can renew orders of protection at the victim's request. Second, the study found that the likelihood of a protective order being issued increased when the offender's criminal history involved certain types of offenses, specifically, sex offenses, misdemeanor assault, and stalking (Jordan, Pritchard, Duckett, & Charnigo, 2010). This finding is consistent with Logan and Walker's (2009) conclusion that stalking is a significant predictor of protective order violations. Their study also found that when an offender's criminal history involved multiple offenses, the likelihood of a protective order being issued increased (an increase of 3.5 percent for every charge). A pattern of multiple offenses within a short time—viewed as a cluster of offenses—may help identify periods when victims are particularly at risk and thus in need of protective orders.

When evaluating the effectiveness of protective orders, it is important to note that not all petitions seeking protective orders are granted. One study found that 7.3 percent of petitions for protective orders filed during a one-year period were denied. The most common reasons for denial included the judge's belief that the petitioner did not meet the statute's eligibility requirements (22.1 percent of petitions); a time lapse between the abuse and the filing of the petition (16.2 percent); the existence of a custody proceeding in another court (15 percent); and problems with the petition itself, such as its being incomplete, incorrect, or illegible (11.5 percent) (Jordan, Pritchard, Wilcox, & Duckett-Pritchard, 2008).

STALKING LAWS

Among the most significant legislative reforms accomplished in the 1990s was the passage of anti-stalking legislation. With regard to rape and domestic violence, advocates had decades of experience and at least a modest body of research as they approached statehouses for reform; that was not true in the case with stalking. Prior to the enactment of legislative reforms, no major study on stalking had been conducted in the general population; the first was the National Violence Against Women Survey, funded by the National Institute of Justice and the Centers for Disease Control and conducted by the Center for Policy Research from November 1995 to May 1996 (Tjaden, 2003). The scientific literature at the time was limited primarily to studies of stalking among persons with a mental illness— so-called erotomania (Harmon, Rosner, & Owens, 1995; Meloy, 1989; Mullen & Pathé, 1994). Erotomania crept into the consciousness of Americans through movies and media stories about celebrities, news anchors, or politicians who were stalked and killed. Domestic violence and rape advocates had certainly seen stalking behavior (e.g., following, surveillance, repeated phone calls), but they were not yet using the term *stalking* to describe these forms of harassment. Legislative reforms were undertaken in response to several high-profile cases, but this happened before the field as a whole had any lengthy experience or empirical data to fully understand the breadth and implications of stalking.

As described in chapter 2, several high-profile stalking cases occurred in California in the 1980s, including the attempted murder of actress Theresa Saldana in 1982, the 1988 murder of seven people by Richard Farley, and the 1989 murder of actress Rebecca Schaeffer by Robert John Bardo. (In addition, four domestic violence victims in Orange County were stalked and killed around the time of Schaeffer's murder; their stories are told in chapter 5.) Thus, legislative reform began in California as well. Prompted by the obvious lack of a means to stop the behaviors of both delusional stalkers and past intimates, the California legislature reacted. Anti-stalking legislation, written by Judge John Watson of Orange County and sponsored by State Senator Edward Royce of Fullerton, took the form of Senate Bill 2184; it was passed in 1990 and became part of the California Penal Code on the first day of January 1991 (Beatty, 2003). To say that the California law started a "movement" is a dramatic understatement: by 1992, twenty-nine states had passed anti-stalking legislation, and by the end of the 1990s, all fifty states and the District of Columbia had done so (Beatty, 2003).

In addition to the unusual timing of this legislative reform (before professionals had any substantial knowledge of or experience with the behavior), the stalking law's structure is singular. Most state penal codes focus on punishing behavior that has already occurred. In the case of stalking, however, the statute intends to prevent more serious crimes, such as murder. "The statute's preventive goal of acting before actual physical injury occurred went beyond the criminal law's traditional preference for providing a remedy only when a victim had actually sustained injury or when a defendant took the substantial step required to commit a criminal attempt to injure (Jordan, Quinn, Jordan, & Daileader, 2000). In addition, the law targets not a single behavior but a pattern of behaviors. The stalking statute speaks to the experience of victims because it recognizes that the offense's repetitive nature is most destructive to victims (Jordan, Quinn, Jordan, & Daileader, 2000). Stalking laws generally have two other elements: the conduct must be intended to make the victim fear for her safety, and the conduct actually does engender fear in the victim (Beatty, 2003).

While anti-stalking statutes were passed more than a decade ago in every state, the specific language varies. In fact, no two states adopted the exact same language in their initial laws. (For a review of state stalking statutes, see Jordan, Quinn, Jordan, & Daileader, 2000.) In particular, they differed in terms of the definition of stalking, the offender's intent (to frighten or not), the victim's reaction (fear or not), the existence of aggravated stalking (e.g., stalking while in possession of a firearm), and the penalties for the offense (Jordan, Quinn, Jordan, & Daileader, 2000). Twelve states classify stalking as a felony for the first offense, and twenty-three states classify stalking as a felony when it involves aggravating factors (e.g., possession of a firearm, prior criminal offenses against the same victim, presence of a protective order in which the court ordered the stalker to stay away from the victim). In the remaining states, the first offense is a misdemeanor, but repeat stalking is prosecuted as a felony (US Department of Justice, 2001). The variability in statutory design among states resulted in some statutory weaknesses that were challenged in court and eventually led to the modification of laws by state legislatures. This prompted Congress to charge the National Institute of Justice to develop a model stalking statute that would be both constitutional and enforceable:

Section 1. For the purposes of this code:

(a) "Course of conduct" means repeatedly maintaining a visual or physical proximity to a person or repeatedly conveying verbal or written threats or threats implied by conduct or a combination thereof directed at or toward a person;

(b) "Repeatedly" means on two or more occasions;

(c) "Immediate family" means a spouse, parent, child, sibling, or any other person who regularly resides in the household or who within the prior six months regularly resided in the household.

Section 2. Any person who:

(a) Purposefully engages in a course of conduct directed at a specific person that would cause a reasonable person to fear bodily injury to himself or herself or a member of his or her immediate family or to fear the death of himself or herself or a member of his or her immediate family; and

(b) Has knowledge or should have knowledge that the specific person will be placed in reasonable fear of bodily injury to himself or herself or a member of his or her immediate family or will be placed in reasonable fear of the death of himself or herself or a member of his or her immediate family;

(c) Whose acts induce fear in the specific person of bodily injury to himself or herself or a member of his or her immediate family or induce fear in the specific person of the death of himself or herself or a member of his or her immediate family; is guilty of stalking. (National Criminal Justice Association, 1993, pp. 43–44)

In addition to criminal statutes, some states (including California, Georgia, and Kentucky) have implemented other reforms to protect stalking victims. In Kentucky, unless a victim requests otherwise, a verdict or plea of guilty for stalking automatically serves as an application for a restraining order that limits the offender's contact with the stalking victim (KRS 508.155). The advantages of this law are that it covers victims who do not qualify for protective orders under existing domestic violence statutes; the duration of a stalking protective order is ten years, rather than the three years for domestic violence orders; and procedurally, it saves the victim from having to access another court to obtain the protection she needs.

Three of the statutory elements noted earlier pose particular challenges to prosecutors and victim advocates: the definition of threat, the element of fear on the part of the victim, and the requirement of intent on the part of the offender. Early on, states required the presence of an explicit threat for stalking behavior to be considered a criminal offense (National Criminal Justice Association, 1993). That requirement precluded the prosecution of many stalking cases, particularly those involving domestic partners, where the offender might be able to communicate threat in more subtle ways. For instance, a stalker might send a photograph of the victim's pet to her to remind her that he had already killed that pet and, at the time, had threatened that she would be next. Arguably, under an explicit threat standard, that person could not be prosecuted for stalking; he would have to communicate more directly to the victim, "I am going to kill you." This difficulty led many states (including Kentucky) to adopt a broader definition that includes implicit threats.

The second essential element in stalking laws is that the behavior of the stalker must cause fear in the victim. States have approached this element in two ways—with a subjective standard or an objective standard (or sometimes with both in the same statute). A subjective standard requires the victim to actually experience emotional distress (Jordan, Quinn, Jordan, & Daileader, 2000). One concern is that, in cases of domestic violence, the victim may be so numb from repeated victimization that she is unable to articulate the necessary fear when she finally seeks help from law enforcement. The subjective standard also sets stalking apart from other crimes. In the case of robbery, for example, the prosecutor must prove that the defendant committed the prohibited act (stealing while threatening to harm or actually harming the victim) with the designated intent.

It is not necessary to show that the robbery victim experienced fear. "Notably, such prosecutions fail to require that the state demonstrate that the victim was reduced to hysterics from the criminal actions of the defendant" (Jordan, Quinn, Jordan, & Daileader, 2000, p. 557). In contrast, some states (Maryland, Pennsylvania, Tennessee) have adopted the objective standard, which does not require the prosecutor to prove that the stalker's behavior elicited fear in the actual victim but rather that such behavior would cause a reasonable person to fear for her safety. As a general rule, victim advocates have pushed for statutory designs that do not focus on the specific victim's behavior. (See chapter 3 for a discussion of the consent standard in rape laws as an example.) This suggests that the objective standard might be the better construction for stalking statutes, but it can be extremely difficult to prove. The "reasonable person" standard might not serve a victim well if she is fearful not because the offender's current behavior is so overtly egregious (in the example cited above, sending a photograph of a pet seems harmless) but because, in the context of past experience, the behavior is terrifying. If the judge or jury cannot fully appreciate the context of stalking in situations of domestic violence, then the prosecutor may be unable to prove the case. Some states (including Kentucky) have adopted both subjective and objective standards for fear in their stalking statutes.

Finally, the offender's intent—the third key element of stalking statutes—can be difficult for prosecutors to prove, and in fact, some authors have opined that this is the most challenging aspect of stalking prosecutions. As Beatty (2003, p. 2-12) notes, "Under such statutes, application of a specific intent standard usually requires prosecutors to prove not only that the stalker intended to commit the alleged acts of stalking, but that he also intended that such acts place the victim in fear. Apart from difficulties inherent in any attempt to prove what was in the mind of a person at the time he or she committed a crime, the challenge is doubly difficult when the stalker insists, as is often the case, that the actions toward the victim were merely displays of affection intended to elicit love rather than fear." To address this concern, some states (and the model code) have adopted a general intent standard that resembles the reasonable person standard applied to fear. In these states, the prosecutor must prove only that the stalker intended to commit the act; it is not necessary to prove that he intended to cause fear or distress in the specific victim.

At the federal level, stalking legislation passed for the first time in 1996. Its primary sponsor was Congressman Edward Royce, who, as a state legislator, had sponsored California's first stalking law (Beatty, 2003). The federal law criminalized stalking behavior when it involves the crossing of state lines and outlawed stalking in federal jurisdictions (18 USC § 2261A). In 2000, as part of the reauthorization of the federal Violence Against Women Act (VAWA), the federal definition was expanded to include international stalking and stalking involving mail and other commerce, which covers cyberstalking and use of the Internet to stalk (VAWA 2000, §1107). In 2005 Congress expanded and strengthened federal criminal remedies for interstate stalking by adding language on surveillance that covers the use of global positioning systems (18 USC § 2261A). The 2005 amendments also toughened federal sentencing provisions, mandating a one-year minimum term of imprisonment for stalking in violation of a court order and increasing the maximum term of imprisonment for a defendant convicted of a prior stalking offense to twice the term otherwise provided (18 USC §§ 2261(b) (6) and 2265A).

The passage of initial stalking legislation was not the end of reform. In fact, the vast majority of states have amended their original statutes, and many have adopted the provisions of the model code. Others have amended their stalking statutes to address legal challenges to their constitutionality. In 1997, in *Monhollen v. Commonwealth*, the Kentucky Court of Appeals upheld the stalking statute passed in 1992, which had been challenged for its vagueness. Most other courts have agreed with *Monhollen*, finding that the reasonable (or objective) person standard protects statutes from constitutional challenges based on vagueness (Jordan, Quinn, Jordan, & Daileader, 2000). Legal experts predict that amendments will continue and states will expand, refine, or replace their existing anti-stalking statutes (Beatty, 2003).

Whether stalking laws are proved effective by research will also impact future statutory changes. The research on stalking is still very young, and so far, findings have addressed the complexity of prosecution for stalking rather than its effectiveness for victims. For example, studies show that although the behavior of stalking may be prosecuted, offenders are often prosecuted for other crimes. In the National Violence Against Women Survey (Tjaden & Thoennes, 1998), for example, stalkers were often charged with harassment, menacing, threatening, breaking and entering, and other crimes. In a review of domestic violence cases, 16.5 percent of all cases described stalking behaviors, but only one case actually resulted in a stalking charge (Tjaden & Thoennes, 2000b). It is possible that prosecutors are reluctant to pursue stalking when other offenses are available that are easier to prove (i.e., that do not require repeated conduct, intent of the offender, and fear in the victim). Prosecution for other crimes may also be preferable because the harm caused by stalking, particularly in the context of domestic violence, is less concrete and more difficult to measure than the harm caused by other forms of violence (Logan & Walker, 2010b).

Studies have also evaluated the outcomes of stalking prosecutions. In one study of Kentucky stalking cases, the most frequent disposition was dismissal (49.2 percent of initial felony charges, 54.0 percent of amended felony charges, 61.2 percent of initial misdemeanor charges, and 62.2 percent of amended misdemeanors). This study also found that of the cases that proceeded through trial, only 28.5 percent resulted in conviction (Jordan, Logan, Walker, & Nigoff, 2003). While this seems low, the felony stalking cases actually had higher rates of conviction than other felony offenses, which ranged from 14 percent for aggravated assault to 16 percent for robbery and 19 percent for rape (Maguire & Pastore, 1999). In summary, early data suggest that while high dismissal rates make it difficult to prosecute stalking successfully, when these cases do make it through the system, there is a reasonable chance of conviction, at least when compared with other felony offenses (Jordan, Logan, Walker, & Nigoff, 2003).

Findings on the civil side of the justice system also raise concerns about the impact of stalking on the outcome of interventions. Logan and Walker (2010b) explored the relationship between stalking and protective orders in Kentucky and found that stalking was robustly associated with violations of protective orders; in addition, women who were stalked reported significantly more harm than women who were not. Another key finding was that many community informants used in the study did not understand the gravity of stalking; for instance, criminal justice professionals took a far less serious view of stalking than did other victim service providers (Logan & Walker, 2010b).

FEDERAL REFORM: THE CONGRESSIONAL RESPONSE

While this book focuses primarily on state reforms, the federal reforms enacted in 1994 were significant and directly impacted state responses. Passage of the federal Violence Against Women Act in

1994, and its reauthorization in 2000 and 2005, dramatically changed the landscape for victims of rape, domestic violence, and stalking. Pushed by the National Network to End Domestic Violence, the National Coalition against Domestic Violence, the National Coalition against Sexual Assault, the National Organization for Women, and others, VAWA was sponsored by Senator Joseph Biden and was enacted as Title IV of the Violent Crime Control and Law Enforcement Act of 1994. President Bill Clinton signed VAWA on September 13, 1994. VAWA provided an initial $1.6 billion to enhance law enforcement and court responses to domestic violence, sexual assault, stalking, and related crimes against women; established new federal crimes and penalties; addressed evidentiary issues in cases of sexual assault; created the National Domestic Violence Hotline; provided grants for battered women's shelters and rape crisis programs; addressed unique rural issues; addressed the purchase and possession of weapons by persons who have committed acts of domestic violence; gave full faith and credit to orders of protection; and allowed victims of domestic abuse to sue for damages in civil court.

For the most part, the provisions of VAWA have withstood constitutional challenges. The exception was a 2000 case in which the U.S. Supreme Court, in a controversial five-to-four vote, held that the civil rights portion of VAWA was unconstitutional on federalism grounds. That provision had given victims of gender-motivated violence the right to sue their attackers in federal court. Specifically, in *United States v. Morrison* (2000), the Court held that Congress exceeded its congressional power under the commerce clause and under section 5 of the Fourteenth Amendment to the Constitution because the acts of domestic violence addressed in VAWA had only an attenuated effect, not a substantial one, on interstate commerce.

REFORMS AGAINST DOMESTIC VIOLENCE AND STALKING: WHAT HAVE THEY WROUGHT?

Early court opinions, in effect, gave violent men immunity and established a veil of privacy around violent families. Men were permitted to "chastise" their wives and could "discipline" them with impunity. As the saying goes, home is where the heart is, but it was also where the violence resided, yet the state could not enter. Feminist reformers of the 1970s challenged the concept of family privacy and worked hard to criminalize acts of violence against women, both in the home and on the street. Their success is evidenced by more than three decades of legislative reforms, the new crimes of domestic violence and stalking, enhanced penalties for domestic violence offenders, the creation of protective orders, and more. These reforms represented the criminalization of domestic violence— its evolution from a shameful family secret to a crime with consistent and stringent consequences. Reforms led to a significant shift in the justice system, from a heavy focus on victims to perpetrator-centric interventions (Barner & Carney, 2011). Increasing the certainty and severity of legal responses was intended to correct the historical, legal, and moral disparities in the protections afforded to battered women (Zorza, 1992).

Research conducted over the past four decades has evaluated civil and criminal justice reforms, with equivocal findings. On the positive side, the criminal justice system has integrated domestic violence into its core, with training for peace officers, prosecutors, and judges and the adoption of stronger policies to guide interventions. Partnerships between grassroots advocates and prosecutors and police are more common. Victim advocates have a greater presence in the justice system as they guide victims through what can be a difficult process. In sheer volume, the number of criminal and civil cases entering the courts has increased exponentially. The increased response of the justice system signals the achievement of early reformers' goals: domestic violence is no longer a private family matter; rather, it is rightfully a matter for the courts, and it is rightly spoken about within communities that will not tolerate violence.

On the empirical side, the findings of early research on the effectiveness of arrest and prosecution, civil or criminal protective orders, batterer treatment, and community interventions have not been positive. To some, they have "generated weak or inconsistent evidence of deterrent effects on either repeat victimization or repeat offending . . . for every study that shows promising results, one or more show either no effect or even negative results that increase the risks to victims" (Fagan, 1996, p. 3).

Future legislative reforms in the areas of domestic violence and stalking must consider two important factors. First, research to evaluate the effectiveness of reforms must be expanded. More studies are needed, and increased state, federal, and foundation funding should be made available to allow larger study samples and longitudinal studies. Researchers also need to forge relationships with advocates; this collaborative approach will ensure the validity of studies and increase the likelihood that findings will be implemented in practice. Additionally, advocates should be involved in determining how success and failure are measured in research studies. If criminal prosecution is not associated with reduced recidivism but is related to increased victim satisfaction, is that a success or a failure? By comparison, would prosecution be a less viable option in murder cases if research showed it did not reduce recidivism? These are key questions for the field as it moves forward.

Second, future reforms must address the unintended consequences of earlier reforms. Advocates are increasingly concerned about the victim disempowerment that has accompanied the adoption of mandatory policies and practices in the justice system. That the reforms instituted over the past four decades are not perfect is no slight to either the advocates and practitioners who designed and pushed for them or the legislators who passed them. Instead, these imperfections speak to the complexity of managing domestic violence through the justice system.

After a pause to celebrate the many successes achieved, advocates and their criminal justice partners must look to the future and continue their work for the women who still need life-saving protections.

5

The Structure and Strategy of Legislative Reform

Legislation is never passed in a vacuum, but in a cultural context.
Regardless of the size of a party's majority . . . certain things simply
can't be done without a cultural consensus.
— Bill Wichterman, former chief of staff of U.S. Senate
Majority Leader (quoted in Gelak, 2008, p. 300)

Legislative reforms to address domestic violence and rape were
born out of a belief among advocates, criminal justice professionals, and their allies that changes in the law would have a direct and
dramatic impact on the lives of battered women and rape survivors.
For many years, advocates had encountered punitive provisions in
existing rape laws and a failure to enforce laws in domestic violence
cases. Without this active grassroots advocacy, nothing would change
for these battered women and rape survivors on whose behalf they
worked. If the system were to improve, advocates had to make their
presence known in state legislatures across the country and in the
halls of Congress.

No matter the importance of legislative reforms, they were not
and are not achieved without sacrifice, hard work, argument, controversy, drama, emotion, and no small amount of guts. It also takes
an astute strategy to overcome the resistance and tough challenges
that will inevitably arise. This chapter turns from reflections on the
history of legislative change and focuses on how to make legal, policy, and legislative reforms happen. The strategies presented here
are not all-inclusive, nor do they adequately capture all the ingenuity brought to bear by reform advocates. Legislative strategies

must adapt to the unique situation in each state: the contemporary makeup of its legislature, the existence of other major public policy issues occurring at the time reforms are sought, the legislative experience of the advocates and the professional criminal justice community, and the historical relationship between advocates and legislators. To provide a baseline of guidance for the next generation of reformers, this chapter begins with a discussion of the broad strategies of legislative reform that have been used in the domestic violence and anti-rape movements over the decades. The next section is more narrowly focused on what Kentucky advocates need to know, including the workings of the Kentucky General Assembly and specific tips and legislative tactics they can employ as they approach the doors of the Commonwealth's capitol. This chapter and the ones that follow are written in a style perceptibly different from that of previous ones. Unlike earlier chapters, which took an analytical, third-person approach, beginning here, the book adopts a more colorful narrative consisting of firsthand accounts and actual stories of Kentucky advocates and their legislative partners. In addition, my perspective as an advocate will be more obvious to the reader.

• • •

Amanda Ross was born in October 1979 in a small county in eastern Kentucky, moving with her family to Lexington at the age of eight. Amanda graduated from high school in 1998 and in 2002 received a degree in business administration and finance from Boston University. Throughout her childhood and young adulthood, Amanda was famous for her good humor, charm, and wit and for having a laugh that could fill a room. She loved art and fashion, and she loved politics, an affection nurtured by growing up in a family where politics was a staple of conversation and activities.

In September 2007 Amanda started dating a man named Steve Nunn, an ex-lawmaker from a well-known Kentucky political family. By March of the following year, Nunn moved into Amanda's residence in Lexington, and plans to marry followed. By October, however, the relationship began to destruct. In February 2009 Amanda Ross broke up with her former fiancé, an act capping a relationship that had become increasingly violent and chaotic. Her act was brave, for she understood in a way that no one else did the harm this man could inflict. In the wake of the deteriorating relationship, Amanda accessed all the legal remedies available to her, including filing assault charges against Nunn and successfully seeking a domestic violence

Amanda Ross, 2008. (Courtesy of Diana Ross)

protective order against him. Amanda was not a timid woman, nor was she easily frightened, but she shared with those close to her that she feared Steve Nunn. She feared for her life. Nunn's refusal to take responsibility for his violence, his alcohol consumption, and his violation of the protective order she had against him were hard evidence of the reasonableness of her fears.

On September 11, 2009, Amanda's worst fears materialized in gunfire. At 6:30 that morning, she was found shot to death outside her home. Steve Nunn was ultimately charged with brutally taking her life. That morning he had stalked her, had waited for her to leave her residence, and then had used a .38-caliber handgun to steal her life. In June 2011, two months before his murder trial was to commence, Nunn pleaded guilty to murder with aggravating circumstances (the latter relating to the presence of a protective order at the time of the homicide). He was sentenced to life without the possibility of parole.

Some time after the shooting, Amanda's mother, Diana Ross, was looking through her daughter's belongings and found an envelope with Amanda's familiar handwriting. What she read there were notes Amanda had made about how the system could improve for victims; her notes were ideas for combating domestic violence. Her notes were also the inspiration Diana was looking for in order to carry on her daughter's legacy. She carried that inspiration to the 2010 Kentucky General Assembly, during which the speaker of the Kentucky house filed House Bill 1 and called it "Amanda's Bill." The legislation would allow a court to impose electronic monitoring as a condition of bail for a person charged with the substantial violation of a protective order. Victims of domestic violence would also have the option of wearing the device, giving them a warning system if the offender came too close in violation of the order. The state senate and house voted unanimously to approve "Amanda's Law," and on April 28, 2010, the governor ceremoniously signed the bill into law.

What about Amanda? Would this legislative reform have saved her life? Speaker Greg Stumbo expressed it well, saying that the bill "would have given her a fighting chance." Amanda's mother Diana says it would have saved her life. So, do legislative reforms matter? Thinking back to Amanda's handwritten notes, it is clear they do.

• • •

LEGISLATIVE REFORM: THREE BROAD STRATEGIES

This section highlights three strategies for achieving legislative reform: public awareness campaigns, public exposure of personal stories, and the formation of coalitions and task forces.

Public Awareness: Waking Communities to Advance Legislative Change

As described in chapter 1, early efforts against rape and domestic violence were characterized by an important connection between advocacy to build local services for women and political activism directed at changing laws. These efforts involved women publicly sharing their stories for the first time—personal stories that, in the hands of advocates, became a force behind legislative reforms. These efforts heightened public awareness, leading an increasingly enlightened public to demand that legislators address the problem of violence against women. There is evidence that these public awareness campaigns have had the desired effect. Public opinion polls suggest that the tolerance for violence against women that once permeated the culture is, in fact, decreasing (Klein, Campbell, Soler, & Ghez, 1997). Messages such as "Domestic violence is a crime," "No means no," and "Real men don't hit women" have been expressed and accepted. One of the most critical messages, however, was the concept that violence can happen to any woman. That message fought the tendency to blame the victim for the violence that befell her, and it taught communities of women to understand that they, too, were vulnerable to victimization. That message united women, who now understood that they had a personal stake in the legislative reform movement's success. This created a natural constituency of legislative advocates who could communicate their desire for change to their local legislators.

While the "it can happen to any woman" message has been successful in the mainstream, it has been argued that it creates a false sense of unity around the experience of gender oppression. As expressed by Beth Richie (2000, p. 1135), "in the end, the assumed race and class neutrality of gender violence led to the erasure of low-income women and women of color from the dominant view . . . it divorced racism from sexism, for example, and invited a discourse regarding gender violence without attention to the class dimensions of patriarchy and white domination in this country." Richie's point is valid, and it heightens an understanding of the complexities of rape and domestic violence, which do not easily lend themselves to slogans and the concise messages of public awareness campaigns.

One of the most effective uses of public awareness as a tool for legislative reform in American history is that of the advocacy group Mothers against Drunk Drivers (MADD). Tragedy gave birth to MADD. On May 3, 1980, thirteen-year-old Cari Lightner was struck and killed by a car as she walked to a church carnival in her neighborhood; the driver then fled the scene. When her mother, Candice "Candy" Lightner, later learned that the driver who killed Cari had been drunk, she and a friend went to the Department of Motor Vehicles in Fair Oaks, California, and asked to see the person's full driving record. She was denied access. Candy soon learned that there were few specific laws against driving while intoxicated, enforcement of existing laws was spotty, and drunk driving was not an issue that the public was aware of. In fact, "partying" and then driving home drunk was considered "normal" behavior. The incentive to create MADD came from the grief over Cari's death, the frustration of an inadequate system response, and the public's ignorance of the number of lives taken by drunk drivers every year. Candy Lightner and her friends set up an office for the fledgling organization, using Cari's bedroom as their starting place (Davies, 2005). The movement started by Candy Lightner and a handful of volunteers caught fire, uniting families with similar experiences from all over the country. That included Cindy Lamb, whose five-month-old daughter Laura was paralyzed and confined to a wheelchair as she aged as a result of a drunk driving crash. In October 1980 Lightner and Lamb went to Washington, D.C., and "riveted the nation during a national press conference on Capitol Hill. It was a seismic shift that catapulted the heartbroken moms into a debate-driving, law-changing force to be reckoned with" (Davies, 2005, pp. 10–11). For MADD, it was exactly this type of public awareness that was central to its mission.

MADD's success was swift and measurable. By 1982, new laws against drunk driving had been passed by half the states; by the end of 1984, MADD had 330 chapters in forty-seven states; by 1990, alcohol-related traffic fatalities had decreased to about 22,400 a year (a drop of nearly 8,000); and by 1993, alcohol-related traffic fatalities had reached a thirty-year low (Davies, 2005). MADD and its network of committed, passionate volunteers worked to achieve their mission through a combination of strategies: adopting a simple and easily defined mission statement; launching public awareness campaigns with standardized, nationally adopted logos; establishing a close relationship with the media; actively involving legislators in their efforts; developing an organizational structure consisting of chapters across the country; and establishing clear and measurable goals (e.g., instituting a 0.08 blood alcohol concentration as the definition of intoxication).

The movement to end drunk and drugged driving is used as an exemplar here because it has interesting parallels to the movements to end rape and domestic violence in America. First, to be successful, all three movements had to face a society that accepted, or in some cases promoted, the issue they fought against. It was the norm to drink and drive, just as it was the norm to ignore the harm done to women behind closed doors or to blame rape victims because of their "provocative" behavior. Second, the movement against drunk driving was created by survivors and family members who told their stories (just as victims of rape and domestic violence did) as a way to galvanize public awareness and create intolerance for inebriated drinking and its costs. Third, all three movements were challenged by a legal system that did not respond consistently or harshly to offenders. In fact, being drunk at the time a driver killed another person with his or her car often mitigated the severity of the crime (resulting in less serious charges or lighter sentences), as did being the husband or boyfriend of the woman he raped or battered.

In addition to these similarities, there are significant differences between the movements against drunk driving and violence against women. Arguably, the anti-rape and domestic violence movements face larger problems with a longer historical reach. Further, statutes at one time expressly and affirmatively allowed men's violent behavior against their wives. The anti-rape and domestic violence movements have also encountered a rabid victim-blaming phenomenon in both the community and the court system, while the casualties of drunk driving crashes are much more likely to be viewed as "innocent" victims. Another fundamental difference has been the ordering of the movements' missions. MADD's original mission was public awareness and legal reform. The provision of crucial services to victims and their families came later, as the organization expanded in size and focus. In contrast, in the battles against rape and domestic violence, victim services were the bedrock.

Public awareness campaigns have a unique relationship with the passage, implementation, and effectiveness of domestic violence and anti-rape laws and policies. Some have argued that, to be effective, laws and policies need to both reflect and impact the social norms of the community. For example, in a recent survey of almost 1,000 residents in four communities, researchers explored the relationship between public perceptions of criminal justice reforms and social norms (Salazar, Baker, Price, & Carlin, 2003). Results from the survey support the contention that perceptions of criminal justice policies have direct effects not only on attitudes toward the policies themselves but also on victim-blaming attitudes and underlying social norms. These findings suggest that it is wise to pair public awareness campaigns with the implementation of new policies or new legislative proposals, because doing so can have the dual effect of advancing a bill's passage while also provoking social change.

The use of public awareness campaigns in combination with legislative reform efforts can be accomplished in many ways: public service announcements, bumper stickers, billboards, and other forms of mass communication. Two strategies of particular benefit are organized public forums in local communities and use of the media. Public forums can be coordinated by the group proposing the legislative changes (e.g., anti-rape and domestic violence coalitions, coalitions of advocates and criminal justice professionals, governmental or legislative task forces) and can involve local advocates, police, prosecutors, educators, researchers, and others. The presence of local legislators at these forums is an ideal first step in lobbying efforts, as these officials can see strong grassroots support for highly visible issues in their own legislative districts. Finally, forums provide an opportunity for the public to offer input and express its views about domestic violence and rape. With that in mind, it is important to present any legislative proposals as being in the idea or draft stage, so that community members feel empowered to influence the final product. Those who coordinate public forums should also be prepared for survivors who disclose their victimization during open dialogues or use the forum as a means to seek help, and advocates and other service providers should be standing by to offer immediate assistance.

The second vehicle for advancing public awareness and legislative reform is the media. To be most effective, advocates should keep in mind that they are not simply talking *to* a journalist during an interview; they are talking *through* that journalist, who has the power to take that message and communicate it publicly in a way advocates cannot. Through the coverage of domestic violence– and rape-related stories, investigative reporting, and editorial writing, the media can bring unique and powerful attention to these important issues and highlight where the systems of protection and intervention have failed. That last function can be extremely useful in underscoring the importance of changing the law. An exceptional example of the power of the press comes from the *Lexington Herald-Leader*. Beginning in 1990, and for more than sixteen months, Maria Henson authored a series of editorials that told the stories of women who had sought protection from Kentucky's court system after being beaten by their husbands or boyfriends.[1] That series, entitled "To Have and to Harm: Kentucky's Failure to Protect Women from the Men Who Beat Them," won Henson the 1992 Pulitzer Prize for editorial writing and lit a fire under the state legislature to pass reforms.[2] The importance of the *Herald-Leader*'s series was twofold. First, by telling the actual stories of Kentucky women through words and photographs, it raised awareness and shone a light on system failures. Second, the editorials included specific recommendations for legislative reform, many of which were later included in a package of legislative proposals offered by the attorney general's task force.

Achieving Legislative Reform through Stories that Rock a Community

Perhaps nothing transfixes the public's attention more than a highly visible case of domestic violence or rape, particularly one that ends in death. These cases often involve victims or offenders known to the community, or they involve violence of such an egregious nature that it shocks all who learn of it. Legislative reform is often inspired by these cases, as communities push public officials to "do something" in the aftermath. At the heart of these impassioned calls for justice are often parents and other family members who want to transform their own worst moments into better protection for others. Undoubtedly, advocates in every state of the nation can cite stories of women whose murder or rape outraged the public and led to legislative reform, often resulting in a law named in honor of the victim.

There are two important cautions when using highly visible cases to motivate legislative reform. First, a woman's murder should not be the only thing known of her. Women's lives are rich, with treasured childhood memories and family members loved; first days in school, awkward first dances, and anxious first kisses; pride at diplomas received and jobs earned; elation at children born; and so much more. What is remembered or reported about a woman should not be limited to the day another person violently ended her life. The full story of a woman is made up of all she did, not only what was taken from her.

* * *

Mary Byron was born on December 6, 1972, in a small community outside of Louisville, Kentucky. She grew up the daughter of John and Pat and was a younger sister to Becky. Mary had a dry sense of humor and loved animals. As a child, she had cats, dogs, even rabbits, and she spent her childhood wanting a horse above all. Mary also loved sports, namely volleyball and softball. Her school days were spent at St. Edwards (Elementary) School and Assumption High School in Louisville, but as she looked toward high school graduation, Mary knew that her life path wasn't to include college. For her, the path would be beauty school. In the course of getting her beauty license, Mary had to find a model on whom to create a hairstyle. She chose her mother, a memory that still makes Pat smile to this day.

While still in high school, Mary met a young man at a teen club and began dating him in her senior year. He took her to her senior prom. Mary dated him for a couple of years, but those years were increasingly filled with jealousy, anger, and growing violence. Her boyfriend's escalating mistreatment led Mary to break up with him, but he was not a man who let go easily. In 1993 her ex-boyfriend stalked, raped, and assaulted Mary—crimes for which he was ultimately arrested and jailed. Mary knew instinctively of the danger posed by her ex-boyfriend, so she asked local police officials to notify her upon his release from jail. She was promised notice by well-intended officers, but they had no real-time way to know when her offender would walk out of jail. As a result, her request was heard but never heeded. On the evening of December 6, 1993, Mary sat in her car as it warmed up after leaving her job at the Mall St. Matthews. She had just left work, where they had celebrated her twenty-first birthday. As her car warmed, in her peripheral vision she saw her former boyfriend approaching the car from the driver's side. She had no chance to fight or even to question why; he fired seven bullets into Mary's head and chest at point-blank range, killing her. Mary died on her twenty-first birthday.

Mary's was a highly visible case that rocked communities across Kentucky. Following her murder, Mary's parents, John and Pat Byron, talked with an attorney and knew they had the right to sue local police for the failure to keep their promise to notify Mary of her ex-boyfriend's release from jail, but they chose a different path. Their path was to create a solution that would prevent the same violent, senseless loss that had damaged their lives from happening to another family. In that choice they would save lives for generations to come, and they would honor their daughter in the most profound way.

Work began in earnest by the Byrons and local elected officials such as county judge David Armstrong; criminal justice experts, including Betsy Helm; and advocates such as Marcia Roth. Their task was to find a creative solution to the notification gap. A decision was ultimately made to create a mechanism to notify victims upon the release of an offender from the

Mary Byron at her sister's wedding, June 1991. (Courtesy of Pat and John Byron)

county jail, and a bid was let for a computer company to create a county-wide automated victim notification system. The local community where Mary was murdered contributed funds to support that contract. Two young men living in Louisville immediately saw the potential such an automated system could provide, so they formed a company called Interactive Systems Inc. and submitted a winning bid. (Mike Davis and Yung Nguyen have gone on to expand their company and to rename it Appriss, Inc.)

With her parents' pleas, the leadership of local elected officials, the passion of advocates, and the ingenuity of computer engineers, a county-wide automated victim notification system was unveiled on Mary's birthday, exactly one year after her murder. It would come to be called the VINE (Victim Information and Notification Everyday) System. As Marcia Roth, director of the Mary Byron Project, remembers, "It wasn't until very late in the process that we knew we had something that no one else in the country had accomplished. And we knew we had to share our innovation outside the walls of Jefferson County" (Roth, 2012). As described in chapter 8, the Jefferson County movement would do just that.

. . .

The second caution is that reforms are also made for women whose cases are not so visible, for women who are not well known. The case of California and the origin of anti-stalking legislation is a good example of the reason for this caution. As detailed in chapter 2, in July 1989, the young actress Rebecca Schaeffer was murdered by an obsessed fan. Her murder received wide coverage in newspapers and on television, riveted national attention to the phenomenon of stalking, and prompted local judges and legislators to draft laws criminalizing stalking behaviors. What is less well known is that Schaeffer was not the only woman stalked and murdered in California that year. Shortly after her death, four other women in Orange County—Patricia Kastle, Manijeh Bolour, Tammy Davis, and Brenda Thurman—died at the hands of men (all former intimate partners) who had stalked them (see chapter 2). Their stories are not as well known, but they, too, influenced the passage of anti-stalking legislation in California.

The murders of these five California women taught important lessons to the public and to those working in the field of violence against women. They showed that stalking can be defined as a set of acts constituting a distinct crime. They showed that these acts, cumulatively, have a terribly negative impact on victims, and that stalking can be associated with significant risk and danger. They illustrated what the literature has now confirmed: stalking is most often perpetrated by someone known to the victim. Finally, they serve as a reminder that legislative changes can be prompted not only by highly visible cases but also on behalf of victims whose names are largely unknown.

Coalitions and Task Forces: Collaborating for Legislative Reform

In the early days of the anti-rape and domestic violence movements, legislative reform efforts were most often an outgrowth of the work of advocates in the field. Collaborations or coalitions with other professionals were rare and, in fact, were often shunned, as advocates believed their status as outsiders and their close alignment with victims and survivors gave them the best perspective on what laws or policies needed to be changed. There was also a distrust of agencies working within the system, which was often seen as the source of further victimization of battered women and rape survivors.

Over time, however, advocates expanded their legislative reform efforts. Among their first partners were researchers whose work documented the extent of rape and domestic violence and measured the effectiveness of criminal justice responses. In the early 1980s, for example, Mary Koss and her colleagues developed and published the Sexual Experiences Survey, which greatly improved how the field defined and counted rape (Koss & Gidycz, 1985; Koss & Oros, 1982). In the 1970s Murray Straus's Conflict Tactics Scale gave a clearer picture of the frequency and severity of domestic violence (Straus, 1977, 1979). One of the earliest and most visible examples of researcher impact came with Lawrence Sherman and Richard Berk's 1984 study of the efficacy of arrest for domestic violence in Minneapolis, Minnesota (see chapter 4).

In some states, criminal justice professionals such as police and prosecutors became legislative allies, as did health and mental health care professionals and educators.[3] Their increasing interest led to the development of broader legislative reform coalitions. In Kentucky, coalitions emerged earlier than they did elsewhere; in fact, one coalition spearheaded the earliest reforms to the Commonwealth's rape statutes. The Kentucky Coalition against Rape and Sexual Assault (informally called the Rape Coalition) was organized in the late 1970s with approximately 500 members across the state; its members included rape crisis center staff and other advocates, police, prosecutors, probation and parole officers, defense attorneys, health care providers, educators, and representatives from the governor's office and other state government agencies. The effort was led by top officials of the Jefferson County government and was staffed by the Louisville–Jefferson County Crime Commission.[4] The Rape Coalition had remarkable legislative success, including laws that provided for public payment for forensic rape examinations (1984), privileged communication status for advocates from rape crisis centers (1986), removal of the term "earnest resistance" from the definitional section of the sexual offense chapter (1988), elimination of the spousal exemption from the sexual offense chapter (1990), expansion of the definition of rape to include penetration with a foreign object (1992), and certification of nurses to perform forensic rape examinations through a statewide sexual assault nurse examiner program (1996).

The Rape Coalition used a number of strategies to advance its legislative agenda. First and foremost, it thrived through its collaboration with rape crisis advocates, women's advocates, child advocates, adult survivors and parents, criminal justice professionals, and state and local government officials. The coalition's structure provided leadership and staffing; its collaborations provided strength and success. Second, during the months between each legislative session,[5] the coalition held public hearings in cities across the Commonwealth to allow local professionals and community representatives to testify about the aspects of the justice and health care systems that were not working. Input from these forums was analyzed and further research was conducted by several working committees of the Rape Coalition. The coalition also surveyed professionals and advocates to elicit ideas and suggestions on the specific design of proposed legislative reforms. In the 1990s, for example, drugs were increasingly being used to incapacitate women and render them incapable of self-protection from rape. Drugs like Rohypnol (flunitrazepam) had sedative, hypnotic, dissociative, and amnesiac effects and were easily administered by offenders. Seeking methods to address this growing threat, the coalition mailed a survey to 629 law enforcement officers, prosecutors, and advocates to determine the importance they attached to the issue of Rohypnol use, whether the coalition should seek a legislative solution, and what changes to law or policy would be best. The survey findings (with a response rate of 25 percent) indicated significant concern over the role of Rohypnol in rape cases (85 percent of respondents) and strong encouragement to pursue legislative action (85 percent of respondents). The respondents also suggested specific statutory amendments (e.g., higher penalties for sexual offenses committed with the administration of a drug) and changes to the statutory scheduling of drugs. Although this survey and others like it were not scientific, they gave the Rape Coalition broad input from across the state (an important aspect, because practices and needs vary in rural as opposed to urban communities) and fought any perception that the coalition was run by a small core of people in only one city.

While coalitions generally involve ongoing collaboration and in some cases permanent organizations, task forces are more limited in duration and more narrowly focused. The advantages of task forces are several, in terms of both the quality of work they produce and the strategic advantages they offer. Certain key characteristics of a task force help ensure that its outcome is maximally effective, including its leadership and staffing, the quality and interdisciplinarity of its membership, the involvement of survivors and advocates as both testifiers and members, the organized and methodical review of systemic weaknesses, the development of comprehensive legislative reforms, and use of the media to ensure public awareness of the task force's work.

Among the first questions to ask when contemplating the creation of a task force is which individual or which office should serve as the body's sponsor or host. That determination must be based on unique factors within the state, but in general, top officers in the executive branch of government, such as the governor or the attorney general, can be advantageous selections. It is critical, however, that the officeholder supports the empowering of women and can be trusted to operate the task force with advocates' substantive input and direction. Another factor is the public perception of that individual; it is essential that the officeholder has a positive public reputation and significant political influence if this model is to be successful. A critical but often overlooked matter is who will staff the task force. In Kentucky, the most efficacious model has been a coupling of office staff (i.e., staff from the attorney general's office or the legislature) with leaders from the advocate movement (the latter both serving on the task force and staffing it). The selection of leadership is also critical. A cochair model is often a good construction because it ensures diversity among the leadership (e.g., in gender and race) and because it can pair advocates with criminal justice professionals. Like the officeholder sponsoring the task force, it is crucial that the chairs have strong reputations and influence in their respective fields. If the legislature is the convener of a task force, there may be less flexibility in selecting leaders, as members of the legislative body will likely be appointed to the leadership roles.

The leadership position on a task force can be a challenging one, making selection of the chair or cochairs a consequential decision. Knowledge of the field is, perhaps, an obvious attribute in a chairperson, but additional skill sets are required. For example, task force proceedings are highly visible, and chairs should have experience with press exposure. Testimony before a task force can also be controversial, causing conflict between members or media scrutiny, both of which need to be managed by the individuals serving as chairpersons. In Kentucky, for example, a task force on domestic violence was created by the Office of the Attorney General in the early 1990s. During one task force meeting, testimony revealed that only about one-third of the civil protective orders issued by a Kentucky court were successfully served. That testimony immediately captured the attention of the media, and significant newspaper and television coverage ensued, causing an outcry from certain law enforcement associations. The fact that testimony or other proceedings are likely to be controversial is no reason to avoid them, but the fallout must be managed effectively by the task force leadership.

The makeup of the task force is also vital to its success. Members should include multiple advocates from several locations: grassroots direct service programs (rape crisis centers and domestic violence programs or shelters), the state's rape crisis or domestic violence coalitions, and state and local governments. Survivors (of domestic violence or rape) should also be represented on the task force. Symbolically, they illustrate that victimization can be overcome and its survivors can be perceptive contributors to change. On the practical side, their stories can capture the attention of the public and the legislative audience that is the task force's final target. The appointment of legislators to the task force is essential; ideally, they should possess significant influence and serve on key committees (e.g., judiciary, human services, appropriations). This gives the task force built-in sponsors for the legislation it will propose. Justice professionals (judges, prosecutors, law enforcement officers, civil attorneys, defense attorneys, and circuit clerks), medical and other health professionals, social services agencies, researchers, educators, and the clergy can also be key members.

Tactical selection of members should take into consideration the work that will need to be accomplished to ensure that the task force's proposals are ultimately passed by the legislature. For example, rather than selecting an unaffiliated physician, choosing a physician who formally represents the state medical association can mean an endorsement of the task force's legislative proposals by an influential lobbying organization. Appointing defense lawyers or others who may oppose some of the task force's proposals can be, paradoxically, a wise move (e.g., a defense attorney may oppose harsher penalties in rape cases, or a prosecutor may oppose leniency for battered women who kill their abusive partners). This, accurately, gives the task force the appearance of fairness, and it provides the opportunity to craft compromises before any proposal reaches the legislature. Some legislative proposals supported by the majority of task force members may not lend themselves to compromise (leading some members to vote in opposition), but the opportunity to thoroughly discuss a proposal is likely to strengthen its design and can reduce the level of acrimony when the legislation goes before the legislature. Astute legislative advocates invest significant effort in avoiding public arguments over proposals during the legislative session, as legislators often shy away from supporting bills that are steeped in conflict or controversy or those that are opposed by influential lobbying groups.

The proceedings of a task force on domestic violence or rape should be well planned, well organized, and designed to provide a methodical review of weaknesses in a state's ability to address domestic violence or rape. A first phase of broad input is useful, accomplished by public forums and invited testimony from individuals and representatives of agencies and associations. Committees can then be established to focus on a range of issues (e.g., criminal justice responses, civil statutes, access to services for survivors, budgetary matters, education, prevention), ultimately leading to a comprehensive package of legislative reforms. The task force should time its work so that final proposals are voted on prior to the beginning of a legislative session, allowing enough time to devise a legislative strategy for the upcoming session while still taking advantage of the momentum and press coverage engendered by the task force's efforts.

TACTICS OF LEGISLATIVE REFORM

The broad strategies detailed above are often designed to create not a single piece of legislation but a package of bills to comprehensively improve the system. There are several advantages to an organized package of bills: they arrive at the legislature with built-in support from the task force or legislative committee that proposed them, they have likely been thoroughly vetted in the interval between legislative sessions, and they tend to attract public attention and enjoy a certain momentum. Despite these advantages, sometimes a single bill is proposed, either because it is the top priority for a coalition or other professional association or because the legislature may not be amenable to multiple bills owing to budgetary woes or other reasons.

Regardless of whether advocates propose a single bill or a complete package, at the end of the day, the large group of individuals that drafted the bill (or bills) must give way to the relatively small number of advocates (or task force or coalition leaders) who spend their days in the halls of the capitol while the legislature is in session. While these advocates and leaders have the support of coalitions, associations, and other constituent groups that play a key role in influencing legislators' votes, it is this smaller team of advocates that selects sponsors, approaches individual legislators for votes, testifies before committees, and deals with the myriad challenges involved in getting a bill passed. This section is dedicated to those front-line legislative advocates. It begins below with a detailed discussion of the Kentucky General Assembly, followed by general and specific tactics for success. The common thread throughout these tactical discussions is the need for advocates to be well informed—informed about the details of the proposal itself, informed about why a specific proposal is so critical, informed about the prior history of related legislative reforms, and informed about the legislative landscape in which they work.

Knowing the Legislative Landscape: The Kentucky General Assembly

Structure and Membership. Although votes on legislative proposals take place during constitutionally structured sessions of the legislature, the work of advocates hoping to reform state statutes on behalf of women victimized by domestic violence, rape, or stalking begins long before the strike of a gavel convenes the session or another strike of the gavel adjourns it sine die.[6] That work starts by knowing the history, structure, rules of procedure, and membership of the legislature. For example, knowing how many times a bill has to be read on the floor of the house or senate before it can be voted on tells advocates when to schedule telephone calls to legislators by key constituents. Knowing the deadline for filing an amendment in committee or on the floor to be eligible for voting is critical both for adding desirable amendments and for avoiding the attachment of undesirable ones. Knowing whether bills have to be posted in a committee and what constitutes a "committee substitute" guides advocates when deciding when to approach sponsors and committee chairs about bringing a bill up for a hearing. Knowing who chairs key criminal justice, human resources, and budget committees; how a given legislator has voted in the past; a legislator's professional background (e.g., defense attorney versus assistant prosecutor); and which legislator has had a falling out with another are the types of wide-ranging information an advocate needs to know to be most effective. The first section of this chapter is designed to provide that knowledge.

· · ·

"Who were these 100 men who laid the foundation of our present Kentucky government? According to the record, 60 were lawyers, 20 were farmers, 13 were doctors, and 7 were bankers or merchants. Most of the delegates were middle aged or older. Quite a few were active in politics. . . . No real radicals were in the group."

—James T. Fleming, past director,
Legislative Research Commission, 1952

· · ·

In Kentucky, the structure of the General Assembly was designed by the state's first constitution, authored in 1792 by delegates to a constitutional convention held in the city of Danville. When Congress approved that document, Kentucky became the fifteenth state in the Union (Aubrey et al., 2003). Kentucky's current constitution—its fourth—was authored in 1892 (Hendrix, 2010). The 1892 constitution gave the name "General Assembly" to the state legislature and provided for two chambers: the state senate, with thirty-eight members and four-year terms,[7] and the state house of representatives, with one hundred members and two-year terms (Blanchard, 2000). While fifteen states have enacted term limits for legislators, Kentucky has not done so (National Council of State Legislatures, 2012b). House and senate members are elected from single-member districts, and the General Assembly is required to redistrict every ten years, ostensibly in a manner that ensures "one person, one vote." The constitution also deemed that the General Assembly would meet every two years in even numbered years for a maximum of sixty days (this would later change).

The Kentucky Constitution stipulates qualifications for members of the General Assembly, setting a minimum age of twenty-four for house members and thirty for senate members and requiring that members be citizens of the Commonwealth at the time of election; prior to election, there is a two-year residence requirement for house members and a six-year requirement for senate members, and they must reside in the district they wish to represent (Aubrey et al., 2003). The length of legislators' service in the General Assembly has increased over the decades, from an average of three years in 1970 to an average of nine years two decades later (Harrison & Klotter, 1997). Some believe this reflects a more professionalized, career-focused legislature, even though the jobs remain part time.

The 1892 constitution included provisions for amendments, and many changes have been made over the years.[8] Of the seventy-eight attempts to amend the Kentucky Constitution, only forty-one have been successful, the most recent in 2012 (Legislative Research Commission, 2013). Also of note, after the U.S. Constitution was amended to reflect women's right to vote, a 1923 attempt to similarly amend the Kentucky Constitution failed. It continued to contain an obsolete "male suffrage" provision until 1955, when it was amended to lower the voting age to eighteen; only then was the "male" requirement eliminated (Legislative Research Commission, 2013). A 1979 amendment established a ten-day planning session of the General Assembly in odd-numbered years and extended its sessions by allowing these ten days to occur any time between January 1 and April 15. (One of the important implications of this change is that the General Assembly can pass the bills it chooses; recess for the ten-day period, during which the governor may exercise the veto power; and then reconvene to consider overriding any vetoes.) One other amendment made in 1979 changed the election of General Assembly members from odd-numbered to even-numbered years. While this change may seem inconsequential—more political than substantive for advocates—understanding when senate and house members will be running for reelection is strategically important in terms of asking members to support a bill or scheduling legislation for a floor vote. For example, for legislators facing reelection, there is a January filing deadline for opponents, and sitting legislators may be reluctant to vote in favor of a controversial bill until they know who is running against them.

By the beginning of the 1980s, the General Assembly was

transitioning into a more independent governmental body. Prior to 1980, governors wielded significant influence over the General Assembly, going so far as to select house and senate leaders and instructing legislators on which bills should be passed on any given day. From the legislative side, that transition was prompted, in part, by a growth in the number of young legislators who had cut their political teeth on the words of President John F. Kennedy. They were idealistic and believed their public service could result in real change. In Kentucky, however, these young, newly elected legislators ran into the brick wall of the governor's office. They learned quickly that they did not have the power they thought they would to change Kentucky for the better (Karem, 2012). Simmering resentment and a chafing against gubernatorial control began to build. By the late 1970s, a group of young senators collectively called the "black sheep squadron" (made up of Democrats John Berry, Lowell Hughes, David Karem, and others) rebelled against the governor's power. They took it upon themselves to pull power back to the legislature, elect their own leaders, and determine for themselves the course of any legislation.

On the gubernatorial side, the term of John Y. Brown Jr. would mark the turning point in legislative independence. Governor Brown did not feel inclined to direct the legislature's work, as his predecessors had done. As the executive branch wielded less clout in terms of controlling votes and directing the progress of legislation, the votes of individual legislators became more important. The relationship between governors and the General Assembly evolved from one in which the governor's edict determined how legislators voted to one in which the governor's legislative agenda might find success in a supportive legislature or defeat in a reticent or even vengeful one. The 1980s would also witness the dark side of legislative independence as votes became commodities, leading to a corruption scandal that would explode in the following decade.

Several key amendments to the Kentucky Constitution passed in 1992, including one requiring the joint election of the governor and lieutenant governor; one allowing the governor to retain the powers of office when absent from the Commonwealth (precluding actions such as Lieutenant Governor Thelma Stovall's efforts on behalf of the Equal Rights Amendment in the absence of Governor Julian Carroll); and one removing the lieutenant governor as presiding officer of the state senate (making Paul E. Patton the last lieutenant governor to serve in that position and John "Eck" Rose, serving at the time as president pro tempore, the first senator to hold the presidency). While proponents of the joint election of governor and lieutenant governor saw that amendment as a way to ensure that both officials were from the same party, some have pointed out that the effect was to stifle women's opportunities to hold elective office (Collins, 2013).

A 2000 amendment to the constitution provided for annual sessions of the General Assembly and required that bills introduced in odd-numbered years that raise revenue or appropriate funds must be agreed to by three-fifths of all senators and representatives—a so-called supermajority (Aubrey et al., 2003). Kentucky's move was part of a trend by state legislatures over the past five decades to change to annual sessions. In the 1960s fewer than twenty state legislatures met annually; a decade later that number had more than doubled. Today, forty-six state legislatures meet annually, with Oregon, Arkansas, and Kentucky being the most recent to adopt this model (National Council of State Legislatures, 2012a). In Kentucky, the proposal to change to annual rather than biennial legislative sessions was not initially embraced by all legislators or all lobbying groups. However, the move to annual sessions was consistent with the growing power and independence of the General Assembly, as meeting more often was seen as a way to temper the power of the executive branch. Proponents of annual sessions also argued that the complexity and intransigence of some issues made biennial sessions unworkable. The bill's primary sponsor also pointed out that annual sessions would reduce the need for specially called legislative sessions. Opponents argued that annual sessions would increase costs, and there would be less time to consider major issues between legislative sessions. Some in the executive branch raised concerns about legislative overreach into strictly administrative matters, and the public opined that "there are enough laws." In the end, the proponents of annual sessions won the day, but some of the opponents' concerns have come to fruition. For example, legislative and lobbying costs have increased, and the number of special legislative sessions has not decreased significantly. Since 2000, there have been ten special sessions; in the 1990s, prior to the amendment, Kentucky had thirteen special sessions—not a precipitous drop (Special sessions, 2012). Additionally, in 1998, prior to passage of the amendment, approximately 40 percent of bills introduced in the session passed; two years after annual sessions were introduced, that percentage had decreased to 27 percent (Legislative Research Commission, 1998). In 2011 increasing numbers of voices were heard, questioning whether the move to annual sessions was a wise policy move for the state (Gerth, 2011).

Leadership. As noted above, a 1992 amendment to the Kentucky Constitution provided that the president of the state senate would be a senator elected by a majority of the membership, rather than the lieutenant governor. That change resulted in similar structures for the senate and house, both of which now have chief presiding officers elected by a majority of the membership—a speaker for the house of representatives (House Rules 27, 28) and a president for the senate (Senate Rule 26), as well as a speaker pro tempore and a president pro tempore, who preside in the absence of the chief presiding officer. Although members vote individually, in practice, the majority party commands more votes and thereby has a greater influence on the election of the chief officer.

Over the years, Democrats have retained the majority in the house (and, through a majority vote, the speakership). The current speaker is Gregory D. Stumbo from Prestonsburg; he has been speaker since 2009, beating Jody Richards from Bowling Green, who had held that position for the longest term in house history. While the house remains Democratic, Republicans have attained the majority in the state senate in recent years. In 1997, in an unexpected and rather controversial move, the sitting president of the senate—Democrat John "Eck" Rose, representing Winchester—was ousted as a result of a political partnership between a dissident group of Democrats and the Republicans in the senate. The agreement was that the Democrats would retain the presidency (in the person of the late Senator Larry Saunders, representing Louisville), but the Republicans would control the chair positions of the standing committees. That agreement lasted for three years, at which time the Republican Party became the majority party in the senate. David L. Williams from Burkesville served as president of the senate from 2000 to 2012 and was succeeded by Senator Robert Stivers from Manchester.

In addition, majority and minority caucuses exist in both chambers, consisting of all the members of each respective party. These caucuses are led by caucus chairs, who are elected by members. The caucuses also elect majority and minority floor leaders (the majority floor leader manages the processing of bills on the floor of the chamber) and whips, who are largely responsible for vote counting. Although most committee meetings of the Kentucky General Assembly are open to the public, technically, caucus meetings are closed (Senate Rule 44B). In recent years, however, caucus meetings have been opened to the public except when a controversial conversation or the election of caucus leaders is on the agenda.

The combined leadership of the two chambers constitutes the leadership of the Legislative Research Commission, the staffing arm of the General Assembly that was created in 1948.

Process and Committee Organization. The principal function of the Kentucky General Assembly is lawmaking, which includes the introduction and enactment of bills that create, amend, or repeal statutes and those that appropriate funds for the operation of the government (Aubrey et al., 2003). The General Assembly is also authorized to pass joint resolutions, which have the force of law, and simple and concurrent resolutions, which do not have the force of law but express the will of one or both chambers.

To engage in its principal lawmaking function, each chamber of the General Assembly adopts rules of procedure at the beginning of each legislative session. House and senate rules set forth the committee structure and the operation of each chamber, and these rules are essential reading for advocates who want to use the legislative process to their advantage and avoid procedural mistakes that jeopardize passage of their legislation. Take, for example, the case of advocates who are considering a proposal to establish a task force to study domestic violence or rape. Although this method was used successfully to advance legislative reform during the 1990s, the General Assembly's receptivity to task forces has changed. By reading the rules, advocates will learn that any proposed resolution for a task force has to go through the committee process, just like any other bill (House Rule 64; Senate Rule 37). Additionally, the senate (Rule 64) now provides that after the passage of such a resolution, the Legislative Research Commission is empowered to assign the study to an existing interim committee rather than establishing a task force (a provision reflecting the senate's dislike of task forces). This kind of information can influence advocates' decisions, given that interim committees of the General Assembly are made up solely of legislators; advocates and professionals in the criminal justice, health, mental health, or other fields cannot sit on the committee, nor can they vote on legislative proposals.

A working knowledge of the rules is also important because they stipulate the deadlines for the introduction of bills (or resolutions having the force of law). These dates are crucial for advocates working with sponsors on the timing of their legislative proposals. (House Rule 51 sets the deadline as the thirty-eighth day of even-year sessions and the twenty-fifth day of odd-year sessions; Senate Rule 51 sets the deadline as the fortieth day of even-year sessions and the thirteenth day of odd-year sessions.) House and senate rules also lay out the process by which a bill that has been defeated on the floor can be brought back by a so-called motion to reconsider (House Rule 14; Senate Rule 14). Specifically, a defeated bill can be reconsidered after two days if a legislator who voted on the prevailing side makes the appropriate motion. Importantly, however, advocates need to work closely with legislators during that two-day period to ensure that a revote will result in a different outcome. (Failure would mean loss of the bill and potential embarrassment for the bill's sponsor.) Finally, the rules provide for where and when lobbying may take place, specifically prohibiting lobbying near the chambers and in the surrounding hallways (Senate Rule 71; House Rule 72). Any eager and well-meaning advocate who violates that rule may be removed by a sergeant at arms.

Senate and house rules provide for three types of committees: procedural, special, and standing committees. Each chamber has three procedural committees. The Committee on Committees (House Rule 37; Senate Rule 37) is composed of the chamber's leadership and is chaired by the chief presiding officer (the speaker of the house or the president of the senate). This committee is empowered to appoint chairs and members of other committees and to select which committees will hear bills when they are introduced. The house and senate rules spell out the jurisdiction of each standing committee that hears bills, thus serving as a guide for the Committee on Committees. Nonetheless, referrals by the Committee on Committees are judgment calls made by a majority of the committee members and can dramatically influence the success of a bill, depending on whether it is sent to a standing committee perceived to be friendly to the bill or a committee where unpopular or controversial bills are sent to languish without being heard. Advocates of all kinds tend to get nervous when their legislative proposals are sent to the Appropriations and Revenue Committee, for example, which is famous for being the final resting place of unwanted legislation. Referral to a committee whose chair has previously expressed animosity for a particular bill would also be worrisome to advocates. For advocates, the lesson is to keep track of when a bill is introduced by a sponsor and to ensure that members of the Committee on Committees are informed and supportive of the bill and aware of which standing committee the advocates prefer. If a bill is sent to an unfriendly committee, advocates should not give up; a bill can be moved to another committee if the chamber leadership is inclined or can be persuaded to do that.

If a bill involves a financial expense to the state (at the local level, at the state level, or to the correction budget), the rules require the preparation of a fiscal impact statement, or fiscal note, by the staff of the Legislative Research Commission (Senate Rule 52; House Rule 52). Fiscal notes that demonstrate a budgetary impact on the state's correctional system can be particularly large. If, for example, a bill increases the penalty for a sexual offense, the staff will calculate the number of offenders who are likely to be subject to that increased penalty and the additional days in prison required to complete those longer sentences. The attachment of a fiscal note to an advocate's bill presents a challenge, for if the cost is significant enough, then the bill may be sent not only to a standing committee of subject matter jurisdiction but also to the Appropriations and Revenue Committee. Although the Legislative Research Commission prepares fiscal notes, advocates should be prepared to provide an estimate of costs. If an advocate group anticipates that a proposal will have a fiscal impact, another strategy is to approach the governor well before the legislative session and ask that the funds be included in the state budget prior to the bill being referred to the legislature. It is easier to pass a bill with a fiscal note attached if the legislature does not have to find the funding in today's universally tight state budgets.

The second procedural committee found in both chambers is the Rules Committee (House Rule 41; Senate Rule 41), which is arguably even more influential than the Committee on Committees. Meetings of the Rules Committees are open (House Rule 41; Senate Rule 44B), so advocates can seek permission to attend them and track their legislation directly. (Note that the senate's rules are more restrictive, limiting attendees to senators, the media, and others invited by the committee, and the only people allowed to speak are committee members and those invited to do so by the chair or a majority of the members.) Sponsors of bills are also given the opportunity to appear before the Rules Committee when their bills are being considered. Even if a bill has been passed by a standing committee, advocates should never assume that this means an automatic vote on the chamber floor. The Rules Committee determines which bills are voted on and when that vote takes place. The Rules Committee is also empowered to return a bill to a standing committee, which may be a sign that it has encountered opposition and is being sent back to committee to die a rather painful legislative death. Additionally, the senate rules stipulate that a bill may be sent back to Appropriations and Revenue "in those instances in which the fiscal implications of the measure may require additional consideration" (Rule 41). If the bill has a funding element or a cost to it, this move should be anticipated; if not, it could be a sign of a negative outcome. In addition, the house rules provide that if a bill includes a penalty that would result in incarceration, it must be heard by the Judiciary Committee (Rule 41). Bills can remain in the Rules Committee for a maximum of five days, after which they must be moved to the floor for a vote or sent back to a standing committee. The chief presiding officer (speaker or president) serves as chair of the Rules Committee, and the majority floor leaders carry out the decisions of the Rules Committee by calling bills.

The third procedural committee is the Enrollment Committee, which oversees the final preparation of bills that have been passed before they proceed to the governor's desk (processes termed engrossment and enrollment of bills).

Special committees, as the name implies, are created during a legislative session to fulfill a unique purpose. Among the most common special committee is the conference committee, which brings senators and representatives together to negotiate and resolve differences when the two chambers have passed different versions of the same bill (Senate Rule 44; House Rule 44). The conference committee is limited in its authority; it may only make recommendations on the primary issues that differentiate the house and senate versions of a bill. If the conference committee cannot reach an agreement, a free conference committee may be appointed by the two chambers. This committee has broader authority to amend the bill, but exceptions include adding significant appropriations or adding the complete text of another bill, both of which are, theoretically, prohibited (but see below). Budget bills (which must be introduced in the house, pursuant to Section 47 of the Kentucky Constitution) almost always end up in free conference committees. Like the majority of other committees, meetings of conference and free conference committees are open.

Attaching the substantial text of one bill to another is prohibited by the rules of both chambers when votes are taken on the floor (Senate Rule 60; House Rule 60). However, advocates may have seen controversial bills that failed to make it out of a standing committee being attached to their bills or to another bill that has significant support in the chamber. In informal terms, such an amendment is called a "piggyback." When this is done, upon the motion of a member, the president or speaker must determine whether the rule has been violated. There are many stories in the history of the house when legislators facing a piggyback bill would, in unison, make noises mimicking a pig's "oink" until the speaker ruled on the measure.[9]

Standing committees operate in both chambers, but they are not exactly the same. The house maintains sixteen standing committees (Rule 40) and the senate twelve (Rule 40) (see table 5.1). As noted above, the Committee on Committees appoints the chairs, vice chairs, and members of these committees. In both the house and the senate, the Appropriations and Revenue Committee uniquely operates with several standing subcommittees called liaison committees (addressing the areas of economic development; general government, finance, and public protection; human resources; justice and judiciary; education; and transportation). The chair of the Appropriations and Revenue Committee has the authority to appoint subcommittee members.

These standing committees are vital to advocates who want their bills to progress through the legislature. Standing committees are where most bills die, either by a majority vote of members or by a failure to be called for a hearing. Standing committees also give advocates a valuable opportunity to publicly testify on behalf of their bills and to directly influence the legislators who will vote on their bills. If a bill is reported favorably out of a standing committee, it progresses to the full floor for a vote after receiving three readings (Senate Rule 56; House Rule 56).

Standing committees of both chambers consider several hundred to more than a thousand bills each session. The majority of bills

Table 5.1. Kentucky House and Senate Standing Committees

Senate Standing Committees	House Standing Committees
Agriculture	Agriculture and Small Business
Appropriations and Revenue	Appropriations and Revenue
Banking and Insurance	Banking and Insurance
Economic Development, Tourism, and Labor	Economic Development
Education	Education
Health and Welfare	Elections, Constitutional Amendments, and Intergovernmental Affairs
Judiciary	Health and Welfare
Licensing, Occupations, and Administrative Regulations	Judiciary
Natural Resources and Energy	Labor and Industry
State and Local Government	Licensing and Occupations
Transportation	Local Government
Veterans, Military Affairs, and Public Protection	Natural Resources and Environment
	State Government
	Tourism Development and Energy
	Transportation
	Veterans, Military Affairs, and Public Safety

Table 5.2. Bills Introduced and Passed in Select Sessions of the Kentucky General Assembly

	1994 Regular Session	1998 Regular Session	2002 Regular Session	2012 Regular Session
Bills Introduced	1,309	1,369	1,169	786
Bills Passed	458	550	314	154
Percentage Passed	35	40	27	20

Source: Legislative Research Commission, 1994, 1998, 2002, 2012.

introduced do not pass; in fact, the percentage of bills passed has decreased over the past few decades. The passage rate dropped to 20 percent in the 2012 regular session, but that legislature also faced the biennial budget and redistricting legislation, causing both the number of bills introduced and the percentage passed to decrease significantly (see table 5.2).

If and when a bill is passed unanimously by a committee, a member of the committee may make a motion to place the bill on consent orders. (If this fails to occur automatically, a quiet reminder to a supportive legislator is worth considering.) Consent orders (House Rule 57; Senate Rule 57) include a list of the noncontroversial bills that have been passed out of committees. They are voted on as a group prior to general orders of the day and do not require discussion or a public floor vote—a great relief to an advocate who fears a bill's failure to pass on the floor. The rules of both chambers provide a procedure for individual legislators to vote against a bill on consent orders and for a bill to be removed from consent orders if an amendment is filed.

How a Bill Becomes a Law. Over the centuries, poets and philosophers have offered less than flattering depictions of lawmaking. As noted by one poet, "Laws, like sausages, cease to inspire respect in proportion as we know how they are made" (Saxe, 1869). The most effective legislative strategies are those based on a meticulous working knowledge of the lawmaking process. This is particularly true late in the legislative session, when the process moves at a rapid pace and any misstep can be ruinous for the success of a bill. Figure 5.1 depicts the process as provided by the Kentucky Constitution and General Assembly rules, offering tips for advocates at each step.

Lobbying: The Tactics of Legislative Reform

In broad terms, lobbying involves advocacy, education, negotiation, and other activities engaged in by an interest or advocacy group as a means of influencing the passage of legislation or the adoption of policy.[10] Lobbying is so essential that it is a protected behavior under the First Amendment to the U.S. Constitution.

The benefits of lobbying are many and include providing policy expertise on complex legislation; providing insight on technical, practical, and long-term ramifications of legislation and public policy; connecting and communicating citizen concerns to lawmakers; informing citizens of impending legislation; holding lawmakers accountable; and uniting citizens with similar concerns (Gelak, 2008). For domestic violence and anti-rape advocates, lobbying and advocacy have always been essential aspects of improving state and federal laws on behalf of rape survivors and battered women.

Legislative activities united advocates at a national level and helped refine and advance the entire women's movement.

Nonprofit advocacy organizations are uniquely positioned to lobby.[11] They have an ideal combination of detailed knowledge (e.g., how the criminal justice or health care system works for battered women and rape survivors in the state's different jurisdictions) and a fervent desire to change laws and policies on behalf of their constituents. They enjoy a great deal of credibility among lawmakers because their mission is honest and pure and because legislators know that advocates have a long-term commitment to their cause and will be there year after year as votes are taken.

In addition to grassroots advocates, the halls of state legislatures are filled with professional lobbyists who are hired and paid by organizations or other interest groups. In fact, over time, the number of professional lobbyists has grown and the amount of money spent on lobbying has increased significantly, influenced in part by the trend toward annual rather than biennial legislative sessions. In Kentucky there were 689 legislative agents at the state level in 2008, placing the Commonwealth in the top twenty states nationwide in the number of lobbyists (Gelak, 2008). From 1994 to 2011 more than $180 million was spent on lobbying in Kentucky—$158 million for legislative agents' salaries and $23 million for lobbying expenses (Legislative Ethics Commission, 2011). In 1994 the total amount of money spent on lobbying in Kentucky was $6.4 million, but the average amount is now more than $15 million annually (Legislative Ethics Commission, 2011). During each legislative session, there is a noticeable trend in the types of lobbyists who appear in the state capital, largely influenced by the major legislation under consideration in a given year by the General Assembly. In the past two years, for example, as the General Assembly has debated legislation to regulate prescription practices and the distribution and sale of certain scheduled drugs (e.g., oxycodone) and other drugs used in methamphetamine production (e.g., pseudoephedrine), the health care industry has been the largest spender with respect to lobbyists' salaries and lobbying expenses.

The ability of large professional organizations (e.g., medical associations, hospital organizations, manufacturing organizations) to invest substantial funds in lobbying can give them certain advantages over grassroots lobbying efforts and can be intimidating to underfunded domestic violence and anti-rape advocates. That

The bill is introduced in the house or senate by the primary sponsor, who must file the appropriate form with the clerk on the floor or in the clerk's office. The Kentucky Constitution requires that bills generating revenue or including a tax must begin in the house. Chamber rules set deadlines for the final day on which a bill may be introduced.

Bills may be cosponsored by more than one legislator. While the senate rules are silent on cosponsorship, in practice, there are often multiple senators sponsoring a bill. House rules provide for a primary cosponsor and other cosponsors. In all cases, cosponsors sign on to a bill with permission of the primary sponsor.

For Advocates
While those of us who have been around the halls of the General Assembly tend to think of proposed bills as ours, only a legislator can actually sponsor a bill. See the text for tips on the selection of sponsors. Only the legislator can direct Legislative Research Commission (LRC) staff to do that work, but I have always found committee staff very open to collaboration. LRC staff are guided by the commission's bill #1 drafting manual. All recommendations for advocates below should be done with knowledge of the sponsor.

The bill is reviewed by the Committee on Committees and assigned to a standing committee for consideration.

For Advocates
Advocates should never just assume that their bill will go to a committee that will be supportive or friendly to their cause; they should approach members of the Committee on Committees to seek help on the referral of the bill.

The bill is heard by the standing committee or may be left unheard. House rules require bills to be posted in committees for three days before being heard; no such requirement exists in the senate. Testimony may be provided before the committee by the primary sponsor and experts. Opponents may also be permitted to testify.

For Advocates
Advocates should request a meeting with the committee chair and ask that a bill be heard. Timed to coincide with when the bill will be heard, advocates should meet with every member of the committee and know the vote count before testimony. See the text for tips on who should testify.

The standing committee reports the bill/resolution out of committee with one of four reports: with the expression of opinion that the same should pass; with the expression of opinion that the same should pass with committee amendment; with the expression of opinion that the same should pass with committee substitute; or with the expression of opinion that the same should not pass.

For Advocates
Remember to seek a motion for placement on the consent calendar for any bill that passes out of committee unanimously.

Figure 5.1. The Process of Lawmaking and Implications for Advocates

The bill must receive three readings on the house or senate floor before being voted on. After two readings, the bill is sent to the Rules Committee. The Rules Committee may recommit the bill or place it on the orders of the day for a floor vote. Chamber rules set deadlines for the final day on which a bill may be placed on the orders of the day for a vote.

For Advocates
As with the Committee on Committees, advocates should approach the majority floor leader to ensure the bill will go on the orders; remember that a bill can remain in the Rules Committee for only five days before action is taken.

If a bill fails to pass, its progression through the legislature ends. To pass, the Kentucky Constitution requires that a bill must receive the votes of at least two-fifths of the members elected to each chamber, and a majority of the members voting; bills with appropriations or emergency clauses must secure the majority of members elected to each chamber.

For Advocates
The day before action will be taken on the floor is a good time for advocates to have their grassroots organizations, other professionals, and constituents make contact with legislators to seek support for the bill.

Upon passage by one chamber, the bill proceeds to the second chamber and goes through the same process outlined above.

For Advocates
The work of advocates outlined above should be repeated in the second chamber. An additional task is to secure a floor sponsor for a bill, as legislators from one chamber cannot speak on the floor of the second chamber.

If the house and senate pass different versions of the same bill, a conference committee may be appointed by the leadership to work out differences. Conference committee reports are sent back to each chamber for final passage. If initial agreement cannot be achieved, a free conference committee may be appointed, which has additional powers to make modifications to the bill.

For Advocates
Advocates may ask to sit in on the open meetings of the conference committees and should devote time to securing the support of the three house and three senate members on the committee.

Upon final passage by both chambers, the bill goes to the governor, who may sign it, allow it to become law without signature, or veto the bill.

If a bill is vetoed by the governor, it is sent back to the house and senate. If the chambers choose to override the veto and secure a constitutional majority in their vote, the veto is overridden and the bill becomes law.

benefit, however, cannot minimize the credibility or effectiveness of what these advocates can accomplish. I once asked a legislator what kind of lobbyist he found most effective, and without hesitation, he said it was advocates: they are "always there, year after year, and their needs are always so heartfelt" (Long, 2012). I confess to being biased, as I served as a legislative advocate for more than two decades, but I do not see any advantage that a professional lobbying firm can offer over effective legislative advocacy by those in the nonprofit arena. (This is not meant to dissuade advocates from partnering with contract lobbyists if that model suits their needs.)

Ten Keys to Success

Advocating for legislative reform—from proposal through passage—is a highly complex process filled with the ebullience of success and the despair of failure. The advocates and lobbyists who have the greatest success with the vagaries of a legislative session are those who plan and strategize. A heartfelt desire to see the law change, though essential to establishing credibility, is not enough to ensure that a bill will eventually reach the governor's desk for signature. While space does not permit a lengthy treatise on effective lobbying methods, the following are some essential guidelines that can serve advocates well as they walk the halls of their state legislatures.

Prepare Well before the Legislative Session Begins. It is axiomatic that the best-prepared advocates are most likely to see their legislative proposals passed by a receptive legislature. Preparation begins by selecting what proposals to put forward. Once a proposal or set of proposals is confirmed, it is essential to develop a broad constituent base of support. For domestic violence and anti-rape advocates, this base starts with their own programs and centers, but broader coalitions of criminal justice professionals, health care and mental health professionals, and others will increase advocates' influence. Developing a communications plan that involves briefing the media on the proposals that will be put forward can also be effective, as legislators are part of the community that reads newspapers, watches television, and listens to the radio.[12]

The production of educational materials should also take place before the session begins. The importance of these materials is frequently underestimated, but a concise, one-page statement of need and what a particular bill does may be the most effective way to communicate with and educate legislators who are not actively involved in the bill's production or movement through the committee process. Narrowing down the bill's provisions to three key statements also allows advocates to explain a bill quickly—making the best use of the three minutes that they have a legislator's attention. Many times a legislator will say to an advocate, "I don't have time to meet with you, just walk with me as I head to this meeting and give me the highlights of the bill" (the legislative equivalent of the elevator speech). Advocates need to be prepared for both long meetings and short moments when they can plead their case.

Build Alliances. Developing strong constituent support for a legislative package is central to a bill's success, particularly when the resulting coalition is broad based. Advocates should consider aligning with groups that already have influence with the legislature. For example, when we proposed legislation in Kentucky to create a sexual assault nurse examiner program, we enlisted heavy involvement and support from the Kentucky Nurses Association; when we proposed legislation to enhance penalties for criminal assaults related to domestic violence, the Kentucky Commonwealth's Attorney Association and the County Attorney Association were key allies.

Legislative staff members can be invaluable allies as well. Generally, staff are assigned to subject matter committees and to the offices of the majority and minority leadership in both chambers. Although they work for members of the legislature and must respect those confidences, they can also be an essential source of information and advice. They likely know more about the legislative process and more about legislators than advocates do. I once asked a staff member why she had been so helpful to our work over the years, and she replied that it was because we always treated her with great respect. As a practical matter, staff also have more time to give advocates than legislators do. As Marie Abrams, a longtime staff member in the state senate's Democratic caucus, remembered, "During a session, I would give lobbyists fifteen minutes to talk about their bill and what they needed; David [Senator David Karem] could only give them two" (Abrams, 2012).

Advocates cannot overlook the fact that not all associations and interest groups will support their legislative proposals. In fact, some proposals will raise fervent complaints from certain corners, and advocates must learn how to manage opposing interests. In Kentucky, legislation we proposed to prohibit shock probation[13] for certain sexual offenders drew the ire of the Kentucky Association of Criminal Defense Lawyers; our legislation to expand insurance reimbursement for mental health services to include licensed psychologists as well as psychiatrists (to make counseling services more accessible to victims in rural counties) elicited vehement opposition from insurance companies. Opposing groups are likely to voice their concerns directly to legislators, which is a fast way for a bill to lose traction and die. Legislators generally prefer to avoid legislation that engenders conflict, based on the belief that a vote for the bill will automatically garner resentment from the opposing group. It is advisable to work with representatives of opposing interest groups in an effort to strike a compromise before a bill ever makes it to a legislative committee. If at all possible, find some type of concession that does not compromise the bill's intent but appeases the opposition. Asking for a large compromise and accepting less is a good way to appear to be flexible without actually weakening a bill. If the compromise bill is introduced and the other interest group still expresses opposition to legislators, then we have used the strategy of explaining that a compromise had already been reached, making us seem infinitely reasonable and the opposing group's position unjustified.

Select the Right Time for a Legislative Proposal. Advocates naturally want to hurry a bill's passage, but it is advisable to assess whether the timing is right. Specifically, what is the climate of the legislature? What other bills will be considered by the house and senate? What is the status of the state's budget? Are there any imminent conflicts on the horizon that might impact legislators? For example, it is not a good idea to introduce a piece of legislation with a large fiscal impact when the state is facing a substantial budget shortfall. During one session, Kentucky legislators were considering their own legislative package designed to reduce sentencing for certain criminal offenses as a means of addressing overcrowded prisons and promoting treatment for drug offenders. This would not have been the best time to introduce legislation enhancing criminal penalties for repeat domestic violence offenders.

Cultivate Strong Relationships with Legislators. This advice may seem obvious, but well-cultivated relationships with legislators will serve an advocate well. Gaining the respect and trust of a legislator often leads to gaining her or his vote. It may be relatively easy to develop good relationships with legislators who have historically supported an advocate's legislation, but that is not sufficient if advocates wish to be most effective. One legislative session, we proposed a bill requiring that if a respondent to a civil protective order attempted to purchase a firearm, then the victim would be notified. One of the first legislators I approached to lobby for the bill was not someone whose support I could count on; instead, it was a legislator widely known for his vociferous support of the Second Amendment right to keep and bear arms. I anticipated that if this legislator opposed our bill based on a perceived infringement of the right to purchase or possess firearms, then we would face an uphill battle getting it passed. I spent a good deal of time explaining that the bill involved a simple notification to protect victims; I also pointed out that federal law already prohibited the purchase and possession of firearms by respondents to protective orders, and our bill instituted no additional infringements. When that legislator publicly endorsed our bill, I knew that his fellow Second Amendment supporters (the majority of the Kentucky legislature) would feel comfortable voting for it. In that case, the vote of a single legislator influenced the bill's ultimate passage.

Relationships with legislators can also be buoyed by showing appreciation when they support the work of advocates. Thanking legislators for their votes and remaining gracious even when they do not support a bill are important. We have also found it effectual to thank legislators after the session is over, such as in local ceremonies in which their constituents can participate. This can be somewhat risky, however, as campaign schedules often follow legislative sessions with May primaries and November general elections. After one legislative session, I succeeded in getting the governor to travel with us to present awards to legislators who had sponsored our bills in their home districts. This put our Democratic governor in the position of praising and raising the profile of a Republican legislator just as another Democrat was trying to unseat him. The governor was exceedingly gracious during the ceremony, but on our way out, he leaned over to the Republican and whispered that he still hoped his fellow Democrat would win the fall campaign. Both men smiled at the remark, acknowledging that the rules of politics reign supreme.

Cultivating strong relationships with legislators also puts advocates in the best position to select primary sponsors for their bills. Picking the right sponsor is one of the most crucial decisions an advocate will make. Several characteristics identify good potential bill sponsors. For example, choosing a member of the majority party can be helpful, not only because that party carries more power than the minority but also because, at a very practical level, a majority-party sponsor has access to more votes. This is not to say that members of the minority party should be ignored; I have often asked key members of the minority to cosponsor bills. Choosing a member of the committee that will hear the bill is also advisable, as those legislators are more likely to understand the bill's subject matter and can more readily influence the committee's vote. A legislator who is powerful or highly respected is also a good choice for a sponsor; in Kentucky, we often requested sponsorship from committee chairs and members of the majority party leadership. There is a flip side to that strategy, however. In the early 1990s, we proposed legislation to include rape with a foreign object as a sexual offense and were pleased to secure the sponsorship of the powerful chair of the senate's Appropriations and Revenue Committee. After sailing through the senate, the bill languished in the house because members wanted to very publicly show their displeasure with the senate's budget, which had been written by our bill sponsor. (The bill was ultimately considered and passed, but not until the end of the legislative session; see chapter 7.)

Similarly, legislators with unique expertise (e.g., a legislator who is a former prosecutor or one who worked in a rape crisis center) are also highly credible bill sponsors. Although it may be tempting to select a sponsor who is a friend to the issue, pragmatically, it is more important to select a sponsor who is influential in the legislature as a whole, in the majority caucus, or on the committee that will hear the bill. Bill sponsors need to be in a position to bring votes with them; their own support of the bill, while highly valued, is not enough.

In addition to these visible characteristics, there is one more essential element of a sponsorship choice: trust. Advocates must be able to trust the legislator who carries their bill. They must trust that the sponsor understands the importance of the bill, will not make unilateral concessions or amendments, and will be honest regarding how the bill is faring with other members of the legislature. But trust goes both ways. Advocates should act responsibly, be honest at all times, keep bill sponsors informed of issues as they arise, and avoid any circumstances that might embarrass the sponsor.

Always (I Mean *Always*) Be Honest. One way to ensure a positive relationship with a legislator is to never, under any circumstances, tell him or her something that is untrue. It may be tempting (but unethical) to do so as a way to secure a vote, but it will likely come to light, causing permanent damage to an advocate's credibility. It is as a lawyer colleague of mine once told me: reckless disregard for the truth has the same legal consequences as lying. In one case, the senate's majority floor leader agreed to bring a bill for a vote on the floor the next day, but only if we could guarantee him at that very moment that we had sufficient votes for its passage. As much as I wanted the bill to be heard, I knew we did not have enough votes. The legislator appreciated my honesty, and he gave me an additional day to secure the rest of the votes.

Being honest includes never guessing at an answer, which can lead to an inadvertent lie and, like an overt lie, will likely come back to haunt you. Even in a political environment, legislators respect honesty. If a question is raised during testimony before a committee and an advocate does not know the answer, simply acknowledging that uncertainty and promising to find the answer before the end of the day (and following through on that commitment) is the best approach. Ensuring honesty also means checking and rechecking any data or statistics offered as justification for a bill and making certain that all information provided is updated.

Being completely forthcoming is not as easy as it might appear. During one legislative session, I was working to secure votes for a bill that would be heard in the Judiciary Committee the following day. As it was rather late in the session, the house of representatives did not adjourn until late in the evening, which meant I was still talking to legislators after nine o'clock that night. I secured the vote of one key member of the committee, but I could not tell him that our sponsor was planning to introduce an amendment to the bill the next day, as the sponsor had sworn me to secrecy. The next day when the bill was heard and the amendment was distributed, the legislator I had spoken to the night before looked straight at me, and I knew he believed I had not been honest with him. At that moment, I could have explained why I had not disclosed the amendment, but I knew that would embarrass the sponsoring legislator, so I chose to remain silent and apologize later for any misunderstanding. The committee member vocalized his displeasure during that public meeting. Fortunately for me, the bill's sponsor ultimately told the truth to the angry legislator, leading him to graciously send me flowers as an apology.

Being honest with legislators does not automatically mean they will be candid with you. While I have had rare occurrences of a legislator flagrantly lying, more commonly, they simply fail to reveal everything they know.

Remain Nonpartisan. As my friends and family well know, I have strong political views. But I never mentioned my personal politics while advocating for legislation, because once you are publicly identified with one political party, you may automatically lose the support of the other. Legislative work is certainly political, but advocates should be seen as nonpartisan experts on their bills and should not assume overtly political positions. This also means that lobbyists or other visible advocates should carefully consider the consequences before assuming a high-profile position in any legislative campaign. Certainly, members of coalitions can do so outside the capitol, but those advocates who are visible in the halls of the legislature should not risk votes by appearing to be partisan. I know of one legislative advocate who became active in a campaign, holding fund-raisers and writing large checks in support of a candidate trying to unseat a particular incumbent. The incumbent prevailed in that race, and when he saw the advocate's name on a list of major donors to his opponent, she was not well positioned to seek support from that legislator, particularly on difficult votes.

To be clear, I am not suggesting that advocates remove themselves from the political process. My cautions are intended to help advocates in the anti-rape and domestic violence movements draw the line between what is political and what is partisan. For instance, sponsoring candidate forums during the political season to ask all those running how they would approach violence-related issues is an outstanding way to be involved politically without being partisan. Holding educational forums, writing letters to the editor, and engaging in other public activities to express what campaigns (plural) should focus on to meet the needs of women in Kentucky and the nation are essential contributions to the electoral process.

Understand the Politics. While advocates should not be politically partisan, it is crucial that they understand the political environment into which their legislation will descend. It is important to know which legislators are battling with one another and when those fights are significant enough to divert or stop the progress of a bill. Advocates need to be aware not only of the political infighting between legislators but also of the quality of the relationship between the legislative and executive branches. Specifically, is the governor in good stead with legislators, or should advocates avoid giving the governor a visible role for fear that his or her presence will cause certain legislators to withdraw their support? Additionally, advocates should never suggest that a positive vote on a particular bill will advantage a legislator politically or (even worse) that failure to support the bill will harm her or him at the polls. Legislators are politically savvy and can determine for themselves how a vote on a bill will help or hurt them. Suggesting that a legislator would vote for or against a measure strictly for political purposes is a fast way to offend that legislator.

Be Familiar with Every Step of the Legislative Process. As detailed earlier, the house and senate rules dictate what will happen to an advocate's bill and when (see figure 5.1). The rules (which are passed each session as a piece of legislation) are essential reading for all advocates. Advocates should know and be involved in every step of the legislative process and should not stop advocating until they are standing as witnesses to the governor's signing of their legislation.

Prepare for the All-Important Legislative Committee Hearing. As noted earlier in this chapter, no more than one-quarter of the bills introduced in a given legislative session will pass—a key reminder of the importance of the committee hearing. If the bill does not make it through the committee, then it will likely die there without extraordinary attempts at resuscitation. As a result, significant attention must be devoted to preparation before the hearing, strategy during it, and follow-up after the hearing takes place.

Once a bill has been assigned to a subject matter committee in the house or senate, all attention should be focused on that committee and its members. Each legislative committee has its own personality, a combination of the chair's style and the makeup of its membership. Knowledge of that personality and familiarity with how bills tend to flow through that committee will help advocates figure out what to expect. In my early days as a legislative advocate in the 1980s, the Senate Judiciary Committee was infamous for being intimidating. The committee chair was an attorney from eastern Kentucky who happily kept to himself what he thought of any particular piece of legislation and the likelihood of its success. Even getting on the committee's agenda, which was tightly controlled by the chair, was a challenge, as was getting a meeting with him. One legislative session when I badly needed a spot on the Judiciary Committee's agenda, I approached a friendly colleague who also served on the committee and asked for his advice and help. He just smiled. A few days later, as I stood with a group of advocates in the hallway outside the legislative offices, my colleague and the committee chair walked by, and my colleague leaned in to whisper that the chair was interested in meeting with me. I grabbed my burgeoning briefcase and whatever confidence I could muster and followed the chair back to his office. It was clear in the first moments of the meeting that he needed no explanation of our bill; he supported the bill and would place it on the committee's agenda. The personality of the Judiciary Committee included this sign of respect toward the chair.

In addition to the committee chair, attention must be paid to each committee member. While I have colleagues who limit their advocacy to the majority members of a committee or to just enough members to secure passage of their bill, I have always approached committees with the belief that every vote counts, minority or majority party, regardless of whether my bill is enjoying unanimous support or is hotly contested. I once had a retiring legislator tell me that there were innumerable times over the years when he had been ambivalent about a bill of ours (not sure whether to vote in favor or not). But when he was in doubt, and sometimes even when he initially opposed the bill, he had been swayed to vote in favor because I always came and respectfully asked him for his vote. He said that, because he was a low-ranking member of the minority party, many lobbyists did not work for his vote. But because I respected him and his vote, he was generally willing to give it when we asked for it.

Before approaching an individual legislator, it is crucial to know her or his legislative priorities and voting record. If the legislator has supported an advocate's bills in the past, it is worth mentioning that fact and expressing appreciation before asking for more help. And if the legislator is an advocate for women's health, for example, discussing how the present bill is consistent with that aim would be wise. Once these preliminaries have been attended to, it is time for the approach and the all-important "ask." Advocates often launch directly into an explanation of the importance of the bill, overlooking the effectiveness of telling a legislator directly that you need his or her individual help. An explanation of the bill comes next (and should include no more than three major points), followed by a reference to the bill's effect on the legislator's constituents. Advocates then need to give the legislator time to ask questions about the bill. After all questions have been answered, advocates should restate the need for the legislator's help. Finally, it is time for the direct question about how the legislator will vote on the bill—for example, "Is this bill something you will be able to help us with?" At this moment, advocates need to listen well. A statement that "It's a great bill" is not a promised yes vote; nor is "It sounds good unless something comes up in the committee discussion." Some legislators will not disclose how they plan to vote, and advocates should not try to compel them to do so. I once heard an advocate demand to know how a legislator planned to vote, even after he had expressed reluctance to share that information. As I anticipated, he was so angered by the advocate's aggressive style that he did not support the bill.

Securing legislators' support is important, but it is meaningless unless they are actually present when the vote is taken. Let the legislator know when the vote is scheduled, and emphasize how important his or her presence is to you. On one occasion, we realized that as the committee convened, two of our "yes" votes were missing. We dispatched advocates to the offices of those members to urge them to come right away to avoid missing the vote.

If you know that a legislator will not support your bill, remain polite and understanding; keep in mind that relationships with legislators carry forward from session to session, and you may be asking for her or his vote again in the future. Even if a legislator cannot be persuaded to vote in favor of your bill, he or she may be willing to at least vote to get the bill out of committee so that it can be debated on the floor. In this case, the legislator has helped you without appearing to be supportive of a controversial bill or one he or she opposes. Another strategy (if you know the legislator well enough) is to ask the legislator to step out of the committee meeting when the vote is taken so you do not receive a "no" vote; this helps the advocate's cause without actually supporting the bill.

Even more influential than state-level advocates when it comes to securing legislators' votes are constituents from their districts. The importance of constituent phone calls, letters, and face-to-face meetings in the capital or in the legislator's hometown cannot be overstated. In one case, we were unsure that a particular legislator would keep his promise to vote in favor of our bill, so we placed one of his constituents in the front row of the audience at the hearing, where she could smile and wave at him.

Another wise place to prepare for a committee hearing is in the office of the committee's legislative staff. Once again, it is important to develop relationships with these individuals. Advocates can best prepare by learning from the staff the totality of the meeting agenda (i.e., what other bills will be heard) and how much time will be available to present their bill. More difficult to learn until the day of the hearing (and staff may not feel comfortable sharing this information), but vital to know, is who will testify against the bill. The general practice is that people who wish to speak must sign in at the beginning of the meeting, but by then, it is fairly late in the process to prepare to address opponents' concerns. Prior to your testimony, provide the committee's staff with all handout materials and written testimony, ensuring that there is a copy for each committee member.

The next strategic decision is who will testify on your bill. The bill sponsor is a de facto presenter, and the second presenter should be the primary expert on the bill's contents. If you are limited to ten minutes, that may cap the testimony. The amount of testimony given by the sponsor is based on his or her individual style. I have worked with sponsors who introduce the bill and then turn the substantive testimony over to advocates or other experts; I have also worked with sponsors who want to be fully briefed and educated so that they can testify in full. If you have more leeway in terms of time, the testimony of additional experts and survivors can be very impactful. Of course, it is essential to seek the input of the bill's sponsor, not only out of respect but also because the sponsor likely knows the personality of the committee and what kind of testimony will sway votes in a positive direction. Admittedly, bill sponsors are not always helpful in this regard. In the first attempt to pass marital rape legislation in 1986, a well-intentioned legislator admonished that an advocate could testify, but she shouldn't get "all emotional and cry because legislators just hate that" (Allen, 2012).

The testimony of an advocate should be well thought out and

structured. The opening line should always be a gracious one, thanking "Mr. Chairman" or "Madame Chair" for the opportunity to testify (and restating that appreciation at the end of the remarks). The rest of the testimony should be structured to fill the exact amount of time allotted; exceeding the time limit could annoy legislators, and you might be cut off before making all your important points. In general, there are five essential points that should be included:

1. A statement of the problem and how your bill solves it.
2. The specific provisions of the bill. If time permits, a brief discussion of the history of reforms made to the relevant section of the statute tends to be particularly well received when testifying in front of attorneys, who generally serve on the Judiciary Committees of the house and senate.
3. An attempt to counter any anticipated negative testimony that will follow (if no opponents will testify, do not mention any opposition). Always be polite when speaking of your opponents, but try to deflate the importance of their comments by showing that their concerns are not valid in your view. If you do not address opposition at this point, you are not likely to have an opportunity to rebut any complaints made by those who testify later.
4. A list of the key associations and individuals who endorse or support your bill.
5. A compelling statement to end your testimony, such as how many victims' lives will be impacted by the bill's provisions.

The most difficult part of legislative testimony can be when the legislators ask questions, because the advocate has no control over the direction those questions will take. Some questions are genuine, well-intentioned efforts to gain additional information; some are framed negatively to expose weaknesses or generate opposition to the bill; and still others are veiled attempts to rattle the testifying advocate. I have found over the years that for any of these scenarios, intense preparation is the best defense. That means knowing every line of the bill verbatim, even sections that refer to statutes not directly related to the bill at hand. Understand why specific language was chosen and is needed, citing court rules or other statutes when relevant. I have found that the appearance of confidence (e.g., the ability to rattle off statute numbers, case citations, and other fine details) can stop questions from legislators whose purpose is to shake the witness. Regardless of whether questions are well intended or not, advocates must remain gracious and appreciative of the interest reflected by the questions, and they should make every effort to answer the questions to the legislators' satisfaction. As noted earlier, if an advocate does not know the answer to a question, he or she should not choose a defensive stance or guess at a reply. Admitting that the advocate does not know and promising to get the answer to the legislator by the end of the day is the best course.

On occasion, the questions asked during committee hearings can test the mettle of even the most seasoned advocate. During one legislative session in the 1990s, the Judiciary Committee was considering a domestic violence bill we had introduced in the house. One legislator from the eastern corner of the state asked whether women might use protective orders to seek retribution against their intimate partners. After all, he said, "You got these honky-tonk women who go out on Saturday night and have fun with their man, have a fight on Sunday, and are down at the courthouse on Monday taking out one of these orders against him." Sometimes there is just no good answer, regardless of the amount of preparation.

Although questions can be tough, the most unnerving moment comes when a legislator brings an amendment or a so-called committee substitute to the committee meeting. Ideally, an advocate will have been tipped off in advance to the likelihood of this happening, but amendments often come without warning. Refusing to concede the point raised by the legislator and refusing to support passage of the amendment must be carefully considered; that position can offend not only the legislator proposing the amendment but also his or her colleagues on the committee, who may see you as inflexible. In advance of the committee meeting, it is helpful to brainstorm with advocate colleagues or the bill's sponsor about amendments that might be raised and to be prepared to take a position on the amendment. Robert Guyer (2003, p. 159) offers the following guidelines to deal with that critical moment:

You should *agree* to accept a proposed amendment if it:
1. Is reasonable;
2. Does not harm your goals;
3. Increases the probability of bill passage;
4. Is being sponsored by a powerful committee member;

5. Receives your sponsor's support; and
6. Will not be defeated by a majority of votes in committee.

You should *disagree* with a proposed amendment if it:
1. Is unreasonable;
2. Would harm your goals;
3. Would decrease the likelihood of bill passage;
4. Is sponsored by a group not supported by a majority of the committee;
5. Is championed by a weak sponsor;
6. Is opposed by your sponsor; and
7. Will be defeated by a majority of votes in committee.

Be Self-Aware and Self-Confident. While the previous guidelines have focused primarily on knowing and managing the legislative process, it is important for advocates to know themselves as well. Not every advocate will make an effective lobbyist. Being a legislative advocate means learning to be comfortable with situations that women often do not like: competition and defeat. It is helpful to remember that positions taken and votes made are not personal, and advocates need to persevere and be prepared to fight another day. That is difficult at times, because we know how great the need is and how many women will suffer without a particular bill, but it is important to try. Exuding confidence and expertise is also crucial; advocates should realize that they understand the issues surrounding domestic violence and rape better than any other lobbyist or legislator. While being confident is a must, having a sense of humor is also key to your survival as a legislative advocate. It is as a colleague of mine once said: "We women need to have a backbone; but just as much, we need to have a funny bone."

6

The Birth of Legislative
Reform in Kentucky

The 1970s

The Commonwealth of Kentucky would experience unprecedented highs and unforgettable lows in the 1970s. The horse industry would celebrate as the fleet-footed Secretariat won the Kentucky Derby in 1973, setting a still unbroken record of 1:59.40. Secretariat was owned and bred by Penny Chenery, another rarity in the horse business—a woman. The early 1970s would also see the first female jockey ride in the Kentucky Derby, Diane Crump. Violence would mar the bucolic grounds of the University of Kentucky, as students protested and a concerned governor called in National Guard troops. Governor Louie Nunn would also send the National Guard to quell demonstrations in Louisville. In another corner of the state, in the darkest hours of the decade, an explosion would bury twenty-six miners in the Scotia Mine in Letcher County, the result of faulty equipment igniting methane in the poorly ventilated mine. Eastern Kentucky would also suffer as rivers and creeks spilled over swollen banks to record a 100-year flood. In northern Kentucky, fire would consume the Beverly Hills Supper Club and 165 people in it, becoming the third deadliest fire in U.S. history.

The 1970s would also bring advances in education to Kentucky. In the 1960s, a man named O. Leonard Press was teaching at the University of Kentucky when he came up with an idea to use television to overcome the geographic obstacles that made education inaccessible to many Kentuckians. Press took his idea to Governor Bert Combs, and their collaboration resulted in a law passed by the General Assembly that established Kentucky Educational Television

(KET). The 1970s brought increased state funding and significant statewide growth for the fledgling educational network. (One of the earliest programs on KET was *Comment on Kentucky*, which aired for the first time in 1974, with Al Smith as its host.) Higher education was advanced in the state when both the University of Louisville and Northern Kentucky University were brought into the state's university system in 1970, followed by Kentucky State University in 1972; this addition followed the 1966 expansion of the system to include the regional state colleges that would become Western Kentucky University, Eastern Kentucky University, Morehead State University, and Murray State University (Klotter, 2000).

The 1970s also brought slow but important changes in the status of women, deriving from the nationwide women's rights movement. Nationally, feminists in the 1960s had been guided by basic goals: equal pay for equal work, enhanced opportunities in the workplace (e.g., more managerial jobs for women), an end to sexual harassment and violence, and a sharing of responsibility for housework and child rearing. As the decade passed, women's participation in the labor force expanded beyond traditional careers such as nursing, teaching, and domestic work. At the national level, women also attained higher levels of education, resulting in higher-paying jobs. However, these gains led to only modest improvements in women's earnings (Bureau of Labor Statistics, 2011). Starting in 1945 and for more than thirty years after, a series of laws mandating "equal pay for equal work" had been passed, but by 1975, the gap between men's and women's wages still ranged from 25 to 35 percent (Legrave, 1998).[1]

Compared with other states, improvements in the economic status of Kentucky women were particularly slow in coming. In 1968 women in the state earned, on average, $2.14 an hour, while the average hourly wage of Kentucky men was $3.18; by 1978, women earned an average of $3.96, while men's hourly pay averaged $6.29 (Berger & Chandra, 1999). Kentucky women's workforce experiences would change dramatically over this and the next decade. The percentage of working-age women in the labor force climbed from 27 percent in 1960 to approximately 50 percent by the end of the 1970s and to 54 percent by 1995—growth that was an improvement for women but still left the state trailing in terms of the percentage of women in the workforce (Harrison & Klotter, 1997). By 1989, Kentucky women employed full time earned an average of $18,352 a year, compared with $29,283 for men—only 62.7 cents on the dollar (Stewart, 1991).

THE POLITICAL LANDSCAPE

As the 1970s dawned, Kentucky voters were supporting the Republican Party at the polls. In one U.S. Senate race, Kentuckians were given a choice: break the religion barrier for the first time by voting for a Catholic Republican man, or shatter the gender barrier for the first time by electing a Democratic woman (Harrison & Klotter, 1997). When the votes were tallied, Marlow Cook had beaten former state commerce commissioner Katherine Peden, and the bar keeping Kentucky women out of the U.S. Senate remained in place (as it does still).

In the state capital as the decade began, a Republican governor was serving the final year of his term. At the time of his victory in 1966, Governor Louie B. Nunn (serving from 1967 to 1971) had been the first Republican elected governor in twenty years.[2] On the campaign trail as he sought the governor's mansion, Nunn's central message had been a pledge to run the state government like a business, along with an assertion that taxes were too high (Sexton & Cross, 2004). Nevertheless, when Governor Nunn faced a significant budget deficit, he proposed a hike in the sales tax to $.05—an increase that politically savvy Democrats would dub "Nunn's nickel." The accomplishments of the Nunn administration included improvements to mental health services for Kentuckians, the addition of the University of Louisville to the state's university system, expansion of the state park system, and growth of KET (Sexton & Cross, 2004).

The 1966 election that sent Louie Nunn to the governor's office also meant a win for Wendell H. Ford, a Democrat from Owensboro who was elected lieutenant governor on that split ticket.[3] Ford was subsequently elected governor, but during the third year of his term, he announced his candidacy for the U.S. Senate—a race he won. Ford thus became the first person in the history of the Commonwealth to be elected to successive terms as lieutenant governor, governor, and U.S. senator (Klotter, 2000). Governor Ford's departure meant that a third governor would lead the state during the 1970s. Lieutenant Governor Julian M. Carroll completed the last year of Ford's term and then went on to win his own full term (serving from 1974 to 1979). Notably, Governor Carroll's administration would give Kentucky its first (but not its last) female lieutenant governor. Thelma L. Stovall was a pioneering and outspoken southern politician who, after winning several statewide offices, capped her career as Kentucky's forty-seventh lieutenant governor (serving from 1975 to 1979; see chapter 1 for more on Stovall's career). The decade would end with the election of Governor John Y. Brown Jr. (serving from 1979 to 1983).

Governor Ford benefited significantly from a supportive General Assembly that was inclined to pass his proposals and block those he opposed (Jones, 2004). His legislative agenda included the advancement of energy research and the implementation of a coal severance tax aimed at putting tax monies derived from the coal counties back in those areas. Ford also convinced the General Assembly to remove the sales tax on food and strengthen the net of social services (Klotter, 2000). Governor Carroll pushed to improve the elementary and secondary education system in the Commonwealth (Harrison & Klotter, 1997). He was not as interested in advancing higher education, however, opining in his 1976 budget message to the General Assembly that "we are no longer in the golden age of higher-education growth" (Sprague, 2004, p. 218). Governor Carroll's legislative agenda also included support for the state park system, energy independence, and a constitutional amendment to drastically change and professionalize the legal system in the Commonwealth. Carroll's administration was the last in which the governor successfully controlled the legislature (Sprague, 2004). (See chapter 5 for further discussion of the General Assembly's independence.)

The attention of the Kentucky General Assembly in the 1970s was heavily focused on energy and the health of the coal industry (Ellis, 2000; Legislative Research Commission 1970, 1972, 1974, 1976, 1978). When Arab (and other) countries implemented an oil embargo in response to what they viewed as the United States' support of the Israeli military, the resulting oil crisis posed a major threat to the nation's economy. In Kentucky, however, the Arab oil embargo meant a boon to the economy of the coalfields (Ellis, 2000; Harrison & Klotter, 1997).

The 1970s also brought enormous reforms in the Commonwealth's justice system. The state's criminal law would be codified, setting out for the first time a Kentucky Penal Code. For the judiciary, the 1970s saw creation of districts for the Kentucky Supreme

Court, organization of the Court of Appeals, designation of the chief justice as head of the Court of Justice, and creation of the Administrative Office of the Courts. In addition, the public defender system was created. For law enforcement, the centralized criminal history information system was established, and new legislation required that coroners investigate all deaths.

Finally, legislative sessions in the 1970s attended to human rights reforms. The Commission on Human Rights was expanded (having been established in 1966). As a measure of social change, the holidays observed by the state were changed: Robert E. Lee Day and Confederate Day were abolished, and Martin Luther King Day was added. (Legislators also eliminated Veterans Day in one session but quickly put it back on the calendar in the next session.)

LEGISLATIVE REFORMS ADDRESSING VIOLENCE AGAINST WOMEN

In a real way, the decade of the 1970s saw the birth of legislation directed at the protection and well-being of Kentucky women. Legislation was passed to codify the existence of a state-level women's advocacy organization and draw attention to the crime of sex discrimination. Protection of adults was also codified in statute during the mid-1970s, laying the groundwork for mandatory reporting in spouse abuse cases—laws that were hailed upon their passage in 1978 but would draw criticism in later years. The decade also saw legislation pass to ensure the availability of forensic examinations for rape victims and to shield rape victims from court proceedings that tended to focus on their irrelevant sexual history rather than on the defendant's behavior. General Assemblies of the 1970s also established a compensation mechanism for crime victims. Select laws passed during the 1970s with a direct impact on rape, domestic violence, stalking, and related crimes against women are described below.

Kentucky Commission on Women (1970)

Although the legislation that established the Kentucky Commission on Women (1970 General Assembly, Senate Bill [SB] 23) did not specifically target violence against women, it takes its rightful place as the first entry in this legislative chronology. For more than forty years, the commission has worked to improve the status of women in the Commonwealth, including those whose lives have been touched by abuse. Its directors and board members have proposed and shepherded legislation and have given battered women and rape survivors an articulate state-level voice.[4]

The Kentucky Commission on Women was initially established in 1964 by Governor Edward T. Breathitt to review and report on the status of women in the state. The governor's act was in response to the creation of President John F. Kennedy's Commission on the Status of Women. The Kentucky commission's report provided compelling evidence that a more permanent state entity was needed to oversee and influence the status of women, and in November 1968 Governor Louie B. Nunn signed an executive order to establish the Kentucky Commission on Women.[5]

• • •

1971—The Lexington Rape Crisis Center becomes the first center of its kind in Kentucky.

• • •

In 1970 SB 23 was introduced to make the commission an agency of the state government. The bill's primary sponsor was Senator Walter Reichert, a Republican from the Thirty-Fourth District, and it did not receive an overly warm welcome. When introduced in the senate, SB 23 was assigned to the State Government Committee, where it languished for more than five weeks. (There were no women on the committee at the time.) The bill was finally passed out of committee after testimony by State Treasurer Thelma Stovall; Katherine Peden, former state commissioner of commerce; and Ledean Hamilton, president of the Kentucky Federation of Business and Professional Women's Clubs (Mrs. Sawyer, 1970). When it reached the senate floor, an amendment was added to remove any funding for the commission in the first biennium; the bill then passed by a

Thelma Stovall presiding as senate president, March 18, 1978. (Courtesy of the Public Records Division–Kentucky Department for Libraries and Archives)

vote of thirty-five to zero, with one senator abstaining. At the other end of the capitol, the house passed the bill seventy-seven to zero; twenty-three legislators either were not present or chose not to vote on the bill.

During the governorship of John Y. Brown Jr., the Kentucky Commission on Women was attached administratively to the governor's office, and in 2008 Governor Steven L. Beshear physically moved the office to the state capitol for the first time in the commission's history.

Minors' Right to Seek Treatment (1970)

SB 193 was an important start for minors' rights in the Commonwealth. The bill, sponsored by Senator Georgia Davis (Powers), a Democrat from the Thirty-Third District, created a new section of KRS Chapter 214 to allow physicians to treat minors for venereal diseases without a parent's consent. A subsequent bill (1972, SB 309) expanded the circumstances to include pregnancy and drug abuse and allowed minors to consent to receive hospital, medical, dental,

Senator Georgia Davis Powers on the senate floor, February 9, 1982. (Courtesy of the Public Records Division–Kentucky Department for Libraries and Archives)

and surgical care without parental or guardian consent. Both SB 193 and SB 309 received a lukewarm reception in the Kentucky house, where legislators were reluctant to support any measure that would infringe on parental rights. Although both bills passed, SB 193 captured only seventy-eight yes votes, and SB 309 passed fifty to nine (the lowest number of votes for any bill in this chronicle). In the 1980s anti-rape advocates would use the statute originally amended by Senator Powers's bill to allow minors to seek mental health counseling services on their own initiative.

Kentucky Penal Code (1972 and 1974)

Creation of the first criminal law in Kentucky dates to its achievement of statehood at the end of the eighteenth century. Kentucky's original criminal law was based on English common law, and except for a reorganization in 1962 (which essentially amounted to renumbering), it had never been substantially rewritten or updated (Brickey, 1972–1973; Lawson, 1969–1970; Renkey, 1971). As the 1970s dawned, cases were tried guided by criminal law buried in case law; criminal law did not exist in any organized statutory form. The amalgamation of case law was anachronistic, disorganized, and sometimes contradictory. Laws overlapped, such that the same criminal conduct could result in prosecution for different offenses and could result in illogically applied, disparate, or discordant sentences and other punishment. No operational definitions existed for criminal acts; defining crime was essentially left to the judiciary and its appellate writings. In short, Kentucky had a criminal law "beset by shortcomings, inequities and, in some cases, nonsense" (Renkey, 1971, p. 1).

Before reform, a significant portion of criminal law in Kentucky consisted of "special crimes" or crimes deriving from special circumstances. Special crimes were extremely limited in their application and often covered only narrow actions or conduct (Lawson, 1969–1970). In the case of homicide, for example, death caused by "stabbing, striking or shooting" resulted in a prison sentence of one to six years (KRS 435.050), while death that occurred "in the course of criminal syndicalism or sedition" resulted in life imprisonment or death (KRS 435.030). Abortion was defined as homicide, and death occurring during an abortion resulted in a sentence of two to twenty-one years, life imprisonment, or death (KRS 435.040). If a homicide-related death resulted from an "obstruction of road," the punishment was life imprisonment or death (KRS 435.060). This conglomeration of narrowly defined acts caused confusion, and they failed to take into account the mental state of the offender. Prior to the 1970s, the mental condition and intent of an offender at the time of the commission of a crime were referred to in the criminal law, but there were no definitions of terms, and multiple terms were used to describe the same mental state. In the case of homicide, for example, three terms were used to describe the offender's mental state—*malice aforethought*, *intentional*, and *willful*—all meaning precisely the same thing (Lawson, 1969–1970). The proliferation of crimes limited to special circumstances and the inconsistent application or understanding of mental states (i.e., the offender's intent) gave rise to the dysfunction that was Kentucky's criminal law.

Battered women and rape survivors were among those for whom the criminal law provided an inadequate remedy. The chapter of criminal law applicable in most of these cases (offenses against persons) offered a "maiming" statute (Chapter 435.160) to address assault, but there were no specific harassment or stalking offenses. The rape statute provided that "any person who unlawfully carnally knows a female of and above twelve years of age against her will or consent, or by force or while she is insensible, shall be punished by death, or by confinement in the penitentiary for life without privilege of parole, or by confinement in the penitentiary for life, or by confinement in the penitentiary for not less than ten years nor more than twenty years" (Chapter 435.090). (Another statute addressed the rape of a child younger than twelve.) By common law, the term *unlawfully* meant that wives could not charge their husbands with rape because sexual behavior, whether voluntary or forced, was not considered an unlawful act when it occurred within a marital relationship.

Someone who killed another person could be charged under a number of relatively confusing statutes, including murder, voluntary or involuntary manslaughter, negligent operation of a motor vehicle, and four types of homicide distinguishable by the circumstances in which death occurred. Battered women shot or stabbed by violent partners prior to 1970 may have learned about a notable distinction in the criminal law: such an offender could be charged either with "malicious and willful shooting, cutting or poisoning" (Chapter 435.170) or with "shooting, wounding or cutting in sudden affray or heat of passion, without previous malice" (Chapter 435.180). Offenders found guilty of a malicious act could be sentenced to up to twenty-one years in the penitentiary, while those adjudged to have acted in the "heat of passion" could be fined up to $500 and/or imprisoned for less than one year.

• • •

Before the existence of the Penal Code, Chapter 436.010 of the Kentucky criminal law read as follows:

(1) Any person who, under promise of marriage, seduces and has carnal knowledge of any female under twenty-one years of age, shall be confined in the penitentiary for not less than one nor more than five years.

(2) No prosecution under subsection (1) of this section shall be instituted where the person charged has married the girl seduced or offers and is willing to marry her unless he willfully and without a cause constituting a ground of divorce provided in KRS 403.020 for the husband, abandons or deserts her within three years after the marriage.

• • •

In the mid-1960s the Kentucky Crime Commission, under the leadership of director Charlie Owen, began to study the status of the state's criminal law and consulted law professors to determine how to improve its structure. The 1968 General Assembly, recognizing the weaknesses in the Commonwealth's criminal law and its justice process, passed a joint resolution directing the Legislative Research Commission and the Kentucky Crime Commission to undertake a revision of the criminal law. As a first step, the Crime Commission prepared a two-volume outline of the problems with existing law. A Kentucky Criminal Law Revision Committee was then created, and attorneys were enlisted to write a new code.[6] The primary objective of the drafters, led by University of Kentucky law professor Robert Lawson, was to create a structure in which all criminal offenses could be organized and defined. That meant eliminating the Commonwealth's existing criminal law and special legislation and providing a uniform classification scheme for all crimes; it meant codifying and defining criminal laws and setting out general principles of criminal liability. Notably, the drafters were not addressing any specific issue (such as domestic violence or rape); rather, they were conceiving a broad reform of criminal law in Kentucky.

The design of the Kentucky Penal Code was influenced by a model code developed by the American Law Institute (ALI) in 1962 to aid in the updating and standardizing of state penal laws across

Senator Michael R. Moloney on the senate floor, 1982. (Courtesy of the Public Records Division–Kentucky Department for Libraries and Archives)

the country (Wechsler, 1968). Under the U.S. Constitution, the power to impose criminal liability is primarily a function of the states (except in the limited circumstances, such as when crimes are committed on the property of exclusive federal jurisdiction or against federal officers, or when they involve more than one state) (Robinson & Dubber, 1999). As such, states act independently to establish criminal laws that their legislatures deem suitable for their respective citizenries.

The final draft of the Kentucky Penal Code was completed in 1971 and passed by the 1972 General Assembly in the form of House Bill (HB) 197. Concurrently, the house and senate adopted resolutions to create the Kentucky Penal Code Study Commission. The 1972 legislation included a delayed enactment date, which gave the commission an opportunity to further analyze and amend the complex draft code in the interim. In 1974 a newly revised draft was submitted to and passed by the General Assembly in the form of HB 232. Key legislators who shepherded the bill through the 1974 General Assembly included Representative William "Bill" Kenton, a Democrat from the Seventy-Fifth District, and Senator Michael R. Moloney, a Democrat from the Thirteenth District. Over the next two decades, Senator Moloney would become well known to the advocate community.

The newly enacted Kentucky Penal Code abolished common-law offenses and established crimes and violations. It was made up of three parts: a section on the general doctrine of the law, twenty-five chapters that codified specific offenses, and three chapters that addressed the disposition of criminal defendants following conviction. In the general doctrine section, four mental states were defined to uniformly apply to all offenses: intentionally, knowingly, wantonly, and recklessly. General principles of liability, justification, and responsibility were also articulated. The new code created an organized structure of offenses, dividing crimes into felonies and misdemeanors and setting out four classes of felony offenses (A, B, C, and D) and three classes of misdemeanor offenses (A, B, and simple violations). Each class was given a range of penalties, reflecting the drafters' belief that not all crimes are of equal severity and not all offenders convicted of a particular offense deserve the same penalty.

The drafting and passage of the Kentucky Penal Code were not without controversy and conflict. Major conflict arose over the death penalty; in fact, the issue was removed from consideration because the drafters feared the controversy might scuttle the entire legislative effort. The management of drug-related offenses was also controversial, with some interest groups pushing for harsh punishments (including a "two-strike" rule that elevated second offenses) and others advocating a more rehabilitative (treatment-focused) model.

Passage of the Kentucky Penal Code in 1974 was a historic moment that improved the Commonwealth's criminal law immeasurably. For rape survivors and battered women, several new statutes were pertinent, including a revised assault statute and the addition of new crimes such as terroristic threatening and harassment. Though the 1974 code was an improvement in many respects for women suffering intimate forms of violence, an ideal criminal law remained elusive. Kentucky's criminal law continued to rely on English common law (as did the ALI Model Code), in which women were valued as the property of their husbands. And the code continued to reflect cultural views of women that would not stand the test of time. The sexual offense chapter of the 1974 code was a prime example of how these archaic views of women would be codified in

Kentucky law, to women's distinct disadvantage. (Similar complaints have been made about the ALI Model Code; see Denno, 2003.) For instance, the 1974 Kentucky Penal Code's rape statute included the following provisions:

1. It incorporated the marital immunity rule (first set out in the writings of Lord Hale, as described in chapter 3), which specified that a husband could not legally rape his wife. The code defined *spouse* for purposes of the immunity rule, but the commentary section interpreted immunity even more broadly, suggesting that it was not limited to those who were legally married but also applied to persons living together as husband and wife (Brickey, 1974). It would take more than fifteen years for the General Assembly to strike marital immunity from the statute.

2. Although it did not require that a woman making a complaint of rape be "chaste" or virginal, its commentary stated that evidence of the victim's "prior unchastity is relevant and admissible on the question of consent" (Renkey, 1971, p. 131).

3. It set a high standard for meeting the definition of "forcible compulsion." The sexual offenses in the new code were (with one exception; see below) predicated on a lack of consent by the victim, which could result from express or implied force (forcible compulsion) or lack of ability to consent (due to age or mental or physical incapacity). The force element required that a rape victim display "earnest resistance," which the code's commentary elaborated on: the victim was not required "to engage in mortal combat to ward off the attack, but token initial resistance will not suffice" (Brickey, 1974, p. 109).

4. It added a fourth degree to the sodomy statute that made sexual contact between persons of the same sex illegal. In this statutory anomaly, consent was not germane; the gender of the parties was the relevant issue. This provision was found unconstitutional by the Kentucky Supreme Court in *Commonwealth v. Wasson* (1992). (Ernesto Scorsone represented Jeffrey Wasson in this case; Scorsone would go on to serve in the Kentucky house and senate before becoming a circuit judge in Lexington.)

. . .

"The 1972 legislative session may be recorded as one characterized by more demonstrative evidence concerning pending legislation than any in history. From the now infamous wild turkey unleashed in the House to stimulate debate on a proposed industrial loan bill, to the homemade brownies intended to sweeten the legislators' dispositions toward transfer of territory of certain school districts, to the diaper pails which bedecked the marble staircase ascending to legislative chambers where hearings on a liberalized abortion law were in progress—it was anything but a dull session. It was in this arena that the criminal law of Kentucky was dragged, screaming, into the twentieth century."

—Kathleen F. Brickey (1972–1973, p. 1)

. . .

These examples and others like them would prompt advocates to seek reforms so that a rapist was criminally liable regardless of his relationship to the victim—that is, a past or ongoing sexual relationship between the complainant and the defendant should not, in and of itself, be a defense to a sexual crime. Advocates believed that the justice system should focus on the acts perpetrated by the offender rather than on whether the victim's resistance was adequate.

There are important lessons to learn from analyzing the process of reforming the criminal law in Kentucky. First, the influence of women in the creation of the Kentucky Penal Code was notably absent. Only two women were officially part of the project: Kathleen Brickey, who would become a law professor at the University of Louisville, was directly involved in drafting the code, and county attorney Gladys Williams Black was the one woman originally on the committee, but she died in an automobile accident in 1972. Additionally, between 1972 and 1974, as the drafters and legislators were working on the final version of the code, public hearings were held across the Commonwealth to allow input on its design. As described by the primary drafter, "In retrospect it is startling that women were not part of the process and further that at no hearing was there testimony on the specific needs of rape victims or battered women" (Lawson, 2012). The absence of advocates was an artifact of time: the penal code reform process predated the creation of rape crisis centers and battered women's shelters in Kentucky, and the strong state coalitions of these programs that exist today would not be created for another decade. One can only speculate how different the 1974 code might have been if more women attorneys had been involved in its drafting and if battered women and rape survivors had been given a public voice.

• • •

1972 HB 30—The General Assembly amends Kentucky's Civil Rights Act to comply with new federal laws and to add sex and age discrimination.

1972 SB 106—The General Assembly passes legislation requiring the state to prepare a marriage manual to be distributed by county clerks to all applicants for a marriage license. The manual must address family planning, proper health and sanitation practices, nutrition, consumer economics, and spouses' legal responsibilities to each other and to their children.

1972 SB 133—The General Assembly amends domestic relations law to establish no-fault divorce.

• • •

A second lesson to be learned is that the legislative process is unpredictable. In this case, all the appropriate steps were taken: the dire condition of the existing criminal law was thoroughly researched and analyzed; the need for a newly constructed criminal code was compellingly argued; an eminent group of attorneys, judges, prosecutors, and law professors was brought together to draft a new penal code; and a distinguished group of legislators was involved in writing, amending, and preparing the legislation. Given this extensive preparation, one might have expected the bill to sail through the 1972 General Assembly on its way to becoming law. But it is axiomatic of the legislative process that nothing proceeds as expected or even as it reasonably should. After exhaustive preparation, on January 20, 1972, the historic legislation (HB 197) was introduced. The bill was almost 400 pages, and its anticipated impact on Kentucky's justice system would be profound. However, as described by Kathleen Brickey: "The following morning the public was informed of this action in an Associated Press article which heralded 'House bill would ease abortions.' Some seven additional column inches were then devoted to describing the 'abortion bill.' Only passing reference was made of the 'entirely new penal code' and the other 35 major areas affected by the legislation" (Brickey, 1972–1973, p. 627). In fact, approximately one of the bill's 373 pages addressed abortion.[7] Although the bill ultimately survived this controversy, the lesson is that, regardless of how well prepared a bill's proponents are, unexpected events can intervene.

Office of the Public Defender (1972)

In an attempt to ensure adequate legal representation for indigent persons "accused of crimes or mental states that may result in their incarceration or confinement" (KRS 31.010), the General Assembly passed HB 461 and created the Office of the Public Defender as a new state agency. In subsequent legislative sessions, the statute would be amended to include representation for a broader group of persons with disabilities.

•   •   •

1974 SB 111—The General Assembly passes legislation to remove language that prohibited a married woman from entering into a contract without her husband's signature.

1974 SB 73—The General Assembly passes legislation requiring that any school with a basketball team for boys provide one for girls as well.

1974 HB 31—The General Assembly repeals a law that prohibited the service of alcoholic beverages by or to females in bars. This was originally part of a sex discrimination bill but was amended out because some legislators found the concept of women in bars unacceptable. The "bar bill" passed as a separate measure and became law without the governor's signature.

•   •   •

The impetus to create a public defender system actually began in the courts of the Commonwealth. Prior to 1972, attorneys were required to represent indigent defendants without pay. Complaints from the bar eventually reached the Kentucky Supreme Court, which ruled on September 22, 1972, that it was an unconstitutional taking of an attorney's property to make him or her represent a defendant without compensation (*Bradshaw v. Ball*, 1972). While an appeal of the Bradshaw case was pending in the Kentucky courts, HB 461, sponsored by Representatives William "Bill" Kenton (Democrat from the Seventy-Fifth District), Ralph Graves (Democrat from the

First District), and John Swinford (Democrat from the Sixty-Second District), was passed by the Kentucky General Assembly, appropriating $1.287 million to create what is now the statewide public defender system.

. . .

1972 HJR 2—The General Assembly passes the Equal Rights Amendment on June 26 by approving House Joint Resolution (HJR) 2.

1978 HJR 20—The General Assembly rescinds its passage of the Equal Rights Amendment on March 17, becoming the fourth state to take such action. Lieutenant Governor Thelma Stovall, in her capacity as acting governor while the governor was out of state, vetoed the rescinding resolution. However, because a governor has no power to override amendments to the U.S. Constitution, her act was primarily symbolic.

. . .

Unified Court System (1976)

Operating under the 1891 state constitution, Kentucky's justice system consisted of police courts, county courts, quarter-session courts, and justice of the peace courts that were locally controlled and exhibited little in the way of uniformity. These lower courts had overlapping jurisdictions, there was no intermediate appellate court, and the former Court of Appeals (now the Supreme Court) was routinely backlogged with cases (Lancaster, 1985). Judges were elected, but they had to run as partisan candidates, meaning they were propelled into the sometimes raucous world of Kentucky politics (Metzmeier, 2006). Jurists serving on the lower courts were not required to have law degrees. Reforming the court system would be no simple task: it would require passage of a constitutional amendment and, perhaps even more challenging, it would require Kentucky voters to give up a significant measure of local control.

Nonetheless, reform efforts began in 1964. As described in detail by Nancy Lancaster (1985), the first step was the creation of a Constitutional Revision Assembly, charged with drafting a new judicial article. The voters rejected that draft in 1968 by a margin of more than four to one. The Kentucky Bar Association then took the lead in shepherding a bill through the legislative process, but its proposal for a constitutional amendment failed to make it out of the Elections and Constitutional Amendments Committee of the 1972 General Assembly.

Notwithstanding these failures, pressure to restructure the courts continued to grow. A series of committees was ultimately created by the governor, the courts, and the bar; the Kentucky Crime Commission provided staff, a statewide survey was completed, and a newly drafted judicial article was readied for the 1974 General Assembly. That session, the constitutional amendment was introduced as SB 183, and it passed out of the senate's Elections and Constitutional Amendments Committee with strong support. On the floor of the senate, the bill passed by a vote of twenty-four to thirteen—barely obtaining the two-thirds majority required for passage of a constitutional amendment. In the house, the legislation also encountered a complicated path but eventually passed on March 15, 1974, by a vote of seventy-nine to four (Lancaster, 1985). On May 27, 1975, the constitutional amendment was put before the voters of Kentucky, who were asked:

> Are you in favor of amending the Constitution of the Commonwealth (by repealing the present sections 109 through 139, 141 and 143, and enacting in lieu thereof sections 109 through 124) to revise the Judicial Branch of Government by establishing one Court of Justice, composed of a Supreme Court, a Court of Appeals, a trial court of general jurisdiction known as the circuit court, and a trial court of limited jurisdiction known as the district court, but retain the non-judicial powers and duties conferred upon the county judge and justices of the peace; providing for the location, composition, administration and jurisdiction of such courts; providing for the eligibility, term of office, election, removal, filling of vacancies, prohibited activities, compensation, and retirement of judges of such courts; providing for the election, selection and removal of the clerks of such courts; and providing a schedule of transition for those judges in office on the effective date of the amendment?

• • •

1976 HB 88—The General Assembly passes legislation to delete from the marriage certificate the distinction between "colored" and "white."

1976 SB 307—The General Assembly passes legislation (sponsored by Senator Georgia Powers) to require motels to provide safety locks on all bedroom doors.

• • •

Public opinion was mixed, but the amendment passed by a vote of 215,419 to 180,124, creating a uniquely styled unified system of trial and appellate courts across the Commonwealth.

The language of the constitutional amendment was codified by the General Assembly in the 1976 legislative session through a series of separate house and senate bills. SB 15 amended all statutory language to change "county court" to "district court"; SB 162 divided the state into Supreme Court districts and provided funding and a structure for the Supreme Court and Court of Appeals; HB 432 created the Court of Appeals; HB 438 defined election procedures for Supreme Court justices and for Court of Appeals, circuit court, and district court judges; and HB 544 made the chief justice the executive head of the Court of Justice and established the Administrative Office of the Courts.

Centralized Criminal History Information System (1976)

The first efforts to collect and distribute criminal identification information and statistics took place in the late 1950s. In 1976 these statutory provisions became substantially more effective when they were amended to create a centralized criminal history information system. The legislation (SB 295) required all city and county law enforcement agencies to obtain a photograph, a set of fingerprints, and a general description of all persons arrested on felony charges and to forward that material to the Department of Kentucky State Police within thirty days of arrest.

Kentucky Crime Victim Compensation Board (1976)

The financial compensation of crime victims was one of the earliest forms of governmental victim assistance in the United States. The first compensation program was created in California in 1965; nine states were operating such programs by 1972; and today, all fifty states, the District of Columbia, and Puerto Rico offer crime victim compensation. By 2012, programs across the country were compensating more than 200,000 victims and spending approximately $500 million annually (National Association of Crime Victim Compensation Boards, 2012).

In 1984 Congress passed the Victims of Crime Act (42 USC § 10601), which, among other things, provided a mechanism for funding crime victim compensation programs operated by the states. Although such programs are run by the government, funding for crime victim compensation generally does not come from state or federal coffers. Instead, a large majority of the funds derive from offender fines, forfeitures, special assessments, and gifts or donations (federal grants provide approximately 35 percent of the payments to victims) (Office for Victims of Crime, 2012).

In 1976 Kentucky became the fourteenth state to create a mechanism to compensate victims of crime. Sponsored by Senator David Karem, a Democrat from the Thirty-Fifth District, SB 58 created new sections of KRS Chapter 346 to permit the compensation of crime victims for out-of-pocket medical expenses and loss of wages; it also established the Crime Victim Compensation Board. (That same session, through HB 639, the board was moved into its current position under the Board of Claims.) Passage was not easy: senators voted twenty-four in favor and nine against; in the house the vote was sixty-one in favor and twenty-six against. Legislators' coolness to the bill resulted from a reluctance to expend state funds on this type of compensation scheme (Karem, 2012). In the 1982 session an additional bill was passed to establish a Crime Victim Compensation Fund administered by the board. Today the Kentucky Crime Victim Compensation Board provides assistance to approximately 1,000 victims annually (Kentucky Crime Victim Compensation Board, 2012).

Adult Protection Act (1976)

The need to protect dependent adults grabbed the attention of the nation in the mid-1970s, leading to the enactment of adult protection laws in states across the country. The primary focus of early adult protection laws was the elderly and others who could not care for themselves and depended on caretakers for sustenance. Although they differed in each state, adult protection laws provided state governments with the authority to investigate and intervene in cases involving the abuse, neglect, and exploitation of adults whose

Senator David Karem with his primary legislative aide, Marie Abrams, on the senate floor, 1982. (Courtesy of the Public Records Division–Kentucky Department for Libraries and Archives)

mental or physical dysfunctioning caused them to require the state's protection. In 1976 Kentucky enacted its first adult protection law when the General Assembly passed SB 230, sponsored by Senators David Karem (Democrat from the Thirty-Fifth District), Gene Huff (Republican from the Twenty-First District), Ken Gibson (Democrat from the Sixth District), and Woodrow Stamper (Democrat from the Twenty-Seventh District). The bill was passed unanimously by both chambers.

Rape Shield Law (1976)

As discussed in chapter 3, the 1970s and 1980s saw the adoption of "rape shield laws" across the United States. In Kentucky this reform would be accomplished by the addition of a new section to the rape statute (KRS 510) by the 1976 General Assembly. Prior to the 1976 session, the justice system operated under the premise that "evidence of the victim's prior sexual conduct was admissible to support the proposition that if she consented to have relations with one or more other persons then she consented to the relations with the defendant" (*Smith v. Commonwealth*, 1978). HB 143 was sponsored by Representatives James B. Yates (Democrat from the Forty-Fourth District), Bob Benson (Democrat from the Thirty-Third District), and Thomas B. Givhan (Democrat from the Forty-Ninth District), and it made evidence about a victim's reputation or prior sexual conduct or habits inadmissible in court proceedings (KRS 510.145).[8] Specifically, Kentucky's first rape shield law provided: "In any prosecution under KRS 510.040 through 510.140, or for assault with intent to commit, attempt to commit, or conspiracy to commit a crime defined in any of these sections, reputation evidence, and evidence of specific instances of the complaining witness' prior sexual conduct or habits is not admissible by the defendant." Under the new statute, the admittance of reputation evidence was limited to cases in which either the victim's prior sexual conduct or her habits with the defendant were deemed specifically relevant by the court, following a hearing on the matter.

The purpose of HB 143 and other rape shield laws across the nation was to eliminate the dynamic by which rape victims were forced to defend themselves at trial. Notably, HB 143 did not pass easily; in the house, eighteen legislators opposed the bill (seventy-one voted in favor). Among those voting against the bill was Representative Willard C. "Woody" Allen (Republican from the Seventeenth District), who would become infamous in the domestic violence community in years to come.

• • •

1977—The YWCA Spouse Abuse Center in Louisville becomes the first center of its kind in Kentucky.

• • •

Uniform Reporting Form for Law Enforcement (1978)

In the 1978 session, a force for women's rights emerged on the legislative scene. Gerta Bendl, representing the Thirty-Fourth District, was an outspoken humanitarian who had cut her teeth on local advocacy before moving to the state level. Her time in Frankfort resulted in some of the foundational legislation on which domestic violence

Representative Gerta Bendl speaking on the floor of the house (note the "Uppity Women Unite" lapel button), January 1982. (Courtesy of the Public Records Division–Kentucky Department for Libraries and Archives)

and anti-rape advocates have built four decades of reforms. In her second legislative session, Bendl (known for her fashionable hats) sponsored five bills related to domestic violence, three of which ultimately passed. Among her successes was HB 496, which created a new section of Chapter 15A that required the Justice Cabinet, the Commission on Women, and any other agency concerned with "particular acts of criminal activity" to design a uniform reporting form for law enforcement that would provide statistical information related to crimes involving domestic violence, child abuse, victimization of the elderly, or "any other particular area of criminal activity deemed by the Secretary to require research as to its frequency." That legislation resulted in creation of the JC-3 form, which is still used by law enforcement officers in the Commonwealth.

Forensic Rape Examinations (1978)

A second bill sponsored by Representative Bendl during the 1978 session laid the groundwork for the services that are now available to rape victims across the Commonwealth. Prior to 1978, rape victims often had to wait for hours in inhospitable, exceedingly public emergency rooms for examinations performed by reluctant physicians. Rape examinations were not considered emergencies by the busy doctors and nurses; these forensic examinations were outside the scope of traditional medical care and did not result in adequate reimbursement for physicians' services, laboratory work, and other costs. Physicians were, by and large, untrained to conduct rape examinations; thus, the evidence collected was not as sound as it could have been, and physicians were loath to testify about their findings at time-consuming court proceedings. The result was that few women sought rape examinations, and for those who did, the experience amounted to a second victimization. A significant number of hospitals even refused to perform forensic rape examinations.

• • •

1978 SB 97—The General Assembly passes legislation defining "abortion referral" and criminalizing the act of charging a woman a fee for an abortion referral.

• • •

The tragic state of affairs for rape victims was illustrated by a case involving the Lexington Rape Crisis Center (later renamed the Bluegrass Rape Crisis Center). A young woman had been viciously raped by a stranger, who then left her lying on the ground severely injured. She managed to walk to the nearest hospital, which treated the victim's broken arm and other injuries but said she would have to go to the University of Kentucky Hospital if she wanted a forensic rape examination. The bewildered and frightened woman walked out of the emergency room, found a pay phone, and called the Rape Crisis Center. The director of the center got in her car, picked up the victim, and took her to the University of Kentucky for the needed examination. That director, Diane Lawless, would become one of the first anti-rape advocates in the halls of the Kentucky General Assembly. As she related the story some thirty years later, she still remembered it in vivid detail. Lawless took that woman's story with her to Frankfort every day as she worked to reform the law that had made the woman's experience so horrific.

Kentucky's medical and forensic response to rape changed in 1978 with the passage of HB 497. The bill amended the hospital licensure law to require every hospital offering emergency services to have a physician available twenty-four hours a day to conduct rape examinations. (The hospital licensure statute, passed in 1974, stipulated that persons in need of emergency care could not be turned away solely because they lacked the ability to pay.) HB 497 not only established the mandate but also defined the elements of a proper forensic examination and created a funding mechanism to reimburse hospitals. HB 497 had the effect of professionalizing the forensic rape examination, and it led to additional changes (e.g., mandated protocols for the examination, the use of forensic nurses). In its day, the bill was controversial, and twenty house members voted against it. Interestingly, among those voting against the bill was Representative William T. Brinkley (Democrat from the Tenth District). Brinkley had also voted against the rape shield law during the 1976 session, yet he would sponsor marital rape legislation in the following decade.

Expansion of the Adult Protection Act to Include Spouses (1978)

In the 1978 legislative session, Kentucky's adult protection act (passed in 1976) was amended to specify that its provisions applied not only to vulnerable adults but to spouses as well. Representative Gerta Bendl was the sponsor of that legislation (HB 501). Subsequently, the mandatory reporting of adult and spouse abuse became a fixture in the Kentucky service system that responds to elder abuse, domestic violence, and the abuse of persons with disabilities.

Interestingly, although the adult protection act was initially intended to help vulnerable adults who could not care for themselves, the amendment to include spouses ended up being the most utilized section of the statute. For example, according to the state's Cabinet for Health and Family Services, reports of spouse abuse (now classified as domestic violence) have averaged approximately 21,000 per year for the past decade, whereas reports related to vulnerable adults have averaged only about half that number. Specifically, in 2011, the cabinet received 11,483 reports related to vulnerable adults, 2,986 (26 percent) of which were substantiated; approximately half the vulnerable adult reports (57 percent) involved female victims, the majority of whom were over seventy years of age (Division of Protection and Permanency, 2012). That same year, the Cabinet for Health and Family Services received 19,061 reports of spouse abuse; those reports related primarily to female victims (80 percent of cases) in the young adult category. (34 percent of the reports involved victims between twenty and twenty-nine years of age.) Of the 19,061 reports, 3,358 (18 percent) were substantiated after an investigation. However, this substantiation rate reflects only cases in which the cabinet was able to contact the victim and the victim was willing to talk. Over the past three years, approximately 50 percent of domestic violence reports could not be investigated because the cabinet could not contact the victim, meaning that, in reality, the cabinet receives closer to 40,000 reports each year (Division of Protection and Permanency, 2012). Of those cases in which the victim was contacted, 54 percent resulted in "no finding," defined by the cabinet to mean that the victim was located but did not wish to talk with an adult protective services worker (Division of Protection and Permanency, 2012).

In recent years, the mandatory reporting of spouse abuse has become more controversial, and some have contemplated an amendment to the statute, but to date, no such legislation has been introduced. (See chapter 4 for a fuller discussion of support for and opposition to the mandatory reporting of domestic violence.)

Civil Protective Orders (1978—Failed)

Although this chronology typically does not include bills that did not pass, some of the early failures are worth noting. In 1978 Representative Bendl introduced legislation to establish a mechanism by which victims could access domestic violence protective orders, but the bill (HB 499) was recommitted to the State Government Committee and never made it out of the house.

• • •

1979—A Lou Harris and Associates poll shows that 21 percent of Kentucky women have experienced spouse abuse at some point in their lifetimes.

• • •

State and Local Domestic Violence Services (1978—Failed)

The 1978 General Assembly also failed to support HB 750, another bill sponsored by Representative Bendl. Bendl's bill, named the Prevention and Treatment of Domestic Violence Act, would have created a governor's commission on domestic violence with fifteen members representing social services agencies, law enforcement, victims, and perpetrators, with at least eight members being victims or former victims of domestic violence. That commission would have been empowered to establish a centralized statewide system of shelters, a statewide program for education of the public, a system for collecting and analyzing data on domestic violence, and an office to ensure the availability of services. The bill required the funding of at least six new shelters during the commission's first year of operation, and it provided $1 million for that purpose. The bill was introduced by Representative Bendl, only to find itself resting, unmoved, against HB 499 for the duration of the 1978 session.

7

Legislative Reform

The 1980s

Secretariat's speed captured the attention of Kentuckians in the 1970s, but in the 1980s it was Derby winners' gender that made news. Only three fillies have won the Kentucky Derby, and two of them did so in the 1980s: Genuine Risk in 1980 and Winning Colors in 1988. Females also brought home trophies in other sports, including Louisville's exceptional Mary T. Meagher, who would win three gold medals for swimming in the 1984 Olympics. The University of Louisville would capture two national collegiate basketball championships for its fans during the decade. Literary-minded Kentuckians would discover two writers with Kentucky ties—Bobbie Ann Mason and Barbara Kingsolver—whose works first appeared during the 1980s.[1] Others would reach for the works of authors lost to the Commonwealth during the decade, including Harriette Simpson Arnow, who wrote *The Dollmaker*; Robert Penn Warren, poet laureate of the United States and author of *All the King's Men*; and Harry Caudill, attorney, defender of the environment, and author of *Night Comes to the Cumberlands* (whose death was in 1990). The decade would be bookended with memorable events from northern Kentucky, where a 5.1-magnitude earthquake would rock the region in 1980 and the collision of a converted school bus and a truck on Interstate 71—known as the Carrolton bus crash—would kill twenty-seven Kentuckians in 1988, because one man chose to drink and drive.

THE POLITICAL LANDSCAPE

On the political front, the 1980s brought a new kind of public servant to the governor's office in the person of John Y. Brown Jr. (serving from 1979 to 1983). Brown beat a pool of well-established political competitors using the media, a well-honed image, his promise to be a salesman for the Commonwealth, and (in an echo of prior races) assurances that he would run the state government like a business (Harrison & Klotter, 1997; Tachau & McClure, 2004). His campaign shunned the traditional Democratic Party process, and his win foreshadowed the political success of wealthy candidates who could fund their own races—a phenomenon Kentuckians would see again before the end of the decade. Brown's first steps as governor also had a feel of newness, as he pledged gender and racial diversity in his cabinet appointees and kept that promise. Faced with nationwide economic stagnation and inflation, Brown cut the state government's organization and payroll and instituted practices that, as promised, resembled those of a business rather than a traditional government (Tachau & McClure, 2004). Among the most lasting effects of the Brown administration, however, was the independence exhibited by the Kentucky General Assembly. Prior to the 1980s the balance of power in the Kentucky government was weighted toward the governor's office (see chapter 5), but Brown preferred a laissez-faire approach and allowed the General Assembly much more independence than any other governor in modern times (Ellis, 2000; Tachau & McClure, 2004). In the area of human services, Brown strongly supported funding for the state's network of spouse abuse centers (discussed later in this chapter).

Following Brown, another new type of public servant would emerge: a female governor. Patiently, waiting her turn after serving as Brown's productive and highly visible lieutenant governor, Martha Layne Collins emerged on top in a highly competitive primary and then comfortably won the general election to become Kentucky's first and the nation's third female governor in 1983 (serving from 1983 to 1987) (Johnson, 2012). Collins brought her love of teaching and her sharp mind for business to the governor's office. During the campaign, she had promised to recruit jobs to the Commonwealth and to reform Kentucky's inadequate education system, and she followed through on those commitments. Her approach of blending education and economic development would be adopted by future governors, but for her, it was based on the very practical opinion that companies considering a move to Kentucky wanted to see the state investing in its people (Collins, 2013).

The inaugural legislative session for the Commonwealth's first

Governor Martha Layne Collins, circa 1985. (Courtesy of Special Collections, University of Kentucky)

woman governor would be a harsh beginning to her governorship. The General Assembly had become more independent under the previous administration, and the timing of the election meant that legislators had a year before Collins took office to elect leaders and become a fully functioning body (Johnson, 2012). Statutory reforms made in 1982 also meant that Governor Collins would be required to present the first biennium budget of her administration by the fifteenth day of the legislative session, only forty-five days after her inauguration. An even greater challenge was the content of the governor's proposal: an omnibus bill to improve elementary and secondary education using a tax increase to support her envisioned reforms (Ryan & Fraas, 2004). With the vast majority of house members up for reelection in the coming year, a tax increase was untenable, and the new and untested governor ultimately withdrew her proposal.

By 1985, however, Governor Collins would set aside that early failure, build a team strategy, call a special session on education, and achieve passage of a $300 million education reform package (Harrison & Klotter, 1997). This paved the way for more sweeping reforms five years later through the Kentucky Education Reform Act (Ryan & Fraas, 2004). In addition, Governor Collins advanced economic development. She recruited Toyota to build its largest manufacturing facility outside of Japan in the Commonwealth—arguably, the highlight of her administration. With that success and others, the state experienced record economic growth under Collins's leadership. Despite a difficult start, by the end of her administration, Governor Collins had developed a strong, collaborative relationship with the General Assembly (a relationship that would not be maintained by the governor who followed her).

Governor Collins's administration was also noteworthy for its nascent efforts to advance the state's response to violence against women. Building on the work of the Kentucky Commission on Women, which had been created by the 1970 General Assembly, Collins devoted a staff position in the governor's office to providing statewide education and training on domestic violence.[2] In doing so, she communicated the importance of protecting women and children from the vantage point of the highest office in the state. She believed in educating Kentuckians about issues that dramatically impacted their health and well-being (Collins, 2013).

The final governor of the decade was another wealthy, self-funded candidate. Like Brown, the first wealthy businessman to live in the governor's mansion in the 1980s, Wallace G. Wilkinson entered a race that was already full of strong, well-established candidates, including former governor Brown himself. Under the political guidance of James Carville (who would later play a role in Bill Clinton's successful run for the presidency), Wilkinson used the idea of a state lottery to win the governorship (Adams, 2004). Wilkinson's victory was widely viewed as an electoral mandate for a constitutional amendment to allow a lottery in Kentucky. This was passed by the General Assembly, despite Wilkinson's contentious relationship with that body (Blanchard, 1993; Harrison & Klotter, 1997).

As leaders at the state level sought and achieved modest reforms of Kentucky's education system in the 1980s, massive reforms were set in motion by a case filed in Franklin Circuit Court in 1985. Sixty-six school districts, seven boards of education, and twenty-two public school students filed a lawsuit claiming that the state's education finance system violated the state constitution (Clark, 2000). In 1989 the Kentucky Supreme Court declared Kentucky's entire system of elementary and secondary schools unconstitutional (*Rose v. Council for Better Education*, 1989). Importantly, the court held that the General Assembly was primarily responsible for ameliorating the deficiencies in the school system, and its remedies had to be in place before the next academic year. This set the stage for the General Assembly's first acts of the new decade (Blanchard, 1993).

While elementary and secondary schools received the most attention in the state capitol during the 1980s, significant changes also occurred in postsecondary education. In this case, progress was measured by an increase in the number of institutions included in the state's public higher education system and a related growth in student enrollment. Between 1970 and 1990, for example, student enrollment in regional universities climbed by 89 percent and in the University of Kentucky by 42 percent (Harrison & Klotter, 1997). Despite this growth in postsecondary education, Kentucky fared poorly when compared with the educational attainment of citizens in other states. The U.S. Census conducted in 1990 showed that Kentucky ranked forty-eighth in the country in the percentage of adults who had earned a bachelor's degree or higher (Sugarman, 1999). That shortcoming weighed even more heavily on women; whereas more than 15 percent of Kentucky men had earned bachelor's degrees, only about 12 percent of Kentucky women had done so. Though this seemed terrible on its face, the 1990 census data obscured an underlying trend that was more positive. As noted by one educational scholar, "The small educational edge that men still held over women in 1990 could be attributed to higher levels of education among the older segments of Kentucky's population. Indeed, reversal of the male dominance of college enrollment and graduation rates was already well underway among younger Kentuckians. A closer look at the educational attainment of young adults today reveals that college women are outperforming men on several key educational indicators" (Sugarman, 1999, p. 47). At the state level, data confirmed that the proportion of women in Kentucky with four or more years of college had increased by 25 percent (Smith-Mello, Childress, Sollinger, & Sebastian, 1999). Although this growth was measureable, substantial reform in the architecture, funding, and success of Kentucky's higher education system would have to await the ideas of a progressive governor in the late 1990s.

LEGISLATIVE REFORMS ADDRESSING VIOLENCE AGAINST WOMEN

The 1980s may be best known for establishing Kentucky's safety net for rape victims and battered women. In the first session of the decade, legislation passed allowing victims of domestic violence to petition the courts for civil protection, foreshadowing passage of the more comprehensive Kentucky Domestic Violence and Abuse Act later in the same decade. General Assemblies in the 1980s would also financially support the state's domestic violence programs (called spouse abuse centers in that era) and rape crisis centers for the first time; when the initiation of funding for spouse abuse centers raised significant public controversy, the initiation of rape crisis center funding was accomplished by keeping it out of the public eye. The beginnings of specialized tools for law enforcement officers responding to domestic violence cases began in the 1980s with passage of a law allowing peace officers to make arrests in domestic violence cases without warrants under specified circumstances. Advocates would see mixed results in response to their push to amend the rape law, achieving changes in the definition of force contained in the sexual offense chapter but failing to eradicate extant barriers to criminal justice protections for victims of marital rape. State financial support for forensic rape examinations was accomplished in the decade, and communications between rape victims and counselors in rape crisis centers became privileged. The rights of crime victims also received significant attention from the General Assemblies of the 1980s (Legislative Research Commission, 1980, 1982, 1984, 1986, 1988). Select laws passed during the decade with a direct impact on rape, domestic violence, stalking, and related crimes against women are described below.

Arrest Powers for Peace Officers in Domestic Violence Cases (1980)

The first legislative session of the new decade began with an effort to strengthen law enforcement's response to domestic violence. Democrats Gerta Bendl (from the Thirty-Fourth District), Jim LeMaster (from the Seventy-Second District), and Alice "Dolly" McNutt (from the Third District) sponsored legislation to give peace officers the authority to make warrantless arrests in cases of domestic violence. Interestingly, as introduced, the bill would have amended the family offense chapter of the Penal Code (KRS Chapter 530) by establishing the crime of domestic abuse and then providing that a peace officer could make an arrest if the officer had probable cause to believe that an act of domestic abuse had occurred. The House Judiciary-Criminal Committee did not agree with that approach, however, and drastically remodeled the bill to amend the provisions of the warrantless arrest statute that was already included in KRS Chapter 431, with no new criminal offense established. The committee's substitute and the final version of the bill as passed by the 1980 General Assembly provided that a peace officer could arrest a person without a warrant if the officer had reasonable grounds to believe that the person had caused physical injury to a spouse, parent, grandparent, child, or stepchild and if the officer had reasonable grounds to believe that the individual would present a danger to others if not arrested.

The bill did not pass without opposition. In fact, to secure passage, proponents had to agree to an amendment that required domestic violence victims to sign a written statement within twelve hours of the arrest confirming that abuse had indeed occurred and that the person who committed it was the victim's spouse. If the victim refused to sign such a statement, then the charges would be summarily dismissed. Additionally, the floor debate on HB 86 was heated, as some of the house's more conservative members

Representatives Gerta Bendl and Vic Hellard on the floor of the house, circa 1980–1982. (Courtesy of the Public Records Division–Kentucky Department for Libraries and Archives)

expressed dismay at the infringement on a man's right to privacy in his home. As Representative Bendl was explaining the critical need for the bill's protections, one male member rose from his seat to exhort his colleagues to vote against the bill because, after all, a man had a right to his castle. Bendl did not even await permission from the speaker to reply to her colleague, as is customary on the house or senate floor. She called out, "Gentleman, sometimes those castles have dungeons in them" (Heleringer, 2013). At the end of the debate, the bill barely made it out of the house, passing by a vote of forty-six to forty-one.

Domestic Violence Protective Orders (1980)

The first effort to provide civil protection to victims of domestic violence had failed to pass the General Assembly in 1978 (HB 499). Just two years later, Representative Gerta Bendl reintroduced her bill, and the effort began anew. The original version of HB 87 created a new section of KRS 403 to allow married persons (if they had been residents of the state for thirty days) to file a verified petition in a court of general jurisdiction (i.e., circuit court) seeking a protective order if they had been abused by a spouse or to seek protection on behalf of children or stepchildren. The bill also created the emergency protective order, which could be issued upon a showing of good cause, and it defined *good cause* to include immediate and present danger of further abuse. Under the original version, the emergency protective order would remain in effect unless and until the parties reunited or converted the order into an action for dissolution of the marriage or legal separation. The final version of HB 87 retained the provisions for the emergency protective order but changed the language to specify that it would remain in effect until further ordered by the court. HB 87 also allowed the court to address support and custody during the course of issuing the civil order. The bill fared fairly well, passing in the house eighty-eight to zero and in the senate thirty-six to zero.

This legislation was notable because it uniquely tailored civil protective orders to address cases of domestic violence, a resource previously unavailable to battered women and their children in the Commonwealth. It represented the first time the Kentucky General Assembly supported the use of civil rather than criminal remedies in domestic violence cases. In addition, HB 87 laid the groundwork for major civil reforms that would appear just four years later.

Further Protection for Adults (1980)

The 1980 legislative session would be the third in a row to address the adult protection act. HB 779 (sponsored by Bendl) amended the definition of *adult* to remove mention of age eighteen, such that married persons of any age who could not care for themselves would be included under the statute. In addition, it eliminated the language that required a victim to sign a statement promising to prosecute the offender before protective services would be made available. It also added law enforcement to the groups of professionals mandated to report abuse, and it empowered representatives of the Cabinet for Health and Family Services to access the medical and mental health records of alleged victims. HB 779 created a new section of the adult protection statute to address the provision of emergency services; amended the statute to create a more severe penalty for caretaker abuse, making it a class C felony; and gave cabinet representatives standing to make criminal complaints. HB 779 did not pass the house easily; in fact, the vote was a cliffhanger—forty-seven to thirty-seven. It fared better in the senate, where the vote was twenty-four to six.

• • •

1981—Directors of the state's spouse abuse centers create the Kentucky Domestic Violence Association.

• • •

State Funding for Spouse Abuse Centers and the Marriage License Fee (1980 and 1982)

The first two legislative sessions of the new decade witnessed the beginning of the state government's financial support for spouse abuse centers. The goal of the directors of these programs, the Brown administration (through First Lady Phyllis George Brown and Jessica Loving and Vicki Dennis from the Commission on Women), and key legislators such as Gerta Bendl and Senator Michael R. Moloney (Democrat from the Thirteenth District) was to support the existing centers and spread the network of shelters for abused women statewide. Toward that end, two efforts were undertaken: the addition of spouse abuse centers to the general fund budget, and the implementation of a novel mechanism to fund these programs through a fee on marriage licenses.

The 1982 General Assembly allocated funding for the shelters, amounting to $686,000 in the first year of the biennium and $794,000 in the second year. The original funds had a split purpose: $200,000 was set aside for challenge grants to create new shelters, and the remainder would be used to support the seven shelters that existed at the time. Securing state funding for the shelters had been a priority, because the directors knew that if battered women lost their lives because they had no safe place to go after fleeing from their violent partners, other legal reforms they might achieve would have little meaning (Walker, 2012).

The shelter directors were surprised by what they could achieve with no formal training or background in lobbying and no experience working in the sometimes odd environment of the General Assembly. One afternoon while sitting in the house gallery, waiting to witness action on their domestic violence legislation, they watched with incredulity as house members debated whether they could attach an amendment naming the coonhound as the state dog

Merle (Holcomb) Van Houten, director of the YWCA Spouse Abuse Center in Louisville, circa 1982. (Courtesy of Merle Van Houten)

Kentucky First Lady Phyllis George Brown (left) touring the YWCA Spouse Abuse Center in Louisville with Jessica Loving (Schickler), circa 1982. (Courtesy of Jessica Loving)

onto a bill making the "Kentucky Opera" the state opera. The ultimately unsuccessful amendment was disconcerting enough, but it was the mocking sound of a coonhound "howling" from the floor of the house that left the biggest impression (Van Houten, 2013). The directors were also aware of the advantage of having a supportive governor and first lady in John Y. Brown Jr. and Phyllis George Brown. Mrs. Brown visited the shelters and gave vocal and influential backing to the statewide spread of these programs. Her presence foreshadowed the influence of future first ladies on the field of violence against women.

The state and grassroots advocates believed that although general fund support was essential to the operation of the shelters, more should be done. Thus, Representative Bendl filed HB 33 on January 8, 1980. The bill would have established a trust and agency account in the state government through the imposition of a fee on the court costs associated with marriage licenses—an innovative idea generated by the Commission on Women in collaboration with the shelter directors. This first effort failed to pass the 1980 General Assembly; in fact, it languished in a house committee for the entire session.

Bendl tried again in the next session, but with a different strategy. HB 141 was introduced in a form that amended KRS 23A.200 to add a $10 filing fee on petitions for dissolution of marriage or for legal separation. (At the time, the fee was $70, so this would have increased the fee to $80.) The day of the hearing was an exciting one for the staff of the Commission on Women and the shelter directors, but they would walk away from the hearing with a completely different feeling.

When HB 141 came before the committee on March 2, 1982, three witnesses had signed up to speak on Bendl's bill: Eugenia Campbell from the Barren River Area Safe Space (the spouse abuse center in Bowling Green), and a minister and his adult daughter (Loving, 2013). Campbell's testimony, naturally, favored passage of the bill, but the other witnesses would not speak kindly of its provisions. The minister's daughter testified that she had been a resident of the YWCA Spouse Abuse Center in Louisville some six or eight months earlier. She admitted that she had not, in fact, been abused at all; she simply wanted a free place to stay. The daughter accused the shelter staff of defaming marriage, of "putting men on the level of animals," and of exposing the residents to "radical literature" (Anonymous, 1982).[3] In short, the minister and his daughter declared that the shelters were anti-family. The bill ultimately passed out of the committee in spite of the negative testimony; days later, it would be passed by the house, but more than one-third of legislators voted against it.

If the bill's proponents thought the measure would now proceed without protest, they were in for an unpleasant surprise. Within days of the committee hearing, Representative Willard "Woody" Allen, a Republican from the Seventeenth District in Morgantown (and famous for his bold and remarkably colored sports jackets), wrote a letter on house stationery imploring constituents to contact their legislators to oppose state funding for spouse abuse centers. The letter read in part: "Many of these government funded spouse abuse centers are run by radical feminists. . . . Nothing in this bill will prevent radical feminists, felons, or even convicted sex offenders from operating or counseling in these spouse abuse centers. Frankly, I'm sick and tired of the government using our taxpayer dollars to promote the anti-family, anti-religious, pro-abortion social agenda of a small group of left-wing activists" (Jones, 1982; Wolfson, 1982).

Unwilling to allow the attack on the spouse abuse centers to go unanswered, the Commission on Women and the Kentucky Domestic Violence Association implemented a powerful telephone campaign and inundated legislators with messages expressing outrage over this characterization of the shelters and urging funding for these programs. The commission watched with pride (and no small amount of relief) as its grassroots effort flooded switchboards with calls, and constituents influenced the votes of their legislators (Loving, 2013).

Although Allen and his supporters failed to prevent passage of HB 141 in 1982, his animosity for domestic violence programs did not end there. In 1987 he spoke publicly during a legislative hearing on the use of state funds to support these programs, arguing that they "recruited clients to justify their state funding." Once again he failed to diminish the General Assembly's support for domestic violence programs. For instance, Senator Helen Garrett,[4] a Democrat from Paducah, spoke at the same hearing and noted that no other programs being funded by the state government spent money more wisely (Chellgren, 1987).

When HB 141 arrived in the senate, the Committee on Counties and Special Districts amended the funding mechanism, reverting to a fee on marriage licenses rather than divorce petitions. The bill ultimately passed in the senate by a vote of twenty-seven to ten. The final version of the bill required each county clerk to remit to

Governor John Y. Brown Jr. signs HB 141 on March 31, 1982. Among the witnesses behind the governor are (left to right) Senator Michael R. Moloney, Jessica Loving (Schickler), Vicki Dennis, and Representative Gerta Bendl. (Courtesy of the Public Records Division–Kentucky Department for Libraries and Archives)

the state, by the tenth of each month, $10 from every $14 collected during the previous month from the issuance of marriage licenses.[5] The bill also created a new section of KRS 209 to establish a trust and agency account in the state treasury that would be known as the spouse abuse shelter fund.

The 1982 session marked the last time Representative Gerta Bendl would serve as the primary sponsor for a bill related to rape or domestic violence. She died of a heart attack in June 1987, cutting short a promising political career and the life of an extraordinary women's advocate. Colleagues and friends speak highly of her to this day. As noted wryly by Senator David Karem, "She could have been speaker [of the house], she was that tough and that articulate. Of course I also think she could have arm-wrestled you" (Karem, 2012). Representative Robert Heleringer still remembers her gallant (but hopeless) fight in 1978 to stop passage of the resolution withdrawing the house's support of the Equal Rights Amendment (ERA). During the floor debate, Bendl noticed that every time she made a motion to forestall passage of the anti-ERA resolution, a house member who was not even present in the chamber voted against her. Realizing that another member was voting for both himself and his absent seatmate, she chose to act. Rather than standing and politely asking the speaker to intervene, she strode across the house floor, assertively closed the rolltop desk belonging to the absent member, and announced, "He's not here!" (Heleringer, 2013).

· · ·

1982, 1984, 1986, 1988—The General Assembly passes legislation to prohibit the use of public funds to obtain an abortion; to require that, after the first trimester, abortions be performed in a duly licensed hospital; to prohibit publicly owned hospitals and health care facilities from performing abortions; to permit abortion only when necessary and after a medical consultation, and to require that a husband be notified when his wife seeks an abortion; and to tighten the rules for abortions for minors.

· · ·

Assault against Peace Officers (1982)

Recognizing the dangerous circumstances peace officers often find themselves in, the 1982 General Assembly created a new crime specific to law enforcement. HB 383 added a new section to KRS

Chapter 508 that defined a new class D felony: assault in the third degree. (The existing crime of assault in the third degree was renamed assault in the fourth degree and remained a misdemeanor.) The new crime required that the act be committed with recklessness and that it be directed at state, county, city, or federal peace officers or probation and parole officers by means of a deadly weapon or dangerous instrument. The bill was sponsored by four Democrats: Representatives Ray Brown (Ninety-Ninth District), L. E. "Gene" Cline (Ninety-Sixth District), Ronald Cyrus (Ninety-Eighth District), and Philip Stone (Fifteenth District).

Criminal Abuse (1982)

A second new crime was established in the 1982 session: criminal abuse. Criminal abuse applied to cases in which a person abused another individual, or permitted someone else to abuse a child or other individual, for whom that person was a custodian. For someone to be found guilty of criminal abuse, the abuse had to cause serious physical injury; place the victim in a situation that could cause serious physical injury; or torture a victim who was physically helpless, mentally helpless, or twelve years of age or younger.

HB 669, sponsored by Representatives Gerta Bendl and Jim LeMaster, amended KRS Chapter 508 and established three levels of criminal abuse: first- and second-degree criminal abuse were class C and D felonies, respectively, and third-degree criminal abuse was a class A misdemeanor. The different levels were based on the offender's state of mind—that is, whether the act was intentional, wanton, or reckless.

• • •

1984—The General Assembly passes legislation to remove the terms *illegitimate* and *bastard* as they relate to children, replacing them with the term *born out of wedlock*.

• • •

Reform of the Mental Health System (1982 and 1986)

In 1824 the Eastern Lunatic Asylum opened in Lexington, a psychiatric facility that still operates today (now called Eastern State Hospital). More than a century would pass before there was any significant change in the approach to mental health care in Kentucky. Congress passed the federal Community Mental Health Centers Act in 1963, and a year later, the Kentucky General Assembly established community mental health and mental retardation boards across the Commonwealth.

The first bill introduced in the 1982 legislative session (HB 1) was called the Kentucky Mental Health Hospitalization Act, and it was sponsored by Representatives Gerta Bendl (Democrat from the Thirty-Fourth District), Raymond Overstreet (Republican from the Fifty-Second District), and Roger Noe (Democrat from the Eighty-Eighth District). It established the processes for voluntary and involuntary hospitalization that are still in effect today. During the same session, Representatives Noe, Overstreet, Bobby Richardson (Democrat from the Twenty-Third District), and Pat Freibert (Republican from the Seventy-Eighth District) sponsored HB 32, which set forth procedures related to criminal responsibility in the commission of crimes. The bill defined terms (which are still in use today), established procedures and time requirements for the evaluation of defendants and for the defenses of mental illness and insanity, and prohibited the prosecution of incompetent defendants.

• • •

1984—Governor Martha Layne Collins establishes the position of liaison for family violence prevention in the governor's office.

1985—The Sexual and Domestic Violence Program is created in the state's Department for Mental Health and Mental Retardation Services.

1985—The Office of Victims Advocacy is established within the attorney general's office.

• • •

Another substantial bill related to Kentucky's mental health care system was enacted in 1986. SB 310, sponsored by Senator Ed O'Daniel (Democrat from the Fourteenth District), passed in the house by a vote of seventy-five to seventeen and in the senate by a vote of twenty-nine to two. It limited the civil liability of qualified mental health professionals for the violent acts of mentally ill persons for whom they were providing care. It also established a "duty to warn and protect," an obligation that arose from a civil lawsuit

(*Tarasoff v. Regents of the University of California*, 1976). Sadly, the story behind the *Tarasoff* case is one that resonates with domestic violence advocates.

Prosenjit Poddar, who had been raised in rural India, arrived in Berkeley, California, in September 1967 to attend graduate school and study electronics and naval architecture. About a year after arriving in the United States, Poddar met a young woman named Tatiana Tarasoff, a community-college student who lived with her parents in the Berkeley community. Poddar quickly developed an intimate attachment to Tatiana, but she was not as interested in him. He imagined the relationship to be much more substantial than it was, leading him to propose marriage in the spring of 1969. Tatiana turned him down and decided to end the relationship completely, since the couple obviously wanted different things from each other. Poddar was angry and humiliated by Tatiana's rejection, and he set out for revenge. He began to stalk Tatiana, including audiotaping their telephone conversations; he also expressed a desire to kill her.

In the summer of 1969 Tatiana traveled to Brazil, and Poddar's mental state seemed to improve. At the urging of his roommate, he sought help through the university's health services, initially seeing a psychiatrist and then a psychologist. During his first therapy session with the psychologist, Poddar revealed that he thought about killing an unnamed young woman with whom he was obsessed. The psychologist ultimately threatened to hospitalize Poddar if he continued to express such feelings, and Poddar was, in fact, involuntarily committed; however, he was quickly released because the psychologist and the campus police believed he appeared to be rational. Although Poddar's psychologist discussed his patient's threats with the campus police and the university administration, at no point did he or any other university official share the threats with Tatiana or her parents.

Upon Tatiana's return from Brazil, Poddar purchased a firearm. One evening just before Halloween 1969, Poddar found Tatiana at home alone, and he shot and killed her. He then called the police and waited at the Tarasoff home to be arrested. Poddar was ultimately convicted of murder in the second degree and served just over five years. Then, with a new attorney, he appealed his conviction to the California Supreme Court. The court vacated Poddar's conviction, ruling that the trial judge should have given a diminished-capacity instruction to the jury. The prosecutor elected not to retry

Poddar. Instead, Poddar agreed to return to India immediately and never again set foot in the United States.

Tatiana's case did not end there. Her parents brought suit against the regents of the university, the university administration, and the mental health professionals involved, alleging that all of them had been negligent in failing to warn them or Tatiana of the danger posed by Poddar. While the original trial court held for the regents, Tatiana's parents appealed to the California Supreme Court, which vacated the lower court's dismissal and ruled in favor of the Tarasoffs. The *Tarasoff* decision (originally released in 1974 and amended in 1976) essentially established a duty for mental health professionals to warn and protect potential victims when their patients voice a threat to harm a reasonably identifiable individual. It was a landmark decision. As one observer noted, "*Tarasoff* thus was a remarkable act of legal genesis in its day, even for the famously activist California Supreme Court of the 1970s. A psychotherapist would now be civilly liable in damages if a patient seriously harmed or killed a third party" after giving the therapist reason to believe that the patient presented a serious danger to a specific victim (Herbert, 2002, p. 419).

Following the *Tarasoff* opinion, twenty-seven states, including Kentucky, adopted language that imposed a duty to breach psychotherapist-patient confidentiality and warn a third person of potential violence (Herbert & Young, 2002). Another ten jurisdictions (nine states plus the District of Columbia) gave psychotherapists permission to warn without explicitly imposing a duty to do so; Virginia rejected *Tarasoff*, at least in the outpatient context; and the remaining thirteen states (plus federal law) do not specifically address a psychotherapist's duty to warn potential victims of violence (Herbert & Young, 2002).

Kentucky's version of psychotherapists' duty to warn was codified in KRS 202A.400. The law specified that no liability would attach to a psychotherapist for not predicting violence unless the patient had communicated an actual threat of some specific violent act (KRS 202A.400(1)). It also released a therapist from liability for violating a patient's confidentiality by warning a potential victim (KRS 202A.400(3)). KRS 202A.400(2) set out how the duty to warn would be satisfied:

The duty to warn of or to take reasonable precautions to provide protection from violent behavior arises only under the limited circumstances specified in subsection (1) of this section. The duty to warn a clearly or reasonably identifiable victim shall be discharged by the mental health professional if reasonable efforts are made to communicate the threat to the victim, and to notify the police department closest to the patient's and the victim's residence of the threat of violence. When the patient has communicated to the mental health professional an actual threat of some specific violent act and no particular victim is identifiable, the duty to warn has been discharged if reasonable efforts are made to communicate the threat to law enforcement authorities. The duty to take reasonable precaution to provide protection from violent behavior shall be satisfied if reasonable efforts are made to seek civil commitment of the patient under this chapter.

Over the years, as the General Assembly enacted additional legislation to certify or license groups of mental health professionals, the duty-to-warn statute has been amended to include those professionals. As a result, the duty now attaches to all certified or licensed mental health professionals in Kentucky (listed in KRS 202A.400(4)).

Domestic Violence and Abuse Act (1984)

As discussed in chapter 4, prior to the domestic violence–related legal reforms of the 1970s and 1980s, the criminal justice system was often insufficient to meet the unique needs of battered women. It was designed to punish criminal behavior after the fact, not to address the ongoing threat of violence posed by offenders. Nationally, advocates began to push for civil reforms in the 1970s to fill the gaps of the criminal justice system; in Kentucky, that move began in 1980 with Bendl's HB 87, noted above.

The issue of civil protective orders was revisited in 1984, this time on a much larger scale. Senator Michael R. Moloney (Democrat from the Thirteenth District) was the primary sponsor of SB 17, which, upon its enactment, became Kentucky's Domestic Violence and Abuse Act (DVAA). SB 17 was noteworthy not only because it would provide new resources to victims but also because it represented the first time the domestic violence advocacy community was directly involved in a bill's preparation and passage. The Kentucky Domestic Violence Association had been formed just three years earlier, and it had an immediate impact. Senator Moloney still remembers those of us he worked with in the summer before the 1984 legislative session, writing bill drafts at his dining room table and in his office in Lexington.[6] The specific language in the bill was based on an analysis of other states' protective order laws and our extensive knowledge of the court system in Kentucky (Moloney, 2012). We shared the initial draft with legislators and constituents well before the session, allowing discussion and compromise before the bill was formally introduced. The involvement of Senator Moloney, an influential legislator, likely played a role in the enormous support the bill attracted. The senate vote on its passage was thirty-four to zero, and the house vote was ninety-one to one.

The intent of the 1984 General Assembly was made clear in the first section of the new law, which stated that its purpose was:

1) To allow persons who are victims of domestic violence and abuse to obtain effective, short-term protection against further violence and abuse in order that their lives will be as secure and as uninterrupted as possible;
2) To expand the ability of law enforcement officers to effectively respond to situations involving domestic violence and abuse so as to prevent further such incidents and to provide assistance to the victims; and
3) To provide for the collection of data concerning incidents of domestic violence and abuse in order to develop a comprehensive analysis of the incidence and causes of such violence and abuse.

SB 17 set out the procedure for obtaining emergency protective orders through ex parte proceedings in the district court, as well as domestic violence orders issued after a hearing. It outlined who was eligible to receive protective orders and provided key definitions. The original DVAA defined *domestic violence and abuse* as "physical injury, serious physical injury, assault, or the infliction of fear of imminent physical injury, serious physical injury, or assault between family members." It defined *family member* as a spouse, parent, child, stepchild, or any other person related by consanguinity or affinity within the second degree. Later legislative sessions would expand both these statutory definitions. Under the provisions of

SB 17, emergency protective orders could be issued upon a finding of immediate and present danger of domestic violence and abuse; domestic violence orders could remain in effect for up to one year; and violation of orders constituted contempt of court.

Importantly, in addition to specifying who could obtain orders and by what process, SB 17 imposed duties on law enforcement officers to report domestic violence and abuse and to use all reasonable means to prevent further abuse by remaining at the location where the violence occurred, helping the victim get medical treatment, and informing the victim of all rights available to her. The requirement that law enforcement officers be trained to handle domestic violence and abuse cases also first appeared in the 1984 DVAA.

For Kentucky's advocates and legislators, SB 17 represented the successful outcome of the Commonwealth's policy debate about civil and criminal remedies. With its passage, civil protection for women and children took its rightful place among the state's responses to domestic violence. In the midst of their celebration in 1984, advocates could not know that this policy debate, fairly won, would arise again more than two decades later.

State Payment for Forensic Rape Examinations (1984)

Kentucky was one of the first states to ban the practice of billing rape victims for forensic rape examinations. HB 196, passed in the 1984 legislative session, directed the state to pay for such examinations. Representative Marshall Long (Democrat from the Fifty-Eighth District), a steadfast advocate for women's rights, was the bill's sponsor. It was his first legislative session, but he chose to take on the controversial bill because he believed in the work of anti-rape advocates. He recalled, "I sponsored a lot of bills during my time in Frankfort, but I'm not sure all of them meant something. When I sponsored something for you all, I always knew I was doing something important" (Long, 2012). Representative Long's legislation accomplished two important reforms: it directed that the attorney general's office would pay for forensic rape examinations at a rate established by regulation, allowing hospitals and health care professionals to be reimbursed for their services, and it explicitly prohibited the practice of charging victims for forensic rape examinations "by the hospital, the victim's insurance carrier, or the Commonwealth" (KRS 216B.400).

• • •

1986—The Kentucky Parole Board begins to provide crime victim assistance services.

• • •

HB 196 was proposed by the Kentucky Coalition against Rape and Sexual Assault and championed by two of the earliest advocates in the anti-rape movement: Grace Erickson from the Rape Relief Center in Louisville and Diane Lawless from the Lexington Rape Crisis Center. While Lawless was testifying before the Health and Welfare Committee, one senator expressed concern about the potential abuse of the bill's provisions. A physician himself, he wondered aloud whether women "would not just use this bill as a way to get a free Pap smear." Lawless did not flinch (nor did she share her actual thoughts at that moment); she simply began to explain, in stark detail, the components of a forensic rape examination. She was interrupted by a supportive legislator who quickly made a motion for passage of the bill. After a speedy majority vote on the motion, the bill sailed out of the committee with no additional questions (Lawless, 2012).

As Representative Long and the advocates were working to get HB 196 passed, they were benefiting from Bendl's 1978 legislation that required all hospitals with twenty-four-hour emergency rooms to make rape examinations available at all times (see chapter 6). Comparing the voting patterns on these two related bills is an interesting exercise. Bendl's 1978 legislation passed the house with an extremely high number of unfavorable votes; the count was forty-six to twenty, with thirty-four legislators declining to vote at all. By 1984, Long's similar bill passed the house by a vote of eighty-two to zero, with eighteen members not voting. (Both bills passed easily in the senate, with no negative votes.) The comparison is striking: in 1978 one-fifth of the house was willing to publicly oppose making rape examinations available to victims; by 1984, no house members openly opposed the state's paying for those same examinations. In both years, a fairly significant number of legislators chose not to vote on the bills, but by 1984, there were fewer abstentions. It is not possible to fully explain the different voting patterns on such similar bills, but cultural changes between the late 1970s and mid-1980s, as well as the more visible presence of anti-rape advocates in 1984, are potential reasons.

Representative Tom Burch speaking on the floor of the house, February 1982. (Courtesy of the Public Records Division–Kentucky Department for Libraries and Archives)

Expansion of Spouse Abuse Centers (1986)

The first notable legislation of the 1986 session was a resolution sponsored by Representative Thomas J. Burch (Democrat from the Thirtieth District). House Joint Resolution (HJR) 1 expressed the sentiment that spouse abuse centers in Kentucky should not only be funded (as they had been since 1982) but also expanded, such that each region of the Commonwealth had a shelter. The resolution read:

A JOINT RESOLUTION directing the expansion of spouse abuse shelters within the Commonwealth.

WHEREAS, nationally six million women and 282,000 men are annually beaten by their spouses; and

WHEREAS, 2 to 4,000 women are annually beaten to death by husbands or boyfriends; and

WHEREAS, surveys show that 43 percent of victimized wives turn to no one for help and 25 percent of women committing suicide had a prior history of being battered; and

WHEREAS, a Lou Harris poll found that 25 percent of abused victims would have welcomed emergency shelter but only 2 percent received it; and of 30 percent of the victims who would have liked to receive counseling, only 5 percent received it; and

WHEREAS, spouse abuse shelters are not available in all regions of the Commonwealth, and further, existing shelters daily turn away victims who ask for help;

NOW, THEREFORE,

Be it resolved by the General Assembly of the Commonwealth of Kentucky:

Section 1. That the Cabinet for Human Resources is directed to request from the 1986 Kentucky General Assembly sufficient funds for the 1986–1988 biennium to expand all spouse abuse shelters in the Commonwealth.

Section 2. Funds for the expansion of the spouse abuse shelters may be made available under the general fund of the Commonwealth, or under the spouse abuse trust fund as set forth under KRS 209.160, or under both.

HJR 1 jump-started the statewide network of comprehensive domestic violence programs that exist today. Enthusiasm for the

Senator Michael R. Moloney on the senate floor, 1984. (Courtesy of the Public Records Division–Kentucky Department for Libraries and Archives)

measure was not shared by all members of the house, however, as three Republicans (the funding controversy of 1982 suggests the name of at least one of them) and one Democrat voted against the resolution. The senate vote was unanimous.

Funding for Rape Crisis Centers (1986)

State funding for rape crisis centers was secured in the 1986 legislative session, but not by an overt request through the governor to the General Assembly, and minus the controversy surrounding the funding of spouse abuse centers. Instead, I quietly asked for the support of Senator Michael R. Moloney, who had served as the powerful chairman of the Appropriations and Revenue Committee for a number of years. Famous for his sharp wit and tough questions during hearings, and known for an occasionally stormy demeanor, Senator Moloney often intimidated those who came before his committee or sought a meeting in his presence. What was also true of the senator, however, was that he had a strong commitment to protecting women and children in Kentucky. When I asked him to help obtain funding for the rape crisis centers, he simply added a line item in the budget of the Department for Mental Health and Mental Retardation Services (where I worked at the time) that read "Program Development" and totaled $100,000. When Dennis Boyd, commissioner of the department, saw the line item in his budget, he asked Senator Moloney to explain its purpose. The senator just smiled in a knowing way and said, "Trust me." He never told Commissioner Boyd or other members of the General Assembly what he had done at the request of a single advocate or what the funds were for, until the session was over. It was a small beginning in terms of funding the rape crisis centers, but it was a beginning.

My strategy was twofold. First, and most important, was simply securing a place in the state budget for the network of rape crisis centers. The specific amount of the funding was less important because, once the rape crisis centers were in the budget, their funding would inevitably increase. The second part of my strategy was more political. I sensed that legislators from districts with minimally funded centers would help us advocate for expanded funding so that their local programs did not receive less than programs in other legislative districts. The collective effect of the individual advocacy of legislators would be equitable funding statewide. It is important to

Directors of the Kentucky rape crisis centers with the author, Carol Jordan (far right), circa 1990. (Author's personal collection)

note that this strategy was successful (resulting in higher budgets for the rape crisis centers every year) because it was based on the state budget's status in the 1980s; arguably, the strategy would have looked very different if we had begun our efforts two decades later, when the budget had been decimated by cuts.

Victims' Appearance before the Parole Board (1986)

Historically, criminal statutes and court rules have assigned specific roles to the professionals involved in any particular case (e.g., law enforcement, prosecutors, judges), and they have provided guidelines for the management of offenders. In the early 1980s, however, that began to change with the recognition that another group deserved to have a role in the process. HB 8 was Kentucky's contribution to a national trend to give victims a voice in the justice system. This legislation, sponsored by Representatives William Donnermeyer Sr. (Democrat from the Sixty-Eighth District), Stephen C. Keith (Democrat from the Ninetieth District), and Pearl Ray Lefevers (Republican from the Eighty-Seventh District), amended the parole statute to require that victims or relatives of victims be notified of any parole hearing related to their case and that they be allowed to offer written or spoken testimony to the parole board. HB 8 also extended the notification and opportunity to testify to prosecutors on the case.

Violent Offenders (1986)

How to manage offenders who had committed the most severe crimes, inflicted the most egregious harm on victims, and were most likely to repeat their criminal behavior drew the attention of the legislature in 1986. HB 76, sponsored by Representative Dorothy "Dottie" Priddy (Democrat from the Forty-Fifth District), created a violent offender statute within KRS 439. For persons serving life sentences for murder, rape, sodomy, or first-degree assault, it prohibited parole until at least twelve years had been served; for those convicted of these same crimes but receiving shorter sentences, the bill required them to serve at least 50 percent of their sentences prior to release.[7] The bill also created a new section of KRS 532 to require a bifurcated trial in felony cases—the first phase for determining guilt or innocence, and the second phase for sentencing. In 1984 Representative Marshall Long had tried unsuccessfully to get similar legislation passed; under his proposal, persons convicted of first-degree rape would have been ineligible for parole until they had served at least two-thirds of their sentences, and shock probation or other conditional release would have been prohibited.

Representative Dorothy "Dottie" Priddy, February 18, 1982. (Courtesy of the Legislative Research Commission)

It was highly appropriate for Representative Priddy to sponsor a "tough on crime" bill. In addition to her renown for wearing hats on the house floor, she often had a revolver strapped to her ankle.

Privileged Communications for Sexual Assault Counselors (1986)

By the second decade of the anti-rape movement, there were still too many victims enveloped by a cloud of shame and too embarrassed to ask for help because they would have to say out loud what had happened to them. After being violated in such a devastating manner, opening up to another person felt like an impossibility. There was also a practical reason for victims wanting to keep their thoughts private: medical or mental health records could be subpoenaed in an effort to embarrass or contradict a victim's testimony during a court proceeding. At the request of the Kentucky Rape Coalition, the 1986 General Assembly provided victims with the protection they needed to share their intimate feelings and experiences with

Governor Martha Layne Collins (right) signs HB 263 in 1986. Looking on are (left to right) the bill's sponsor Representative Marshall Long, Diane Lawless, and Grace Erikson. (Courtesy of Diane Lawless)

a sexual assault counselor without fear that others might learn the details of that communication.

For legislative assistance, the coalition again turned to Representatives Marshall Long and Gerta Bendl. Their HB 263 created a new section of KRS 421 to define sexual assault counselors as only those working through a rape crisis center and to identify all information transmitted between a victim and a sexual assault counselor in the confines of that protected relationship as "confidential communications." The bill also protected sexual assault counselors by exempting them from being examined as witnesses in any civil or criminal proceeding without the prior written consent of the victim. Exceptions to the rule were also articulated. The privilege for sexual assault counselors would be dramatically expanded over the years. KRS 421 was eventually restructured as the Kentucky Rules of Evidence (KRE), and KRE 506 extended the privilege to victim advocates and other certified counselors.

Marital Rape (1986)

Following passage of the Kentucky Penal Code in 1974, the General Assembly would be asked to address the rape of married women on numerous occasions. The effort to pass marital rape legislation in Kentucky can be traced to a feisty, five-foot-tall lawyer from Louisville named Bonnie Brown. In 1981 she attended a training program at the Rape Relief Center only to find that Kentucky law provided an exception for spousal rape. When she learned that, Brown recalls, "I couldn't breathe and I was mad for fifteen years" (Brown, 2012). Brown began to study the issue, and in the process she contacted Laura X, who was the primary advocate on a national level for abolishing the marital rape immunity. That contact was fateful, as just four years later, Laura X got in touch with Brown and asked her what was going on in the small western Kentucky town of Madisonville. Brown did not know, but she followed up and learned that the county attorney in Madisonville, Logan Calvert, had attempted to prosecute a marital rape case, only to be told by the judge that the law did not allow it.

In 1985 Calvert was contacted by a woman who had been severely assaulted and raped by her husband. They were separated at the time—and had been for quite a while—but they were still legally married. Calvert was eager to prosecute the husband, and the case got as far as the preliminary hearing before the court declared to the shocked prosecutor that the rape charge could not go forward because KRS 510 provided a marital immunity for acts committed by a spouse. Calvert was appalled and was very receptive when Bonnie Brown contacted him a short time later and suggested they work on a solution (Calvert, 2012).

While the ruling in the criminal case was on appeal, Calvert contacted his local legislator, William T. "Bill" Brinkley (Democrat from the Tenth District), who agreed to sponsor a bill on marital rape "as long as it was narrowly constructed and did not go too far" (Calvert, 2012). Representative Brinkley worked diligently on HB 311, seeking cosponsorship by both conservative and liberal legislators. When the bill died in the Judiciary Committee, he convinced its chair, Representative Dottie Priddy, to bring the bill back for a second hearing.[8]

Prior to passage of the Kentucky Penal Code, the rape statute was limited to "unlawful" sexual assault—language that, by definition, gave a married woman no legal right to charge her husband with rape. The Penal Code incorporated the marriage immunity rule (see chapter 6 for a detailed discussion) by defining a married couple as persons living together as husband and wife, regardless of the legal status of their relationship. The 1974 version of the sexual offense chapter excluded only "spouses living apart under a decree of judicial separation" from the definition of married (such that only legally separated wives could file rape complaints against their husbands). The original version of HB 311 as filed in 1986 attempted to extend that exclusion to include circumstances in which the spouses were living apart, with or without a decree of judicial separation. It was the narrowly constructed bill Representative Brinkley sought, but it would provide important protections to a wider range of women who had physically separated from their abusive husbands but had not yet filed for divorce. The bill that came out of the full house and senate, however, had been modified, such that the exception would apply to spouses who were living apart *and* had filed a petition under KRS 403. By requiring both circumstances—living separately and having filed a petition—the bill narrowed protections rather than expanding them. More troubling, the bill amended the perjury statute (KRS 523.020) to specify that if a spouse's accusation of rape included a material false statement, then it would be a class D felony. By the end of the session, the bill had also been amended to require that the arrest record of any person accused by a spouse under KRS Chapter 510 would be expunged if the charges were dismissed with prejudice or a verdict of not guilty was entered. These were just the first of many compromises advocates would be asked to accept as they sought to protect married women from rape.

The story of HB 311 includes some valuable lessons for advocates. If the bill had passed in its original form, it would have expanded protections to a larger group of married women. But, as sometimes happens during the legislative process, the bill's proponents lost control of its provisions, and punitive language was the end result. Although the 1986 effort was an important first battle to end the marital rape exemption in Kentucky, the bill in its final form, with its perjury and expungement language, seemed to codify the negative cultural attitudes toward women. Perhaps the harshest of these was the view that women lie. HB 311's reception by the 1986 Kentucky General Assembly made it clear that a negative portrayal of the feminine image still existed.

Crime Victims' Bill of Rights (1986)

The 1986 General Assembly had already given crime victims the right to appear before the parole board (see earlier). The next step was a comprehensive crime victims' bill of rights. Attorney General David Armstrong believed in the need for such legislation, and he sought the sponsorship of Representative Fred Cowan (Democrat from the Thirty-Second District) on what would become HB 390. Under the sponsorship of Cowan and thirteen other house members, the bill set out several key rights for crime victims:

1. The right to receive critical information. Specifically, the bill made it the responsibility of law enforcement officers and prosecutors to inform victims of the services available to help them and to provide information about the status of their cases at key points in the criminal justice process. That information included the arrest of the accused; judicial proceedings, such as the release of a defendant on bond; the defendant's plea; trial dates; and any hearing at which victims were permitted to testify.
2. The right to provide victim impact statements to the parole board and to any probation or parole officer preparing a presentence investigation.

3. The right to receive information about how to be protected from intimidation, harassment, and retaliation from the defendant or others associated with the defendant.
4. The right to be consulted on the disposition of their cases, particularly dismissal, negotiated pleas, and entry into a pretrial diversion program.

The bill also required the attorney general's office to assist prosecutors in establishing victim assistance programs and to prepare a concise brochure explaining the criminal justice system to victims and witnesses.

Sex Offender Treatment Program (1986)

Representative Fred Cowan sponsored a second bill during the 1986 session that did not attract as many cosponsors as the crime victims' bill of rights, perhaps reflecting legislators' reluctance to appear "soft" on crime. HB 535, which had been recommended to Cowan by the Kentucky Rape Coalition, amended KRS 197 to authorize the state's first formal sexual offender treatment program within the Department of Corrections. Cowan thought the bill was essential, as it allowed the state to address the reality that sex offenders will be "back on the street and likely to commit another sex crime if they have not been rehabilitated" (Cowan, 2012). The bill also prohibited parole for certain offenders who refused to participate in the program. The bill passed the house with seventeen legislators voting against it and thirteen not voting at all; it fared better in the senate, where it passed by a vote of twenty-nine to zero.

Expansion of Civil Protection for Victims (1988)

By 1988, Representative Tom Burch had already spent fifteen years in the Kentucky house and had become a well-known advocate for women, children, and families. As the powerful chair of the Health and Welfare Committee, Burch's primary target for legislative reform was the child protection system, but he also made his mark in the development of spouse abuse centers and the expansion of protections for battered women and their children.[9] During the tense floor debate in 1982 on Representative Bendl's legislation to fund spouse abuse centers with marriage license fees, Burch had stood and asked all present who had been abused during their childhoods to raise their hands. In that poignant moment, only his hand would be raised. He then went on to share with house members the terror of his childhood, the battering of his mother, and the violence he had endured at the hands of his alcoholic father (Burch, 2012). Owing to his experiences with violence and alcoholism, Burch was closely connected to the domestic violence community.

In 1988 Representative Burch sponsored HB 87. Although the bill focused primarily on children, it also amended the Domestic Violence and Abuse Act to expand eligibility for civil protective orders to ex-spouses and to members of an unmarried couple who had a child in common. HB 87 made the same change to the warrantless arrest statute and expanded the definition of peace officer to include full-time police officers at Kentucky's universities.

The "Earnest Resistance" Standard (1988)

As described in chapter 3 (see the discussion of *Brown v. State*), the specific behaviors described in the rape statute (e.g., intimate touching or intercourse) entered the realm of criminal conduct when they were forced by one party on another. Without the element of force, those behaviors were not criminal. To differentiate the consensual from the criminal, rape statutes necessarily included language related to force. Although advocates understood the need for such language, they were growing increasingly concerned because the language in Kentucky's rape statute not only defined force (specifically termed "forcible compulsion") to describe an offender's behavior but also required victims to "earnestly resist" an assault. At the time, it was not enough that the victim asked the offender to stop or even that she tried to get away. As noted in court opinions at the time, the standard required the victim to fight off the rape and to "mean it."

Members of the Rape Coalition believed that this extra burden on only one type of victim in the entire penal code was unreasonable. What about victims who froze in the midst of an assault or did not have the physical ability to fight off the offender? What about those who made a strategic decision to comply rather than place their lives at greater risk? Did the statute really require a victim being raped at knifepoint to attempt to physically overcome her attacker? The coalition believed it did and set out to amend the law.

HB 288 of the 1988 General Assembly was sponsored by Jon David Reinhardt (Republican from the Sixty-Ninth District), Ray H. Altman (Republican from the Fifty-First District), Bill Lile (Republican from the Twenty-Eighth District), and Dan Seum (Democrat from the Thirty-Eighth District). The bill made a small change in the language of the law, but its impact would be substantial for rape victims. HB 288 removed "earnest resistance" on the part of a victim from the definition of forcible compulsion. Once legislators in both chambers learned the specifics of the bill and its implications, it garnered strong support. The bill passed ninety-five to zero in the house and thirty-eight to zero in the senate.

Prevention of Family Violence through Education (1988)

In the 1988 legislative session, the successful partnership between domestic violence advocates and Kentucky educators resulted in HB 345, sponsored by Representative Walter Blevins (Democrat from the Seventy-First District). HB 345 created a new section of KRS Chapter 158 to require parenting and life skills education in kindergarten through twelfth grade. The curriculum, which included information on domestic violence and child abuse, consisted of modules that had been developed by educators and advocates. The family life skills curriculum lasted only two years in Kentucky schools, however, as the adoption of the Kentucky Education Reform Act, passed by the 1990 General Assembly, repealed all mandatory curricula.

Complete Removal of the Spousal Exemption for Rape: The First Attempt (1988)

The second marital rape bill of the decade was, in fact, the first attempt to completely remove the marriage immunity from the rape statute. HB 390 simply struck the definition of marriage from the statute, making any act of rape a criminal act, regardless of the relationship between the victim and the offender. The bill was pushed by the Kentucky Rape Coalition and sponsored by Representatives Marshall Long and Harry Moberly (Democrat of the Eighty-First District), but it did not attract support from other house members. The bill went down to a resounding defeat on the house floor by a vote of forty-two in favor and forty-nine against, with nine legislators not voting. Not to be dissuaded, Long promised to try again in the first session of the new decade.

Minors' Right to Seek Counseling (1988)

Two bills from the 1970s sponsored by Senator Georgia Davis Powers (SB 193 in 1970 and SB 309 in 1972) laid the groundwork for statutorily empowering minors to make medical decisions without their parents' consent under certain conditions. In the 1988 legislative session, we built on those accomplishments by proposing legislation to expand those rights to include counseling services for minors. The primary purpose of HB 574, sponsored by Representative Walter Blevins (Democrat from the Seventy-First District), was to make counseling services available to teenaged victims of sexual abuse or physical violence. The original language of the bill as I drafted it, along with the rape crisis centers, did not contain any restrictions with regard to the victim's age or the purpose of counseling. As the bill moved through the legislative process, however, the General Assembly—traditionally reluctant to diminish parental rights—restricted the bill's provisions to include only minors aged sixteen and older and only those minors who had been sexually or physically abused by a parent or guardian (from whom the child otherwise would have had to obtain consent).

8

Legislative Reform

The 1990s

The 1990s would see the Commonwealth celebrate 200 years of statehood. Other celebrations would follow when the University of Kentucky men's basketball team achieved stunning success on the court, bringing home national championships in 1996 and 1998. And the decade would be capped by another extraordinary achievement by a Kentuckian when Victoria "Tori" Murden McClure became the first woman to row solo across the Atlantic Ocean.[1]

Darker moments would be seared in the memories of Kentuckians, such as the cold December morning when fourteen-year-old Michael Carneal opened fire on a group of fellow students at Heath High School in Paducah, killing three and wounding five. The Commonwealth would also see an increase in the abuse of oxycodone, a powerful narcotic pain reliever, leading to disastrous consequences.

Among the national news items that would impact the Commonwealth in the 1990s was the murder of Nicole Brown Simpson and Ronald Goldman and the subsequent murder trial of her ex-husband, former football star and actor O. J. Simpson. Although the events took place in California, Kentuckians were transfixed by television coverage of what would become the most publicized criminal trial in American history. Ultimately, Simpson was acquitted after a nine-month trial, an acquittal that riveted the nation's attention to the issue of domestic violence.

The Political Landscape

As the 1990s began, the term of Governor Wallace Wilkinson (serving from 1987 to 1991) had passed its midpoint. The issue of gubernatorial succession was causing friction between the governor and the General Assembly. Wilkinson held the view that any governor deserved the opportunity to serve a second term to ensure that new programs were carried through to fruition; moreover, he believed that any constitutional amendment to permit succession should include the incumbent governor (Adams, 2004). Legislative leaders, in contrast, feared that succession would result in an imbalance of power in the executive's favor and objected even more stringently to inclusion of the sitting governor if the constitutional amendment were to pass. The confrontation that ensued only fueled the already contentious relationship between the executive and legislative branches. The governor's wife, Martha Wilkinson, announced in 1990 that she would seek the Democratic gubernatorial nomination in order to succeed her husband in office, but she ultimately withdrew when her candidacy got little traction.

Notwithstanding the tense relationship between Governor Wilkinson and the General Assembly, the 1990 session brought passage of one of the most important reforms in the state's history: the Kentucky Education Reform Act (KERA). Education reform was the state's response to the 1989 *Rose* decision declaring the state's system of elementary and secondary schools unconstitutional. KERA would restructure the system by vesting local councils of parents, teachers, and administrators with more authority; expanding the power of the Kentucky Department of Education to take over failing school districts; implementing a statewide testing system; and substantially increasing revenues to local school districts (Harrison & Klotter, 1997).

Wilkinson's successor, his lieutenant governor Brereton C. Jones, would also make financial investments to continue the reforms begun under KERA. Jones had bested his competitors in the primary and general election to become the state's fifty-fourth governor (Miller, 2004). At the end of Governor Jones's administration (which ran from 1991 to 1995), the state would have a budget surplus (even though Jones had inherited a $400 million revenue imbalance), declining welfare rolls, and lower unemployment rates.

Jones's reforms would dramatically impact women. During the 1980s, the proportion of separated and divorced women had risen steadily, and by 1990, almost 16 percent of all Kentucky households were headed by women. Only four in ten divorced mothers received child support from their ex-husbands (Garkovich & Zimmerman,

1999), meaning that these women were the sole economic support for their families. Not surprisingly, labor force participation rates spiked among mothers with young children (Negrey, 1999). During the 1990s, the percentage of children living in poverty increased from just under 22 percent to 27 percent, with more than half the children in Kentucky's female-headed families living in poverty (Stewart, 1991).

Governor Jones also championed government and ethics reform policy, legislation for gubernatorial appointees, and campaign finance reform. He appointed the first woman to the Kentucky Supreme Court and, overall, appointed three times the number of African Americans and far more women than previous administrations (Miller, 2004). While making advances in these areas, Jones fell short of achieving his primary goal: comprehensive health care reform. Specifically, although his efforts during a 1992 special legislative session led to reforms that prohibited denial of insurance coverage based on preexisting conditions and allowed Kentuckians to keep their health insurance if they changed jobs (i.e., portability), he failed to accomplish universal coverage. Arguably, this failure was influenced by his deteriorating relationship with the General Assembly. Conflicts around ethics reforms and particularly Jones's public statements about the federal BOPTROT investigation (including his opinion that the scandal would lead to a "cleansing process" in the General Assembly) soured that relationship dramatically and permanently (Miller, 2004).[2] Governor Jones also supported the once-controversial gubernatorial succession amendment, upping its chance of passage by endorsing a provision that exempted the sitting governor—a step that would dramatically impact Jones's successor.

• • •

1993—Sara Walter Combs becomes the first female justice of the Kentucky Supreme Court.

• • •

That governor was Paul E. Patton (serving two terms: 1995 to 1999 and 1999 to 2003). When Patton easily won reelection, he became the first governor in the state's history to be elected to two consecutive four-year terms (Blanchard, 2000, 2004).[3] Like his Democratic predecessors since the 1970s (Brereton Jones, Martha Layne Collins, Julian Carroll, and Wendell Ford), Patton secured the office after serving as lieutenant governor. Upon assuming the governorship, Patton set a tight agenda with a limited number of priorities, chief among them being reform of the system of higher education in the Commonwealth. In a special session called in 1997, Governor Patton proposed legislation to reform the postsecondary education system, creating a seamless system of higher education with two research institutions (University of Kentucky and University of Louisville), six regional universities (Eastern Kentucky University, Kentucky State University, Morehead State University, Murray State University, Northern Kentucky University, and Western Kentucky University), and a comprehensive community and technical college system. His proposal deliberately set the University of Kentucky on a path toward prominence as a nationally ranked comprehensive research institution, and it enabled substantial financial investments in research through an innovative Research Challenge Trust Fund (totaling $110 million in 1998 and $120 million in 2000 through direct appropriations, and $120 million in 2002 through a bonding mechanism) (Ellers, 2003). Reform of the workers' compensation system and the criminal justice system, as well as multiple initiatives targeting economic reform, rounded out Patton's list of achievements.

Governor Patton's first term was highly successful and benefited from a positive relationship with the General Assembly. He would be called one of the most politically skillful and persuasive governors in a quarter of a century (Blanchard, 2004). His success can be attributed to a unique ability to show respect to legislators, lobby them personally, and be accessible to both leaders and members, regardless of party. That positive relationship would not extend through his second term, however. One reason was the Republican Party's takeover of the Kentucky senate—the first time in the state's history that this once minority party would flip to the majority. With a divided (and often conflicted) legislature and the rise of a formidable opponent in the person of senate president David Williams, Patton's ability to influence the legislature ebbed. Patton was also hurt by a personal scandal that became public in 2002.

The Patton administration was marked by the visible and influential role of First Lady Judi C. Patton, who brought the issues of domestic violence and sexual assault, child maltreatment, and breast cancer to the forefront. The Patton administration's reforms on behalf of women included creation of the Governor's Office of Child

Editorials

Friends in high places

Creation of domestic violence office is a good move

To every woman numb with dread of the next beating, to every child betrayed by an adult's sexual advance, to every victim of rape or incest, we wish we could personally convey this message from first lady Judi Patton: "You are viewed as extremely important."

Her remarks were occasioned by Gov. Paul Patton's creation of the Office of Sexual Abuse and Domestic Violence Services. The governor signed the order last Friday and announced that his wife will serve as its volunteer adviser.

Significantly, the new office will be part of the governor's office, located on the same floor of the Capitol as Patton. We hope this attachment and access lend it clout beyond its modest budget.

Kentucky can be proud of progress made in recent years to safeguard our most vulnerable citizens. But there remains a long way to go before we have protected children and women from the violence and abuse that are handed down through generations like a family curse.

Under the able leadership of its executive-director, Carol Jordan, the new office can keep pushing in the right direction and help coordinate various efforts to protect victims.

Jordan, a wise choice for the job, was part of the legislative task force that labored for almost two years to produce a package of improvements in domestic violence laws. That process provided one of the few reminders during the last General Assembly of how well government *can* work for people.

But legislative action is just the first step. An obvious job for Jordan and her staff is to watch to see if the laws are working for the lowliest victim on the most local level.

For the first time, judges and other professionals who work with victims of domestic violence must undergo training. We hope Jordan will keep a close eye on the quality of the training.

The recent changes also stiffen penalties for repeat offenders, strengthen victims' advocates roles in courts, create a system for notifying victims when their attackers are released and allow children under 12 to testify about sexual abuse on videotape. Properly carried out, all of these changes should underscore Judi Patton's message: Victims are important.

The most dangerous time for an abused woman is when she finally takes her children and makes the break from her abuser. Kentucky's spouse abuse shelters already are brimming, operating at capacity or beyond. Patton's continuation budget provided no money to expand shelters. This points up another challenge for the Pattons and Jordan before next year's special session: Come through with funding to provide victims with safe havens.

> **Significantly, the new office will be part of the governor's office, located on the same floor of the Capitol as Patton. We hope this attachment and access lend it clout beyond its modest budget.**

"Friends in High Places," *Lexington Herald-Leader* editorial, April 10, 1996.

Abuse and Domestic Violence Services, an office visibly connected to the chief executive by its location just doors away from the governor's office.[4] Mrs. Patton became a special adviser to the office and made legislative reform a priority, testifying on bills and meeting with legislators. During the Patton administration, twenty separate pieces of legislation were proposed and passed by the General Assembly.

In conjunction with the state domestic violence coalition, the sexual assault coalition, and partners among judges, prosecutors, health and mental health professionals, educators, and others, significant improvements were made during the eight years of the Patton administration through substantial legislative reforms, innovative policies, and elevated public awareness. Governor Patton also earmarked significant additional funds for domestic violence programs and rape crisis centers. In fiscal year 1995, when he took office, domestic violence programs (spouse abuse centers) were receiving $3,415,046 a year in state general funds. By the end of his administration in fiscal year 2003, the level of funding had grown 42 percent, to $4,851,852. In addition, the governor allocated a one-time capital construction fund of $1,075,000 to improve the structures of the domestic violence programs. Even more dramatic changes were seen in funding for rape crisis centers, which, at the beginning of the Patton administration, were receiving $916,462 a year in state general funds. By fiscal year 2003, that appropriation had grown to $2,100,656, a 129 percent increase.

The General Assemblies of the 1990s took on major reforms, including health care reform, primary and secondary education reform, postsecondary education reform, and campaign finance and election reform (Legislative Research Commission, 1990, 1992, 1994, 1996, 1998). By the midpoint of the decade, legislators also faced a federal investigation that ultimately slimmed their ranks by 10 percent through criminal convictions, reaching all the way to speaker of the house Don Blandford. Also of note, the 1996 General Assembly enacted a redistricting plan that was challenged by Thomas Jensen (Republican from the Twenty-First District), the minority floor leader of the house. He claimed the plan did not create a whole district within either Pulaski or Laurel County, but the Kentucky Supreme Court ultimately upheld the redistricting plan, determining that it satisfied the requirements of section 33 of the Kentucky Constitution.

Kentucky First Lady Judi C. Patton surrounded by children on the lawn of the governor's mansion, October 15, 1998. (Author's personal collection)

LEGISLATIVE REFORMS ADDRESSING VIOLENCE AGAINST WOMEN

The General Assemblies of the 1990s achieved more legislative advances on behalf of battered women than any in the history of the Commonwealth. This accomplishment was largely the result of the continued presence of the Kentucky Coalition against Rape and Sexual Assault; two task forces on domestic violence, one organized by the executive branch and the other by the legislative branch; a task force on child sexual abuse; and a governor's office that was active on crime victim legislation. Select laws with a direct impact on rape, domestic violence, stalking, and related crimes against women are described below, but unlike previous chapters, which were organized chronologically, the laws discussed here are organized by the bill's source.

Kentucky Coalition against Rape and Sexual Assault

The Kentucky Coalition against Rape and Sexual Assault (the Rape Coalition) offered four major legislative proposals during the 1990s, including a second effort to pass a bill that had suffered a resounding defeat in the 1980s and three more that would be attempted for the first time.

Marital Rape (1990). True to his word, Representative Marshall Long filed HB 38 to remove spousal immunity from the rape statute at the beginning of the 1990 legislative session, this time with Representative Gregory D. Stumbo (Democrat from the Ninety-Fifth District) as the lone cosponsor. The timing of Stumbo's support was particularly meaningful. He had watched the verbal bloodbath in 1988 during the floor debate on the first bill, and he knew that, as majority floor leader, his support this time around would signal to the rest of the Democrats that a vote in favor of the bill would be politically safe (Stumbo, 2012). History would prove him right.

This second attempt to remove spousal immunity mirrored the earlier bill, but by this time, a statewide alliance supporting the bill had built a substantial voice around the Commonwealth and in the halls of the capitol. Bonnie Brown continued to represent the Rape Coalition in the effort and beat her proverbial drum incessantly, leading some legislators to say they would "vote for the danged bill" if it meant they wouldn't have to listen to her "go on and on about it again."

Also prominently involved in the marital rape fight were the domestic violence programs, through the leadership of Sherry Currens, their coalition's executive director, and the rape crisis centers I had organized through the Department for Mental Health and Mental Retardation Services.[5] Together, the programs conducted a survey to gather data on the prevalence of marital rape among the women who came to them for aid. Their findings revealed that close to half the women seeking shelter had experienced rape as part of their partners' victimization. This information allowed each program to tailor its services to meet its clients' needs and provided more Kentucky-specific data to give to legislators.

The moment Representative Long introduced the bill in the house, the challenges began. Its first stop was the Judiciary Committee, where it received its first hearing on February 16, 1990. The Judiciary-Criminal Committee was chaired at that time by Louis E. Johnson (Democrat from the Thirteenth District), a devout Catholic attorney from Owensboro who had voted against the marital rape legislation in 1988. Notwithstanding his earlier vote, the chairman allowed the bill to be heard, and he eventually voted in favor of it. The committee hearing was colorful. Representative Herbie Deskins (Democrat from the Ninety-Fourth District) expressed concern that passage of the bill would give women a powerful tool to use during divorce proceedings. According to Deskins, "If you don't think there's some mean women, you get one that's in a divorce case who has the opportunity to use a statute against them. If we pass a statute like that out there's going to be some mean divorces in the state" (Marital-rape bill, 1990). Ray Larson, longtime Commonwealth's attorney (Twenty-Second Circuit) from Lexington, replied to that claim by providing national data and explaining that false reports could be easily detected. Representative Tom Kerr (Democrat from the Sixty-Fourth District) cited biblical references in support of his opposition: "The Bible says that in a marriage contract the husband's body is not his, it's the wife's and the wife's is not hers, it's the husband's. And neither shall withhold their body from each other except by mutual agreement for a limited period of time" (ibid.). In a profound retort, assistant Commonwealth's attorney Keith McCormick (Twenty-First Circuit) said, "I took some vows seventeen years ago. Mine were to honor, not to rape. Mine were to cherish, not to sodomize" (ibid.). As we advocates held our collective breaths, the bill passed out of committee by a vote of eleven to two.

As HB 38 advanced through the legislative process, the media followed it closely, quoting both advocates and opponents:

> When you are married, you've already had sex. The element of degradation is removed. If a man goes home and holds his wife down and forces her to have sex, I don't think the criminal justice system should frown on that in the same way that it does if the man goes out and grabs a woman off the street and forces her to have sex (Gordon Germain, a Monticello lawyer, quoted in Sponsor, 1990).

> A rape is a rape and the relationship should not be a factor in prosecuting the crime (Sherry Currens, Kentucky Domestic Violence Association, quoted in Marital-rape bill, 1990).

> Rape is an act of violence that a husband can inflict as easily as a stranger (Diane Lawless, Lexington Rape Crisis Center, quoted in Sponsor, 1990).

If women can charge their husbands with rape, it's going to be hard to defend men falsely accused. The charge of rape is one that's very easy to make and very hard to disprove (Vince Aprile, Kentucky Department for Public Advocacy, quoted in Sponsor, 1990).

Probably the best argument is that there will be an increase in false reports; but other states that have passed similar legislation have had no problems with false reports (Bonnie Brown, Kentucky Coalition against Rape and Sexual Assault, quoted in Marital-rape bill, 1990).

It's an excruciating process, women don't do that on a whim (Carol E. Jordan, Kentucky Department for Mental Health and Mental Retardation Services, quoted in Sponsor, 1990).

In fact, rape is considered the most under-reported of all crimes and marital rape even more so. Marital rape victims do not discuss it and they don't report it because the law will not help them (Carol E. Jordan, quoted in Marital rape permissible, 1989).

On Thursday, March 1, the bill arrived on the house floor, and we sat on the edge of our seats in the gallery. In the midst of the debate, Representative Dottie Priddy (Democrat from the Forty-Fifth District) rose to her feet, and silence ensued. Priddy, a no-nonsense, tough-on-crime legislator, had voted against the Equal Rights Amendment, and at the time, she was one of only five women in the house. Priddy announced that she had gone along with her male colleagues for twenty years on other bills, and now it was her turn to ask them to stand with her. She stated, "I am appalled at some of my fellow colleagues who stand here today and indicate that a marriage license gives a husband the right to abuse. . . . Just because a woman is married she should not be denied the same rights as a single woman. There is no law in statute today that treats you men that way. I'm asking you to come out of the Dark Ages and make the statement 'all persons are created equal' a true statement and all laws will be the same for all women" (Bill outlawing, 1990). Her speech got a standing ovation that echoed throughout the house chamber.

Representative Marshall Long on the house floor during the debate on marital rape legislation, March 1, 1990. (Courtesy of the *Lexington Herald-Leader*)

• • •

1990, 1996—The General Assembly passes legislation to require health insurance policies to cover mammograms and mastectomies and to cover the treatment of breast cancer by high-dose chemotherapy.

• • •

On the house floor, HB 38 engendered a flurry of amendments. Some were poorly veiled attempts to kill the legislation, including an amendment to strip guns from men who were charged under the rape statute, a second repealing Kentucky's "concealed and carry" gun law, and a third prohibiting corporal punishment. Others were successfully added to the bill, to the dismay of advocates. These included amendments requiring victims to report the crime to law enforcement within one year (a statute of limitations not applied to any other felony offense); requiring victims to sign a complaint; prohibiting the introduction of evidence of marital rape in any proceeding related to child custody or visitation; and exempting intercourse or deviate sexual intercourse with a spouse from being criminal if the only element of criminality is that the victim is younger than sixteen or mentally retarded. At the end of the debate, with the amendments attached, the marital rape legislation passed by a vote of eighty-eight to nine, with three members not voting. After a brief celebration, advocates looked down the hallway toward the senate, wondering what fate awaited the bill in that chamber.

Managing the marital rape legislation in the senate was Michael Moloney (Democrat from the Thirteenth District), chair of the Appropriations and Revenue Committee and former chair of the Judiciary Committee. Only one amendment was attached to the bill by the senate's Judiciary Committee, and that one came from Moloney, who was concerned that the house's provision regarding custody proceedings could keep reports of child sexual abuse from reaching the ears of the judges deciding custody or visitation arrangements. With the amendment attached, the bill passed out of the committee by a vote of five to one.

On March 27 the marital rape bill arrived on the senate floor, where it would be amended by another of its opponents, Senator Dan Seum (Democrat from the Thirty-Seventh District). Seum was still concerned that men would be falsely accused, asking, "What happens to a rape charge when the charges are dropped and the

Governor Wallace Wilkinson signs the marital rape law. Looking on are (left to right) Travis Fritsch, unknown, Bonnie Brown, Sherry Currens, Tamara Gormley, Representative Marshall Long, Phyllis Alexander, and Helen Kinton. (Courtesy of the Public Records Division–Kentucky Department for Libraries and Archives)

lady thirty days later decides to go back and live with the fellow? Is he stuck with this stigma for the rest of his life?" (Spousal rape bill, 1990). Seum's amendment stipulated that if charges against a defendant were dismissed or the defendant was found not guilty, then all records would be expunged. The amendment even went so far as to allow any person in this position to answer "no" if asked whether he had ever been arrested.

Senator Moloney's simple but elegant floor speech in favor of the legislation belied the controversy and angst surrounding it. He said, "HB 38 brings Kentucky in line with 44 other states that make rape of a spouse a crime. Why it has taken us this long, I don't know. It's a very simple piece of legislation; one that we probably should have enacted a number of years ago" (Spousal rape bill, 1990). With that, the senate passed the marital rape legislation by a vote of thirty-two to two, and the house concurred with the senate changes later the same day. When Governor Wallace Wilkinson signed the law,[6] the rape of married women became a crime in Kentucky.

Advocates were not happy with the amendments, however, which they believed would harm women. Addressing those shortcomings in the rape statute would take another decade.

• • •

1990—The Kentucky Rape Crisis Center Association is created; it would be renamed the Kentucky Association of Sexual Assault Programs in 1997.

• • •

Rape with a Foreign Object (1992). A top priority for the Rape Coalition during the 1992 legislative session was expansion of the rape statute to address sexual assault committed with an object other than the rapist's body. This was not the coalition's first try at passing "foreign object" legislation, as the advocacy group had proposed similar legislation in both 1986 and 1988. An omnibus sexual offense bill in 1986 had attempted to add rape with a foreign object, remove the "earnest resistance" requirement from the definition of force, and expand the definition of sexual contact to include contact by sexual organs over clothing (HB 931). Earnest resistance legislation passed on its own in 1988 (see chapter 7), but an attempt to create an entirely new offense under KRS 510 called "sexual assault with a foreign object" was unsuccessful. It took a third stand-alone effort, a different statutory approach, and a new sponsor in Senator Moloney to achieve passage. Kim Allen (representing the Rape Coalition) and I served as staff to this legislative effort.

Since passage of the Penal Code in 1974, rape had been limited to "intercourse in its ordinary sense" (KRS 510.010(8)), meaning that the object penetrating a victim during a sexual assault had to be the sexual organ of a man. But coalition members and rape crisis center staff from across the state were hearing horror stories of rapes involving objects other than body parts, which could be prosecuted only as lesser or nonsexual assaults. To gather information that I could then share with the General Assembly, I sent a survey from the Department for Mental Health and Mental Retardation Services to the ten rape crisis centers in existence at the time. They reported serving eighty-one victims of foreign object rape during 1991, including the following: a thirty-four-year-old woman who was raped with a Coke bottle, a cucumber, a douche consisting of bleach and vinegar, and a barbell; a twenty-five-year-old woman who was raped with a coat hanger and a broom handle; and a thirty-three-year-old

The author (left) with First Lady Judi C. Patton (center) and Kim Allen (right), 1996. (Author's personal collection)

woman who had small explosives inserted into her pelvic cavity. None of these offenders could be charged with rape under the existing Kentucky statute. The legal solution was to amend the definition of sexual intercourse by adding "penetration of the sex organs of one person by a foreign object manipulated by another person" (KRS 510.010(8)). The original version of SB 160 also stipulated that this did not include penetration during the performance of generally recognized health care practices. During the legislative process, the bill was amended to remove the term "female" and replace it with "sex organ or anus," a change that expanded foreign object rape to include male victims. SB 160 defined foreign object to mean "anything used in commission of a sexual act other than the person of the actor" (KRS 510.010(9)).

The bill moved quickly through the senate, ultimately passing unanimously by a vote of thirty-five to zero. Although the senate was very supportive, a few of its members could not resist the opportunity to joke with a young female advocate. In one case, I found myself explaining SB 160 to a senator who I knew supported its provisions; he was a seasoned attorney and a long-standing member of the Judiciary Committee. But he pointed to a specific sentence in the bill, looked perplexed, and asked me, "What's that thing called 'deviant' intercourse?" In fact, the sexual offense chapter included a definition of *deviate* sexual intercourse (referring to oral or anal sex)—a distinction I knew was not lost on the senator. Nevertheless, I explained the specific meanings of the definitions in the statute. After listening to my answer, the senator exclaimed (with a sardonic smile), "My mama would slap my ears if she heard me talking this way." I replied that she probably should, confirmed his aye vote for the bill, and left his office to the sound of his chuckling. On the house side, SB 160 received a majority vote when it was heard in the Judiciary Committee, but there too, a few legislators couldn't resist asking if "foreign" objects meant they were made in Japan.

When SB 160 hit the house floor, all humor left the capitol, and the bill was stopped dead in its tracks. For advocates, it was a painful reminder that legislation can be expedited or delayed for political reasons that have nothing to do with the content of a bill or its supporters. In this case, Senator Moloney, who chaired the Appropriations and Revenue Committee, had raised the ire of house members by dramatically changing their version of the state budget. We waited outside the house chamber each day, hoping the bill would be voted on, but to no avail. Every day for three weeks, Representative Marshall Long reassured me that as soon as the house was done expressing its displeasure over Senator Moloney's budget modifications, our legislation would sail through the house. For all anti-rape advocates, it was a long wait as the end of the session neared. But on March 30 the bill passed by a vote of ninety-two to two, making Kentucky the forty-fourth state in the nation to pass foreign object rape legislation.

Access to Sex Offender Presentence Investigations by Mental Health Professionals (1996). As early as 1986, the Rape Coalition saw the wisdom in creating specialized treatment programs for convicted sex offenders. The idea was not to advocate treatment instead of prison, but to ensure that while the offender was incarcerated, he would be engaged in a program that addressed his highly recidivistic offending behavior.

As described later in the section on the Attorney General's Task

Governor Brereton Jones signs the foreign object rape law surrounded by staff from Kentucky's rape crisis centers, 1992. On the far right is Kim Allen, standing next to the author. (Author's personal collection)

Force on Child Sexual Abuse, the 1994 General Assembly passed legislation to implement specialized assessments of sex offenders. To improve on these provisions, the Rape Coalition proposed in 1996 that mental health professionals who have been authorized by the Department of Corrections or the Department for Mental Health and Mental Retardation Services to evaluate sex offenders have access to information gathered by probation and parole officers. Sponsored by Representatives Mary Lou Marzian (Democrat from the Thirty-Fourth District), Joni Jenkins (Democrat from the Forty-Fourth District), Jon Ackerson (Democrat from the Forty-Seventh District), and Bill Lile (Republican from the Twenty-Eighth District), HB 406 amended KRS 532.045 to specify that information on a specific sex offender that is part of a presentence investigation conducted by probation and parole officers be provided to mental health professionals for use in their court evaluation of that individual. The bill also amended KRS 532.050 to require sex offenders

Representatives Mary Lou Marzian (left) and Joni Jenkins in the Health and Welfare Committee, January 2011. (Courtesy of the Legislative Research Commission)

to pay the costs related to presentencing, probation, and conditional discharge evaluations, based on their ability to pay.

The second part of HB 406 made important changes to the sexual offense chapter of Kentucky law. Back in 1988, the definition of "forcible compulsion" had been amended to remove the requirement that a victim "earnestly resist" being raped (see chapter 7). HB 406 built on that success by clarifying that a rape victim does not have to physically fight off her attacker for the offense to be legally defined as rape (KRS 510.010). The bill also amended the definition of "substantial sexual conduct" in KRS 532.045 to clarify that penetration may occur by the penis of either the victim or the offender, to address cases in which males are the victims of sexual abuse.

• • •

1998—The General Assembly passes legislation to criminalize partial birth abortion and to require that women be given information about the nature of the procedure and alternatives to it twenty-four hours prior to an abortion.

• • •

The legislature strongly supported HB 406. It passed in the house by a vote of ninety-three to zero and in the senate by a vote of thirty-eight to zero.

Creation of the Kentucky Sexual Assault Nurse Examiner (SANE) Program (1996). Earlier reforms required hospitals with twenty-four-hour emergency rooms to make forensic rape examinations available at all times (1978) and required the state to pay for such examinations (1984). These reforms dealt with access to rape exams but did not address quality. Rape crisis centers across the Commonwealth continued to report survivors' negative experiences, including one case in which the physician put the instructions from the rape kit on the victim's stomach while he conducted the examination (Recktenwald, 2012).

Together, the Rape Coalition and the rape crisis centers decided to address this concern by establishing a certification program that would allow nurses to perform these examinations—an idea that drew significant support from the Kentucky Board of Nursing. Sponsored by Representatives Joni Jenkins, Mary Lou Marzian, and twelve cosponsors, HB 495 amended KRS 216B to allow specially certified nurses to conduct forensic rape examinations. The bill required the chief medical examiner to issue a forensic protocol to be used by the physicians and nurses who conducted forensic rape examinations. (Thanks to a Victim of Crime Act grant, we were able to begin the program in the chief medical examiner's office.) It also required the Kentucky Board of Nursing to establish a certification program for sexual assault nurse examiners, with training and education requirements. A thirteen-member advisory council would provide consultation to the program.

The SANE legislation garnered significant support from legislators, passing ninety-three to zero in the house and thirty-eight to zero in the senate. Its passage made Kentucky the first state in the nation to offer a statewide certification program for sexual assault nurse examiners.

Attorney General's Task Force on Domestic Violence Crime

Kentucky's first domestic violence task force of the 1990s was convened by Attorney General Frederic J. Cowan on March 12, 1991. While Cowan was running for attorney general, a supporter asked him to speak to a victim of domestic violence, in the hopes that he would address this type of crime if elected. He was significantly influenced by that conversation, as he was by a domestic violence–related homicide-suicide that occurred in Henderson after he took office

(Cowan, 2012). At the time, Travis Fritsch was on the staff of the Victims' Advocacy Division within the Office of the Attorney General, and when she approached Cowan about creating a committee to address domestic violence, her proposal fell on receptive ears.[7] The attorney general charged the resultant Task Force on Domestic Violence Crime with "the responsibility of comprehensively analyzing and evaluating Kentucky's laws and services as they relate to domestic violence crime; and proposing realistic changes to measurably improve the effectiveness of the ability for criminal justice and community service professionals to intervene in these cases" (Office of the Kentucky Attorney General, 1991). The task force was chaired by two Kentucky judges: circuit judge Julia Adams and district judge Stanley Billingsley. Among its legislative members were Senator Walter Baker, Senator Susan Johns, Senator David Karem, Representative Richard Lewis, and Representative Marshall Long. Its multidisciplinary membership (see appendix C for a complete list) met regularly, heard extensive testimony, and reviewed statistical data. The task force used an effective model to advance its agenda by issuing what were termed emergency recommendations on May 14, 1991. By doing so, the task force drew the media's attention to its work before it issued a final report, and framing these recommendations as emergent attached additional importance to them. These ten recommendations included twenty-four-hour access to civil protective orders; creation of an electronic file in the Law Information Network of Kentucky (LINK), which is the Commonwealth's criminal justice database, to allow law enforcement officers to validate the existence and status of orders any time of the day or night and on weekends; provisions related to custody and visitation to ensure the safety of children living in homes where domestic violence exists; and a number of recommendations related to improved policies by criminal justice professionals. After issuing these emergency recommendations, the task force went on to publish hundreds more in thirty distinct areas of reform.

The Task Force on Domestic Violence Crime then convened a legislative committee to determine which of its proposals merited attention in the 1992 General Assembly.[8] The committee chose four of the task forces' most critical recommendations and proposed them in a package. These four bills would strengthen protections for children living in abusive homes when custody and visitation were under consideration by a court, make significant changes to the civil protective order statute, add self-defense provisions in cases in which battered women killed their abusive husbands, and create the crime of stalking. There were many controversial provisions in this package, but the momentum of the task force and the sense of urgency surrounding these bills helped make the 1992 legislative session so successful (Currens, 2012).

Protecting Child Witnesses to Domestic Violence (1992). The first of the four bills in the package (SB 80) was introduced in the senate and was sponsored by Senator David Karem (Democrat from the Thirty-Fifth District) and David LeMaster (Democrat from the Twenty-Fifth District). It was an overt acknowledgment of the danger to which children are exposed in cases of domestic violence. The bill amended KRS 403.150 to include information related to

Senator David Karem. (Courtesy of the Public Records Division–Kentucky Department for Libraries and Archives)

domestic violence in petitions for the dissolution of marriage or legal separation. It required courts to consider the existence of domestic violence when making custody decisions and determine the extent to which such domestic violence had affected the children. The bill also provided that, if domestic violence had been alleged, any visitation arrangements prescribed by the court must avoid endangering the child's or the custodial parent's physical, mental, or emotional health. SB 80 moved through the senate with relative ease, passing unanimously in the Judiciary Committee and on the floor. Its route through the house was not as easy, but it passed by a vote of sixty-three to twenty-five.

Expanding Protections under the Domestic Violence and Abuse Act (1992). It had been eight years since passage of the Domestic Violence and Abuse Act, and advocates knew the time had come to reform that seminal legislation: more victims needed protection from a broader range of abuse, remedies needed to be expanded, law enforcement officers needed the authority to respond more effectively to violations of protective orders, and the issuance of orders binding victims to the same court orders as offenders was problematic. Solutions to these weaknesses were crafted into HB 115, which was sponsored by task force member Representative Marshall Long and Representative Mark Farrow (Democrat from the Sixty-Second District).

One of HB 115's key reforms was to expand the categories of victims eligible to obtain civil orders of protection to include members of an unmarried couple who were living together or had lived together in the past (a parallel change was made to the state's warrantless arrest law) and to include victims of sexual abuse (by adding that form of victimization to the act's definition of "domestic violence and abuse"). The bill also extended protection to victims who had fled to Kentucky to escape their abusers, eliminating the thirty-day residency requirement for filing a petition for protection. To address the problem of victims being subject to the conditions of protective orders, HB 115 limited a court's ability to issue "mutual orders," allowing them only when a respondent had filed a cross-petition and, following a hearing, a court had made specific findings of domestic violence and abuse. HB 115 also required that protective orders be available twenty-four hours a day, and it expanded what orders a court could impose after a finding of domestic violence and abuse;

this included restraining the respondent from further abuse and other orders to prevent additional abuse (for emergency protective orders and domestic violence orders). HB 115 also added language to the statute that would allow either party to amend a protective order after it had been issued by a court.

A significant portion of HB 115 addressed the role of law enforcement officers in enforcing domestic violence protective orders. Significantly, the bill improved how protective orders were entered into the LINK system following their issuance.[9] HB 115 also required law enforcement agencies to establish written policies to ensure that officers fully complied with their responsibilities under the protective order statute. Critical sections of the bill created the crime of violating a protective order, making it a class A misdemeanor, and it required peace officers who had probable cause to believe that a protective order had been violated to arrest the respondent, without a warrant, for contempt of court.

The provisions relating to the enforcement of violated protective orders created a significant stir in the senate. The bill had passed out of the house unanimously (although eleven representatives did not vote), but it encountered so much opposition in the senate that advocates feared the bill would be lost. The controversy centered around one portion of the legislation, and the critique was raised by one legislator, Senator Walter Baker (Republican from the Ninth District). Baker, a Harvard-trained lawyer, was highly respected by the bench and the bar in Kentucky and by his senate colleagues. He had a reputation as a gentleman scholar and a wise counsel on legal matters.[10] What made his opposition even more difficult for advocates was that he had, ironically, served as a member of the attorney general's task force. Specifically, Baker objected to allowing a peace officer to arrest a person for an act that was not a criminal offense—authority the senator publicly decried as "appalling" (Honeycutt, 1992, p. A9). After a tense standoff with Travis Fritsch outside the senate chamber in the closing hours of the session, a political détente led to a compromise amendment and passage of the bill.[11]

Imminent Danger from the Perspective of Battered Women (1992). Addressing the issue of battered women who kill their violent partners after a history of abuse was an essential part of the task force's legislative package. (See chapter 2 for a more detailed discussion of "victim-precipitated homicides.") The original Penal Code had been written to acknowledge that there are circumstances in which force against another person is justifiable (e.g., when a person believes such force is necessary to protect himself or herself against the use or imminent use of unlawful physical force by the other person). That original law was designed to accommodate self-defense in the traditional sense; as such, it focused on the immediacy of the act and the specific set of circumstances that would lead a reasonable person to believe that his or her life was in danger (e.g., a dangerous person holding a weapon and threatening to kill her or him). Self-defense in the context of domestic violence, however, was more difficult to accommodate in the law because a person's interpretation of current facts might be influenced by past experience. The classic example is a battered woman who shoots her sleeping husband because the pattern of his prior abuse clearly communicates to her that he will kill her when he wakes. Even more challenging than crafting a new statute to incorporate these complexities was convincing reticent legislators that such an accommodation was appropriate. As articulated by one vehemently opposed legislator, "I don't want to give spouses a hunting license to go out and shoot each other. . . . It seems we have enough people killing each other without giving them some limb to hang on that makes it more justifiable" (Senator Walter Baker quoted in Honeycutt, 1992, p. A9).

The task force accepted the legal and political challenge and drafted HB 256, sponsored by task force member Representative Richard H. Lewis (Democrat from the Sixth District). First, the bill amended Kentucky's self-defense statute to define the term *imminent* to mean impending danger and, in the context of domestic violence and abuse, to allow imminent danger to be inferred from a past pattern of repeated serious abuse (KRS 503.010). The addition of that term, in essence, expanded the meaning of self-defense as engaged in by severely battered women. The bill went on to amend the probation and parole statute to exempt a person who has been determined by a court to be a victim of domestic violence or abuse (pursuant to KRS 533.060) from the prohibition on probation, shock probation, or other conditional discharge when a class A, B, or C felony was committed with a weapon. Similarly, the violent offender statute was amended so that a victim of domestic violence or abuse (pursuant to KRS 533.060) was exempt from the requirement that violent offenders serve 50 percent of their sentences prior to consideration for parole. This applied to offenses involving death or serious physical injury; it did not extend to rape or sodomy in the first degree (KRS 439.3401). HB 256's provisions were retroactive, so they applied to persons convicted prior to the effective date of the legislation (July 1992), and the bill set out procedures for such persons to apply for relief under the new law.

Creation of the Crime of Stalking (1992). California's passage of anti-stalking legislation in 1990 started a nationwide movement to design a criminal justice response to this unique crime. (See the discussion in chapter 4.) Within two years of California's pioneering act, almost thirty states had addressed stalking through legislative action (Beatty, 2003), and the task force was intent on making Kentucky one of them.

HB 445, the fourth bill in the legislative package, was sponsored by Representative Richard Lewis. The version of the bill introduced in the house and considered by the Judiciary Committee added a definition for "harass" in a new section of the assault statute, such

Representative Richard Lewis, circa 1989. (Courtesy of the *Lexington Herald-Leader*)

that a course of conduct involving following, harassing, and threatening became the essential elements of stalking; it also created two felony levels and one misdemeanor level of the new crime. The Judiciary Committee amended the bill's construction to mirror more directly the Model Code. (See chapter 4 and Jordan, Quinn, Jordan, & Daileader, 2000, for a discussion of the statutory construction of Kentucky's stalking statute.) It defined "stalking" directly and maintained the three levels of criminal behavior (two felony, one misdemeanor). In an unrelated amendment, the house committee also included a new definition of "sexual contact," which had been requested by prosecutors as a means of addressing abuse that involved fondling over the clothing. The house version of HB 445 passed out of that chamber without any floor debate and without a dissenting vote (ninety to zero). HB 445 was amended in the senate to simplify the levels of the offense to one felony level and one misdemeanor level and to remove the revised definition of sexual contact added by the house. Upon amendment, the bill passed out of the senate by a vote of twenty-seven to zero, and the house subsequently agreed to the final version.

Attorney General's Task Force on Child Sexual Abuse

As Cowan's Task Force on Domestic Violence Crime was finalizing its work, his successor, Attorney General Chris Gorman, made two important decisions. First, he would allow the task force's work to continue through the 1992 General Assembly, even though Cowan's term had already ended; second, he would convene a task force of his own. Specifically, in April 1992, Gorman created a task force to "restore accountability to a criminal justice system that has frequently failed children" (Office of the Kentucky Attorney General, 1995, p. 1). The findings and legislative proposals of the Attorney General's Task Force on Child Sexual Abuse are summarized here because many of its bills impacted adult victims of criminal sexual offenses as well.

The Task Force on Child Sexual Abuse was, in part, a governmental response to a group of stories published by the *Lexington Herald-Leader* in December 1991, aptly titled the "Twice Abused" series.[12] Its membership represented survivors, advocates, justice professionals, health and mental health care professionals, and legislators. (See appendix C for a complete membership list.) After extensive work over a two-year period, the task force published more than a hundred recommendations, two-thirds of which would require legislative action to implement. The task force prioritized its goals and incorporated twenty-eight of its recommendations into fourteen legislative proposals that it submitted to the Kentucky General Assembly. Among the proposals that passed the General Assembly and impacted both child and adult victims were the establishment of a sex offender registry and other provisions related to risk assessment and the treatment of offenders, mandates for professional licensure boards to improve their response to sexual misconduct by professionals, legislation to permit prosecutors to employ victim advocates, and an expansion in the types of mental health professionals whose services would be reimbursed by insurance companies. (The remainder of the bills addressed state and local multidisciplinary teams, statutory definitions of incest, and the prevention of child abuse.)

Registration of Convicted Sex Offenders (1994). In the early 1990s the Kentucky Coalition against Rape and Sexual Assault began to explore programs that would expand the tools available to law enforcement officers who investigated sex crimes. Among the options studied by the coalition was the creation of a registry containing the location of and other information about persons convicted of certain sexual offenses. By 1992, sixteen states had established registries precisely for this purpose, but an effort to pass such a law in Kentucky that year did not succeed (HB 546 died in the senate Judiciary Committee). By 1994, the congressional response to the kidnapping of a young boy in Minnesota would give new momentum to the idea of sex offender registries and would influence the recommendations of the Task Force on Child Sexual Abuse.

On October 22, 1989, eleven-year-old Jacob Wetterling, his younger brother Trevor, and their friend Aaron were riding their bicycles home from the video store when a masked gunman approached the three boys and ordered them to throw their bikes into a ditch and lie down on the ground. After asking their ages, the gunman instructed Trevor and Aaron to run away, threatening to shoot them if they looked back. By the time the two boys were far enough away that they felt it was safe to turn back toward the ditch, Jacob and the masked man were gone. Jacob's whereabouts and the identity of the gunman remain a terrible mystery to this day (Johnson, 1990). Following Jacob's abduction, his parents Patty and Jerry became advocates for the creation of state sex offender registries across the country, and in 1994 Congress passed the federal Jacob Wetterling Crimes Against Children and Sexually Violent Offender Registration Act.[13] It was the first federal law to require states to create sex offender registries, and it provided the motivation Kentucky needed to act in kind.

Legislative reform is often a unique combination of substantive need and the luck of timing, and this was the case with the effort to create a sex offender registry in Kentucky. As the Task Force on Child Sexual Abuse was deliberating, the Kentucky State Police received a telephone call from an individual inquiring whether Kentucky had a sex offender registry. The caller was the parent of a convicted sex offender and was canvassing surrounding states to find one without a registry so that the offending son could move there.[14] When task force cochair Kim Allen learned about the phone call, her response received widespread media coverage: "There are a lot of things we want Kentucky to be known for, but being a safe haven for sex offenders is not one of them" (Allen, 2012). This provided the necessary momentum to include a sex offender registry in the task force's legislative package. The sponsor of SB 43 was Senator Jeffrey R. Green (Democrat from the First District in far western Kentucky). Green had been appointed to the task force during his first year as a senator, and he would become one of the champions of the domestic violence and anti-rape movements during his short time in the legislature.

The legislation limited access to registry data to law enforcement officers, and it applied only to sex offenders who had committed the felonies of rape, sodomy, or sexual abuse in the first degree; incest; unlawful transaction with a minor; or use of a minor in a sexual performance. As the bill progressed through the legislative process, members of the house Judiciary Committee, particularly those who were also defense lawyers, raised the concern that the legislation was too burdensome with regard to persons convicted of certain crimes. During testimony, one committee member unexpectedly proposed an amendment such that the law would apply only to offenders who committed their offenses after the effective date of the act. The committee chair asked Senator Green, the bill's sponsor, whether he believed the amendment to be "friendly"—that is, whether he supported the amendment. It was one of those difficult moments when a bill's sponsor looks to the advocate to ask what to do. In this case, the advocate, Kim Allen, used good instincts and agreed to the amendment. She knew that the Judiciary Committee regularly blocked the retroactive application of new penalties to persons already convicted of an offense. Additionally, allowing the amendment served as a compromise that stilled any further opposition. In the end, SB 43 passed out of the senate and house without a dissenting vote.

Subsequent to the 1994 legislative session, the sex offender registry statute was substantially amended to expand the types of offenders included in the registry, to allow public access to registry information, and to provide for public notification of the release of sex offenders.

Addressing Sexual Misconduct by Certified and Licensed Professionals (1994). As the Task Force on Child Sexual Abuse worked, some of us focused on how to make mental health services more accessible to child victims, adult victims, and adult survivors of sexual abuse and how to expand specialized assessment of and treatment services for sex offenders. During the course of information gathering, the task force heard testimony on misconduct by health and mental health care professionals who should have been serving this vulnerable population of clients and patients. In response, the task force proposed legislation to strengthen the role of licensure boards in responding to and preventing sexual misconduct by professionals. Specifically, the task force proposed SB 107, sponsored by Senator Gerald A. Neal (Democrat from the Thirty-Third District), and HB 115, sponsored by Representatives Robert R. Damron (Democrat from the Thirty-Ninth District), Bill Lile (Republican from the Twenty-Eighth District), and Tommy Todd (Republican from the Eighty-Third District), to require professional licensure boards for physicians, nurses, chiropractors, psychologists, social workers, and educators to develop guidelines to improve investigation, inquiry, and hearing procedures for sexual misconduct cases involving professionals licensed or certified by them.

The legislation also stipulated that if a licensure board could substantiate that sexual contact had occurred between a professional and a client, patient, or student while the person was under the care of that professional, then such a finding was grounds for revocation of the professional's license or certificate. Revocation was also allowed if a board learned that a professional under its auspices had committed certain felony sexual offenses involving a client, patient, or student. The legislation also required training for all the named licensure boards. Both bills passed in both chambers without any negative votes, although in the house, roughly fifteen legislators did not vote.[15]

Victim Advocates in the Offices of Commonwealth's Attorneys and County Attorneys (1994). Today, victims of crime whose cases are being prosecuted by county attorneys or Commonwealth's attorneys are routinely supported by victim advocates located in those offices. Prior to 1994, however, prosecutor-based victim advocates were not available statewide; they could be found only in select prosecutors' offices where the prosecutor was personally committed to victim advocacy and where the budget could pay for specialized staff (e.g., the office of the Fayette County Commonwealth's attorney). Legislation proposed by the Task Force on Child Sexual Abuse changed that. HB 95, sponsored by Representative Paul Mason (Democrat from the Ninety-First District), authorized Commonwealth's and county attorneys to employ at least one victim advocate in their offices.[16] The bill set forth education, training, and

Representative Paul Mason in the Health and Welfare Committee, circa 1994. (Author's personal collection)

experiential qualifications and job descriptions for victim advocates. To address concerns raised during testimony on HB 95, its language was amended to specifically prohibit victim advocates from engaging in political activities while performing their duties or to engage in the practice of law. (In addition to provisions related to victim advocates, HB 95 addressed the participation of prosecutors on multidisciplinary teams for child sexual abuse cases and the collection of data related to the prosecution of such cases.)

Assessment of Sex Offenders (1994). In addition to recommending the creation of a sex offender registry, task force members believed that the effective management of sex offenders required changes at the point of their release from prison. To accomplish that goal, the task force offered HB 96, which was sponsored by Representatives Bob Damron (Democrat from the Thirty-Ninth District), Bill Lile (Republican from the Twenty-Eighth District), and Tommy Todd (Republican from the Eighty-Third District). This legislation specifically prohibited the probation or shock probation of the most serious sex offenders (those convicted of class A, B, or C felonies) and required court-ordered mental health evaluations of any class D felon being considered for probation or shock probation. HB 96 also stipulated that if a court chose to suspend a sex offender's sentence, then outpatient treatment would be a mandatory condition of probation. It also required that specialized assessments of sex offenders be part of the presentence investigations conducted by the Department of Corrections. The bill required that all specialized mental health assessments be conducted by trained professionals through the Sex Offender Treatment Program operated by the Department of Corrections (a program created during the 1986 legislative session) or by a provider approved by the Department of Corrections or the Department for Mental Health and Mental Retardation Services.

HB 96 passed out of the house with no dissenting votes, but the bill's journey was more complicated in the senate, where it was assigned to the Judiciary Committee, chaired by Senator Kelsey E. Friend (Democrat from the Thirty-First District). Friend was a seemingly unapproachable man with the air of a stern father figure, and he ruled his committee with an iron hand. As described in chapter 5, with the aid of a friend in the senate, I had been introduced to Friend, and he had agreed to place HB 96 on his committee's agenda, a move that generally meant he supported the bill and

Senator Kelsey Friend at his desk on the senate floor, circa 1984. (Courtesy of the Public Records Division–Kentucky Department for Libraries and Archives)

believed it would pass. I spent the next several days working each member of the Judiciary Committee, ensuring that I had a majority of votes in hand.

The day of the hearing for HB 96 came late in the session, and the halls of the capitol annex were filled with anxious legislators and apprehensive lobbyists who were fearful that the session would end before their bills were heard and passed. For legislators, advocates, and lobbyists whose bills were in the senate's Judiciary Committee, the tension was particularly palpable, as this was its last scheduled meeting of the session. Among those feeling the clock ticking down were proponents of measures to restrict abortion rights in Kentucky. This lobbying group's efforts had been bottled up in the Judiciary Committee the previous session, and all signs pointed to a repeat of that outcome in 1994. Adding to the drama was the fact that pro-life forces had taken to wearing buttons sporting the words "Protect Women," a maneuver that apparently reflected their view that our legislation tended to pass, but it offended many domestic violence and anti-rape advocates who did not support the pro-life groups' efforts. As a result, the Judiciary Committee's small meeting room was thick with tension—and packed with button-wearing supporters of the abortion legislation—when Chairman Friend called HB 96 as the next item on the agenda.

Since it was common practice for the Judiciary Committee to hear only those bills that already had members' support, testimony on any given piece of legislation generally did not last long. With that prior experience in mind, and having the support of the chairman and what I believed to be the majority of the committee members, I anticipated only a brief discussion as I joined our sponsor, Representative Damron, at the testimony table. What we did not know was that the committee had privately decided to draw out the questioning on HB 96 to take up time, thus avoiding a hearing on the abortion legislation. As the senators' questions continued, one after another, and the minutes passed, I could only respond to their inquiries and wonder why things had taken such a bad turn. To heighten my anxiety and perplexity, one of the senators who had voiced strong support of the bill just the day before suddenly switched his position, ditching his support of rehabilitation and espousing an extreme "tough on crime" approach that would send all sex offenders to prison indefinitely. It was at that point in the testimony that I realized what was happening: that particular senator was playing to the audience of pro-life lobbyists and supporters, whom I could hear rustling in their seats behind me, and the committee as a whole was simply attempting to draw out the testimony and end the hearing.

As I left the committee room after what turned out to be a successful hearing on HB 96, I heard the surreal sound of "Happy Birthday" being sung to the committee chair by the (unsuccessful) pro-life supporters.

Accessibility of Mental Health Services for Victims (1994). The attorney general's task force was particularly concerned with increasing the accessibility of mental health services for victims of rape and other forms of sexual assault. At the time, few resources existed, particularly in the rural areas of the Commonwealth. HB 514, sponsored by Representatives Jesse Crenshaw (Democrat from the Seventy-Seventh District), Bob Damron (Democrat from the Thirty-Ninth District), E. Porter Hatcher Jr. (Democrat from the Forty-Third District), and Paul Mason (Democrat from the Ninety-First District), was an innovative approach to increased accessibility. At the time of the bill's introduction, insurance companies generally reimbursed covered parties only for mental health care services that had been provided by psychiatrists. Testimony before the task force had emphasized the limited number of psychiatrists in the state and the small percentage of clinicians within that profession who specialized in providing services to sexual assault victims. The remedy contained in HB 514 was to require any individual, group, or blanket health insurance policy and any health maintenance organization that covered mental health care to reimburse for services provided by licensed psychologists and licensed clinical social workers, in addition to psychiatrists.

HB 514 was a controversial bill that garnered the immediate opposition of insurance companies, a relatively powerful lobbyist group. However, we gathered a strong coalition of supporters, particularly the Kentucky Psychological Association and the Kentucky chapter of the National Association of Social Workers, both of which joined me in testifying on the bill. Our joint effort ultimately succeeded in securing its passage by a vote of eighty-seven to six in the house and thirty-eight to zero in the senate.

Legislative Task Force on Domestic Violence

In September 1994 the leadership of the Kentucky General Assembly publicly announced the creation of the decade's second task force on domestic violence. Planning and strategizing had actually begun weeks earlier in Lexington, when a group of well-known domestic violence advocates gathered in the conference room of a local hotel.[17] We were momentarily transfixed by newspaper accounts of a case in which a victim of domestic violence had been murdered, but we quickly turned our attention to the hunt for answers. The walls of the room were soon papered with creative ideas and possible solutions, and we set about brainstorming how to transform those ideas into legislative action. We explored who had the best contacts to facilitate the creation of a task force by the Kentucky General Assembly. The group decided to approach a long-standing supporter of the movement—Senator Michael Moloney—and asked me to follow up. Never one to let the proverbial grass grow under his feet, and always looking to improve the justice system, Senator Moloney immediately took the group's idea of a task force and a list of suggested names to the General Assembly's leadership.[18] On September 26, 1994, the Legislative Task Force on Domestic Violence was publicly announced. This unusually quick movement was emblematic of

Senator Jeffrey R. Green (left) and Representative Leonard Gray cochairing a meeting of the Legislative Task Force on Domestic Violence, 1994. (Author's personal collection)

the advocates' impatience to make change happen and the General Assembly's responsiveness during the 1990s.

The legislative task force was cochaired by Senator Jeffrey R. Green (Democrat from the First District) and Representative Leonard Gray (Democrat from the Forty-Second District).[19] Not unlike the task forces that preceded it, its members included advocates and representatives from the legislature, the judiciary, prosecution, law enforcement, social and protective services, mental health, victim services, and court administration. (See appendix C for a complete list.) The task force held thirteen meetings from its creation through October 1995, concluding its work by voting on sixteen recommendations.

The task force was a high-profile undertaking, with public figures from both national and state governments offering testimony. Among the national figures was U.S. Attorney General Janet Reno, who offered remarks on the Violence Against Women Act (VAWA), which had just been signed into law by President Bill Clinton.[20] Reno touted Kentucky's commitment to women, as evidenced by its attention to the crime of domestic violence. In the midst of her testimony, cochair Jeff Green offered the Commonwealth as a "laboratory" for the development of a model response to the full faith and credit provisions of VAWA (see below). Sherry Currens, executive director of the Kentucky Domestic Violence Association (KDVA), and I had prompted and prepared Green to make that offer to Reno. Her positive response led to the preparation of a federal grant proposal to the U.S. Department of Justice; that grant was ultimately awarded, and a program called Project Passport was implemented under the leadership of the KDVA.

Through legislation proposed by the task force, protective orders would be enforced across state lines, a victim notification system would be implemented, higher education would become a tool to address violence against women, the role of victim advocates would be formalized, and domestic violence training for professionals would be bolstered.

Civil Protection Twenty-Four Hours a Day and across State Lines (1996). Passage of the federal Violence Against Women Act (Title IV, §§ 40001–40703, of the Violent Crime Control and Law Enforcement Act) in 1994 made it clear that addressing domestic violence and rape was a national responsibility. Among the key provisions of the act was the addition of language giving "full faith and credit" to domestic violence protective orders. Simply speaking, the provision meant that orders issued in one state would be enforceable in other states to which a victim might travel, move, or flee. In Kentucky, which is bordered by seven other states, this was critical. The task force believed that implementing the full faith and credit provisions of VAWA would require procedural language in Kentucky's Domestic Violence and Abuse Act. To that end, SB 105 was proposed and sponsored by Senator Jeff Green. Senator Michael Moloney, who had sponsored the original 1984 legislation that created the Domestic Violence and Abuse Act, was an active consultant in drafting and managing the legislation. From the advocate side, Sherry Currens took the lead in working with the Legislative Research Commission to draft and staff the bill. SB 105 established a process for authenticating out-of-state domestic violence protective orders, and it required protective orders issued in Kentucky to certify that the issuing court had jurisdiction over the parties when the order was granted. This latter provision was intended to ensure

Senator Jeffrey R. Green announcing the task force's legislative package on the senate floor, January 1996. (Author's personal collection)

Sherry Currens speaking to a group that includes Governor Paul Patton, Judge Peter Macdonald, First Lady Judi Patton, and Carol Jordan, March 9, 1998. (Author's personal collection)

that when Kentucky victims fled to another state, that state would enforce the Kentucky order.

SB 105 made other changes to Kentucky's Domestic Violence and Abuse Act. To aid in entering protective orders into LINK, the bill required the use of standardized forms created by the Administrative Office of the Courts for the issuance of protective orders. It also lengthened the duration of protective orders from one year to three and allowed the reissuance of protective orders an unlimited number of times without requiring a violation of the existing order. To many judges, reissuing a protective order when there had been no violence was counterintuitive, in that no violation meant the order was not needed. We advocates believed the opposite was true: no violation meant the order was working and should be extended without requiring the victim to suffer additional violence. SB 105 also required district and circuit courts to establish local protocols to ensure that protective orders could be obtained twenty-four hours a day, and it addressed how joint jurisdiction between the two courts would be managed. Finally, SB 105 prohibited the use of mediation in domestic violence cases, except at the request of the victim, when a court found that the victim's request was voluntary and not the result of coercion, and when mediation was a realistic and viable alternative or adjunct to the issuance of a protective order.

SB 105 was amended during the legislative process, but it garnered wide support from the 1996 General Assembly.[21] Although the bill passed through the senate with no opposition, a well-meaning senator created some discomfort for advocates. He filed a floor amendment that would add violation of a protective order to the list of aggravators in death penalty cases. In other words, if an offender committed certain felony offenses against a victim while a protective order was in place, then the death penalty could be in play. As a general rule, domestic violence advocates support any amendment that requires a strict response from the justice system, but some advocates vehemently oppose capital punishment. Our unwillingness to support this amendment caused its sponsor significant frustration.[22]

There was also some drama on the house side. There, one legislator stood on the house floor to express his opposition to the bill. (His was the sole vote against it.) The legislator, touching the U.S. Constitution he always carried in his front pocket, expressed his fear of enforcing protective orders from "foreign" countries, apparently misunderstanding that "foreign protective orders" were those issued by the courts of other states or territories of the United States, not orders from other countries.

The First Statewide Automated Victim Notification System (1996). Chapter 5 told the story of Mary Byron and how her violent death inspired the creation of an innovative system to notify crime victims when offenders were released from the Jefferson County correctional system. Mary's parents, Pat and John Byron; Judge David Armstrong; and Mike Davis and Yung Nguyen, the founders of a small computer firm called Interactive Systems Inc., unveiled the Victim Information and Notification Everyday (VINE) system exactly one year after Mary's murder.

Marcia Roth, director of the Jefferson County Office for Women, easily convinced the task force that VINE's life-saving features were good not just for Jefferson County but for the entire Commonwealth. To accomplish the statewide expansion of this victim notification system, two steps were needed: passage of enacting legislation, and funding from the state budget. Senator Jeff Green sponsored

Mary Byron's mother, Pat (bottom left), celebrates passage of SB 108 from the senate gallery, March 8, 1996. Behind her are Carol Jordan (giving the thumbs up) and Sherry Currens. (Courtesy of the *Louisville Courier-Journal*)

SB 108, which established what would become the nation's first statewide computerized victim notification system. It required the Department of Corrections to create the system, and it required jails and detention facilities to provide information on the release of offenders to the department. The bill essentially gave victims the right to be notified of an offender's release from prison or jail. During the legislative process, two major amendments were added to the bill: one to provide immunity to jailers who acted in good faith to notify victims (i.e., they could not be sued if a good-faith attempt to notify a victim was unsuccessful), and a second to extend notification to the victims of juvenile offenders who had committed violent felonies. The VINE legislation was passed unanimously by the 1996 General Assembly.

The next step was to secure state funding for the program. Just one year earlier, the Jefferson County government had taken the unprecedented step of giving $100,000 to the state to support the expansion of VINE. As Governor Brereton Jones accepted that

Governor Paul Patton and Judge David Armstrong at the public announcement of VINE. Behind them are (left to right) Secretary of the Cabinet for Health Services John Morse, First Lady Judi Patton, Lieutenant Governor Steve Henry, Senator Jeff Green, Pat Byron, and John Byron. (Courtesy of Creative Services, Office of the Kentucky Governor)

check from Judge Armstrong at a press conference, he quipped that while he was very accustomed to giving state funds to counties, this was the first time he could recall a county giving money to the state. Governor Jones pledged to use the $100,000 toward the creation of a statewide victim notification system, but full funding would not be obtained until after the election of a new governor.

As the 1996 legislative session began, Governor Paul Patton was giving speeches to audiences across the state about the "structurally imbalanced" budget he faced, and he vowed that no new state general fund dollars would be made available in his executive branch budget proposal. On January 16, 1996, I had the opportunity to meet with Governor Patton and First Lady Judi Patton to describe the task force's entire legislative package. At the beginning of the meeting, I told the governor that I hoped to secure his support for all our legislation, and I asked for his permission to state publicly that he endorsed the package. Patton was quick to agree to both. Then came the time to address funding for the VINE legislation, and all I could hear were the words "structurally imbalanced" ringing in my ears. When I asked for the governor's financial support, he smiled and started to respond, only to have Mrs. Patton quickly say that "of course" he would add the item to the budget. That unexpected voice was just the opening act of the first lady's substantial platform on child abuse, domestic violence, and rape during her husband's administration, and it resulted in funding for the VINE legislation.[23]

Building a University Response to Violence against Women (1996). Arguably, the primary focus of the legislative task force's package was improving the civil and criminal justice system on behalf of women facing domestic violence: it was intended to expand existing protections in the law and create new ones. Senate Resolution 47, however, offered something different. In short, the resolution urged Kentucky's public universities to include curricula addressing domestic violence and child sexual abuse for undergraduate and graduate students in psychology, social work, counseling, law, and medical programs. Senator Jeff Green was joined by nineteen other senators in sponsoring the resolution.

Strengthening the State's Response to Domestic Violence (1996). HB 309 reflected the task force's desire to elevate the working knowledge of professionals in the Commonwealth. The bill established training requirements for licensed and certified health and mental health professionals, social workers in the Cabinet for Human Resources (now the Cabinet for Health and Family Services), staff in domestic violence programs, prosecutors, and law enforcement officers[24] on the dynamics of domestic violence, the effects of domestic violence on adult and child victims, legal remedies for protection, lethality and risk issues, model protocols for addressing domestic violence, community resources and victim services, and mandated reporting requirements. The bill also required the Justice Cabinet, the Office of the Attorney General, the Administrative Office of the Courts, and the Cabinet for Human Resources to develop appropriate training curricula for the professions under their auspices and to ensure the quality and consistency of training provided to all relevant professionals.

The task force was able to target health, mental health, and criminal justice professionals through statutory changes because their licensure and oversight were controlled by the executive branch of government. We could not manage judicial education the same way, however. To ensure that judges and clerks were included in the mandatory training requirements, I sought the assistance of Chief Justice Robert Stephens, who, through comity,[25] agreed that the Kentucky Supreme Court would implement court rules related to the training of court personnel.

HB 309 also required the Cabinet for Human Resources to establish certification standards for mental health professionals who provide court-ordered services to domestic violence offenders. Before proposing this portion of the bill, I conducted a survey of therapists working in community mental health centers, seeking information about how they provided such services. The results were disturbing: almost half had no set standards of care, 20 percent did not assess homicide or suicide risk, 13 percent did not assess the protective needs of victims, almost 30 percent had no contact at all with the victims of the offenders they were treating, and the therapists were using twenty-five different assessment tools. HB 309 set out to remedy the inconsistency and ineffectiveness of the mental health care provided to these offenders. The bill laid out standards of care based on three principles: that domestic violence is a pattern of coercive control that constitutes criminal conduct; that the primary goal of treatment programs is the cessation of domestic violence to ensure the safety of victims and their children; and that domestic violence offenders are responsible and accountable for the violence they perpetrate. HB 309 created an application process for mental health professionals wishing to obtain certification from the Cabinet for Human Resources to allow them to accept court referrals to assess and treat domestic violence offenders.

Finally, HB 309 required the Kentucky attorney general to develop a manual for Commonwealth's and county attorneys related to the prosecution of domestic violence–related crimes.

HB 309 was sponsored by Representative Stephen R. Nunn (Republican from the Twenty-Third District) and was cosponsored by Paul Mason (Democrat from the Ninety-First District), Michael D. Bowling (Democrat from the Eighty-Seventh District), Thomas J. Burch (Democrat from the Thirtieth District), Mary Lou Marzian (Democrat from the Thirty-Fourth District), Ruth Ann Palumbo (Democrat from the Seventy-Sixth District), and Ernesto Scorsone (Democrat from the Seventy-Fifth District). It passed in the House by a vote of ninety to one and in the senate by a vote of thirty-seven to zero.

Strengthening the Criminal Justice Response to Domestic Violence (1996). For the first two decades of reform, domestic violence advocates prioritized funding to make shelter available and provide civil protections for battered women. Criminal remedies did not become a primary focus until later (the exceptions being warrantless arrest powers in 1980, creation of the crime of stalking in 1992, and amendments to the violent offender act in 1992). The legislative task force chose to put reforms to the criminal justice system back on the front burner by proposing HB 310.

The primary sponsor of HB 310 was Representative Mike Bowling (Democrat from the Eighty-Seventh District), along with fourteen cosponsors.[26] Bowling, who was serving his first term as chair of the house Judiciary Committee, had served on the task force and considered his sponsorship of the bill a natural outgrowth of his role as a public servant. What he did not anticipate was the opposition he encountered when trying to toughen the law for battered women. In his words, "If we'd have been trying to pass this stuff in California, it would have sailed through, but here in Kentucky we had our work cut out for us. I never met so many men who believed that women were going to lie about them" (Bowling, 2012).

The criminal reforms proposed by HB 310 included harsher penalties for domestic violence offenders. This effort was viewed as particularly important because these offenders often committed multiple and repeated offenses that were usually prosecuted at the misdemeanor level. For the prosecution of felony cases, Kentucky law had several provisions that addressed the severity of crimes that occurred on a repeated basis—most notably, KRS 532.055 (the so-called truth-in-sentencing provision) and KRS 532.080 (the persistent felony offender provision). These provisions, however, did not apply to the prosecution of misdemeanor domestic violence cases. Yet, by their recidivistic and patterned nature, these crimes inflicted severe harm on victims. To address this inadequacy in the law, HB 310 provided a penalty enhancement for third and subsequent fourth-degree assaults committed against family members or members of an unmarried couple as defined in KRS Chapter 403. (The bill originally sought the penalty enhancement after the second assault, but that was revised during the committee hearing process.) In cases of harassment involving strikes, shoves, kicks or other physical contact between the victim and the offender, the bill increased the crime from a violation to a class B misdemeanor.

HB 310 expanded the types of peace officers who can carry out warrantless arrests. In addition, it removed the requirement that a peace officer predict whether a person presents a future danger before making a warrantless arrest.

The task force also had a keen interest in statutory measures to improve victim safety immediately following the arrest of a domestic violence offender. Stories from victims illustrated the real danger they were exposed to when angry and vengeful offenders were quickly released after an arrest. The first proposal considered by the task force seemed utterly reasonable and effective, but it quickly drew the ire of defense lawyers, who reacted as if we were recommending a life sentence for a misdemeanor. The proposal would have instituted a twenty-four-hour holding period following the arrest of a domestic violence offender—a cooling-off period that would allow victims an opportunity to seek safety. The reaction to the proposal was so negative that it was excluded from the final version of HB 310. Our backup plan was to target the point at which a court was deciding whether to release a person who had been arrested for a crime covered by KRS Chapter 508 (e.g., assault or stalking) or KRS Chapter 510 (e.g., rape or sodomy). The bill required the court to review the facts of the arrest and determine whether the person would be a threat to the victim and whether the offender was reasonably likely to appear in court for trial. The court could then impose one or more conditions of bail or release, including issuing a no-contact order, enjoining the offender from committing further acts of violence or threatening to do so, requiring the offender to vacate a shared residence, prohibiting gun possession or the possession or consumption of alcohol or controlled substances, or any other conditions necessary to protect the safety of the victim and ensure the offender's appearance in court. HB 310 required any peace officer with probable cause to believe that a person had violated a condition of release to effect a warrantless arrest, and it made the violation of bond conditions a class A misdemeanor.

Finally, in recognition of the danger posed to social workers investigating domestic violence cases, HB 310 amended KRS 508.025 to expand assault in the third degree to include employees of the Department for Social Services who are assaulted while carrying out their duties. It further amended the statute to define assault in the third degree as intentional conduct that does not include a deadly weapon or dangerous instrument.

Governor Paul Patton signs HB 310 as Representative Mike Bowling (at the podium) and task force members watch and applaud, 1996. (Author's personal collection)

HB 310 would ultimately pass in both the house and the senate by wide margins (eighty-three to two in the house, and thirty-seven to zero in the senate), but these overwhelming majorities did not reflect the experience of those of us who worked on the bill. Outside the public view, we encountered significant pushback, and some legislators expressed reluctance to support HB 310 because they saw it as "special legislation" that treated domestic violence cases differently from other assaults. There was general concern that the bill's statutory provisions would harm the structure of the Penal Code, and a few legislators were opposed, on principle, to penalty enhancements. One house member was vehemently opposed to the bill on these grounds, and task force member and prosecutor Jerry Bowles attempted to speak to this legislator before the bill's hearing. When Bowles handed him a copy of the bill, hoping to explain its provisions, the legislator actually threw it back at him, leading Bowles to lean toward the advocate standing next to him and whisper, "Hmm, that didn't go so well" (Bowles, 2012). The legislator abstained when the bill was voted on in committee.

Formalizing the Role of Victim Advocates in the Criminal Justice System (1996). The final bill proposed by the legislative task force was designed to empower victim advocates who helped victims as they maneuvered through the justice system. HB 315 was sponsored by Representative Paul Mason, an extension of the victim advocate legislation he had sponsored in 1994 (HB 95); it was cosponsored by eight other representatives.[27]

During hearings held by the task force, advocates had testified about being required to leave court proceedings, which diminished their ability to support victims at a crucial time. As a result, HB 315 provided that victim advocates could accompany victims during court proceedings. It also strengthened the training requirements for victim advocates and specified that their training include the topic of domestic violence. Finally, the bill amended the Kentucky Rules of Evidence (KRS 422A.0506; KRE 506) to add victim advocates to the counselor-client privilege.

As HB 315 progressed through the legislative process, there were two points of contention. The first was expressed by legislators who were also attorneys; they were concerned that authorizing advocates to accompany victims into court proceedings was tantamount to allowing them to practice law. As a result, the bill was amended to specify that victim advocates could not provide legal advice or counsel to crime victims for whom they were advocating. The second point of contention was raised by prosecutors, who did not want the privileged communication provisions to apply to victim advocates working in their offices. They reasoned that whatever information a victim shared with her advocates had to be shared with the prosecutor and, upon the discretion of the prosecutor, might be used in court. As a result, the bill was also amended to exempt prosecutor-based victim advocates from the counselor-client privilege.

The end of the 1996 legislative session brought celebration and a brief pause that allowed us to relish everything our task force had accomplished. Our celebration was short-lived, however, for in September 1997, advocates and the Commonwealth would be shocked by the death of Senator Jeff Green.

Green had become a state senator in 1992, and he could have

chosen to lend his name to any cause. For him, that cause was the protection of women and children. I first met Jeff when he was named to the Attorney General's Task Force on Child Sexual Abuse. During the 1994 session of the General Assembly, he sponsored much of the key legislation proposed by that task force, including the controversial bill to allow the testimony of child victims to be videotaped for use in court, rather than requiring the child to testify in front of the offender. I worked diligently to secure votes for the bill, but on the day of its hearing in the house Judiciary Committee, my count told me we had insufficient votes for passage. I broke the news to Jeff that morning and told him which legislators were likely to vote against the bill. When he arrived at the hearing room, the meeting had already begun. One by one, he asked those legislators to step down from their seats and follow him to the back of the room for a chat. I can only imagine what Jeff said to them. He was a charismatic and charming man, but he could be a fiery opponent when he cared deeply about an issue. Perhaps he cajoled or teased; maybe he inspired or pushed. But one way or another, he changed some votes that day, and the bill passed. So when he was appointed cochair of the Legislative Task Force on Domestic Violence in 1994, that was great news to all of us.

In 1997 we lost one of our greatest champions. Jeff was a remarkable man in his public life and in his family life. He had a remarkable way of making the battles against domestic violence and child abuse seem winnable. He used his talents, his sense of humor, his unwavering energy, and his dogged determination to make us all believe we could end violence against women and children in Kentucky. He finds his rightful and honorable place in this book.

Legislation Proposed by the Governor's Office

The Governor's Office of Child Abuse and Domestic Violence Services (1998). In 1996 Governor Paul E. Patton first established the Governor's Office of Child Abuse and Domestic Violence Services to ensure that his administration prioritized the issues of domestic violence, rape, and child maltreatment. By its second anniversary, the success of the office was clear, and the governor wanted to make it a permanent part of the state government through SB 274, which was sponsored by Senator David K. Karem (Democrat from the Thirty-Fifth District). The bill established the office in

Governor Paul Patton signs SB 274 on April 13, 1998. Standing behind him, from left to right, are First Lady Judi Patton, Marie Abrams, Lisa Beran, Kim Allen, Marigail Sexton, Jill Seyfred, Karen Quinn, and Carol Jordan. (Author's personal collection)

Kentucky statute, set out its duties, and named the first lady of the Commonwealth its special adviser.[28]

Protecting Children from Domestic Violence (1998). Among the priorities of Governor and Mrs. Patton was advancing the protection of children. To pursue this interest, the Pattons relied on Viola Miller, secretary of the Cabinet for Human Resources, and Representative Tom Burch (Democrat from the Thirtieth District), a staunch defender of children's rights. From their collaboration came HB 142.

HB 142 was intended to make substantial and enduring changes to Kentucky's child protection statute, particularly with regard to court decisions about the best interests of a child and the termination of parental rights. At the time, KRS Chapter 620 stipulated that, in order to remove a child by means of an emergency custody order, the child had to be in danger of imminent death or serious physical injury or experiencing sexual abuse. That language set the standard so high that a child might suffer extreme harm before child protective services was authorized by law to act. HB 142 strengthened the courts' ability to remove a child from extremely dangerous circumstances. In addition, the language authorizing a court to place a child with a relative was amended to require consideration of the child's wishes.

HB 142 also added a new section to the child protection statute to guide courts when rendering decisions about a child's best interest. It enumerated six standards for the court to consider: any mental illness that would render a parent unable to care for the immediate and ongoing needs of a child; the presence of abuse or neglect; alcohol or other drug abuse that results in the parent's incapacity to care for or protect the child; the existence of any guardianship or conservatorship of a parent; a finding of domestic violence and abuse in the child's home, regardless whether the child was witness to it; and any other crime committed by a parent that results in the permanent physical or mental disability of a member of that parent's family or household. The bill also addressed the timing and adequacy of permanency plans in child protection cases.

The section of the child protection statute relating to the termination of parental rights was also substantially strengthened by HB 142. A year earlier, the Cabinet for Human Resources had been stymied from petitioning for termination of the parental rights of a father who had killed his child and been incarcerated for that crime. The existing law required that prior to termination, the child who was the subject of the petition had to be abused or neglected. In the case described here, that essentially meant that until the father was released from prison and abused or neglected his murdered child's sibling, his parental rights remained intact. To tighten the law, HB 142 allowed a circuit court to terminate a person's parental rights based on the pleadings and by clear and convincing evidence that the child named in the petition has been abused or neglected; the parent has been convicted of a criminal charge relating to the physical or sexual abuse or neglect of any child; that physical or sexual abuse, neglect, or emotional injury to the child named in the petition is likely to occur again if parental rights are not terminated; and termination is in the best interest of the child.

Legislation to protect children was usually embraced by the

Representative Tom Burch chairing the Health and Welfare Committee, November 2007. (Courtesy of the Legislative Research Commission)

General Assembly, but that was not the case with HB 142. For some legislators, the problem was a clash of parental rights versus child protection. The bill was first heard in the house by the Health and Welfare Committee, where it was amended and resubmitted to the committee for further amendment. It was then recommitted to the Judiciary Committee and voted out as another committee substitute. By the time HB 142 reached the floor of the house, thirteen floor amendments had been filed. Some of these compromises and floor amendments addressed the concerns of conservative legislators that the definition of "emotional injury" was not measurable or adequately defined; the sponsor therefore agreed to add language stipulating that a qualified mental health professional had to testify to the presence of emotional injury. Significant concern was also raised about parents' right to discipline their children, so the sponsor agreed to clarify that physical or emotional injury to the child "shall not include reasonable and ordinary discipline recognized in the community where the child lives" (KRS 620.060). Amendments to HB 142 also made it a class A misdemeanor for anyone to knowingly and with malice make a false report of child abuse or neglect.

Although HB 142 was introduced on January 6, the full house did not vote on it until February 19, when it passed eighty-nine to two. The bill had an easier time in the senate, passing thirty-five to zero, with no amendments.

Governor's Omnibus Crime Bill (1998). Since his time as a county judge executive in Pike County, Governor Patton had believed the state's criminal justice system needed to change. During his second full legislative session as governor, he would turn that belief into comprehensive legislative reform, with the help of Representative Mike Bowling (Democrat from the Eighty-Seventh District) and twenty-four cosponsors.[29]

The sponsors of HB 455—otherwise known as the governor's omnibus crime bill—envisioned a way to make ongoing reforms, as needed, by creating a Criminal Justice Council with representatives from all three branches of government. The council would, among other things, review legislation to be considered by the General Assembly prior to every session.

HB 455 also addressed juvenile justice by establishing delinquency prevention councils and a statewide detention program with graduated sanctions. For instance, secure detention would be employed in severe cases, but alternatives to incarceration, such as community-based programs, mentoring, and counseling, would be available to help rehabilitate juveniles. In addition, anti-gang provisions would allow judges to add one, two, or three years to any sentence for a violent felony, gang recruitment, or trafficking in destructive devices if the crime was committed in furtherance of criminal gang activity. Gang activity was also included as one of the factors a juvenile court judge could consider when deciding whether to allow a child to be tried as a youthful offender.

Hate crimes were addressed in the bill by creating the offense of institutional vandalism, covering the burning of churches and other places of worship. The bill also provided that when specific types of crimes (e.g., assault, certain sex offenses, kidnapping, arson) are committed because of a victim's race, color, religion, sexual orientation, or national origin, early release is prohibited (KRS 532.031). When the governor's crime bill began the legislative process, the hate crime provisions included crimes directed at a woman because of her gender. Notably, this provision was so controversial (even more controversial than sexual orientation) that the reference to gender was removed from the bill during the amendment process and is still absent in the law today.

The qualifications of law enforcement officers were addressed in the crime bill by establishing a certification program. Other provisions included increases in the stipend and eligibility for the Kentucky Law Enforcement Program Fund.

The new crime of fleeing or evading the police was created by HB 455, as were the offenses of disarming a peace officer and impersonating a peace officer. Also, as a means of protecting law enforcement officers, offenders who used body armor in the commission of certain offenses were excluded from early release.

Drugs were addressed in the crime bill by increasing the seriousness of manufacturing, possessing, and trafficking in methamphetamines. In addition the existing crime of unlawful transaction with a minor in the first degree was amended to cover the use of a child to conduct illegal drug activity.

The bill toughened the system's response to violent offenders by requiring them to serve 85 percent of their sentences (up from 50 percent) prior to release. It added the sentence of life without parole in capital cases and added aggravators to capital cases—for example, if a murder victim had a domestic violence protective order against the offender or a court had issued other orders or conditions of bond against the offender. This specific provision had been proposed, unsuccessfully, as an amendment to domestic violence legislation in 1996 (SB 105), and it would become a highly visible provision in a murder case in the following decade. HB 455 also set up alternative sentencing, home incarceration, work release, and pretrial diversion programs to allow nonviolent offenders to remain in the community, when appropriate.

The bill addressed drunk driving by establishing minimum jail time for drivers with blood alcohol levels of 0.18 or higher. It also added the offense of drunken hunting.

The bill addressed the rights of crime victims by requiring restitution as a condition of pretrial diversion, probation, shock probation, conditional discharge, and parole and by prohibiting an offender's final release from probation or other discharge until restitution was paid. (This section had been pushed by prosecutors and the attorney general.) The bill amended the law relating to the Crime Victim Compensation Board to ensure that at least one member was a victim or a victim advocate and to require that all new members be trained on the dynamics of domestic violence, child abuse, sexual assault, homicide, and other violent crimes and have an understanding of the criminal justice process. Other critical reforms related to victim compensation included increasing the offender fee from $10 to $20; redefining court costs to include the victim's fee; extending the time for a victim to file a claim from one year to five years; removing the requirement that victims turn in a six-month progress report on mental health services, since no similar progress reports were required for physical health services; and increasing the award for funeral expenses from $3,500 to $5,000.

The bill also renamed KRS 421 the Crime Victim Bill of Rights; strengthened victims' rights by adding stalking, unlawful imprisonment, additional sex offenses, terroristic threatening, and other crimes to the definition of victim; and added language about the duties of prosecutors to notify victims of their rights. The bill established the Victim-Witness Program, which had been proposed and would be administered by the attorney general's office. This program was intended to help prosecutors protect victims who were participating in the criminal prosecution of cases; services paid for through this program included physical protection for a victim, security measures for her home or workplace, and short-term relocation.

•   •   •

1998—The General Assembly passes legislation prohibiting the marriage of a person younger than sixteen unless the female is pregnant and a district judge grants permission for the marriage.

•   •   •

The bill amended the psychiatric hospitalization statute to allow the notification of victims when persons charged with or convicted of violent offenses and then involuntarily hospitalized are released, are transferred, or escape from a psychiatric or forensic psychiatric facility. The bill amended KRS Chapter 532 to allow elocution during the sentencing process—in other words, it allowed victims to introduce evidence about the crime's impact on them, including the nature and extent of any physical, psychological, or financial harm suffered.

With regard to Kentucky's sex offender registry, the crime bill specified that high-risk sex offenders must register for a lifetime instead of the ten years required for other sex offenders. It established a process for the sentencing court to determine whether a sex offender is a high risk, moderate risk, or low risk for purposes of registration and community notification requirements. For purposes of public notification, information about a high-risk sex offender's release and any special conditions of bond would be provided to the local sheriff, who would then notify the local law enforcement agency, the victim, designated community groups, and the public; for moderate-risk sex offenders, that information would be given to the local law enforcement agency, the victim, and designated community groups; and for low-risk sex offenders, the information would be given to the local law enforcement agency and the victim.

The bill established a mandatory three-year conditional discharge for released sex offenders, and it allowed that conditional discharge to be revoked for any violation of the release conditions. The bill restricted the crediting of good time for sex offenders who had not successfully completed sex offender treatment. The bill also required the Criminal Justice Council to study the feasibility of the civil commitment of sexual predators.

Other Legislation Passed in the 1990s

Kentucky Rules of Evidence (1990 and 1992). In the same way that passage of the Penal Code marked the 1970s, passage of the Kentucky Rules of Evidence (KRE) marked the 1990s. Prior to the passage of an organized set of court rules, laws governing the use and introduction of evidence in court proceedings consisted of two centuries of statutes and court rulings embedded in common law. Legal practitioners had to "deal with the problem of 'finding' the law, distilling from a morass of conflicting common law precedents the ones applicable to the issue at hand, a task regularly producing contention rather than agreement and, more often than not, a level of uncertainty as to the correct rule for the problem" (Lawson, 1998–1999, p. 517). As a practical matter, the lack of any true guidelines meant that even the most seasoned jurists could rule in an inconsistent fashion on how and whether evidence could be introduced. To ensure fair application of the law and to improve the courts' efficiency, a set of organized rules of evidence was needed.

The process began in 1987 with the appointment of an Evidence Rules Study Committee by the Kentucky Bar Association. Chaired by University of Kentucky law professor Robert Lawson (who was also the primary drafter of the Kentucky Penal Code; see chapter 6), the committee was comprised of judges from the trial and appellate benches, trial attorneys, law professors, and members of the General Assembly. Its charge was to create a structure (and, arguably, a function) for the tangle of case law that governed the use of evidence in civil and criminal cases. The study committee made two early decisions. First, Kentucky's rules would track, to the extent possible, the Federal Rules of Evidence (Lawson, 1998–1999); having been adopted in 1975, the federal rules were firmly established, and a substantial body of case law had already been developed (Evidence Rules Study Committee, 1992). A number of other states had taken the same approach. Second, it would be necessary to revise the more than fifty rules that already existed in statutes at the time (including the rape shield law, which had passed in 1976).

The committee worked for two years and submitted its first draft of proposals to the Kentucky Supreme Court in June 1989 (Lawson, 1998–1999). This draft was widely circulated for input and modified to incorporate suggestions from various parties. As the draft was being completed, debate ensued regarding whether the final rules of evidence would be adopted by the Kentucky Supreme Court or whether the General Assembly would assume authority for rule making. In the case of the Federal Rules of Evidence, Congress had taken responsibility for creating the rules, but the Kentucky Constitution explicitly delegated to the state supreme court the authority to "prescribe . . . rules of practice and procedure for the Court of Justice" (Kentucky Constitution § 116; Lawson, 1998–1999). In the end, the rules were enacted jointly by the court and the legislature.

By the fall of 1989, the rules were finalized and readied for consideration by the 1990 General Assembly. The rules of evidence passed the 1990 General Assembly in the form of HB 214, with an enactment date of July 1992. The delayed effective date provided additional time for public hearings and input. Final passage of the Kentucky Rules of Evidence occurred during the 1992 session in the form of HB 241, sponsored by Representatives William M. Lear (Democrat from the Seventy-Ninth District) and Joseph P. Clarke (Democrat from the Fifty-Fourth District). Following legislative enactment, on May 12, 1992, the Kentucky Supreme Court entered an order adopting the Kentucky Rules of Evidence, and they became law. Among the statutory evidence law that became part of the Kentucky Rules of Evidence was the rape shield law (KRS 510.145

became KRE 412) and the sexual assault counselor privilege (KRS 421 became KRE 412).

Hands and Feet as Dangerous Instruments (1990). Prior to the 1990s, intimate partner violence perpetrated with the hands or feet did not rise to the level of felony assault; most cases were prosecuted as misdemeanor assaults. The highest levels of assault were reserved for cases involving the use of a "dangerous instrument," defined under the statute as a gun or other weapon. SB 305, sponsored by Senator Tim Shaughnessy (Democrat from the Nineteenth District), amended the assault statute (KRS 500.080) to include human body parts in the definition of "dangerous instrument." With that amendment, individuals who assaulted their intimate partners with their hands or feet could expect to be charged with a second-degree felony if their victims were physically injured and a first-degree felony if they were seriously physically injured.

HIV Testing of Convicted Sex Offenders (1992). Representative Paul Mason's drive to address the harm inflicted by sex offenders did not begin with an interest in criminal justice. It began, instead, with a petite young woman from Whitesburg who contracted HIV through a blood transfusion in 1987. The young woman's name was Belinda, and she was Mason's daughter. Belinda had evidenced a gift for language at an early age, and by the time she contracted HIV, she had already embarked on a fine career as a fiction writer. When her life changed in the late 1980s, the activist in Belinda emerged, and she cofounded the Kentuckiana People with AIDS Coalition and served as president of the National Association of People with AIDS. Belinda worked with her father to pass the AIDS Act, which protected the rights of persons infected with HIV and mandated AIDS education for health care professionals in Kentucky. Just after her death in 1991 at age thirty-three, Mason told me that he saw Belinda in me, that his daughter and I were "kindred spirits" through our activism and our quest for justice. Belinda's story, as a result, feels comfortably placed in this book.

Representative Mason was joined in sponsoring HB 481 in 1992 by Representative Russell Bentley (Democrat from the Ninety-Second District). The legislation created what is now KRS 510.320, and it required that a defendant convicted of a sexual offense be court-ordered to take an HIV test; that the victim of the sexual offense be provided with the results of the HIV test; and, if the test was positive for HIV, that the Cabinet for Human Resources (now the Cabinet for Health and Family Services) provide counseling to the victim.

• • •

1998—The General Assembly passes legislation to render same-sex marriage illegal, void, and unenforceable in Kentucky.

• • •

Out of respect for Mason and the importance of the issue, the bill passed without a single "no" vote. Since its original enactment, KRS 510.320 has been amended on four occasions to include pre-conviction provisions, to specify that the Cabinet's role in counseling relates to physical health issues, to clarify that filing of a notice of appeal does not stay a court's order for HIV testing, and to make other changes.

DNA Testing of Convicted Sex Offenders (1992). A second bill passed in 1992 created Kentucky's centralized DNA data bank and required the DNA testing of convicted sex offenders. The purpose of HB 631, sponsored by Representatives Steve Riggs (Democrat from the Thirty-First District), Gregory D. Stumbo (Democrat from the Ninety-Fifth District), and Jon Ackerson (Republican [formerly Democrat] from the Forty-Seventh District), was to provide a tool for law enforcement officers investigating sex crimes. DNA identification records produced from samples taken from sex offenders were exempted from public records by the legislation. Since the bill's enactment, the types of offenders whose samples are collected and maintained has been expanded to include all violent crime offenders and juveniles, and the purpose of the data bank has been expanded to include the search for missing persons.

Family Courts (1996 and 1998). The 1996 legislative session marked the beginning of a six-year effort to establish family courts in Kentucky. Under the sponsorship of Senator Michael Moloney (Democrat from the Thirteenth District), SB 60 was a simple bill that allowed the establishment of a family court within the circuit courts of Kentucky. It was a relatively popular idea, and the bill passed in the senate by a vote of thirty-four to two and in the house by a vote of ninety-three to two. The bill was intended to authorize the family court pilot project that had begun in Jefferson County in 1991—the first Kentucky court designed to focus solely on the needs of families and children. That project's success would serve as a model for the creation of more family courts statewide.

Two years later, the General Assembly took a second major step in the creation of a family court system by passing HB 544, sponsored by Representative Michael D. Bowling (Democrat from the Eighty-Seventh District) and sixteen other legislators. That bill added a new section to KRS Chapter 23A to allow the creation of eight family court pilot projects. While allowing concurrent jurisdiction in the district and circuit courts at the discretion of the chief justice, the bill carved out a special jurisdiction for family courts that included dissolution of marriage; child custody and visitation; support and equitable distribution; adoption and termination of parental rights; domestic violence, including emergency protective orders; noncriminal juvenile matters, including juvenile mental inquests and self-consent abortions; paternity and the Uniform Reciprocal Enforcement of Support Act (URESA), related to spousal and child support matters; dependency, abuse, or neglect; and status offenses such as truancy and running away.

The final step in the creation of a statewide family court system would await the next decade and a change in the Kentucky Constitution

Full-Time System of Commonwealth's Attorneys (1996). HB 161, sponsored by Representatives Gross C. Lindsay (Democrat from the Eleventh District) and Jon Ackerson (Republican from the Forty-Seventh District), authorized and then implemented a full-time prosecutorial system for Commonwealth's attorneys.

There is a lesson to be learned from the relationship between advocates and Representative Gross Lindsay, who chaired the house Judiciary Committee from 1999 until his retirement in 2006. Lindsay served in the General Assembly from 1970 to 1980 and again from 1993 to 2006, acting as general counsel to the majority floor leader in the interim. It was said that he "wielded the Roberts Rules of Order like Excalibur whenever a question of parliamentary procedure came up" (Rep. Gross Clay Lindsay, 2008). He was much admired by his legislative colleagues and staff. In fact, there was a Gross Lindsay Fan Club that came with a membership card containing a photo of Lindsay and the club's motto: "It's Great to Be Gross" (Brammer, 2008).

• • •

1998—The General Assembly passes legislation to require insurance coverage for breast reconstruction following mastectomy, for bone density testing for women aged thirty-five and older to promote the early detection of osteoporosis, and for the diagnosis and treatment of endometriosis. The bill also prohibited insurance providers from making domestic violence a preexisting condition; required a biennial survey by the Cabinet for Health Services on the status of women's health; and required, by the year 2000, the creation of an Office of Women's Health.

• • •

Lindsay was central to the creation of the Penal Code, making him extremely protective of its statutory construction and wary of any revisions to it. Not unlike his senate counterpart Kelsey Friend, Lindsay guarded changes to the law vigorously. He would point out that even the minutest change in the wording of the Penal Code would have a profound impact on the prosecution of cases, because attorneys practiced down to the letter of the law. As chairman of the Judiciary Committee, he found many amendments to the law unnecessary and refused to call them for a vote in his committee. Even for bills he did support, he often redrafted the legislation in the form of a committee substitute. Not liking to show his hand in advance, he often sprang the new version of the bill on the sponsor and the bill's supporters in the midst of their testimony.

To succeed in Representative Lindsay's committee, which we usually did in the era of his chairmanship, advocates had to know their bills' exact wording, and they had to know how the broader law would be impacted by the bill. Advocates had to be familiar with legal jargon (or get the help of an attorney if they were not). And they had to be wholly prepared to answer questions before testifying and to respond to unexpected amendments.

9

Legislative Reform

2000 through 2012

During the first decade of the new century, destructive weather events would be imprinted into the memories of Kentucky families. In 2003 and again in 2009, ice storms descended on the Commonwealth, leaving a frozen tundra and death. In the middle of the decade and again in 2012, Kentucky would experience brutal summer droughts and stretches of record-breaking triple-digit heat. On primary election eve in 2008, tornadoes would blow through Kentucky, foreshadowing the spiraling tornadic winds of 2012 that would kill more than twenty Kentuckians and completely flatten the town of West Liberty (Honeycutt & Warren, 2012; National Weather Service, 2012). The end of the 2000s would also bring spring flooding to western Kentucky, swamping fields and roads and leaving residents to fill thousands of sandbags in an attempt to hold back the rising water.

In the sports world, Kentucky would become the first state with African American head coaches at all of its collegiate Division 1 football teams: Joe "Joker" Phillips at the University of Kentucky and Charlie Strong at the University of Louisville. In fall 2010 the state would host more than half a million guests at the Fédération Equestre Internationale (FEI) World Equestrian Games, the first time the games would be held in the United States. Sponsored by Alltech, the games would decide the world championships for eight equestrian sports, with fifty-seven countries represented by approximately 800 equestrians and their horses (Alltech, 2010). Although the World Equestrian Games were largely successful, they ended with controversy when it was revealed through tax returns that the foundation supporting the games had closed the year more than

$1.3 million in the red (Patton, 2012). One more major sports event would occur in 2012, to the delight of the so-called Big Blue Nation (the name given to University of Kentucky basketball fans). The UK men's basketball team, the Wildcats, won the national championship in New Orleans, Louisiana, besting the University of Kansas in the final game. It would be the eighth national title for the Wildcats, this one brought home by a talented group of underclassmen, most of whom cut down the nets and then took their talents to the professional basketball ranks (Schneider, 2012).

The Wildcats' win would not be the only story involving the state's flagship institute of higher education. In September 2010 Dr. Lee T. Todd Jr., who had served as president of the University of Kentucky for a decade, announced that he would step down effective June 30, 2011. Todd's resignation led to a national search and the installation of UK's twelfth president in the person of Dr. Eli Capilouto.

On the legal scene, the U.S. Supreme Court would uphold Kentucky's lethal injection protocol, which led to the 2008 execution of Marco Chapman. Chapman had pleaded guilty to killing two children and wounding their mother and another child in their northern Kentucky home in a 2002 attack.[1]

THE POLITICAL LANDSCAPE

The beginning of the new millennium brought the end of the Patton administration and the temporary end of Democratic control of the governor's office. Although the Democratic Party had generally prevailed in state elections since the mid-nineteenth century, the 2000s would see a Republican majority in the Kentucky senate and the election of Ernest L. Fletcher as governor (serving from 2003 to 2007)—the first Republican to win that office in more than three decades. (The last had been Governor Louie Nunn.)[2] Fletcher began his administration with a pledge of "no new taxes" and a promise to reform the tax code (Cross, 2004). In 2004 he sent a reform package to the General Assembly, but his proposals were not well received. (His tax reform legislation would fare better in 2005.) The 2004 session was also the second consecutive session in which the General Assembly failed to pass a biennium budget. (The first occurred in 2002 under Governor Patton.) This ultimately led to a 2005 Kentucky Supreme Court ruling that both the General Assembly and the governor had acted counter to the state's constitution by failing to pass a budget and by spending funds that had not been allocated by the legislative branch. Notwithstanding the court's decision, this would not be the last time the Kentucky legislature failed to pass a budget.

Governor Fletcher also reorganized the state government, scaling back its cabinet structure from fourteen to eight and implementing cost efficiencies. He also demoted the Governor's Office of Child Abuse and Domestic Violence Services, created statutorily under the previous administration, to a smaller division in the Cabinet for Health and Family Services. In addition to saving money through reorganization, Governor Fletcher made economic development a priority.

Early in his campaign for governor, a key part of Fletcher's public message had been a vow to "clean up Frankfort." Two years into his administration, in an ironic turn of events, Attorney General Gregory D. Stumbo began an investigation of allegations that the Fletcher administration had circumvented the state employee merit system by hiring and firing employees based on their connections and donations to the Republican Party. In what the media dubbed the "Blackberry Jam" (because evidence of inappropriate actions had been captured in e-mails sent by BlackBerry phones), members of Fletcher's administration were indicted by a grand jury, and the governor issued blanket pardons to protect them. While the investigation was still under way, Governor Fletcher announced that he would run for reelection in 2007. However, his lieutenant governor, attorney Stephen B. Pence from Louisville, declined to run for reelection on Fletcher's ticket. Ultimately, Fletcher beat his primary opponents, including Congresswoman Anne Northup, but lost in the general election to another former lieutenant governor, Steven L. Beshear (serving from 2007 to 2011 and 2011 to the present).

• • •

2011—Deputy Chief Justice Mary C. Noble becomes the first woman to preside during oral arguments in the Kentucky Supreme Court.

• • •

Governor Beshear's political and public service history is lengthy and diverse. He served as a state representative for three terms (1974–1979), attorney general (1980–1983), and lieutenant governor (1983–1987). After unsuccessful campaigns for governor in 1987 and for U.S. senator in 1996, Beshear returned to political prominence in 2007 by winning a competitive six-contestant primary race for governor and then the general election against the incumbent, Fletcher.

A plan to expand casino gambling in Kentucky had been Beshear's major campaign platform, and he introduced legislation to achieve that aim in the first legislative session of his administration. The proposal encountered significant difficulty in the Democratic-led house, however, and ultimately failed to be called for a vote. The governor was unsuccessful in accomplishing that goal during his first term. Governor Beshear's first legislative session was also marred by conflict with the Republican-controlled senate. During the 2008 session, both chambers of the legislature had used the practice of "stopping (or unplugging) the clock" so they could continue to conduct business without going beyond the constitutional limit of sixty days (ending at midnight on April 15). Among the bills passed during this legislatively constructed time warp was one to design and fund Kentucky's road plan. The governor vetoed the bill on April 26, but senate president David Williams claimed that because the legislative record showed the bill had passed on April 15, the governor's veto was outside the ten-day period allowed for vetoes. Governor Beshear won the case in court, with an opinion that the road plan bill was invalid and that the General Assembly could no longer use the clock-stopping mechanism. This would not be the last time Beshear and Williams found themselves on opposite sides of an issue, and in fact, their conflicts would carry into the next gubernatorial election.

Thanks to the 1992 changes to the state constitution, Beshear was eligible to run for a second term as governor, and in July 2009 he announced that he would do so. Because sitting lieutenant governor Daniel Mongiardo had decided to challenge Republican Mitch McConnell for a seat in the U.S. Senate, Jerry Abramson, the long-time mayor of Louisville, became Beshear's running mate. Beshear faced no primary challengers in 2011, but the winner of the Republican primary was none other than David Williams, setting up a dramatic election battle. Perennial candidate Gatewood Galbraith from Lexington also threw his hat into the ring, resulting in a three-way race for the governor's seat. When the votes were tallied on November 8, 2011, Beshear won handily with more than 55 percent of the vote, making him the second governor to win consecutive terms. (The first was Paul Patton.)

During his governorship, Beshear would encounter a General

Assembly vastly different from the one he had worked with as lieutenant governor or the one he had served in as a house member. Beshear was only the second governor to face the challenge of working with a split legislature, with the house in Democratic hands and the senate in Republic hands. He would also find that the General Assembly of the 2000s was much more independent, leaving the governor with markedly less influence on legislative matters. The 2009 organizational session impacted the Beshear administration's relationship with the General Assembly when Gregory D. Stumbo, a long-term, politically powerful legislator, ousted Jody Richards as speaker of the house, a position Richards had held for well over a decade.[3]

• • •

2012—Representative Ruth Ann Palumbo becomes Kentucky's longest-serving woman in the General Assembly.

• • •

Governor Beshear's administration targeted economic development, Medicaid reform, and legislation to raise the high school dropout age (a bill pushed by First Lady Jane Beshear), with mixed results. However, the greatest influence during the Beshear administration was the economy's drastic downturn. Upon taking office in 2007, Beshear cut the state budget by almost $80 million, citing a projected budget deficit of almost five times that amount. The 2008 legislative session focused heavily on the budget, for it was anticipated that the deficit would approach $1 billion during the 2008–2010 biennium. In fact, throughout Beshear's first term in office and into his second, substantial budget cuts were required. Beshear's second term was notable for his decision to fully implement the federal Affordable Care Act, thereby extending health care coverage to thousands of Kentuckians.

The General Assemblies of the early twenty-first century undertook a number of major issues (Legislative Research Commission, 2000–2012). These included establishing family courts, prohibiting racial profiling by law enforcement officers, restoring civil rights for convicted felons, and reforming Kentucky's juvenile justice system. After reports emerged showing that Kentucky's prison population had grown unchecked, increasing by 600 percent since 1970 (Lawson, 2005), the General Assembly undertook Penal Code reform, with the goal of changing the penalties for certain criminal offenses to reduce the prison population. The General Assemblies also addressed the synthetic and prescription drug epidemics in the Commonwealth. In the final sessions of this period, state lawmakers passed a law that bolstered prescription monitoring and focused on pain management clinics—an urgent need, given the pervasiveness of pill abuse and the suffering it causes in a state where more people die from drug overdoses than from car crashes (Schneider, 2012).

LEGISLATIVE REFORMS ADDRESSING VIOLENCE AGAINST WOMEN

Yet another task force, this one instituted by the governor, would signal the beginning of significant legislative advances on behalf of rape victims. The work of the Governor's Task Force on Sexual Assault would result in stricter laws related to sexual offenses, improvements in the state's victim notification mechanism, and a civil right of action for stalking victims. Rape crisis centers would be formally established in statute, and at least some of the controversial provisions of the marital rape law would be repealed. A state-level coordinating body for services and policies related to domestic violence and rape would be established and would later propose important legislation. The most visible domestic violence–related legislation of this period would bear the name of the victim: the Amanda Ross Domestic Violence Prevention Act.

Although there were some important legislative contributions to the field of domestic violence during this period, it would perhaps become better known for what was not achieved. As early as 1992, domestic violence advocates had sought to expand eligibility for civil orders of protection to women in dating relationships. By the 2000s, this goal had become a top priority. However, thus far, repeated calls for legislation to extend civil protection to victims harmed by their dating partners have gone unheeded.

Select laws passed from 2000 through 2012 with a direct impact on rape, domestic violence, and related crimes against women are described below, organized by the source of the legislation.

Governor's Task Force on Sexual Assault

For eight years, advocates for rape victims had watched as two task forces on domestic violence achieved reforms on behalf of battered women and children in the Commonwealth. Believing that the same level of attention was warranted for rape cases, I approached Governor Patton in 1999 and asked him to establish a time-limited task force to study the state's response to sexual assault. He agreed, and on September 21, 1999, he established the Governor's Task Force on Sexual Assault and instructed it to study the effectiveness of the criminal and civil justice systems for victims of sexual assault and make recommendations for change by January 1, 2000. Governor Patton named his wife honorary chair of the task force; the cochairs were Representative Joni Jenkins (Democrat from the Forty-Fourth District) and Commonwealth's attorney Steve Wilson.[4]

The membership of the Governor's Task Force on Sexual Assault

Representative Joni L. Jenkins, August 26, 2010. (Courtesy of the Legislative Research Commission)

resembled that of earlier task forces. It had a multidisciplinary makeup that included legislators, state and local victim advocates, judges, prosecutors, law enforcement, Court of Justice staff, criminal justice planners, corrections personnel, and nurses (see appendix C). At the task force's first meeting, members heard testimony on the historic treatment of sexual assault cases in Kentucky, were provided with state and national crime data on sexual assault and a summary of how such data are collected in Kentucky, heard testimony about the psychological impact of rape on a victim, and received an overview of the operation of rape crisis centers in Kentucky. Powerful testimony was provided at the October 1999 meeting by women and men who had survived sexual assault. The task force also heard detailed presentations on the Crime Victim Compensation Board, DNA testing, and the forensic sexual assault examination kit.

The November 1999 meeting focused on the investigation and prosecution of rape cases. Testimony from law enforcement officers and administrators addressed the training provided by state and local agencies to ensure the effective investigation of such cases. The task force raised significant questions about the use of polygraphs with sexual assault victims and heard testimony from a polygrapher. Police officials and prosecutors recommended changes to the Penal Code to respond more appropriately to the severity of rape cases, additional training for law enforcement officers, more sexual assault nurse examiners, and enhanced tools for investigation. At its final regular meeting, the task force heard testimony regarding the Sexual Assault Nurse Examiner (SANE) Program and the use of sexual assault response teams. Probation and parole officers pointed out the need for specialized officers to track sex offenders and the importance of the polygraph as a clinical tool in sex offender treatment. The task force also heard testimony from the judiciary related to the organization of the sexual offense chapter and potential weaknesses in its statutory language. The task force also invited a representative of the defense bar to respond to all the recommendations received. Finally, a national expert provided the task force with an evaluation of the civil remedies available to sexual assault victims and offered recommendations on how to enhance those options in Kentucky.

On December 9 the full task force met for the last time to consider all the recommendations offered. It voted on a total of eighty-seven recommendations involving changes to Kentucky statutes,

The author, Carol Jordan, chairing a meeting of the Governor's Task Force on Sexual Assault, with Judi Patton and John Y. Brown III to her left and Steve Wilson and Senator Marshall Long to her right, circa 2000. (Author's personal collection)

rules of the court, and various programs and policies. From those recommendations, the task force chose to propose legislation to create by statute the Governor's Council on Domestic Violence and Sexual Assault and expand its scope to include crimes of sexual violence, repeal the inadmissibility of marital rape charges in custody cases, remove the one-year reporting requirement for marital rape and sodomy, designate the date-rape drug gamma hydroxybutyric acid (GHB) a schedule 1 controlled substance, allow forensic rape examinations to be conducted in "sexual assault examination facilities," statutorily establish rape crisis centers, and create a civil right of action for stalking.

Victim Notification (2000). Building on earlier groundbreaking reforms, such as notifying victims of an offender's release from jail or prison and informing victims of an offender's HIV status, the task force proposed SB 116, sponsored by Senator (formerly Representative) Marshall Long (Democrat from the Twentieth District and a task force member). The first section of SB 116 strengthened the VINE system created in 1996 by requiring jailers to enter information about an inmate's impending release into the system before the actual release, giving victims time to ensure their safety before the offender is back on the streets. It also amended KRS 196.280 to require public notification when an incarcerated person is being released from a penitentiary; KRS 431.064 to facilitate entry of any conditions of release into the Law Information Network of Kentucky (LINK); and KRS 438.250 and 510.320 to more specifically require that crime victims receive the results of certain HIV tests performed on offenders. SB 116 also expanded the protections available to stalking victims by creating a new section of KRS Chapter 411 to specifically allow a stalking victim to sue the stalker.

SB 116's first stop in the legislative process was the senate's Judiciary Committee. I spoke to each member of the committee and received their verbal support, with the exception of one member who indicated that he did not have time to meet with me. I then asked committee chair Robert Stivers (Republican from the Twenty-Fifth District) to place the bill on the agenda. The day of the bill's hearing, First Lady Judi Patton and I joined Senator Long at the table to offer testimony. After a brief explanation of the bill and a few questions by committee members, I was optimistic that the bill would pass favorably out of committee at any moment. At that very second, however, the single senator I had not talked to entered the room, sat down, and made a motion that the bill be passed over instead of receiving a vote that day. His motion was immediately seconded by a legislator who, less than an hour before, had reassured me of her support, and the motion was passed with the aye votes of every member of the senator's party.

I learned later that the senator was angry at our bill's sponsor for some unrelated grievance and wanted to embarrass him in the presence of Mrs. Patton and the public. It was a harsh reminder that the legislative process is unpredictable and sometimes painfully political. The bill was brought back at the committee's next meeting and passed easily, although the committee made two major changes before the final vote was taken: it strengthened the bill by stipulating that a stalking victim could sue a stalker for civil damages even if the stalker had not been convicted of the crime of stalking, and it deleted the bill's original provision granting the victim access to the presentence investigation report prepared by probation and parole officers. With these changes, the bill passed in the senate by a unanimous vote.

On the house side, a different kind of challenge surfaced for SB 116. It became clear that members of the Judiciary Committee had concerns and very detailed questions about the bill's civil right of action for stalking victims. Worried that neither the sponsor nor I would be able to answer all the questions raised during the hearing, I sought at the last minute the support of Robert L. Elliott, a lawyer with the firm Savage, Elliott, Houlihan, Mullins, & Skidmore in Lexington. Elliott was a colleague who supported the bill and was knowledgeable on the subject, but more important, he was highly respected by legislators and had served as president of the Kentucky Bar Association. On the day of the meeting, I watched as the committee members warmly greeted Elliott before he even sat down to testify, and I knew our bill would be fine. Indeed, it was passed by the committee with only modest changes. SB 116 went on to pass the full house by a vote of ninety-four to zero; the senate later concurred with the house changes by a vote of thirty-seven to zero.

Omnibus Sexual Offense Bill (2000). Any controversy over SB 116 paled in comparison to our experience with the next task force bill. SB 263 revised the sexual offense chapter, the stalking law, and the violent offender statute, and it changed the management

Senator Robert Stivers speaking in the Judiciary Committee, circa 2011. (Courtesy of the Legislative Research Commission)

of sex offenders in the criminal justice system. It also included a victim notification provision when respondents to protective orders attempted to purchase firearms. One of the amendments to the sexual offense chapter attempted to extract the punitive language on marital rape that had been attached as a compromise to HB 38 in 1990. Anticipating some controversy, I secured the sponsorship of Senator Robert Stivers (Republican from the Twenty-Fifth District), chair of the Judiciary Committee. To this day, Senator Stivers good-naturedly complains that I did not prepare him for the battle this bill would entail—admittedly a fair complaint.

The first section of SB 263 addressed the use of so-called date-rape drugs. The task force's approach was to amend KRS 218A.050 to include GHB, the most well-known date-rape drug, on the list of schedule 1 drugs.

The second section of SB 263 focused on the management of sexual and other violent offenders before and after incarceration. It was, in part, an effort to codify the applicable federal law.[5] First, the bill amended various statutes to prohibit shock probation for violent offenders. It also strengthened the sex offender registry (KRS Chapter 17) to provide for community notification through a website maintained by the Kentucky State Police; in addition, it required ten-year rather than lifetime registration for those convicted of sexual abuse in the first degree and clarified the provisions regarding lifetime registrants. SB 263 prohibited convicted sex offenders from residing within 1,000 feet of a school or day-care facility. It also required courts to order comprehensive sex offender presentence evaluations for those convicted of sex crimes, unless one had been completed within the past six months.

The next section of SB 263 addressed the problem of guns in the hands of domestic violence offenders. The bill created a new section of KRS 237 to require victim notification when a respondent to a protective order attempted to purchase a firearm. At the federal level, Congress had passed the Gun Control Act of 1994 (18 USC § 922), making it illegal for a person subject to a court order that prohibits harassing, stalking, or threatening an intimate partner or engaging in conduct that places an intimate partner in reasonable fear of bodily injury to self or to a child to purchase, possess, or transfer a firearm. The federal law specifies that the order must have been issued after a hearing for which the respondent received actual notice, and the order has to include a finding that the person represents a credible threat to the physical safety of an intimate partner or a child. The act also provides that persons convicted of misdemeanor assaults are banned from firearm possession. (Preexisting law already prohibited felons from possessing firearms.)[6]

SB 263 was designed to make the federal gun law maximally effective in Kentucky by adding a notification provision. Specifically, if a respondent to a protective order issued in Kentucky purchased or attempted to purchase a firearm in violation of the federal law, any agency with responsibility for entering domestic violence records into the LINK system was required to notify the court in the jurisdiction where the order was issued and the law enforcement agency with jurisdiction in that county. The bill also required the law enforcement agency to make a reasonable effort to notify the victim who obtained the domestic violence protective order of the respondent's purchase of or attempt to purchase a firearm. Upon further reflection after the bill's passage, advocates realized that this latter provision was not forceful enough, and it would be remedied at the earliest opportunity (2002).

As the 2000 legislative session began, we knew that the "notification upon attempt to purchase firearms" provision of SB 263 could

Judi Patton and Carol Jordan discussing their work on SB 263 in the hallway of the capitol annex, with Marigail Sexton and a trooper (not in uniform) from the Kentucky State Police. (Author's personal collection)

have a disastrous effect on the overall bill. Kentucky prides itself on protecting the Second Amendment right to bear arms, and any law perceived as infringing on that right would never see the light of day. Notably, SB 263 did not restrict a person's right to possess a firearm (the federal law did that); rather, it simply added a notification provision when the federal law was breached. We knew, however, that such a distinction could easily be overlooked, leading to the bill's early demise. To me, the strategy was clear. I would approach the most well-known advocate of Second Amendment rights in the house. If I could get him to support the bill, then I knew other legislators would not worry about it being an attempt to ban guns. The success of that approach is explained in chapter 5.

The rest of SB 263 involved changes to the stalking law and the sexual offense chapter. With respect to stalking, the bill clarified two provisions in the law. First, at the time, KRS 508 provided that a prior felony or class A misdemeanor conviction elevated a subsequent stalking case to a felony. It specifically excluded misdemeanor stalking as a prior offense resulting in elevation to a felony—an exception removed by SB 263. Second, the bill provided that stalking while a protective order was in place elevated the crime to a felony. SB 263 made a variety of other changes to KRS 510 to clarify how sexual offenses would be prosecuted, including elevating third and subsequent sexual offenses to felony status and amending the sodomy statute to include foreign object penetration.

So far, SB 263 had addressed guns, sodomy, pedophiles, and stalkers. Only after that did the bill become controversial. The first controversy related to SB 263 involved the addition of sexual offenses perpetrated by the offender's hands rather than a sexual organ or foreign object. Advocates knew of many cases in which an offender had used one or both hands to penetrate an adult or a child, but the statute treated so-called digital penetration as if it did not have the same devastating impact as penetration by an object or other body part. Legislators vehemently opposed the effort to elevate digital penetration to a felony. In fact, SB 263 did not even make it out of the senate with that provision; that language was removed by a floor amendment. This would not be the only session in which digital penetration legislation was scuttled. In one memorable effort, a committee member made odd hand gestures in reference to the bill following a victim's testimony. At this time, no digital penetration bill has been passed by even one chamber of the General Assembly.

The controversy over digital penetration was just a warm-up for the reaction in the house when legislators learned that SB 263 revisited marital rape. As described in chapters 7 and 8, the 1986 (HB 311) and 1990 (HB 38) General Assemblies passed legislation related to marital rape. The 1986 bill added language to the sexual offense chapter that allowed defendants' records to be expunged under certain circumstances and stipulated that if a victim's claim of rape were materially false, then she could be charged with felony perjury. The 1990 legislative effort had been a tremendous success, in that it removed the so-called spousal exclusion from the sexual assault chapter; however, a by-product of that bill's passage had been the addition of three more amendments that were not to advocates' liking. As drafting was under way for SB 263, we realized that a decade had passed and the time had come to repeal those five amendments. SB 263 did that by amending KRS 500.050 to delete the one-year reporting requirement for marital rape; repealing KRS 510.310, which prohibited allegations of marital rape from being raised in custody proceedings; repealing the language requiring the expunging of all records of marital rape cases that resulted in dismissal with prejudice or a not-guilty verdict; removing language allowing a person in that circumstance to answer "no" to questions about a prior arrest; and repealing the language in KRS 523.020 providing that perjury in the first degree includes making a materially false statement accusing a spouse of an offense under KRS Chapter 510.

All of us working on SB 263 viewed these provisions as harmful to victims and fundamentally unjust. We also knew that they were based on the fear among some legislators that women might fabricate stories of violence to punish their partners or achieve some legal advantage. We hoped that the passage of time had tempered that view, but we were wrong. The reaction of conservative house members was swift and certain. I was stopped in the hallway by a legislator who had often been supportive in the past, but this time, he was livid that SB 263 was even being proposed. With a raised voice (loud enough for everyone in the hallway to hear), he told me I was the best lobbyist he knew, but he could not understand why I was trying to destroy the state's families. The challenge for any advocate in this situation is to choose her words very carefully when responding. Although I vehemently disagreed with his point of view, I knew that his beliefs were genuinely held and based on his reading of scripture. I knew that nothing I said could persuade him otherwise; nor could I criticize his beliefs without seeming highly disrespectful. Instead, I quietly said that since he thought so highly of my work, perhaps he would consider that this was not what we were trying to accomplish. The end of the conversation came quickly. When the bill ultimately passed in the house by a vote of eighty-one to thirteen (the second highest number of "no" votes on any bill during my tenure), he was not among the eighty-one.

Notably, the bill was only partially successful in repealing the objectionable provisions. Although the language regarding custody and the statute of limitations were removed, the expunging of records remains in the law (applicable only to marital rape), and the perjury statute still uniquely references marital rape cases.

Extending the Rape Shield Law to Civil Cases (2003). In June 1992 the Governor's Office of Child Abuse and Domestic Violence Services submitted a proposal to the Kentucky Supreme Court requesting two changes to the Kentucky Rules of Evidence (KRE). I coauthored this proposal with Commonwealth's attorney Steve Wilson (vice chair of the Governor's Task Force on Sexual Assault), using legal research prepared by Mary Jo Gleason, the office's legal counsel. The primary proposal involved extending the protections afforded under the rape shield law to include civil cases. As we explained:

> As the Court is well aware, Rule 412 of the Kentucky Rules of Evidence currently prohibits introduction of evidence of a victim's past sexual behavior at a criminal trial except under certain situations. Rule 412 of the Federal Rules of Evidence, however, extends the rape shield law's protections to civil cases which involve alleged sexual misconduct. Kentucky should extend KRE 412 to encompass civil actions which come within the ambit of the federal Rule's protection. By extending KRE 412 to civil cases, Kentucky would protect the privacy of victims subjected to sexual misconduct and encourage victims to report misconduct, while giving trial court judges more discretionary power to determine whether such evidence should or should not be admitted or discovered. (Jordan & Wilson, 2002, p. 2)

Submitting such proposals inevitably leads to the rather ominous task of testifying before the court itself. I tried to think of the Kentucky Supreme Court as just a supersized senate Judiciary Committee, which I had stood in front of innumerable times. So I wore my highest high-heeled shoes and appeared before the court along with Steve Wilson and civil attorney Robert Elliott, who had helped us with legislative testimony in the past. The court approved our proposal and submitted it to the 2003 General Assembly for codification as HB 263, sponsored by Representative Gross Lindsay (Democrat from the Eleventh District).

HB 263 amended KRE 412, relating to the admissibility of character evidence in certain sex crimes prosecutions. Specifically, it expanded the shield to alleged victims in all civil and criminal cases involving sexual misconduct and provided that certain proffered evidence in criminal and civil cases is admissible unless its probative value is substantially outweighed by the danger of unfair prejudice against the alleged victim. The bill also required that the alleged victim be notified of an in-camera hearing on the admissibility of evidence in criminal and civil cases, that the alleged victim be permitted to attend and be heard at such a hearing, and that a motion for such a hearing must be filed at least fourteen days before the trial date.[7]

Council on Domestic Violence and Sexual Assault (2000). In the late 1970s and early 1980s Representative Gerta Bendl was an outspoken advocate for the protection of women. In 1978 she tried unsuccessfully to create a statewide council to oversee domestic violence and rape services (see chapter 6), and two decades later, the task force would try again. HB 427, an effort to develop a statewide structure to respond to the crimes of rape, stalking, and domestic violence, was sponsored by Representatives Stephen R. Nunn (Republican from the Twenty-Third District), Kathy Stein (Democrat from the Thirteenth District), Kevin Bratcher (Republican from the Twenty-Ninth District), Tom Burch (Democrat from the Thirtieth District), Ron Crimm (Republican from the Forty-Seventh District), Jim Gooch (Democrat from the Twelfth District), Joni Jenkins (Democrat from the Thirty-Fourth District), Susan Johns (Democrat from the Thirty-Second District), Thomas M. McKee (Democrat from the Seventy-Eighth District), and Susan Westrom (Democrat from the Seventy-Ninth District).

HB 427 had two major foci: establishing a statutory council to oversee the state's efforts, and training the state's professionals. Specifically, the bill added new sections to KRS Chapter 403 to establish the Council on Domestic Violence and Sexual Assault and ensure a broad, interdisciplinary membership. The bill stated that the council would be established "for the purpose of planning and direction of legal, protection, and support services related to domestic violence and sexual assault, and to increase the awareness of all Kentuckians regarding the prevalence and impact of these crimes." It set forth the duties of the council, which included facilitating coordinative work among criminal justice, advocacy, health, and mental health agencies and assisting in the development of local councils and response teams by creating model protocols. The bill specifically permitted local domestic violence coordinating councils to create fatality review teams and stipulated that the proceedings of these team were privileged. In the area of training, HB 427 built on earlier legislative proposals related to mandatory training for professionals who encounter cases of domestic violence, rape, stalking, and child maltreatment (in particular, adding rape where it had previously been omitted). It expanded the list of professionals for whom training was required and clarified the topics to be covered in those educational programs. The bill amended KRS 194B.540 to require domestic violence training courses for alcohol and drug counselors, psychiatrists, paramedics, emergency medical technicians, coroners, and medical examiners; it amended KRS 403.784 to require that training for police dispatchers, probation and parole officers, and law enforcement officers include the dynamics of child physical and sexual abuse, rape, and the effects of crime. The bill also amended KRS 15.718 to update the statutory language related to the training of Commonwealth's attorneys and county attorneys (as well as victim advocates), specifying that educational programs should include the dynamics of child physical and sexual abuse, rape, and profiles of offenders. Finally, HB 427 prohibited any mental health professional or organization from operating a program for domestic violence offenders (court-ordered) without first obtaining certification from the Cabinet for Human Resources (now the Cabinet for Health and Family Services).

HB 427 had little trouble as it moved through the legislative process. Despite some modest grumblings about "yet another state government council," the bill passed in the house by a vote of ninety-one to zero (after the Judiciary Committee added the language on domestic violence offender treatment), and it passed in the senate by a vote of thirty-eight to zero. On the senate side, the bill lost the provisions related to judicial education through a floor amendment.

Following passage of HB 427, the Council on Domestic Violence and Sexual Assault was attached to the governor's office, and for the duration of the Patton administration, it was used as a vehicle to create model policies and propose additional legislation. Since that time, however, the council has become largely irrelevant, with only its subcommittee on sexual assault response teams continuing to function effectively (Recktenwald, 2012).

HB 427 would be the last time Representative Steve Nunn served as the primary sponsor of any legislation related to crimes of violence against women. As described later in this chapter, his life would become a mockery of and a horrific affront to all his past accomplishments.

Creating a Statutory Structure for Rape Crisis Centers (2000). The fourth measure proposed by the Governor's Task Force on Sexual Assault strengthened the presence of rape crisis centers in Kentucky. It was sponsored, quite appropriately, by Representative Joni Jenkins, who not only had established a robust reputation as a woman's advocate but also had worked in a rape crisis center herself (the

Center for Women and Families in Louisville). She was joined by fifteen cosponsors. HB 448 began by creating new sections of KRS Chapter 211 to require the Cabinet for Health Services to designate one nonprofit corporation in each area development district to serve as the regional rape crisis center. This was an extremely important provision because it gave a high profile to each of these centers and allowed the state to fund one central program in each region rather than funding multiple disparate agencies throughout the region. HB 448 also required the establishment of nonprofit boards to oversee the centers' operation, and it stipulated which services were to be provided by rape crisis centers, including crisis counseling, mental health services, advocacy, consultation, public education, and training for professionals. Mental health records that identified center clients were accorded confidential status.

The second part of HB 448 brought the rape crisis centers into the service system for forensic sexual assault examinations. Kentucky's first reforms in this area were now more than two decades old. They had begun with passage of HB 497 in the 1978 session, a bill that required hospital emergency rooms to provide forensic examinations for rape victims (see chapter 6). The next step had been HB 196 in the 1984 session, a bill that recognized the exams' purpose as evidence collection and required the state to pay for them (see chapter 7). With 1996 came passage of HB 495, the third component of Kentucky's reforms in this area, which made it the first state in the nation to create a statewide certification program for sexual assault nurse examiners (see chapter 8). Expanding the locations where these examinations could be performed and allowing them to be conducted outside the traditional hospital setting were the goals of our proposals in 2000. HB 448 amended KRS 216B.015 to define a "sexual assault examination facility" as a licensed health facility, emergency medical facility, primary care center, or children's advocacy center or rape crisis center regulated by the Cabinet for Health and Family Services. The bill went on to permit sexual offense victims to be examined in these facilities, where the presence of rape crisis counselors would provide a more victim-sensitive environment.

Governor's Council on Domestic Violence and Sexual Assault

During his first month in office, Governor Paul Patton issued Executive Order 96-68, creating the Kentucky Council on Domestic

Violence. He took that action to focus high-level governmental attention on the incidence of domestic violence and to increase awareness of the prevalence of that crime and its harmful effects on the Commonwealth's citizens. I first met with Governor Patton in January 1996 (to discuss proposals from the Legislative Task Force on Domestic Violence; see chapter 8), and I asked him to create such a council because Kentucky needed a stronger mechanism to implement legislative reforms. Although task forces had worked well in the past, a permanent entity was required to ensure continuity of effort and implementation of those task forces' proposals. Patton agreed and established the Kentucky Council on Domestic Violence. He named First Lady Judi Patton as its chair, and I staffed it.

On December 9, 1997, Patton renamed the body the Governor's Council on Domestic Violence.[8] In 1998 former governor John Y. Brown Jr. joined Mrs. Patton in the role of cochair. Some months earlier, Brown had asked Governor Patton to give him some role in the state's efforts against domestic violence. The former governor had shown a prior interest in the issue, having supported the expansion of domestic violence programs during his administration, but the crime became real to him in September 1997 when his sister, Betty "Boo" McCann, was severely assaulted by her live-in boyfriend. Responding to a phone call from his sister, Brown went to her home, where he found blood on the wall and Boo with a broken nose, cuts to her scalp and limbs, and bruises on her body. The offender was ultimately convicted of his crime. Later, Brown said, "It has always been my conviction that this society is made up with laws that protect everyone according to a sense of justice, fairness, protection, and equality. But when I witnessed my sixty-six-year-old sister beaten up by a man, without provocation or cause, it crystallized for me that our society still treats domestic violence as though it was a different crime" (Brown, 2013).

The membership of the Governor's Council on Domestic Violence was designed to emphasize a multidisciplinary approach; it included legislators, judges, clerks, prosecutors, law enforcement officers, social workers, health and mental health professionals, domestic violence advocates, child advocates, and community representatives (see appendix C). Its specific goals were to assess the availability of services to victims; to advance coordination among the multiple agencies responding to the crime; to create training curricula, protocols, and policies; and to promote public awareness.

Shortly after the 2000 General Assembly made the council a statutory entity and renamed it the Governor's Council on Domestic Violence and Sexual Assault, it became embroiled in controversy. On September 4, 2001, Detective Frank Smith, a police officer assigned to the Third District in Louisville, was arrested for the abuse of his estranged wife. In addition to being a law enforcement officer, Smith had recently been appointed to serve on the council. Detective Smith had investigated domestic violence cases and had developed positive working relationships with victim advocates in Louisville, the local domestic violence programs, and others in the county's criminal justice system. Once his case became public, the media reported that Smith had also been suspended from the police force in 1993 after he allegedly hit a former wife and drew his service weapon during an argument with her (Tangonan, 2001). Smith would not be the last man associated with Kentucky's domestic violence movement to violate the trust of advocates with ruinous outcome.

The Governor's Council on Domestic Violence and Sexual Assault actively proposed legislation during the years of the Patton administration. These proposals included strengthening the stalking statute; creating a protective order for stalking victims; expanding the triggers for victim notification of an offender's release from incarceration; notifying victims when respondents to protective orders attempt to purchase firearms; creating local domestic violence coordinating councils; expanding the types of professionals required to have training on domestic violence, sexual assault, and child maltreatment; and improving the SANE Program.

Notification of Attempts to Purchase Firearms (2002). The bill passed by the General Assembly in 2000 (SB 263) placed the burden of victim notification on local law enforcement agencies when respondents to protective orders attempted to purchase firearms. In 2002 the council proposed an automated system to provide that information directly to victims, increasing the likelihood of them receiving it and improving its timeliness. SB 89 allowed the Justice Cabinet to contract with a private entity to notify victims who had registered for notification of attempted firearm purchases.

The second portion of SB 89 strengthened HB 309 from the 1996 session as it related to the certification process for mental health professionals providing court-ordered domestic violence offender treatment. To ensure program effectiveness and victim safety, SB

89 amended KRS Chapter 403 to specify which information these treatment providers must provide to the Cabinet for Health and Family Services to enhance monitoring and to ensure the quality of services provided to offenders.

SB 89 was sponsored by Senator Marshall Long, who was joined in testifying on the bill by Mrs. Patton and me. The bill passed in the senate (thirty-six to zero) after one amendment that clarified that immunity from civil liability did not limit liability for negligence. On the house side the bill proceeded through a supportive Health and Welfare Committee and passed the full house by a vote of ninety-eight to zero.

Oversight of the Sexual Assault Nurse Examiner Program (2002). Recognizing the effectiveness of the SANE Program, which had been in existence for six years, and wanting to promote an interdisciplinary team approach to the investigation of sexual assault cases, the council (in collaboration with the Kentucky Association of Sexual Assault Programs) proposed legislation to create a state-level oversight body. HB 308 was sponsored by Representatives Kathy Stein (Democrat from the Seventy-Fifth District), Joni Jenkins (Democrat from the Thirty-Fourth District), Tom Riner (Democrat from the Forty-First District), Steve Nunn (Republican from the Twenty-Third District), and Susan Westrom (Democrat from the Seventy-Ninth District). The bill moved the SANE Advisory Council, which had been attached to the Board of Nursing by the 1996 enacting legislation, and placed it under the Governor's Council on Domestic Violence and Sexual Assault. It also set out the membership of that advisory council to include representatives from the state police, the Kentucky Association of Sexual Assault Programs, the Board of Nursing, the Kentucky Nurses Association, the Kentucky Medical Association, the Kentucky Hospital Association, the state police crime lab, the chief medical examiner, the Governor's Office of Child Abuse and Domestic Violence Services, and the attorney general's office, as well as a sexual assault nurse examiner, a member of a sexual assault response team, a physician, and a Commonwealth's attorney. The SANE Advisory Council continues to play an active oversight role and is routinely credited with the overall effectiveness of Kentucky's programs in this area (Recktenwald, 2012). The bill also clarified the statute to specify that the Rape Victim Assistance Fund would pay for examinations conducted at out-of-state hospitals

Carol Jordan, Judi Patton, and Representative Marshall Long testifying on SB 89, February 19, 2002. (Author's personal collection)

if the rape occurred in Kentucky. The bill passed easily through the General Assembly—ninety-seven to zero in the house, and thirty-six to zero in the senate.

Protective Orders for Stalking Victims (2002). Representatives Rob Wilkey (Democrat from the Twenty-Second District) and John Vincent (Republican from the 100th District) sponsored HB 428, designed to strengthen the statutory provisions related to stalking under KRS 508. The bill represented an acknowledgment that stalking offenders are exceptionally recidivistic and that those who become obsessed and continue to follow or harass their victims over long periods may be the most dangerous type of stalker. It also addressed the fact that not all victims of stalking were eligible for protective orders under the Domestic Violence and Abuse Act.

The major aim of the bill was to increase victim protection. Specifically, the bill amended KRS Chapter 508 to allow the court to enter a restraining order on behalf of a stalking victim upon a criminal conviction for stalking. Under the provisions of HB 428, the defendant would be notified and afforded an opportunity to be heard prior to entry of the order, and the victim would be able to request that an order not be entered or could ask that it be dismissed at any time. The legislation directed that stalking protective orders be entered into the LINK system, and it allowed warrantless arrests for violations, similar to the provision already in place for domestic violence protective orders. To address anticipated opposition from those concerned about convicted stalkers' gun ownership rights, the bill included specific language that stalking protective orders did not fall under the federal gun ban related to domestic violence protective orders.

The bill's journey through the legislative process was, at times, quite difficult. As early as the 2002 session, some legislators were demonstrating an increased reluctance to support the use of protective orders, and the amendments they made to HB 428 represented some of that growing antipathy. The first change was to shorten the proposed permanent stalking order to no more than ten years, the specific duration of the order being determined by the court. With that amendment, the bill passed in the house by a vote of ninety-six to zero. On the senate side, the bill raised some concerns among attorneys on the Judiciary Committee, who amended the bill to specify that the provisions of the stalking order did not apply to contact by an attorney with regard to a legal matter. After passing the Judiciary Committee on March 6, the bill sat in the Rules Committee for a week, and on March 13 it was recommitted to the Appropriations and Revenue Committee. In this case, that action had little to do with the bill itself; rather, it was the result of unrelated political issues. On March 21 the bill was revived from the Appropriations Committee and passed the next day by a vote of thirty-seven to zero. The house concurred with the senate changes by a vote of ninety-five to zero.

OTHER LEGISLATION PASSED DURING THE 2000s

Other laws passed in the early twenty-first century that were more indirectly related to violence against women are outlined below.

Women's Education and Research (2000)

In March 2000 Nine West Group Inc., one of the country's largest suppliers of women's shoes, agreed to settle a nationwide lawsuit alleging that the company had engaged in resale price fixing in violation of federal and state antitrust laws. The outcome of the settlement was that Nine West would pay $34 million to fifty-six U.S. states, territories, commonwealths, and possessions. The funds from the settlement flowed through the office of the attorney general in each state and were earmarked for women's health, educational, vocational, and safety programs. In Kentucky, Attorney General Albert B. "Ben" Chandler III believed the funds should be used to address domestic violence, rape, and stalking. With Chandler's backing, support from the Kentucky Association of Sexual Assault Programs and the Kentucky Domestic Violence Association, and the sponsorship of Representative Susan Westrom (Democrat from the Seventy-Ninth District), the funds were ultimately used to create the Center for Research on Violence Against Women at the University of Kentucky.

Insurance Discrimination in Cases of Domestic Violence (2000)

In 2000 Representative Robert Damron (Democrat from the Thirty-Ninth District) sponsored legislation to ensure that domestic violence and abuse would never be used as a reason to limit or deny insurance coverage for a victim. Specifically, HB 3 provided that no insurer can use the fact that an applicant or an insured incurred bodily injury as a result of domestic violence or abuse as the sole reason for making rating or underwriting decisions, refusing to insure, refusing to continue to insure, or limiting the amount, extent, or kind of coverage available to an applicant or an insured. Additionally, the bill provided that if a property or casualty insurance policy excluded coverage for intentional acts, then the insurer cannot deny payment to an innocent coinsured if the loss arose from a pattern of domestic violence and abuse and the perpetrator was criminally prosecuted for the act causing the loss.

Office of Women's Physical and Mental Health (2001)

During the years of the Patton administration, the Commission on Women was strongly focused on women's health, particularly under the directorships of Virginia Woodward (who spearheaded breast cancer legislation with the women's caucus in the house), Eugenia Potter, and Betsy Nowland-Curry. In 2000 Governor Patton created

Carol Jordan announcing the creation of the University of Kentucky Center for Research on Violence Against Women at the governor's mansion, 2002. (Author's personal collection)

the Office of Women's Physical and Mental Health by executive order. In 2001, through the sponsorship of Representative Gregory D. Stumbo (Democrat from the Ninety-Fifth District), the executive order became a statutory entity attached to the Office of the Secretary within the Cabinet for Health Services. HB 124 passed with relative ease, encountering only one "no" vote on the house floor.

Safety and Security at Universities (2000)

As described in chapter 3, the murder of Jeanne Clery on a college campus led to passage of a federal law requiring institutions of higher education to track and report on-campus crimes.[9] Specifically, the federal law requires universities to collect and publish data on crimes occurring on their grounds and to their students. In Kentucky, Michael Minger, a Murray State student, died in his dormitory room when someone set the building ablaze. After his death, Michael's mother, Gail, became a visible advocate, pushing for reforms to increase transparency about fire offenses and other criminal occurrences on the campuses of public and private universities in Kentucky. The result was HB 322, sponsored by Representative Jim Wayne (Democrat from the Thirty-Fifth District). HB 322, which became known as the Michael Minger Act, codified many of the provisions of the federal Clery Act by creating new sections of KRS Chapter 164 relating to safety and security at postsecondary educational institutions. The bill, which took effect as the 2000 academic year started, required each such institution to maintain a public daily log recording all crimes occurring on campus, required campus authorities to immediately report a fire or threat of fire to the state fire marshal, and required each university to report its crime and fire data and policies annually to the Council on Postsecondary Education.

Family Courts (2001–2003)

During the 1990s, the legislature had taken several steps toward creating family courts. In 1996 Senator Michael R. Moloney (Democrat from the Thirteenth District) had sponsored SB 60 to allow the establishment of a family court pilot project, and in 1998 Representative Michael Bowling (Democrat from the Eighty-Seventh District) had sponsored legislation to spread pilot projects to eight total jurisdictions. By 2001, it was clear that the family court model was beneficial to families and to the justice system. However, the Kentucky Constitution (§109) stated, "the judicial power of the Commonwealth shall be vested exclusively in one Court of Justice which shall be divided into a Supreme Court, a Court of Appeals, a trial court of general jurisdiction known as the Circuit Court and a trial court of limited jurisdiction known as the District Court." Therefore, to allow family courts, the constitution would have to be amended. That was the purpose of SB 58, sponsored by Senator Robert Stivers (Republican from the Twenty-Fifth District). The bill, which provided for a resolution to amend the Kentucky Constitution, was passed by the 2001 General Assembly. The resolution was placed on the ballot in November 2002 and was passed in 120 counties with more than 75 percent of the vote. The constitution would ultimately be amended to read: "The Supreme Court may designate one or more divisions of Circuit Court within a judicial circuit as a family court division. A Circuit Court division so designated shall retain the general jurisdiction of the Circuit Court and shall have additional jurisdiction as may be provided by the General Assembly" (Kentucky Constitution §109).

In 2003 the final step in the process was taken when Representative Jody Richards (Democrat from the Twentieth District) sponsored HB 380, which gave the specific statutory structure to family courts in Kentucky. The family court concept and the bill continued to receive strong support from the General Assembly, passing ninety-five to zero in the house and thirty-eight to zero in the senate. In 2010 the Kentucky Supreme Court adopted uniform rules for family law cases statewide (Minton, 2010); those rules became effective in January 2011. As of 2012, family courts serve 3.2 million citizens in seventy-one Kentucky counties, and the Commonwealth's system is considered a model for the nation (Administrative Office of the Courts, 2012).

Creation of the Crime of Terroristic Threatening (2001)

In the early morning of September 11, 2001, nineteen hijackers flew four commercial airliners carrying passengers into buildings in New York and Washington, D.C., and into the ground in Pennsylvania. Those acts of terror gripped the nation and caused significant concern in the Kentucky General Assembly. HB 1 was the response, adding a section to KRS Chapter 508 to define the new crime of terroristic threatening, consisting of three levels (first degree, second degree, and third degree). The new offense covered the use or threatened use of weapons of mass destruction, particularly when targeted at schools and other public buildings. The bill also amended KRS 527 to define weapons of mass destruction and amended KRS 532.025 to add use of a weapon of mass destruction as an aggravating circumstance in death penalty cases.

Date-Rape Drugs (2002)

In 2002 Senator Dan Kelly (Republican from the Fourteenth District) sponsored legislation to increase the seriousness of possessing date-rape drugs and of committing sexual offenses through the use of these drugs. Specifically, SB 25 amended KRS Chapter 218A, relating to the trafficking and possession of a controlled substance, to add flunitrazepam (commonly known as Rohypnol) and gamma hydroxybutyric acid (commonly known as GHB). Through a house committee substitute, the bill made trafficking in GHB a class C felony for a first offense and a class B felony for a second or subsequent offense; it made possession of GHB a class D felony for a first offense and a class C felony for a second or subsequent offense. The bill also amended the definitional section of KRS Chapter 510 to move "controlled substances" from the definition of "mentally incapacitated" to the definition of "physically helpless." The effect of that change was to leave rape committed through the use of an intoxicating substance a class D felony and to elevate rape committed through the use of a controlled substance to a class B felony.

Expansion of the Kidnapping and Violent Offender Act (2002)

Senator Dan Kelly also sponsored SB 26, which amended the kidnapping statute (KRS 509.040) to add the circumstance of taking a child for the purpose of depriving a parent or guardian of that minor. An exception was included to cover those persons exercising custodial control or supervision as defined in the statute. The bill also amended the violent offender statute (KRS 439.3401) to add the crimes of robbery in the first degree and (by a floor amendment in the house) burglary in the first degree when accompanied by the commission or attempted commission of a felony sex offense or certain felony assaults (KRS 508.010, 508.020, 508.032). The bill's latter provisions were not retroactive.

Creation of the Crime of Video Voyeurism (2002)

Representative Jimmie Lee (Democrat from the Twenty-Fifth District) had proved himself a strong advocate for women and children through his role as chair of the budget review subcommittee for human resources. In 2002 he sponsored HB 130 to create the new crime of video voyeurism under KRS Chapter 531. The bill defined video voyeurism, a class D felony, as the videotaping of a person in various sexual acts or states of undress without the person's permission. The bill exempted telephone companies, television stations, and Internet providers from provisions of the statute and created a new provision of KRS Chapter 531 to require the destruction of videotapes and other materials violating this statute.

Sexual Assault Victim Assistance Fund (2004)

SB 138 was sponsored by Senator Julie Denton (Republican from the Thirty-Sixth District) and was designed to secure funding for forensic rape examinations paid for by the Crime Victim Compensation Board (CVCB). In 1984 the state was mandated (through HB 196) to pay for forensic examinations through a Rape Victim Assistance Fund, managed by the Office of the Attorney General. During the Patton administration, the fund was moved to the CVCB because expenditures by the board would receive matching federal funds. SB 138 created a new section of KRS Chapter 346 to formally establish the Sexual Assault Victim Assistance Fund under the auspices of the CVCB. It required that state funds and matching federal funds be deposited into an account that would be used to pay for rape examinations for adults and forensic medical examinations for children through the state's network of children's advocacy centers. To protect victims and those performing examinations, the senate's Health and Welfare Committee stipulated that the CVCB was prohibited from conducting its own investigations but was allowed to require proof that such examinations had been conducted. The legislation received strong support from the General Assembly, passing

Senator Julie Denton speaking on the senate floor, circa 2011. (Courtesy of the Legislative Research Commission)

in the senate by a vote of thirty-seven to zero and in the house by a vote of ninety-four to zero.

Creation of the Crime of Indecent Exposure (2004)

In 2004 Senators Damon Thayer (Republican from the Seventeenth District) and John D. "Jack" Westwood (Republican from the Twenty-Third District) sponsored SB 145. The bill added a new section to KRS Chapter 510 to create the crime of indecent exposure in the first degree, defined as occurring when a person indecently exposes himself under circumstances in which he knows or should know that his conduct could cause affront or alarm to a person under the age of eighteen years; it amended KRS 510.150 to define indecent exposure in the second degree as occurring under the same circumstances but when the victim is eighteen years of age or older. The bill passed in the senate by a vote of thirty-five to one. In the house, the Judiciary Committee was concerned that the penalties were too high; therefore, through a committee substitute, it amended the bill to make the first offense a class A misdemeanor and the second and subsequent offenses a class D felony. As amended, SB 145 passed in the house by a vote of eighty-seven to zero, and the senate subsequently concurred with those changes.

Creation of the Crime of Fetal Homicide (2004)

In the 2004 session, Representative Robert Damron (Democrat from the Thirty-Ninth District) and forty-two cosponsors proposed to create the new crime of fetal homicide. HB 108 added a new section to KRS Chapter 507A to include an unborn child from the point of viability in the statutory definition of "person" as it applied to the criminal homicide statutes, thus establishing the crimes of fetal homicide in the first, second, third, and fourth degrees. HB 108 included two exceptions: the law would not apply to health care providers in certain circumstances, and the acts of a pregnant woman that caused the death of her unborn child would not fall under the new law. The house Judiciary Committee amended the bill to prohibit imposition

Senator Kathy Stein speaking on the senate floor, January 11, 2012. (Courtesy of the Legislative Research Commission)

of the death penalty for fetal homicide cases. The bill also included an emergency clause, which meant it would become law upon the signature of the governor.

HB 108 encountered no real difficulty in passing the General Assembly, although a block of liberal legislators voted against it. It mustered eighty-five votes in favor and five against in the house. On the senate side, no amendments were made, and the bill passed by a vote of thirty-three to four. The modest opposition to HB 108 resulted from the belief that the crime of fetal homicide was being used across the nation to outlaw abortion. Notably, many in the domestic violence community, though aware of research that points out the risk of violence to pregnant women, did not support the bill.

Elder Abuse and Domestic Violence (2005)

In the 2005 session, Representative Jimmie Lee (Democrat from the Twenty-Fifth District) and twenty-one other legislators joined in sponsoring HB 298 to substantially improve the state's response to elder abuse. Because the provisions of HB 298 were placed in KRS 209, the domestic violence provisions that had previously been included in the Kentucky Adult Protection Act were moved to their own chapter of KRS 209A. When that new chapter was created,

Helen Kinton, Eileen Recktenwald, and Sherry Currens, December 2011. (Courtesy of the Kentucky Association of Sexual Assault Programs)

language was added to require the Cabinet for Health and Family Services to designate a nonprofit corporation in each area development district to serve as the primary service provider and regional planning authority for domestic violence shelter, crisis, and advocacy services. This language established the domestic violence programs in statute, as had been done for the rape crisis centers in the 2000 General Assembly.

Kentucky's Stand-Your-Ground Law (2006)

In the 2000s, an increasing number of states passed so-called stand-your-ground laws. The rationale for such laws is that a person should be allowed to use force in self-defense when there is a reasonable belief that another is person unlawfully entering a residence or vehicle with the intent to cause that person harm (based on the concept that one's home is one's castle). Approximately half the states have such laws, and Kentucky's was proposed to the 2006 General Assembly in the form of SB 38, sponsored by Senators Richard "Dick" Roeding (Republican from the Eleventh District) and Damon Thayer (Republican from the Seventeenth District). Under that law, a person is presumed to have a reasonable fear of imminent peril of death or great bodily harm (to him- or herself or another person) when using defensive force that is intended or likely to cause death or great bodily harm to a person unlawfully entering a residence, dwelling, or occupied vehicle. The provisions extend to guards or peace officers who use deadly force to prevent the escape of a person from jail, prison, or some other detention facility or from a vehicle. Some exceptions were built into the law, including a person who has a lawful right to be in a dwelling, as long as there is no domestic violence protective order requiring him to vacate the residence, and a person seeking to remove a child or grandchild when that person is the lawful guardian of that child. In addition, the right to use defensive force is not applicable when the person using it is engaged in unlawful activity. Finally, the law does not apply when a law enforcement officer is attempting to enter a residence. The law also stipulates that a person who is lawfully in his or her own residence, dwelling, or vehicle does not have a "duty to retreat." Finally, civil and criminal immunity applies to actions taken in self-defense, as provided under the law. Law enforcement agencies are permitted to use standard investigative procedures related to the use of force, but no arrest or prosecution can be commenced unless there is probable cause to believe the actions taken were unlawful. SB 38 was slightly modified in the Judiciary Committee and went on to pass in the senate by a vote of thirty-six to two; in the house, the vote was eighty-eight to eight. Stand-your-ground laws have a complicated relationship to the domestic violence movement, drawing both supporters and opponents. (See the discussion in chapter 10 and section below related to firearms.)

Division of Child Abuse, Domestic Violence, and Human Trafficking Services (2007)

SB 43 was sponsored in the 2007 General Assembly by Senators David Boswell (Democrat from the Eighth District), Walter Blevins (Democrat from the Twenty-Seventh District), Perry Clark (Democrat from the Thirty-Seventh District), Denise Harper Angel (Democrat from the Thirty-Fifth District), Jerry Rhoads (Democrat from the Sixth District), Richard Roeding (Republican from the Eleventh District), Ernesto Scorsone (Democrat from the Thirteenth District), Tim Shaughnessy (Democrat from the Nineteenth District), and John D. Westwood (Republican from the Twenty-Third District). The bill created in statute the Division of Child Abuse, Domestic Violence, and Human Trafficking Services within the Cabinet for Health and Family Services. That division had been created in statute in 1998 and placed in the governor's office by Governor Paul Patton; however, that law had been repealed and the office moved to the cabinet under Governor Ernest "Ernie" Fletcher. SB 43 set out the division's duties, which included public education, training, and the granting of funds.

With regard to human trafficking, the bill called for the development of policies and programs to prevent these acts, and it added counselors for human trafficking victims to those provided privilege under the Kentucky Rules of Evidence. The bill also created a new section of KRS Chapter 431 to establish a policy of nonincarceration for victims of human trafficking, meaning that (with limited exceptions) such victims cannot be held in a detention center, jail, or other secure facility pending trial for an offense arising from the experience of being trafficked. It also specified that business enterprises can be held liable in human trafficking prosecutions. It amended the criminal syndication statute to include the new offense of exploitation of persons and created several new sections of law to add an offense involving commercial sexual activity and to criminalize forced labor or services.

The bill passed in the senate by a vote of thirty-seven to zero and in the house by a vote of ninety-six to zero.

No Polygraphs for Rape Victims (2008)

SB 151, which prohibited the use of polygraphs for victims of rape, was the first bill proposed and staffed by the Kentucky Association of Sexual Assault Programs (KASAP). The idea of prohibiting polygraphs had first been raised in 2000 by the Governor's Task Force on Sexual Assault, but there had been significant pushback from some law enforcement entities and some legislators. KASAP continued to work on the proposal, and in 2008 it proposed SB 151, sponsored by Senator Robert Stivers (Republican from the Twenty-Fifth District).The bill stipulated that law enforcement officers and prosecutors cannot request or require a victim of an alleged sexual offense to submit to a polygraph examination or any other device designed to determine whether a person is telling the truth. Similarly, police officers and prosecutors cannot charge or threaten to charge the victim of an alleged sexual offense with a criminal offense for refusing to submit to a polygraph examination. The bill specifically applied to Commonwealth's attorneys and county attorneys (KRS Chapter 65), officers of the Kentucky State Police (KRS Chapter 16), other police officers (KRS Chapter 95), and sheriffs, deputy sheriffs, constables, and county police officers (KRS Chapter 70).

SB 151 had the distinction of making it through the entire legislative process without a single amendment. It passed in the senate by a vote of thirty-three to zero and in the house by a vote of ninety-one to three. Among the three opponents was a legislator who had previously served as a law enforcement officer.

Sexual Offenses and Social Media (2009)

HB 315 enjoyed significant support, with twenty-nine cosponsors joining the primary sponsor, Representative Johnny Bell (Democrat from the Twenty-Third District). The purpose of HB 315 was to interdict cases of stalking and acts of obscenity that use the Internet or social media. The bill amended KRS Chapter 510 to provide that solicitation of a minor for criminal sexual activity through electronic communications is prima facie evidence of that person's intent to commit the offense, even if there is no meeting between the offender and the child. The bill also amended the stalking statute pursuant to KRS Chapter 508 to include the use of computers, the Internet or other electronic networks, cameras or other recording devices, telephones or other personal communications devices, and scanners or other copying devices in the description of a course of conduct that has no legitimate purpose. In addition, HB 315 amended the obscenity statutes to include live images transmitted over the Internet, and it specified that convicted, registered sex offenders cannot intentionally or knowingly use social networking websites. It amended the website maintained by the Kentucky State Police to include a function whereby the public can enter an e-mail address or other electronic identity and learn whether an individual is a convicted sex offender. A person is guilty of phishing under HB 315 if he or she knowingly or intentionally solicits, requests, or takes any action to induce another person to provide identifying information by means of a Web page, e-mail message, or other use of the Internet, by representing himself or herself to be a third person without the authority to do so.

Sexual Assault against Incarcerated Persons (2010)

SB 17 was sponsored by Senators Julie Denton (Republican from the Thirty-Sixth District), Denise Harper-Angel (Democrat from the Thirty-Fifth District), Perry Clark (Democrat from the Thirty-Seventh District), and Gerald Neal (Democrat from the Thirty-Third District) as a means to better protect incarcerated individuals from specified sex crimes. Specifically, the bill amended KRS 510.060, relating to rape in the third degree, and KRS 510.090, relating to sodomy in the third degree, to prohibit specified employees and volunteers of an agency or facility responsible for detention or treatment from having sexual intercourse or deviate sexual intercourse with persons who are incarcerated, supervised, evaluated, or treated by those agencies. The language of KRS 510.120, relating to sexual abuse, was also amended to make it consistent with the rape and sodomy language. SB 17 passed in the senate by a vote of thirty-seven to zero and in the house by a vote of eighty-seven to zero.

Amanda's Law (2010)

The story of HB 1 began not in the state capitol but on a street in Lexington, where gunfire rang out early one morning in September 2009. Chapter 5 told the story of Amanda Ross, a vivacious young woman who was murdered by her ex-fiancé, former state representative Stephen R. Nunn. This chapter now tells the story of Nunn's downfall.

Steve Nunn came from a well-known political family headed by his father, former governor Louie Nunn. In 1990 Steve won a seat in the Kentucky house of representatives and served there as a moderate Republican for fifteen years. His term ended in 2006 amid whispers of his increasingly inappropriate personal behavior, which helped propel a Democratic newcomer into the seat (Alessi, Estep, & Clark, 2009). In 2003 Nunn ran an unsuccessful campaign for governor, losing in the primary to Ernie Fletcher, who would go on to win the governorship that year. Soon after this significant electoral defeat, Nunn was stunned by the unexpected death of his father in January 2004. Thus began a five-year descent in Steve Nunn's character and behavior.

Nunn divorced his second wife in 2006, but in 2007 his life seemed to brighten when he met and began dating Amanda Ross, with whom he shared a love of politics. That year, Nunn drew public attention when he announced his support for Democratic gubernatorial candidate Steve Beshear—a move some viewed as politically controversial. Nevertheless, the longtime Republican backed the Democrat in the race rather than supporting his own party and endorsing incumbent Ernie Fletcher, who had bested Nunn in the primary. Upon Beshear's win, he appointed Nunn deputy secretary of the Cabinet for Health and Family Services, a position that gave him a leadership role in the funding of programs serving victims of domestic violence, rape, and child abuse. By 2008, Nunn had a job he seemingly loved, and he and Amanda became engaged.

The apparent improvement in Nunn's life would be short-lived. Alcohol, depression over his father's death, and jealousy in his relationship began to consume him. After a violent incident between Steve and Amanda in February 2009, she broke up with him and filed an emergency protective order against him. Within forty-eight hours of the protective order being granted by a court in Fayette County, Nunn resigned his position with the cabinet. He also entered an Alford plea (admitting no guilt, but acknowledging there was enough evidence for a jury to find him guilty) to a misdemeanor assault charge associated with his violence against Amanda (Alessi, Estep, & Ward, 2009). Nunn then sank even lower into a morass of alcoholism, sexual promiscuity, and a seething desire for revenge against Amanda.

As detailed in chapter 5, on September 11, 2009, Nunn stalked Amanda Ross and shot her to death as she left her condominium for work. After originally pleading not guilty, on June 28, 2011, Nunn pleaded guilty to Amanda's murder and to violating the protective order she had against him. He received a life sentence. Ironically, in 1998 Nunn had cosponsored a criminal justice bill (HB 455; see chapter 8) that made violating a protective order an aggravating circumstance in death penalty cases. His vote on that bill would affect his own life, making his murder of Amanda a death penalty case. In fact, throughout Nunn's career in the legislature and in state government, he had been a visible supporter of reforms to protect women and children. He served on several task forces and was a regular sponsor or cosponsor of domestic violence and child abuse legislation. Advocates trusted him as a friend of their cause, making his brutality all the more shocking.

Within days of the murder, Speaker Gregory D. Stumbo (Democrat from the Ninety-Fifth District) knew he would sponsor a bill to honor Amanda Ross. Within two months, a bill had been filed and introduced before the Interim Joint Committee on Judiciary. Stumbo not only had a long history of advocating for domestic violence and rape legislation; he also had a personal connection to the Ross family. He felt compelled to act for them and for all Kentucky victims. Stumbo also had a long history in the Kentucky house, serving as a state representative from 1980 to 2004, when he became the state's attorney general. For almost twenty of those years, he served as majority floor leader. Stumbo returned to the house in 2008 and would ultimately be elected speaker. As floor leader, Stumbo quietly shepherded many of our bills through the legislative process. During the Patton administration, Mrs. Patton and I would brief him at the beginning of every session on the bills we were proposing, and he would make sure those bills were heard on the house floor. He was the single brave cosponsor when Representative Marshall Long introduced the marital rape legislation in 1990 (HB 38).

In the sponsorship of HB 1, Stumbo was joined by forty-five

Representative Greg Stumbo with Amanda Ross's mother, Diana, upon HB 1's passage from the Judiciary Committee (with Mary Karen Stumbo looking on), January 7, 2010. (Courtesy of the Legislative Research Commission)

other legislators, all sharing a desire to honor Amanda, give strength to her mother, Diana, and change the law to save future victims. HB 1 created a new section of KRS Chapter 403 to permit a court, as part of a domestic violence protective order, to order a respondent to wear or carry a global positioning system (GPS) monitoring device. The bill also gave petitioners the option of carrying a similar device that would notify them if the respondent was nearby. The bill was slightly modified in the house to permit the use of GPS devices in other situations, including upon the pretrial release of a person on house arrest or a person with a substance abuse problem, for those enrolled in felony pretrial diversion programs, and upon an order of probation or shock probation. The house also amended the bill to allow a county or contiguous group of counties to jointly operate a GPS monitoring system. HB 1 passed in the house by a vote of ninety-seven to zero, taking only seven days from introduction (January 5) to passage (January 12).

Upon arrival in the senate, the bill stalled; it would sit in the

Judiciary Committee for more than two months before receiving a hearing (not entirely unusual, as one chamber often does not take up bills from the other chamber until March). Meanwhile, the house introduced bill after bill related to domestic violence, including legislation to criminalize trespassing on the grounds of shelters operated by domestic violence programs and to amend KRS 403.740 to allow an emergency protective order to remain in place until service on the adverse party (sponsored by Mike Denham, Democrat from the Seventieth District); to require respondents to protective orders to surrender their firearms to the local sheriff (sponsored by Joni Jenkins, Democrat from the Forty-Fourth District, and Mary Lou Marzian, Democrat from the Thirty-Fourth District); to require data collection related to domestic violence offenses (sponsored by Jimmie Lee, Democrat from the Twenty-Fifth District); and two bills to allow dating partners to obtain protective orders (one sponsored by Jenkins, and the other by Jody Richards, Democrat from the Twentieth District).[10] House leaders and members, working with the Kentucky Domestic Violence Association, chose to consolidate these bills, so Lee's bill was amended to absorb key provisions of all of them. His HB 189 then passed in the house by a vote of ninety-six to zero, but it never made it out of the senate's Judiciary Committee. Although none of these bills passed, several of their provisions were ultimately amended onto HB 1.

HB 1 arrived in the senate's Judiciary Committee on January 14, 2013, and began to move by the second week of March. The committee, chaired by Senator Tom Jensen (Republican from the Twenty-First District), took the opportunity to amend not only HB 1 but also the Domestic Violence and Abuse Act. The Judiciary Committee's version of HB 1 narrowed the eligibility for protective orders by removing persons related by consanguinity and affinity in the second degree (but did not add dating couples), and it amended KRS 403.740 to allow an emergency protective order to remain in place until service on an adverse party. It made significant changes to the provisions related to GPS devices, limiting their use to "substantial violations" of protective orders. The committee was sending an important message with this change, one that advocates would encounter again—namely, that many senators did not like the civil protective order process. They believed that victims of acts constituting criminal conduct should use the criminal side of the justice system, not the civil side. Therefore, they ensured that respondents to protective orders would not be ordered to wear tracking devices if their violation of the order did not rise to the level of criminal conduct. By the time HB 1 was voted out of the senate, it looked considerably different than it had upon arrival.

When the bill returned to the house for concurrence, members and advocates were unhappy with a number of the senate's amendments. As a result, the house chose not to concur with those changes and sent the bill back to the senate. The senate refused to remove its amendments, thus creating the need for a conference committee of legislators and then a free conference committee that would draft a final version of HB 1.

The free conference committee removed the bill's provisions related to risk assessment; allowed the extension of an emergency protective order for a maximum of six months, after which time the order would be rescinded unless the petitioner filed a new petition; and specified two years as the total time an emergency protective order could be extended and a hearing reset. It also added language to restrain the adverse party from approaching the petitioner or a minor child of the petitioner within a distance specified in the order, not to exceed 500 feet. With these and other changes, the free conference committee report on HB 1 was finalized on April 10, 2010. By April 14, the bill was back in the individual chambers, passing in the senate by a vote of thirty-seven to zero and in the House by a vote of 100 to zero.

Rape Examinations and Qualified Medical Professionals (2010)

HB 500, based on work by the state's Sexual Assault Response Team, was sponsored by Representatives Kevin Sinnette (Democrat from the 100th District), Marie Rader (Republican from the Eighty-Ninth District), Ruth Ann Palumbo (Democrat from the Seventy-Sixth District), Tom Riner (Democrat from the Forty-First District), Sal Santoro (Republican from the Sixtieth District), Fitz Steele (Democrat from the Eighty-Fourth District), John Tilley (Democrat from the Eighth District), and Addia Wuchner (Republican from the Sixty-Sixth District). The bill expanded the persons who are authorized to conduct forensic rape examinations to include other qualified medical professionals (as defined by administrative regulations promulgated by the Justice and Public Safety Cabinet). It also removed the statutory requirement that victims report the offense to law enforcement; specifically, it stated that no victim can be denied an examination because she chooses not to file a police report, cooperate with law enforcement, or otherwise participate in the criminal justice system. HB 500 also addressed the storage of samples collected during forensic rape examinations. The bill passed easily: ninety-five to zero vote in the house, and thirty-eight to zero in the senate.

Gun Bans Applicable to Persons Involuntarily Committed (2011)

HB 308, sponsored by Representatives Robert Damron (Democrat from the Thirty-Ninth District), Royce Adams (Democrat from the Sixty-First District), Will Coursey (Democrat from the Sixth District), Dennis Keene (Democrat from the Sixty-Seventh District), Terry Mills (Democrat from the Twenty-Fourth District), Rick Rand (Democrat from the Forty-Seventh District), Arnold Simpson (Democrat from the Sixty-Fifth District), and Brent Yonts (Democrat from the Fifteenth District), addressed the purchase of guns. It added a new section to KRS Chapter 237 to establish a procedure by which information about an individual who has been declared mentally ill by a court and has been committed to a mental institution is reported to the Kentucky State Police; in turn, the state police must transmit the person's Social Security number and date of birth and a copy of the commitment order to the FBI National Instant Criminal Background Check System. The bill also set out how a person can obtain relief from the prohibition on firearm possession as permitted by the federal National Instant Criminal Background Check System Improvement Amendments Act of 2007. The bill passed in the house by a vote of ninety-seven to one and in the senate by a vote of thirty-seven to zero.

Although not all gun-related bills are included in this book, the totality of Kentucky legislation focused on gun possession is worthy of mention. There are generally two types of laws: those that protect or extend the rights of gun owners, and those that restrict individuals from possessing firearms (specifically, felons and the mentally incompetent). Within the first category of laws, the 1970 General Assembly ensured the right to bear arms in the form of KRS Chapter 237 (language that already existed in the Kentucky Constitution as ratified in 1891).[11] In 1996 the legislature enacted a licensing process for Kentuckians to carry concealed deadly weapons, and in 2006 the primary gun law (KRS 237) was amended to allow employees to keep firearms or ammunition in vehicles parked on company property. The 2006 General Assembly also passed legislation to prohibit any person, unit of government, or governmental organization, during a period of disaster or emergency or at any other time, to revoke, suspend, or limit the right of any person to purchase, transfer, loan, own, possess, carry, or use a firearm, ammunition, or any deadly weapon or dangerous instrument.

The third significant gun measure passed in 2006 was Kentucky's version of a national trend to protect persons who use force or deadly force against intruders (KRS 503.080), based on the so-called castle doctrine. Kentucky's "stand-your-ground" law was broader than that of many states, as it applied to any place a person might legally be, rather than just a person's homestead. Interestingly, domestic violence advocates across the country have split on such laws. Opponents have raised concerns that they limit law enforcement's ability to enter a home where a victim may be held or harmed. Proponents have argued that these laws protect victims who kill offenders, allowing them to justify the deadly act. The latter outcome has yet to occur in a criminal trial, however. In a Florida case, for example, Marissa Alexander fired a weapon into the wall of her home as a warning shot when her ex-husband refused to leave the premises (Stacy, 2012). Court records showed that Alexander had a protective order against the man, who had violently abused her on multiple occasions and threatened her on the day she fired the weapon. Her defense attorneys unsuccessfully argued the applicability of the stand-your-ground law. Alexander was convicted of aggravated assault with a deadly weapon and sentenced to twenty years in prison under the state's mandatory sentencing law. (The jury deliberated twelve minutes before convicting her.)

The most recent major gun-rights legislation was passed in 2012, and it placed a proposal on the ballot to amend the Kentucky Constitution to mandate that hunting and fishing cannot be outlawed in the state without the vote of the people. The ballot measure passed with overwhelming support, although proponents acknowledged that no apparent threat to this right existed.

When the Kentucky General Assembly has acted to restrict gun rights in any way, it has usually been based on a requirement of federal law. For example, the 1994 General Assembly passed legislation to prohibit the sale of a firearm to a felon and to make the manufacture or sale of armor-piercing ammunition illegal—provisions that were already included in federal law (18 USC § 922(g)(8)). Legislation in 2011 also tightened the process by which the Kentucky State Police is notified that a person has been adjudicated mentally ill or committed to a mental hospital—information that must be entered into the National Instant Criminal Background Check System database.

The Kentucky General Assembly has also elevated the seriousness of criminal offenses when they are committed with a firearm or other deadly weapon or dangerous instrument. For example, the crime of stalking is elevated to a felony when the act is committed while the stalker has a deadly weapon on or about his person (KRS 508.140); the controlled substances law raises the offense by one class if the person possessed a firearm at the time of the crime (KRS 218A.992); and receiving stolen property is a class A misdemeanor unless the property is a firearm, in which case the crime is a class D felony (KRS 514.110).

Reform of the Criminal Justice System (2011)

More than thirty years after passage of the Kentucky Penal Code, a task force of legislators took a long look at its sentencing and penalty provisions. They focused on penalties that had become more stringent over the years, their goal being to more effectively manage the prison population and to institute a broader rehabilitative approach to offenses related to the use and abuse of drugs. The task force was led by the two chairs of the Interim Joint Committee on the Judiciary, Senator Tom Jensen (Republican from the Twenty-First District) and Representative John Tilley (Democrat from the Eighth District). When the task force completed its review, its final report took the form of HB 463, which was sponsored by Tilley and cosponsored by Greg Stumbo (Democrat from the Ninety-Fifth District), Rocky Adkins (Democrat from the Ninety-Ninth District), Tom Burch (Democrat from the Thirtieth District), Larry Clark (Democrat from the Forty-Sixth District), Jesse Crenshaw (Democrat from the Seventy-Seventh District), Robert Damron (Democrat from the Thirty-Ninth District), Martha Jane King (Democrat from the Sixteenth District), Arnold Simpson (Democrat from the Sixty-Fifth District), Tommy Thompson (Democrat from the Fourteenth

District), and Brent Yonts (Democrat from the Fifteenth District). The legislative intent of HB 463 was laid out clearly in its first part, which reformulated the state's sentencing policy in a new section of KRS Chapter 532:

(1) The primary objective of sentencing shall be to maintain public safety and hold offenders accountable while reducing recidivism and criminal behavior and improving outcomes for those offenders who are sentenced;

(2) Reduction of recidivism and criminal behavior is a key measure of the performance of the criminal justice system;

(3) Sentencing judges shall consider:
   (a) Beginning July 1, 2013, the results of a defendant's risk and needs assessment included in the presentence investigation; and
   (b) The likely impact of a potential sentence on the reduction of the defendant's potential future criminal behavior;

(4) All supervision and treatment programs provided for defendants shall utilize evidence-based practices to reduce the likelihood of future criminal behavior; and

(5) All supervision and treatment programs shall be evaluated at regular intervals to measure and ensure reduction of criminal behavior by defendants in the criminal justice system.

With that policy as a guide, HB 463 inserted offender risk assessments and treatment into the justice system, with an eye toward rehabilitation and risk reduction. It promoted community-based treatment, therapeutic interventions, and individualized treatment plans for drug offenders. The bill went so far as to establish a presumption that community-based treatment was appropriate unless the sentencing court found substantial and compelling reasons why a defendant could not be safely and effectively supervised in the community, was not amenable to community-based treatment, or posed a significant risk to public safety.

HB 463 also reduced sentences for certain drug offenders by amending KRS 218A so that a second or subsequent charge of possession of a controlled substance would not be elevated to a felony. Similarly, sentences for the illegal possession of a controlled substance were capped at three years, and options were provided for deferred prosecution (the preferred alternative) or presumptive

Representative John Tilley chairing the Judiciary Committee, January 19, 2011. (Courtesy of the Legislative Research Commission)

probation. Deferred prosecution meant that the charges would be set aside for up to two years and subsequently dismissed if the offender completed the deferred prosecution program. The bill also amended the maximum penalties for possession of marijuana and salvia: incarceration not to exceed forty-five days for the former and thirty days for the latter. Sentencing laws were also changed to exempt drug possessors from the category of persistent felony offenders. HB 463 expanded the conditions under which an offender could accrue credit toward a sentence to include obtaining a general equivalency diploma (GED), college degree, or technical certification; successfully completing a drug treatment program; or engaging in exceptionally meritorious service. Finally, HB 463 required the Department of Corrections to document the cost savings resulting from these changes and reinvest those funds in jail- and prison-based treatment and community-based recovery services for offenders. HB 463 also required the Kentucky Supreme Court to operate a drug court program.

HB 463 was largely embraced by the General Assembly, passing in the house by a vote of ninety-seven to two and in the senate by a vote of thirty-eight to zero.

Notes on a Bill That Did Not Pass

Legislation to amend the Domestic Violence and Abuse Act to allow members of a dating couple to obtain protective orders was introduced in at least eleven different bills over the decade (by primary sponsors Representatives John Tilley, Jody Richards, Joni Jenkins, Jimmie Lee, and Rob Wilkey and Senators Denise Harper Angel, Ray S. Jones II, and Kathy Stein), but it failed every time. The dating violence legislation was strongly supported by domestic violence advocates and was led for many years by the Kentucky Domestic Violence Association. Their determination was so single-mindedly robust that this was the only proposal they put before the General Assembly; as a result, only two major domestic violence bills were passed between 2002 and 2012 (Amanda's Law in 2010, and the elder abuse/domestic violence bill in 2005). Failure of the dating violence bills did not represent a lack of bill management or poor legislative advocacy; rather, it resulted from a growing hostility toward the entire civil protective order process. A growing number of legislators wanted to reopen the national debate, begun in the early 1980s, about providing a civil resource to support victims of domestic violence. The implications of revisiting that policy debate are addressed in chapter 10.

10

Violence against Women Legislative Reform

Past and Future

The legislation chronicled in previous chapters peels back layers of time to reveal the stories of just over 100 bills passed by the Kentucky General Assembly from 1970 to 2012. The bills included in this chronicle were chosen because they were proposed by the anti-rape and domestic violence movements in Kentucky[1] or because they dramatically impacted rape victims and battered women (e.g., the Kentucky Penal Code). These bills, in total, illustrate the building of Kentucky's justice system, and they give a face to the state's legislative response to domestic violence, rape, and stalking. The legislation that created the Kentucky Commission on Women as a state agency appropriately takes its place as the first reform described, for the totality of this book is an essay on women's accomplishments and women's empowerment.

FOUR DECADES OF LEGISLATION

Following creation of the Kentucky Commission on Women, the earliest reforms from the 1970s laid the foundation for the justice system of today. Work had begun in the late 1960s to write the state's first formal criminal law, leading to passage of the Kentucky Penal Code in 1974. This was instrumental to the construction of a fair and efficient justice system because, prior to the 1970s, criminal law was buried in case law, which was disorganized and sometimes contradictory, often leading to overlap and illogical application. The inherent unfairness and anachronistic nature of criminal law in Kentucky were eliminated by the Penal Code, providing a firm statutory structure for the first time in the state's history. The public defender system was also created in 1972, pushed by the Kentucky bar as practicing attorneys statewide grew weary of judicial orders to handle cases for indigent defendants. (Interestingly, the transformation of felony prosecutors to full-time Commonwealth's attorneys would await more than two decades, a supportive governor, and the 1996 General Assembly.) The unified court system in Kentucky was structured and funded by the 1974 and 1976 General Assemblies through another seminal set of bills that abolished the police courts, county courts, quarter-session courts, and justice of the peace courts; created the Administrative Office of the Courts; and gave the system uniformity and a two-tiered appellate process for the first time. (The next substantial reform of the court system—the establishment of family courts—took six years to accomplish and was finally passed in 2003.) For law enforcement, the centralized criminal history information system was established in 1976, and in subsequent years, officers would be empowered with the ability to make warrantless arrests in felony cases. (Warrantless arrest powers for misdemeanor assaults would be obtained through domestic violence reforms, described later.)

Less than a decade after passage of the Penal Code, and to the chagrin of its drafters, the General Assembly began to add new crimes to the code. Beginning in 1982, new offenses included criminal abuse, terroristic threatening, assault in the third degree, indecent exposure, institutional vandalism, fleeing or evading a peace officer, disarming a peace officer, drunken hunting, and video voyeurism. The new offense that drew the most visible support from legislators was fetal homicide in 2004 (with more than forty cosponsors), a crime that garnered the backing of pro-life proponents and left women's advocates worried about the implications for the pro-choice movement. In the 1980s the violent offender statute was created to address the most serious repeat offenders, and it has grown stronger and more expansive over the years as public sentiment has become tougher on crime. Legislatures in the 1980s also provided guidelines for determining the criminal responsibility of individuals with serious mental disorders.

By 1992 the second most significant reform of Kentucky law (after the Penal Code) was codified as the Kentucky Rules of Evidence. Just as the criminal law and the court system had once been a confusing morass of conflicting crimes and multiple courts, the rules guiding the use and introduction of evidence in court proceedings consisted of two centuries of statutes and court rulings embedded in common law and largely undecipherable by legal practitioners. The solution was a formal set of rules passed by the legislature in 1992 and subsequently adopted by the Kentucky Supreme Court.

Following adoption of the Penal Code, the General Assembly passed two major reforms to the criminal law and the management of criminal cases. During the Patton administration, the "governor's omnibus crime bill" created a state-level criminal justice planning body; established prevention programs and a statewide detention program for juveniles and added penalties for gang activity; designated certain offenses as hate crimes;[2] toughened penalties on serious and repeat offenders, including sex offenders; and created a certification program for law enforcement officers. The bill addressed the rights of crime victims by requiring restitution as a condition of pretrial diversion, probation, shock probation, conditional discharge, and parole, and it began to address the state's drug problem by increasing the penalties for possessing and trafficking in methamphetamines. The second major contemporary reform of the justice system was an outgrowth of this latter provision. Recognizing the breadth of the drug problem in the Commonwealth, a 2011 law reviewed how these cases were managed in the court system, in particular the sentencing and penalty provisions; instituted more effective management of the prison population; and required a broader rehabilitative approach to offenses related to the use and abuse of drugs. It reduced sentences for certain drug offenders, eliminated the elevation of a second or subsequent charge of possession of a controlled substance to a felony, and promoted the use of deferred prosecution.

Beyond building and amending the criminal justice system, a second category of legislation enacted over the past four decades relates to the rights of crime victims. As early as the mid to late 1970s, the General Assembly passed legislation to establish the Crime Victim Compensation Board and to protect vulnerable adults. In 1986 a crime victims' bill of rights was established under Kentucky law (KRS 421.500), and victims were permitted to testify before the parole board. Between 1994 and 2000, several bills proposed by anti-rape and domestic violence advocates benefited the larger population of crime victims, including a bill empowering victim advocates to escort crime victims into the courtroom and multiple bills to notify victims of an offender's release from jail or prison.

Rape Legislation

Kentucky's first anti-rape legislation was passed by the General Assembly almost forty years ago. Of the approximately thirty rape laws enacted since that time, a majority relate to criminal law and criminal procedure. These include measures proposed by the Kentucky Coalition against Rape and Sexual Assault to create the rape shield law in criminal cases (it was later extended to civil cases) and amendments to the sexual offense chapter to remove the term "earnest resistance," to amend the definition of "forcible compulsion," and to eliminate the spousal exclusion. The sexual offense chapter was also amended to elevate foreign object penetration to a rape offense and, in more recent years, to address the rape of incarcerated persons. Through the leadership of the Kentucky Association of Sexual Assault Programs (KASAP), rape victims cannot be forced or pressured to submit to a polygraph examination in the course of an investigation or prosecution. Newer statutes reflecting social and technological trends include human trafficking legislation and creation of the crime of using the Internet or social media to commit sexual offenses or to stalk a victim.

Following legislation pertaining to criminal law and procedure, the second largest group of rape-related bills passed over the decades involves the interdiction, prosecution, and management of sex offenders. (Arguably, these bills are also related to the criminal law and procedure as they apply to the processing of arrested and convicted sex offenders.) The first bill, proposed by the Rape Coalition and passed by the Kentucky legislature in 1986, defined sex offenders and created the sex offender treatment program. Subsequently, several bills proposed by the Attorney General's Task Force on Child Sexual Abuse were passed, providing for risk assessments of sex offenders and creating a sex offender registry in Kentucky. The initial law designed the registry to serve as an investigative tool for law enforcement, following passage of the federal Jacob Wetterling Crimes Against Children and Sexually Violent Offender Registration Act in 1994; it was expanded into a public notification resource in the next session, following Congress's passage of Megan's Law and the Pam Lychner Sex Offender Tracking and Identification

Act in 1996. Innumerable other measures have been passed over the years to restrict the release of sex offenders, and sex offenders are included in laws related to violent offenders.

The third group of rape laws covers the aftermath of sexual assault and victim intervention. As early as 1978, legislation required hospitals with twenty-four-hour emergency departments to offer forensic rape examinations, and in 1984 the state was required to pay for those examinations. In 1996 the Governor's Office of Child Abuse and Domestic Violence Services worked with KASAP to make Kentucky the leader in developing a statewide Sexual Assault Nurse Examiner Program, and over the next several years, three more laws would address payment and provider issues. Counseling services have also been facilitated legislatively, first by establishing that communications between a rape crisis counselor and a rape victim are privileged. (This privilege would eventually be extended to a broader group of victim advocates, including domestic violence counselors.) Legislation that altered insurance reimbursement for mental health care and gave minors the right to receive counseling without parental consent was designed to make therapeutic intervention more accessible to rape victims. Finally, legislation proposed by the Governor's Task Force on Sexual Assault established rape crisis centers in statute, organized the regional distribution of these centers, provided for their funding, and set out the types of services they would provide.

In addition to legislative reforms, anti-rape advocates (inside and outside government) have been able to secure funding for rape crisis centers in Kentucky. In 1986, $100,000 in seed money was quietly placed into the budget of the Sexual and Domestic Violence Program in the Department for Mental Health and Mental Retardation Services. (At the time, the rape crisis centers also received $87,994 in preventive health and health services block grant funding.) Funding for the centers experienced slow growth over the next decade as their number more than tripled, from four to thirteen. Their funding grew substantially during the administration of Governor Paul Patton, when state general funds increased by almost 130 percent (from $916,462 in 1995 to $2,100,656 in 2003).[3]

Domestic Violence and Stalking Legislation

As the anti-rape movement began its reform of the criminal justice system in the mid-1970s, the domestic violence movement began to focus on police procedure, protective services, and funding for shelters. The first piece of legislation in 1978 created the uniform reporting form for law enforcement, and the second added spouses to the mandatory reporting laws in Kentucky. Warrantless arrest powers for law enforcement appeared in the 1980 session, and during the 1982 session, fueled by the leadership of the newly formed Kentucky Domestic Violence Association (KDVA), two major accomplishments improved the budgets of the shelters by instituting a marriage license fee and supporting state funding for shelters (now called domestic violence programs). Four years later, that funding was significantly increased to allow the development of a statewide network of shelter programs. The most significant increase in funding for domestic violence programs came during the Patton administration, when general funds increased by 42 percent (from $3,415,046 in 1995 to $4,851,852 in 2003). In addition to increasing general funding, Governor Patton allocated a one-time capital construction fund of $1,075,000 to improve the structures of the domestic violence programs. Many of these improvements were accomplished with the help of First Lady Judi C. Patton, whom I affectionately called my "secret weapon." During the Beshear administration, as the state's economic downturn made general funds scarce, First Lady Jane Beshear worked with the KDVA on an innovative "shop and share program" to bolster in-kind giving to domestic violence programs and the women they serve.[4] Finally, in 2005 the regionalization of domestic violence programs as "primary service providers" for battered women was enshrined in statute (as part of a bill addressing elder abuse), adding new language to KRS Chapter 209A. In 1984 the KDVA was also instrumental in advancing passage of the Domestic Violence and Abuse Act, which would serve as the chief legal resource for battered women and their children.

The Attorney General's Task Force on Domestic Violence Crime was the first broad-based, interdisciplinary legislative effort in the domestic violence field. In the 1992 session it advanced legislation to address cases of self-defense in which a battered woman killed an abusive partner; to require domestic violence to be considered during custody decisions; to create the crime of stalking; and to expand the Domestic Violence and Abuse Act. Four years later, the Legislative Task Force on Domestic Violence proposed another strong portfolio of bills that passed, including legislation to provide full faith and credit for domestic violence protective orders and to ensure their twenty-four-hour availability; to mandate training for criminal justice, health, and mental health care professionals; to create a certification program for domestic violence offender treatment providers; and to enhance penalties for repeated domestic violence–related assaults. (The bills creating a victim notification mechanism and authorizing advocates to accompany victims into court were described earlier but were actually part of the task force package.) In the late 1990s and early 2000s, the Governor's Council on Domestic Violence and Sexual Assault took the lead in legislative advocacy, proposing bills to expand training for more professionals and to include rape as a topic of training, in addition to domestic violence, and to notify petitioners when a respondent to a domestic violence order attempts to purchase a firearm. Stalking has been addressed three times by the Kentucky General Assembly: the law's creation in 1992, the creation of a stalking protective order, and the creation of the crime of stalking using the Internet.

PATTERNS IN RAPE, DOMESTIC VIOLENCE, AND STALKING LEGISLATION: 1970–2012

Just over half of the approximately one hundred bills included in this chronicle relate specifically to rape, domestic violence, and stalking. (The rest have a more general purpose, such as penal code reform and family court legislation.) A comparison of these roughly fifty bills reveals some interesting patterns. First, over the past four decades, the General Assembly has passed more bills related to rape (approximately 55 percent of the approximate 50 bills) than to domestic violence (40 percent) or stalking (5 percent). Of the twenty-eight legislative sessions portrayed in the chronicle, eighteen included at least one bill related to rape, twelve had bills related to domestic violence, and three addressed stalking. Anti-rape bills were spread fairly evenly among sessions, with one or two bills being proposed during each of the eighteen sessions, whereas domestic violence legislation tended to be clustered in groups of bills, with more sessions in which no domestic violence bills were introduced.

Targets of Reform

The anti-rape and domestic violence movements (both nationally and in Kentucky) did not approach legal reforms in exactly the same way, as each had very different priorities. The anti-rape movement began by advocating for the repeal of provisions in the criminal sexual offense statutes that had a harmful effect on rape survivors (e.g., statutes of limitations on rape but not on other felonies, spousal exclusions, the victim-resistance requirement) and for the addition of victim protections in the legal process (e.g., the rape shield law). Anti-rape reforms also addressed interdiction and the management and treatment of sex offenders, as well as statutory provisions related to forensic rape examinations.

Domestic violence reforms, in contrast, started with a different priority and addressed a wider range of reforms. Among the first was the effort to secure funding to create and expand shelters across the Commonwealth. Advocates in the domestic violence movement chose funding as a first priority because they knew that if women did not have a safe place to flee their partners' lethal violence, then other legal reforms would be of little consequence (Walker 2012). Early efforts also included policy and practice reforms directed at law enforcement and prosecutors; these reforms were less about amending existing criminal law and more about ensuring its effective enforcement. Domestic violence reforms have also focused heavily on adding civil justice options to the array of protections available to battered women. Other topics have included professional certification and mandatory training, adult protection, domestic relations, and prevention.

Sources of Reform

It is notable that legislative reforms have rarely been the result of a combined effort of the anti-rape and domestic violence movements. Even in the case of marital rape (the one exception), that effort was actually commenced by one group (the Rape Coalition); only later did it benefit from the addition of domestic violence and other women's advocates to the broader advocacy group. For the first twenty-five years outlined in this book, legislation related to rape was primarily initiated by the Rape Coalition and its legislative allies. In fact, nearly one-third of all rape-related bills passed in the last forty years were initiated by that advocacy organization. The coalition ceased operations in 1994 in the belief that the statewide coalition of rape crisis centers (KASAP) could and should take the lead in advancing rape-related legislation.[5] During the Jones and Patton administrations, task forces, the Governor's Council on Domestic Violence and Sexual Assault, and the Governor's Office of Child Abuse and Domestic Violence Services actually led that effort, and the majority of anti-rape legislation in the past four decades was accomplished during their active years (1994–2003). More recently, KASAP has assumed a more active legislative role, advancing its first stand-alone legislative effort in 2008.

The first reforms in the domestic violence arena were initiated in the late 1970s by individual domestic violence programs and the Commission on Women, in partnership with key legislative allies. Beginning in 1982 and for the next decade, the Kentucky Domestic Violence Association led domestic violence reforms in the state. Beginning in the 1990s, however, the majority of domestic violence–related reforms were accomplished through task forces and councils rather than one single association. The 1992 Attorney General's Task Force on Domestic Violence Crime, the 1996 Legislative Task Force on Domestic Violence, and the 1998–2002 Governor's Council on Domestic Violence and Sexual Assault were the primary legislative advocacy groups in the domestic violence field. Following the 2002 legislative session, the number of domestic violence reforms dropped significantly, a trend covered in the next section of this chapter.

The most active years of legislative reform to address rape and domestic violence in Kentucky stretched from 1992 through 2003 (see figure 10.1). Before 1992, one or two rape or domestic violence bills would pass in each legislative session, reflecting the work of early, brave advocates. Beginning in 1992, legislative accomplishments

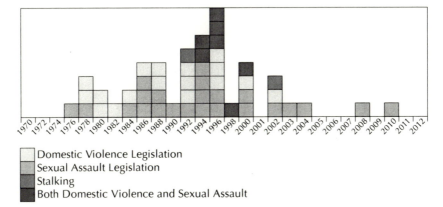

Domestic Violence Legislation
Sexual Assault Legislation
Stalking
Both Domestic Violence and Sexual Assault

Figure 10.1. Advocate-Proposed Legislation by Legislative Session

largely resulted from task forces, coalitions, and councils with powerful conveners (attorney general, governor, or General Assembly) and influential members (legislators and leaders of numerous advocacy, criminal justice, and health and mental health organizations). Importantly, a major strength of this model was that advocates did more than simply serve on these bodies; they were also involved in staffing—a critical way to influence the direction of a task force or council. During this productive era, an average of four to six bills passed each legislative session as a comprehensive package. That number has now declined. Between 2003 and 2012, only two domestic violence bills were passed (the elder abuse/domestic violence bill in 2005, and Amanda's Law in 2010), and fewer than five rape-related bills were passed, only one of which was initiated by an advocacy organization.

Legislators and Their Votes

A review of all legislation proposed by the anti-rape and domestic violence movements over the past forty years reveals that we relied on the support of approximately two dozen key legislators to accomplish all that we have. These individuals include house and senate members who served as bill sponsors, committee chairs who let our bills be heard, and legislative leaders who shepherded our bills through the legislative process. Legislative sponsors have been Democrat and Republican, women and men, conservative and liberal, but they all shared a commitment to justice and to protecting Kentucky's women and children.

Beyond the small group of legislators we depended on as bill sponsors, the success of any bill we proposed always came down to voting patterns by all legislators. For each bill, we had to achieve support from a majority of legislators. The evolution of voting patterns on domestic violence and rape legislation over the past four decades has been interesting to witness. It began with large numbers of "no" votes by legislators who felt no significant external pressure to support our legislation. For example, the 1978 legislation requiring hospitals with twenty-four-hour emergency rooms to provide forensic rape examinations passed in the house, but it did so by a heart-stopping count of forty-six in favor, twenty opposed, and thirty-four not voting at all. To be sure, the 1970s and 1980s brought significant legislative success, but our wins were hard fought, and more often than not, we worked in a culture that was unsupportive of women.

The second phase in voting patterns began as the 1990s dawned, and we began to see a change in attitude in our state. It became less permissible to publicly oppose legislation intended to protect women and children. The vote totals for rape, domestic violence, and stalking bills reflected that change, and by the 1990s, there were significantly more bills passing unanimously or with almost no opposing votes in the house and senate. (For example, the marital rape bill of 1988 was defeated by the house 42–49; the 1990 version passed 81–7.) As a practical matter, beginning in the early to mid-1990s, legislators may have felt more external pressure to support rape and domestic violence legislation because a majority of these bills were proposed by highly visible coalitions, task forces, and councils; they often offered bills as packages that benefited from an element of momentum that swept all the individual bills through the legislature together. Task force and council bills also had prior legislative involvement through their membership (legislators often served on these task forces and councils), and they were staffed by effective, well-organized, and persuasive advocates who, by this time, were well known and trusted by legislators. These practical factors certainly influenced more legislators to vote in favor of our proposals.

Although a measurable cultural shift toward intolerance of violence and support for women has benefited the anti-rape and domestic violence movements, there are sharp exceptions. Certain types of legislation are still resisted by the Kentucky General Assembly, regardless of cultural shifts, the political influence of the bill's sponsor, or the persuasiveness of advocates. A review of voting patterns shows that legislation addressing marital rape and domestic relations continues to draw significant opposition from the General Assembly. On their face, these two types of bills seem quite different: one is criminal and the other civil; one is handled as a felony in a circuit court, while the other is adjudicated in family court. What they share in common, however, is the pervasive and persistent view that women routinely make false claims of victimization and use false allegations of rape or domestic violence to punish their partners in criminal court or to benefit themselves in custody or divorce proceedings—in short, that women lie. This negative view of women, once embedded in seventeenth-century English common law, is still flourishing today.

THE FUTURE OF REFORM: REFLECTIONS OF ONE ADVOCATE

A chronicle such as this one compels a question regarding the future of legislative reform and how lessons from the past can inform our work in coming decades. Reenergizing legislative reform related to domestic violence and rape is a timely undertaking, for in many states, the successes of the past have waned. This is true in Kentucky, where the number of bills passed since the early 2000s has dropped.

What has caused the slowing of legislative reform in Kentucky in the past decade? The first factor involves the General Assembly itself. One could argue that the increased partisanship displayed in the 2000s has created an environment that is less supportive of significant legislative reform. This is a problem that goes beyond our movement; it impacts a broad range of legislative efforts at both the state and national levels. Second, years of hard work and cultural shifts resulted in voting pattern changes, as it became less acceptable to oppose what were viewed as women's issues; more recently, however, there appears to be a shift back, with an increase in legislative efforts perceived to be against women, gays and lesbians, and other minority groups (Marzian, 2013).[6]

Additionally, I believe there is a "fatigue factor." As pointed out by one legislative leader, "The legislature works on the 'squeaky wheel' theory; we react to what is brought to us. It's the nature of the legislature to address a significant policy or budget issue, solve it, and then move on to the next crisis. You're challenged because you want to keep coming back to get more bills passed; it's not just domestic violence (and rape), all issues are treated like that" (Stumbo, 2012). For advocates, this suggests that our future success depends on our ability to convince the public (and, by extension, their elected representatives) that the rape and battering of women are still pertinent issues. We must fight the false argument that nothing substantial is left to be done, for as we achieve a deeper understanding of the nature of these offenses and the efficacy of interventions, laws must change accordingly. Some recent examples include extending protections to immigrant women and to dating couples, addressing cyberstalking, and removing the statute of limitations on rape cases because of the availability of DNA testing. As humorously expressed by former governor Martha Layne Collins: "It's kind of like housework, it's never done" (Collins, 2013).

Another major factor in the slowing of reform in Kentucky is the role of advocates. Historically, we served as the bedrock of legislative reform; we were the instigators who persuaded top executive and legislative branch leaders to hear our concerns. These days, however, advocates are less visible in the halls of the capitol. As expressed by a legislator who also served as an advocate, "Advocates are much less present and behind the scenes; like they're letting the legislators they always counted on do it alone. They seem more timid, more afraid of losing state funding at a time when their budgets are rock bottom and the economy is as well (Jenkins, 2012). That sentiment is echoed by top advocates as well. Said one, "We feel a need to protect what we've won before now and to protect our budgets. I think we have more access, but we're fearful of using it (Currens, 2012). In addition, advocates are scarcer within state government; the specialized offices that once flourished in Kentucky government and partnered with advocates outside of government have now been eliminated or downsized and underfunded.

Finally, at a practical level, there are no active interdisciplinary coalitions, task forces, or councils currently working on legislative reform. Their absence means an absence of their advantages: early involvement of multiple legislators, visible support from governors, media support, and momentum. One legislative leader, reflecting on past years, said, "These days I couldn't even tell you what provisions were in which bills back then, but it was obvious there was a concerted effort to pass a coordinated, well-thought-out, comprehensive package of bills. That influenced how well those bills fared" (Stivers, 2012).

Fear of funding cuts, partisanship, the fatigue factor, and the absence of interdisciplinary task forces and councils may explain a decline in the passage of legislation, but they do not mean that resurgence is impossible. Although the relevant factors differ in states across the country, the following guidelines can advance our efforts in coming years.

Know Your History

For today's advocates, there are lessons to be learned from the almost hundred-year history of the women's movement in the United States. As detailed in chapter 1, women sought the right to vote and fought for legal and economic equality in the early 1900s. As these priority reforms were achieved, however, the women's movement became less visible and seemed less urgent, and the progression of women's freedoms slowed for decades. It was not until the 1970s that women started to rebuild momentum for reform and reignite the battle for women's rights. This second wave of the women's movement in the 1970s gave birth to the anti-rape and domestic violence movements, which would go on to achieve remarkable improvements in women's lives. In Kentucky, the 1970s through 1990s brought a torrent of reforms, but in the following decade, legislative reform slowed again. One can only wonder what reforms were delayed or lost because the movement was stuck on pause for so many years. What might have been accomplished if the women's movement had maintained its fierce determination between 1920 and 1970?

The first lesson for today's advocates, then, is that sporadic reforms can mean delayed or even denied reforms. When addressing something as ubiquitous and damaging as domestic violence and rape, advocates cannot afford to accept gaps in legislative reform. Ours must be a continuous, ever-adapting movement that evolves with our knowledge but never subsides.

Second, advocates of today need to know their history and recognize that they are the daughters and granddaughters of earlier reformers. Chapters 3 and 4 offer that history and reveal what worked and what did not and how improvements were achieved in state houses and courthouses. Advocates, particularly those in state leadership roles and those involved in legislative work, must be fluent in that history and capable of using its lessons to inform the work ahead. But today's young advocates should not shoulder that responsibility alone. Those of us who have been part of the reform effort from its earliest years must teach the next generation of advocates. As one long-standing advocate put it, "We didn't even know we were making history" (Johnson, 2013). Yet we were, and we have been making history for more than four decades. That history must be known and owned by the generation of advocates that follows us.

Build a Legislative Powerhouse

As a practical matter, building an effective legislative response to rape and domestic violence means that advocates need to be savvy about how the state legislature works and how to turn an idea into a law signed by the governor. As explored in chapter 5, ideas for legislative reform come from two levels: individuals and groups. At an individual level, advocates need to have representatives at the state level with "lobbying" expertise. They also need to know legislators and be familiar with the process by which a bill becomes a law. A good idea will fall short if the proposal cannot make it through the legislative process. At the group level, the model of state task forces and coalitions has worked very well in Kentucky.[7] Therefore, it would be wise to explore how interdisciplinary legislative coalitions can be implemented again and how the power they bring in terms of numbers and influence can support anti-rape and domestic violence advocates. Historically, Kentucky task forces have been created at the top levels of government (General Assembly, governor, attorney general), but this is not the only model. Coalitions of domestic violence or anti-rape groups can assume the leadership role, create effective interdisciplinary legislative reform groups, and access all the advantages discussed in chapter 5. It is also wise to pair public awareness campaigns with the proposal of new legislation; this can have the dual advantage of advancing the bill's passage and playing an instrumental role in effecting social change.

A third important level is the grass roots, where the anti-rape and domestic violence movements were born. A grassroots network of advocates, women's organizations, and community members who oppose violence and support healthy families, paired with legislative advocates at the state level, builds the broadest powerhouse to ensure that legislators listen to our proposals. For us, grassroots movements are advocates, but to legislators, they are influential constituents.

Be Constantly Aware and Responsive

In the 1970s, as the anti-rape and domestic violence movements were growing, there was no word and no specific criminal offense to describe what women experienced when abusive intimates or strangers followed them, left notes on their car windshields, sent them unwanted packages, or watched their every movement. It was not until 1990 that the field responded with law and policy changes to address stalking. Back in the early days of reform, the pervasive use of date-rape drugs could not have been predicted, and the notion of cybercrimes could not have been imagined. Thus, we must stay attuned to evolving influences and interests and respond accordingly. However, awareness cannot be limited to types of crimes or the methods by which they are committed. Not all women experience or react to victimization in the same way, so our legislative changes must also reflect new knowledge about race, ethnicity, culture, poverty, and related issues.

This book is intended to celebrate the work of advocates and our legislative allies over the past four decades. While celebratory, this book should also serve as a reminder that our work is never done. As a state and as a nation, we have much to be proud of in the measure of our accomplishments and much to be grateful for. The systems that serve and respond to victims of domestic violence and rape are demonstrably better than they were four decades ago. Our prior success, however, cannot make us complacent about the future. Complacency can lead to a loss of progress, the repeal of taken-for-granted reforms, and an inability to respond to the newest forms of victimization. Knowledge and awareness are vital if advocates hope to maintain their relevance at the state level and if victims and survivors are to be protected and well served.

We advocates also have to deal with factors such as devastating budget cuts, increasing partisanship, and loss of interest in our cause. But advocates can take heart: the fears confronting today's advocates are not unlike those that rattled our sisters in the earliest days of reform. They found strategies to make their work successful, and in solidarity with them, today's advocates can do so as well. We have learned from them, and we have learned from our own experiences of the past four decades. In that knowledge, we will find continued success. As the mighty reformer Susan B. Anthony once said, "Failure is impossible" (Sherr, 1995).

Appendix A

Interviews Conducted by the Author

Note: Legislative and executive branch titles are used for current and retired legislators and governors.

Marie Abrams, Louisville, Kentucky
Kim Allen, Louisville, Kentucky
Jerry Bowles, Louisville, Kentucky
Representative Michael D. Bowling, Middlesboro, Kentucky
Bonnie Brown, Louisville, Kentucky
Governor John Y. Brown Jr., Lexington, Kentucky
Representative Thomas Burch, Louisville, Kentucky
Patricia Byron, Louisville, Kentucky
Logan Calvert, Madisonville, Kentucky
Governor Martha Layne Collins, Versailles, Kentucky
Representative Fred Cowan, Louisville, Kentucky
Sharon A. Currens, Frankfort, Kentucky
Senator Julie Denton, Louisville, Kentucky
Paul Doyle, Louisville, Kentucky
Representative Robert Heleringer, Louisville, Kentucky
Representative Joni Jenkins, Louisville, Kentucky
Pam Johnson, Louisville, Kentucky
Senator David Karem, Louisville, Kentucky
Diane Lawless, Lexington, Kentucky
Robert Lawson, Lexington, Kentucky
Senator Marshall Long, Shelbyville, Kentucky
Jessica Loving, Louisville, Kentucky
Representative Mary Lou Marzian, Louisville, Kentucky
Burniece Whitaker Minix, Salyersville, Kentucky

Senator Michael R. Moloney, Lexington, Kentucky
Lisa Murray, Lexington, Kentucky
First Lady Judi Patton, Pikeville, Kentucky
Governor Paul E. Patton, Pikeville, Kentucky
Holly Dunn Pendleton, Evansville, Indiana
Senator Georgia Davis Powers, Louisville, Kentucky
Eileen Recktenwald, Frankfort, Kentucky
Diana Ross, Lexington, Kentucky
Marcia Roth, Louisville, Kentucky
Senator Kathy Stein, Lexington, Kentucky
Senate President Robert Stivers, Manchester, Kentucky
House Speaker Gregory D. Stumbo, Prestonsburg, Kentucky
Merle Van Houten, Tucker, Georgia
Edwina Walker, Savannah, Georgia

Select Anti-Rape and Domestic Violence Legislation: 1970–2012

General Assembly	Bill Number	Recorded Sponsor (Party, District)	Subject Matter
Governor Louie B. Nunn (1967–1971)			
1970	SB 23	Sen. Walter Reichart (R, 34), J. C. Carter (R, 9)	Creation of the Kentucky Commission on Women
	SB 193	Sen. Georgia Davis Powers (D, 33)	Minors' right to consent to select medical procedures
Governor Wendell Ford (1971–1974)			
1972	SB 309	Sen. Georgia Davis Powers (D, 33)	Minors' right to consent to select medical procedures expanded
	HB 197	Rep. Bill Kenton (D, 75)	Initial creation of the Kentucky Penal Code
	HB 461	Reps. Bill Kenton (D, 75), Ralph Graves (D, 1), John Swinford (D, 62)	Creation of the Kentucky Public Defender's Office
Governor Julian M. Carroll (1974–1979)			
1974	SB 183	Sens. William L. Sullivan (D, 4), John C. Cornett (D, 29), Kelsey Friend (D, 31), Tom Garrett (D, 2), William Gentry Jr. (D, 14), Carroll Hubbard Jr. (D, 1), Gus Sheehan (D, 23)	Constitutional amendment to create new judicial article
	SB 334	Sen. Michael R. Moloney (D, 13)	Funding for a unified court system

General Assembly	Bill Number	Recorded Sponsor (Party, District)	Subject Matter
	HB 232	Reps. Richard Lewis (D, 6), William Kenton (D, 75), Gross C. Lindsay (D, 11), Allen, Benson, Beshear, Hancock, Hopkins, Overstreet, Quickert, Stone	Creation of the final version of the Kentucky Penal Code
1976	HB 143	Reps. James B. Yates (D, 44), Bob Benson (D, 33), Thomas B. Givhan (D, 49)	Creation of the statutory rape shield law
	HB 432	Reps. Charles Wible (D, 13), Bobby Richardson (D, 23)	Unified court system: court of appeals
	HB 438	Reps. Charles Wible (D, 13), Bobby Richardson (D, 23)	Unified court system: election of judges
	HB 544	Rep. Charles Wible (D, 13)	Unified court system: role of chief justice
	SB 15	Sens. Walter Baker (R, 9), Gus Sheehan (D, 23)	Unified court system: county courts to district courts
	SB 58	Sen. David Karem (D, 35)	Creation of the Crime Victim Compensation Board
	SB 162	Sens. William L. Sullivan (D, 4), Tom Garrett (D, 2)	Unified court system: supreme court
	SB 230	Sens. David Karem (D, 35), Huff, Gibson, Stamper	Creation of the Adult Protection Act
	SB 295	Sen. Tom Garrett (D, 2)	Creation of the Centralized Criminal Justice Information System
1978	HB 501	Rep. Gerta Bendl (D, 34)	Addition of "spouse abuse" to Adult Protection Act
	HB 496	Rep. Gerta Bendl (D, 34)	Mandate to create uniform reporting forms for law enforcement
	HB 497	Rep. Gerta Bendl (D, 34)	Amendment to hospital licensure law to require hospitals with 24-hour emergency departments to make forensic rape examinations available

General Assembly	Bill Number	Recorded Sponsor (Party, District)	Subject Matter
Governor John Y. Brown (1979–1983)			
1980	HB 86	Reps. Gerta Bendl (D, 34), J. LeMaster (D, 72), A. McNutt (D, 3)	Authorization of warrantless arrest in cases of domestic violence
	HB 87	Reps. Gerta Bendl (D, 34), J. LeMaster (D, 72)	Early protective order
	HB 779	Rep. Gerta Bendl (D, 34)	Adult Protection Act: removal of requirement that victims sign a statement prior to receiving protective services
1982	HB 1	Rep. Gerta Bendl (D, 34)	Creation of involuntary commitment proceedings
	HB 32	Reps. Roger Noe (D, 88), Richardson, Overstreet, Freibert, Priddy	Creation of provisions for criminal responsibility
	HB 141	Rep. Gerta Bendl (D, 34)	Marriage license fee for spouse abuse center funding
	HB 383	Reps. Ray Brown (D, 99), Cline, Cyrus, Stone	Creation of felony 3rd-degree assault when the person assaulted is acting in a professional capacity
	HB 669	Reps. Gerta Bendl (D, 34), J. LeMaster (D, 72)	Creation of crime of criminal abuse
Governor Martha Layne Collins (1983–1987)			
1984	SB 17	Sen. Michael R. Moloney (D, 13)	Creation of Domestic Violence and Abuse Act
	HB 196	Rep. Marshall Long (D, 58)	Mandate that the state (not victims) pay for forensic rape examinations
1986	SB 310	Sen. Ed O'Daniel (D, 14)	Creation of duty-to-warn responsibilities for mental health professionals
	HJR 1	Rep. Thomas J. Burch (D, 30)	Expansion of funding for statewide spouse abuse centers (now domestic violence programs)
	HB 8	Reps. William Donnermeyer Sr. (D, 68), Stephen C. Keith (R, 90), Pearl Ray Lefevers (D, 87)	Authorization for crime victims to speak before parole board

General Assembly	Bill Number	Recorded Sponsor (Party, District)	Subject Matter
	HB 76	Reps. Dottie Priddy (D, 45), Clark, Guenthner, Kerr, Lile, Reinhardt, Seum, Steward, Yates	Creation of violent offender statute
	HB 263	Reps. Marshall Long (D, 58), Gerta Bendl (D, 34), Bill Lile (R, 28)	Creation of sexual assault counselor privilege
	HB 311	Reps. Bill Brinkley (D, 10), Gerta Bendl (D, 34), Tom Riner (D, 41), Gregory D. Stumbo (D, 95)	Marital rape (attempt to expand types of cases to which the spousal exclusion would not apply)
	HB 390	Reps. Fred Cowan (D, 32), Blevins, Caldwell, Harper, Johnson, Kerr, Lear, Nett, Priddy, Pritchett, Reinhardt, Richards, Riner, Seum	Creation of Crime Victim Bill of Rights
	HB 535	Rep. Fred Cowan (D, 32)	Creation of sex offender treatment program

Governor Wallace G. Wilkinson (1987–1991)

General Assembly	Bill Number	Recorded Sponsor (Party, District)	Subject Matter
1988	HB 87	Rep. Thomas J. Burch (D, 30)	Expansion of definition of "family member" under Domestic Violence and Abuse Act and warrantless arrest statute
	HB 288	Reps. Jon David Reinhardt (R, 69), Ray Altman (R, 51), Bill Lile (R, 28), Dan Seum (D, 38)	Removal of the term "earnest resistance" from rape statute
	HB 345	Rep. Walter Blevins (D, 71)	Creation of family violence prevention curriculum for schools (removed with passage of KERA 2 years later)
	HB 574	Rep. Walter Blevins (D, 71)	Minors' right to consent to counseling under select conditions
1990	HB 305	Sen. Tim Shaughnessy (D, 28)	Expansion of statutory definition of "dangerous instrument" to include hands and feet
	HB 38	Reps. Marshall Long (D, 58), Gregory D. Stumbo (D, 95)	Marital rape (removal of spousal exemption)

General Assembly	Bill Number	Recorded Sponsor (Party, District)	Subject Matter
	HB 214	Reps. William Lear (D, 79), Joe Clarke (D, 54)	Initial codification of Kentucky Rules of Evidence

		Governor Brereton C. Jones (1991–1995)	
1992	SB 80	Sens. David Karem (D, 35), David LeMaster (D, 25)	Requirement that domestic violence be considered as a factor in custody
	SB 160	Sens. Michael R. Moloney (D, 13), Dick Roeding (R, 24), David Karem (D, 35)	Expansion of definitional section of rape statute to include penetration with a foreign object
	HB 115	Reps. Marshall Long (D, 58), Mark Farrow (D, 62)	Expansion of Domestic Violence and Abuse Act
	HB 241	Reps. William Lear (D, 79), Joe Clarke (D, 54)	Final codification of Kentucky Rules of Evidence
	HB 256	Rep. Richard Lewis (D, 6)	Expansion of statutory meaning of imminent danger as applied to domestic violence homicide cases
	HB 445	Rep. Richard Lewis (D, 6)	Creation of crime of stalking
	HB 481	Reps. Paul Mason (D, 91), Russell Bentley (D, 92)	Requirement for HIV testing of sex offenders
	HB 631	Reps. Steve Riggs (D, 31), Gregory D. Stumbo (D, 95), Jon Ackerson (R, 47)	Requirement for DNA testing of sex offenders
1994	SB 43	Sen. Jeffrey Green (D, 1)	Creation of Kentucky sex offender registry
	SB 107	Sen. Gerald Neal (D, 33)	Strengthening response of licensure boards to acts of sexual misconduct by professionals
	HB 95	Rep. Paul Mason (D, 95)	Creation of victim advocates in statute, including authorization to accompany victims in court proceedings
	HB 96	Reps. Robert Damron (D, 39), Jesse Crenshaw (D, 77), William Donnermeyer (D, 68), Bill Lile (R, 28), Tommy Todd (R, 83)	Mandate for courts to order assessment of sex offenders

General Assembly	Bill Number	Recorded Sponsor (Party, District)	Subject Matter
	HB 115	Reps. Robert Damron (D, 39), Bill Lile (R, 28), Tommy Todd (R, 83)	Strengthening response of licensure boards to acts of sexual misconduct by professionals
	HB 514	Reps. Jesse Crenshaw (D, 77), Robert Damron (D, 39), Porter E. Hatcher (D, 43), Paul Mason (D, 95)	Extension of insurance reimbursement to licensed psychologists and licensed clinical social workers to make mental health services more accessible to victims
Governor Paul E. Patton (1995–1999, 1999–2003)			
1996	SB 60	Sen. Michael R. Moloney (D, 13)	Authorization for pilot family court within circuit court
	SB 105	Sen. Jeffrey Green (D, 1)	Full faith and credit for domestic violence protective orders
	SB 108	Sen. Jeffrey Green (D, 1)	Statutory creation of the statewide victim notification system (VINE)
	SR 47	Sen. Jeffrey Green (D, 1) and 19 cosponsors	Resolution to include domestic violence, rape, and child maltreatment in university curricula
	HB 161	Reps. Gross C. Lindsay (D, 11), Jon Ackerson (R, 47)	Allow Commonwealth's attorneys to become full-time prosecutors
	HB 309	Reps. Steve Nunn (R, 23), Paul Mason (D, 91), Michael D. Bowling (D, 87), Thomas J. Burch (D, 30), Mary Lou Marzian (D, 34), Ruth Ann Palumbo (D, 76), Ernesto Scorsone (D, 75)	Creation of certification for mental health professionals who treat domestic violence offenders; expansion of domestic violence training mandates
	HB 310	Reps. Michael D. Bowling (D, 87), Geveden, Callahan, L. Clark, D. Graham, Jenkins, Lile, Marzian, Mason, Nunn, Palumbo, Rapier, Richards, Stengel, Stumbo	Domestic Violence Omnibus Crime Bill

General Assembly	Bill Number	Recorded Sponsor (Party, District)	Subject Matter
	HB 315	Reps. Paul Mason (D, 91), Nunn, Bowling, L. Clark, Lile, Crenshaw, Jenkins, Marzian, Palumbo, Scorsone	Expansion of statutory provisions related to victim advocates
	HB 406	Reps. Mary Lou Marzian (D, 34), Joni Jenkins (D, 44), Jon Ackerson (R, 47), Bill Lile (R, 28)	Access to sex offender presentencing investigation reports by mental health professionals conducting court-ordered assessments
	HB 495	Reps. Joni Jenkins (D, 44), Mary Lou Marzian (D, 34) and 12 cosponsors	Creation of Sexual Assault Nurse Examiner Program
1998	SB 264	Sen. David Karem (D, 35)	Creation of Governor's Office of Child Abuse and Domestic Violence Services
	HB 142	Rep. Thomas J. Burch (D, 30)	Child protection legislation, including consideration of domestic violence as factor in termination of parental rights
	HB 455	Reps. Michael D. Bowling (D, 87), Adkins, Bratcher, Bruce, Callahan, Clark, Ford, C. Geveden, J. Gooch, J. Haydon, S. Johns, J. Lee, J. Lovell, H. Moberly, R. Murgatroyd, S. Nunn, T. Pope, J. Richards, S. Riggs, A. Simpson, J. Stacy, G. Stumbo, T. Turner, M. Weaver, Yonts	Governor's Omnibus Crime Bill
	HB 544	Rep. Michael D. Bowling (D, 87) and 16 cosponsors	Authorization for pilot family courts in multiple jurisdictions
2000	SB 116	Sen. Marshall Long (D, 20)	Strengthening of statutory victim notification provisions
	SB 263	Sen. Robert Stivers (R, 25)	Omnibus Sex Offense Bill
	HB 3	Rep. Robert Damron (D, 39)	Prohibition of insurance discrimination in domestic violence cases

General Assembly	Bill Number	Recorded Sponsor (Party, District)	Subject Matter
	HB 322	Rep. Jim Wayne (D, 35) and 11 cosponsors	Safety and security at universities
	HB 427	Reps. Steve Nunn (R, 23), K. Stein, K. Bratcher, T. Burch, R. Crimm, J. Gooch, J. Jenkins, S. Johns, T. McKee, S. Westrom	Establishment of Governor's Council on Domestic Violence and Sexual Assault; expansion of training mandates related to domestic violence and rape
	HB 448	Rep. Joni Jenkins (D, 44) and 15 cosponsors	Creation of rape crisis centers in statute as regional primary service providers
2001	SB 58	Sens. Robert Stivers (R, 25), Katie Stine (R, 24)	Legislation for a constitutional amendment to allow establishment of family courts
	HB 1	Rep. Jody Richards (D, 20)	Creation of crime of terroristic threatening
	HB 124	Rep. Gregory D. Stumbo (D, 95)	Creation of Office of Women's Physical and Mental Health in Cabinet for Health and Family Services
2002	SB 25	Sen. Dan Kelly (R, 14)	Sex offense bill, date-rape drugs, trafficking
	SB 26	Sen. Dan Kelly (R, 14)	Amendment to violent offender statute, including application to rape cases
	SB 89	Sen. Marshall Long (D, 20)	Notification to victims for attempt to purchase firearms
	HB 130	Rep. Jimmie Lee (D, 25)	Creation of crime of video voyeurism
	HB 308	Reps. Kathy Stein (D, 75), Joni Jenkins (D, 44)	Reimbursement for sexual assault nurse examiners
	HB 428	Reps. Rob Wilkey (D, 22), John Vincent (R, 100)	Creation of stalking protective orders
2003	HB 263	Rep. Gross C. Lindsay (D, 11)	Amendments to Kentucky Rules of Evidence, including expansion of the rape shield law to civil cases
	HB 380	Rep. Jody Richards (D, 20)	Creation of statutory structure for family courts

General Assembly	Bill Number	Recorded Sponsor (Party, District)	Subject Matter
Governor Ernest Fletcher (2003–2007)			
2004	SB 138	Sen. Julie Denton (R, 36)	Creation of Sexual Assault Victim Assistance Fund within Crime Victim Compensation Board
	SB 145	Sens. Damon Thayer (R, 17), Jack Westwood (R, 23)	Creation of crime of indecent exposure
	HB 108	Reps. Robert Damron (D, 39), R. Adams, R. Adkins, A. Arnold, E. Ballard, J. Barrows, K. Bratcher, B. Buckingham, J. Callahan, M. Cherry, L. Clark, P. Clark, J. Coleman, H. Collins, T. Edmonds, C. Embry Jr., B. Farmer, D. Ford, J. Gooch, D. Graham, J. Gray, K. Hall, M. Harmon, C. Hoffman, S. Lee, P. Marcotte, L. Napier, R. Nelson, F. Nesler, D. Pasley, R. Rand, J. Richards, S. Riggs, A. Simpson, D. Sims, A. Smith, R. Thomas, T. Thompson, C. Walton, M. Weaver, R. Webb, R. Wilkey, B. Yonts	Creation of crime of fetal homicide
2005	HB 298	Reps. Jimmie Lee (D, 25), T. Feeley, J. Barrows, C. Belcher, T. Burch, L. Clark, J. Crenshaw, M. Denham, W. Hall, J. Jenkins, M. Marzian, T. McKee, R. Meeks, H. Moberly Jr., R. Nelson, S. Nunn, R. Palumbo, J. Richards, T. Riner, K. Stein, T. Thompson, M. Weaver	Elder abuse; established KRS 209A, including designating domestic violence programs as regional primary service providers
2006	SB 38	Sen. Damon Thayer (R, 17)	Amendments to justification/self-protection statute

General Assembly	Bill Number	Recorded Sponsor (Party, District)	Subject Matter
2007	SB 43	Sens. David Boswell (D, 8), W. Blevins Jr., P. Clark, D. Harper Angel, J. Rhoads, D. Roeding, E. Scorsone, T. Shaughnessy, J. Westwood	Human trafficking; creation of Division on Child Abuse, Domestic Violence, and Human Trafficking in Cabinet for Health and Family Services
Governor Steven L. Beshear (2008–2012, 2012–2016)			
2008	SB 151	Sen. Robert Stivers (R, 21)	Creation of statutory prohibition on polygraphing rape victims
2009	HB 315	Reps. Johnny Bell (D, 23), W. Stone, R. Adams, H. Collins, L. Combs, W. Coursey, R. Damron, T. Edmonds, K. Flood, K. Hall, R. Henderson, J. Jenkins, D. Keene, T. McKee, R. Meeks, B. Montell, F. Nesler, D. Osborne, R. Palumbo, J. Richards, C. Rollins II, A. Simpson, D. Sims, A. Smith, G. Stumbo, T. Thompson, T. Turner, D. Watkins, S. Westrom	Creation of crime of using the Internet and social media to stalk or commit sex offenses
2010	SB 17	Sens. Julie Denton (R, 36), Denise Harper Angel (D, 35), Perry Clark (D, 37), Gerald Neal (D, 37)	Increased penalties for rape of incarcerated persons

General Assembly	Bill Number	Recorded Sponsor (Party, District)	Subject Matter
	HB 1	Reps. Gregory D. Stumbo (D, 95), R. Palumbo, R. Weston, R. Adams, R. Adkins, M. Cherry, L. Clark, H. Collins, W. Coursey, J. Crenshaw, R. Crimm, R. Damron, M. Denham, M. Dossett, T. Edmonds, T. Firkins, K. Flood, J. Greer, K. Hall, R. Henderson, C. Hoffman, J. Hoover, D. Horlander, D. Keene, M. King, Ji. Lee, T. McKee, C. Miller, S. Overly, D. Owens, D. Pasley, J. Richards, S. Riggs, T. Riner, S. Santoro, K. Sinnette, A. Smith, J. Stacy, F. Steele, K. Stevens, W. Stone, T. Thompson, D. Watkins, S. Westrom, B. Yonts	Amanda Ross Domestic Violence Prevention Act
	HB 500	Reps. Kevin Sinnette (D, 100), M. Rader, R. Palumbo, T. Riner, S. Santoro, F. Steele, J. Tilley, A. Wuchner	Use of qualified medical professionals to conduct forensic rape examinations
2011	HB 308	Reps. Robert Damron (D, 39), R. Adams, W. Coursey, D. Keene, T. Mills, R. Rand, A. Simpson, B. Yonts	National instant background checks upon attempt to purchase firearms for persons involuntarily committed
	HB 463	Rep. John Tilley (D, 8)	Reform of criminal justice system; including primary focus on drug offenses
2012			No substantial legislation related to domestic violence, rape, or stalking passed

Appendix C

Membership on Task Forces and Councils

ATTORNEY GENERAL'S TASK FORCE ON DOMESTIC VIOLENCE CRIME (1991)

Cochairs

Honorable Julia H. Adams
Honorable Stanley Billingsley

Legislative Membership

Senator Walter Baker
Senator Susan Johns
Senator David Karem (designee: Marie Abrams)
Representative Richard H. Lewis
Representative Marshall Long

Office of the Attorney General Staff

E. Blair Bottom
Travis Fritsch
Marcia Johnson
Barbara Whaley

Membership

Mary Acklin, Department for Employment Services
Honorable Karen Alfano, Appalachian Research & Defense Fund of Kentucky Inc.

Major Neal Brittain, Kentucky State Police

Honorable Don Buring, Commonwealth's attorney, Sixteenth Judicial Circuit

Betsy Coffey, Corrections Cabinet

Honorable Michael E. Conliffe, county attorney, Thirtieth Judicial District (represented by Hon. Jerry Bowles, Domestic Violence Unit)

Sharon A. Currens, executive director, Kentucky Domestic Violence Association

Barbara Curry, commissioner of social services, Lexington-Fayette County, KY (represented by Teri Faragher, Domestic Violence Prevention Board)

Kathy W. Frederich, adult protection specialist, Department for Social Services

Jim D. Greene, Jefferson County sheriff

Honorable Barbara Gregg, alderman, Louisville, KY

Honorable Margo Grubbs, Florence, KY

Doug Hamilton, chief, Louisville Police Department (represented by Officer Jackie Taylor, domestic violence liaison; Hon. Paul Guagliardo, legal counsel)

Honorable Ernest A. Jasmin, Commonwealth's attorney, Thirtieth Judicial Circuit

Sherry Johnson, Hebron, KY

Carol E. Jordan, director, Sexual and Domestic Violence Program, Department for Mental Health and Mental Retardation Services

Betty Lawrence, circuit court clerk, Fifteenth Judicial Circuit

Malinda Martin, director, Science and Human Development, Department of Education

Honorable Dan Mason, Northeast Kentucky Legal Services

Honorable Keith McCormick, assistant Commonwealth's attorney, Twenty-First Judicial Circuit

Robert McKinney, commissioner, Department of Criminal Justice Training, Eastern Kentucky University

Honorable Stephen K. Mershon, Thirtieth Judicial Circuit, Family Court Division

Ralph Orms, president, Kentucky Fraternal Order of Police

Honorable Gary Payne, Twenty-Second Judicial District

Marcia Roth, director, Jefferson County Office for Women

Tom Scillian, sheriff and president, Kentucky Sheriffs' Association

Honorable Stephen M. Shewmaker, Fiftieth Judicial Circuit

Honorable Norrie Wake, county attorney, Twenty-Second Judicial
    District
Larry Walsh, chief, Division of Police, Lexington-Fayette Urban
    County Government (represented by Lt. Jack Gurnee)
Marsha Weinstein, executive director, Kentucky Commission on
    Women
Honorable C. Renee Williams, Fifth Judicial District

LEGISLATIVE TASK FORCE ON DOMESTIC VIOLENCE (1994)

Cochairs

Representative Leonard Gray
Senator Jeff Green

Legislative Membership

Representative Mike Bowling
Senator Fred Bradley
Representative Paul Mason
Senator Michael Moloney
Representative Stephen R. Nunn
Representative Ruth Ann Palumbo
Senator John David Preston
Representative Frank Rasche
Senator Elizabeth Tori

Legislative Research Commission Staff

Mac Lewis
Scott Varland
Susan Lewis Warfield

Professional Staff

Sharon A. Currens, executive director, Kentucky Domestic
    Violence Association
Carol E. Jordan, director, Sexual and Domestic Violence
    Program, Department for Mental Health and Mental
    Retardation Services

Membership

Honorable Jerry Bowles, director, Domestic Violence Unit, Office of the Jefferson County Attorney

Baretta Casey, MD, chair, Domestic Violence Committee, Kentucky Medical Association

Sharon A. Currens, executive director, Kentucky Domestic Violence Association

Kathy Frederich, adult protection specialist, Department for Social Services

Major Dennis Goss, Information Services Branch, Kentucky State Police

Honorable Lana Grandon, assistant attorney general, Office of the Attorney General

Paul Isaacs, director, Administrative Office of the Courts

Susan Johns, former state senator

Carol E. Jordan, director, Sexual and Domestic Violence Program, Department for Mental Health and Mental Retardation Services

Honorable Peter C. Macdonald, Third Judicial District

Honorable Steve Mershon, Thirtieth Judicial Circuit, Family Court Division

Honorable Lewis Paisley, Twenty-Second Judicial Circuit

Marcia Roth, director, Jefferson County Office for Women

Chuck Sayre, commissioner, Department of Criminal Justice Training

Tom Scillian, sheriff and president, Kentucky Sheriffs' Association

Marsha Weinstein, executive director, Kentucky Commission on Women

Honorable Virginia Whittinghill, Thirtieth Judicial District

Major Kathy Witt, Office of the Fayette County Sheriff

GOVERNOR'S COUNCIL ON DOMESTIC VIOLENCE AND SEXUAL ASSAULT (1996–2000)

Leadership

Former governor John Y. Brown Jr., cochair

First Lady Judi Conway Patton, cochair

Carol E. Jordan, executive director, Office of Child Abuse and Domestic Violence Services, Office of the Governor, vice chair

Honorable Julia Adams, Twenty-Fifth Judicial Circuit, First
    Division, vice chair (1996–1998)
Honorable Jerry Bowles, Thirtieth Judicial Circuit, Family
    Division, vice chair (1998–2000)

Staff

Carol E. Jordan, executive director, Office of Child Abuse and
    Domestic Violence Services, Office of the Governor

Legislative Membership

Senator Robert L. Jackson
Representative Stephen R. Nunn
Representative Kathy W. Stein
Senator Elizabeth Tori
Representative Rob Wilkey

Membership

Kim Allen, executive director, Kentucky Criminal Justice Council
Clayton Bradley, Franklin County Council on Family Abuse
Ed Brady, chief of police, Henderson Police Department
Honorable A. B. Chandler III, Office of the Attorney General
    (designee: Hon. Tamara Gormley)
Sharon A. Currens, executive director, Kentucky Domestic
    Violence Association
Teri Faragher, executive director, Fayette County Domestic
    Violence Prevention Board
Becci Fulks, assistant service region administrator, Cabinet for
    Family and Children
Sharon Green, victim advocate, Graves County
Becky Hagan, president, Kentucky Domestic Violence Association
Jimmy D. Helton, secretary, Cabinet for Health Services
Pam Johnson, client services representative, Center for Women
    and Families
Carol E. Jordan, executive director, Office of Child Abuse and
    Domestic Violence Services, Office of the Governor
Honorable Cicely Lambert, executive director, Administrative
    Office of the Courts

Honorable Ernie Lewis, Office of the Public Advocate

Honorable Peter C. Macdonald, Third Judicial District, First Division

Viola P. Miller, secretary, Cabinet for Families and Children (designee: Bonnie Hommrich)

Honorable George Moore, Office of the Commonwealth's Attorney, Twenty-First Judicial Circuit

Genie K. Potter, executive director, Kentucky Commission on Women

Honorable H. B. Quinn, Office of the County Attorney, Fifty-Sixth Judicial District

Doug Sapp, commissioner, Department of Corrections

Honorable Robert F. Stephens, secretary, Justice Cabinet

Diane Thompson, circuit clerk, Tenth Judicial Circuit

Annette Toler, physician, Shelby County

Robert Walker, assistant professor, University of Kentucky

Kathy Witt, Office of the Fayette County Sheriff

GOVERNOR'S TASK FORCE ON SEXUAL ASSAULT (1999)

Honorary Chair

First Lady Judi Conway Patton

Cochairs

Honorable Joni L. Jenkins
Honorable Steve A. Wilson

Legislative Membership

Representative Charles Geveden
Senator Marshall Long
Senator Robert Stivers

Governor's Office Staff

Carol E. Jordan, executive director, Governor's Office of Child Abuse and Domestic Violence Services

Karen Quinn, legal counsel, Governor's Office of Child Abuse and Domestic Violence Services

Membership

Kim Allen, executive director, Kentucky Criminal Justice Council
Beverly Bleidt, PhD, therapist, Louisville, KY
Honorable Michael Bowling, Bowling, Johnson, & Costanzo
Honorable Glenda Bradshaw, assistant county attorney, Thirtieth Judicial District
Paul Carter, assistant chief, Paducah City Police Department
Ed Crockett, Administrative Office of the Courts
Sergeant Alecia Edgington, Kentucky State Police
Carol E. Jordan, executive director, Governor's Office of Child Abuse and Domestic Violence Services
Honorable Tom Lockridge, Commonwealth's attorney, Thirteenth Judicial Circuit
Honorable John G. McNeill, Landrum & Shouse
Phyllis Millspaugh, executive director, Rape Crisis and Prevention Center
Honorable Lewis G. Paisley, Twenty-Second Judicial Circuit, Division 6
Doug Sapp, commissioner, Department of Corrections
Marigail Sexton, executive director, Kentucky Association of Sexual Assault Programs
Miriam Silman, Rape Victim Services Program
Tom Thomas, RN, SANE, King's Daughters Medical Center

Notes

1. Kentucky Women and the Advocates Who Fought for Them

1. The Eighteenth Amendment, the first to restrict rather than ensure a right, was repealed in 1933 by ratification of the Twenty-First Amendment, the only instance in U.S. history in which a constitutional amendment was repealed.

2. Historical documents reflect two spellings for Nation's name: Carrie and Carry. She appears to have used Carrie until later years, when the symbolism of "carry a nation" led her to change the spelling.

3. While the history provided in this book focuses primarily on state elections and state officeholders, at the federal level, Republican Katherine G. Langley of Pikeville became the first woman to represent Kentucky in the U.S. House of Representatives, serving from 1927 to 1931 (taking the seat formerly held by her husband). It was nearly seventy years before another woman from Kentucky would serve in the House. Republican Anne Northup won election in the Third Congressional District in 1997; she would serve for a decade. As of 2012, Kentucky has never had a female U.S. senator, and no person of color has represented Kentucky in the House or Senate.

4. The 92nd Congress passed the Equal Rights Amendment in 1972, and the states had seven years to ratify it. The ERA ultimately fell three states short of passage (thirty-five of the thirty-eight states needed).

5. Charles W. Anderson was the first person of color elected to the Kentucky General Assembly. He won a seat in the Kentucky house of representatives in 1935.

6. Only one woman has ever served in the top leadership of either chamber: Katie Kratz Stine, who became senate president pro tempore in 2005.

7. This book uses the term *domestic violence* to refer to all forms of physical assault against women. It is the term used most frequently in the past two decades in discussions of legislative reform, and it is the term used in most statutory definitions.

8. The founding directors of the programs were Diane Lawless, Lexington Rape Crisis Center; Grace Erickson, Rape Relief Center; Sue Cassidy, Rape Crisis Center of Northern Kentucky; and Lexie Hicks, Rape Victim Services Program.

9. I was the first director of the Sexual and Domestic Violence Services Program and served in that capacity from 1985 to 1995. The rape crisis centers fell under this program.

10. In 1996 KASAP hired its first executive director, Marigail Sexton. Eileen Recktenwald took over in 2001 and continues to serve in that capacity.

11. Carol Morse served as the first director of the YWCA Spouse Abuse Center in Louisville, followed by Merle Holcomb.

12. Travis Fritsch served as the first director of the YWCA Spouse Abuse Center in Lexington.

13. Pennie Smith served as the first director of the Barren River Area Safe Space from 1980 to 1981, followed by Eugenia Campbell from 1981 to 1987.

14. Edwina Walker was serving as director of the Women's Crisis Center in Northern Kentucky at the time its rape and domestic violence services were merged.

15. In 1987 Sherry Currens was hired as director of the Kentucky Domestic Violence Association and continues to serve in that capacity.

16. Other than local support, the earliest funding (circa 1977–1978) for spouse abuse centers in Kentucky came from the federal Comprehensive Education and Training Act (CETA, Pub. L. 93-203) and the Law Enforcement Assistance Administration (LEAA). CETA was enacted in 1973 with the purpose of training workers and providing them with jobs in public service. The LEAA was established by the Omnibus Crime Control and Safe Streets Act of 1968 and was abolished in 1982. It was preceded by the Office of Law Enforcement Assistance (1965–1968) and followed by the Office of Justice Assistance, Research, and Statistics (1982–1984) and the Office of Justice Programs (1984–present). The LEAA primarily administered federal funding to state and local law enforcement agencies and funded educational programs, research, state planning agencies, and local crime initiatives.

2. The Prevalence of Violence and the Stories of Women Who Lived It

1. In February 2010 France became the first country to outlaw "psychological violence" between members of a couple, making it an offense punishable by up to three years in prison. This occurred as part of new measures aimed at improving protection for victims of domestic violence.

2. The 1979 Harris survey (Schulman, 1979) also included findings related to the women's attempts to seek help, such as reports to law enforcement, access to battered women's shelters, and medical treatment, as well as other descriptors of their experience with violence. Although prevalence data are still meaningful over time, these others descriptions

and the women's responses are too dated to provide accurate insights, so they are not cited here.

3. The grant for the Intimate Partner Violence Surveillance System was awarded to the University of Kentucky Survey Research Center in collaboration with the Kentucky Department of Public Health. Carl Spurlock served as the original principal investigator.

4. The Center for Research on Violence Against Women at the University of Kentucky was created in 2002 as a partnership between the university and the administration of Governor Paul E. Patton. It was formally established by the University Board of Trustees in 2003. I served as its first director.

5. The Governor's Office of Child Abuse and Domestic Violence Services was established by Governor Paul E. Patton and existed during his two terms in office. First Lady Judi C. Patton served as special adviser to the office, and I served as its executive director. Under the subsequent administration, the office was moved to the Cabinet for Health and Family Services and ultimately merged with other programs.

6. As director of the Center for Research on Violence Against Women (CRVAW), I was one of the principal investigators for the Women's Safety Study, along with Pamela Wilcox, then-professor in the UK Department of Sociology (Jordan, Wilcox, & Pritchard, 2007; Wilcox, Jordan, & Pritchard, 2006, 2007). The Women's Safety Study was a joint project of the CRVAW, the Office of the UK President, the Office of the Provost, the President's Commission on Women, the Student Government, Student Affairs, and the Graduate School.

3. Rape and Sexual Violence: A Nation's Reform

1. Kentucky's law never required corroboration to prosecute a sex crime.

2. The victim's surname was not included in the judicial opinions. This retelling of the case relies heavily on *Rusk v. State* (1979) and *State v. Rusk* (1981).

5. The Structure and Strategy of Legislative Reform

1. Maria Henson began her work at the *Lexington Herald-Leader* in 1989. She left after more than two decades to become associate vice president and editor-at-large at her alma mater, Wake Forest University.

2. The *Lexington Herald-Leader* also received a Pulitzer Prize for a series of articles focusing on child sexual abuse. That series, entitled "Twice Abused: How Kentucky Denies Justice to Sexually Violated Children," exposed system failures and recommended legislative reforms, many of which were passed in 1994 by the Kentucky General Assembly.

3. Judges cannot participate in such coalitions because doing so would

violate judicial codes of ethics. Federal judges must abide by the Code of Conduct for United States Judges, which guides them on issues of integrity and independence, diligence and impartiality, permissible extrajudicial activities, and the avoidance of impropriety or its appearance. The American Bar Association also has a Model Code of Judicial Conduct (2010) with four canons that address independence, impartiality, conflict of interest, and political activity.

4. Ernie Allen served as the original chair of the Rape Coalition. He was a former director of public health and safety and then chief administrative officer for the City of Louisville; he now serves as president and CEO of the International Center for Missing and Exploited Children in Washington, D.C. The Rape Coalition was staffed by Kim Allen in her role as executive director of the Crime Commission. By the 1980s, Kim Allen and I had become partners in that effort.

5. Until the end of the 1990s, the Kentucky General Assembly met on a biennial basis; in 2000 the General Assembly amended the Kentucky Constitution to allow annual legislative sessions.

6. A legislative body adjourns sine die when it adjourns without appointing a specific day on which it will reconvene.

7. In Kentucky, the four-year senate terms are staggered so that half the senators face election every two years.

8. The Kentucky Constitution provides that amendments can be made by constitutional convention or by a three-fifths vote of the General Assembly. If the latter approach is taken, the amendment must be submitted to the voters for ratification at the next general election.

9. Under the rules, members can move to "suspend the rules" to allow the placement of a piggyback on a bill. If a majority of the membership agrees, the new text may be added to the bill.

10. Lobbying takes place in a multitude of locations (both houses of Congress; state legislatures; federal, state, and local governments); is focused on a broad range of governmental decisions or proceedings (law, regulation, policy, budget); and includes both communication with constituents and advocacy with policy makers (Gelak, 2008). Discussions of lobbying in this book are limited to lobbying efforts or advocacy with elected members of state legislatures. Additionally, the term *lobbying* is used to describe the activities of both registered agents and nonregistered advocates.

11. Whether lobbying efforts are conducted by grassroots organizations or professional lobbyists, federal tax laws dictate how funds can be used and in what amounts for 501(c)(3) and (c)(4) organizations.

12. Advocates should remember that media contacts need not be limited to a state's largest newspapers. Constituents and legislators, particularly in rural states, are also influenced by local daily and weekly newspapers.

13. Shock probation is a practice whereby a court incarcerates a

convicted offender for a brief period and then suspends the remainder of the sentence and places the offender on probation. The theory behind the practice is that the "shock" of prison is an effective deterrent to recidivism.

6. The Birth of Legislative Reform in Kentucky: The 1970s

1. Even today, men's wages still surpass women's. In a recent comparison of the wages of women and men one year out of college, women earned, on average, 82 percent of what men earned, even after controlling for college majors and employment differences (Corbett & Hill, 2012).

2. In 1972 Governor Nunn was a candidate for the U.S. Senate, but he was defeated by Walter Dee Huddleston, effectively ending his formal political career.

3. Until a constitutional amendment in 1992, candidates for governor and lieutenant governor ran separately.

4. Beginning in 1968, the first two chairs of the Kentucky Commission on Women were Marie Humphries and Jean Sawyer. Once the commission became a state agency, its executive directors have been Marie Abrams (1971–1974), Helen Howard Hughes (1974–1979), Jessica Loving (1979–1983), Robin Crigler (1983–1987), Phyllis Alexander (1987–1991), Marsha Weinstein (1992–1996), Virginia Woodward (1996–1998), Eugenia Potter (1998–2000), Betsy Nowland-Curry (2000–2004), Glenda Woods (2004–2007), and Eleanor Jordan (2008–present)

5. Executive orders exist only during the administration of the governor who signs them. Without legislation codifying the language in Nunn's order, the Kentucky Commission on Women would not have become a permanent entity.

6. The members of the Kentucky Criminal Law Revision Committee included Court of Appeals judge John Palmore (in 1970 the Kentucky Court of Appeals was the state's highest court); attorney general John Breckinridge; judges Robert Lukowsky and Caswell Lane; Commonwealth's attorney Frank Benton; county attorney Gladys Williams Black; attorneys James Jernigan, Frank Haddad, and Joseph Huddleston; University of Kentucky dean emeritus W. L. Matthews Jr.; and University of Louisville dean James Merritt. The drafting group consisted of Robert Lawson, acting dean of the University of Kentucky College of Law; Kathleen Brickey, professor of law at the University of Louisville; Carl Ousley Jr., assistant Commonwealth's attorney; and attorney Paul K. Murphy. Attorney Norman W. Lawson of the Legislative Research Commission also provided staff support.

7. In *Roe v. Wade* (1973), the U.S. Supreme Court's landmark decision on abortion, the Court ruled that a right to privacy under the due process clause of the Fourteenth Amendment extends to a woman's decision to have an abortion.

8. As described in chapter 8, in 1992 the Kentucky Rules of Evidence

(KRE) were adopted. As a result, KRS 510.145 was repealed, and KRE 412 became the rape shield law applicable in Kentucky.

7. Legislative Reform: The 1980s

1. Bobbie Ann Mason's books from the 1980s include *Shiloh and Other Stories* (1982), *In Country* (1985), *Spence + Lila* (1988), and *Love Life* (1989). Barbara Kingsolver's include *The Bean Trees* (1988) and *Animal Dreams* (1990).

2. Travis Fritsch served in this position, which was titled the liaison for family violence prevention and services. The position would not last past the Collins administration.

3. Although the hearing records of the Legislative Research Commission provide the name of the shelter resident who testified before the committee, I have chosen not to identify her by name.

4. Garrett represented the Second District in the state senate from 1979 to 1990. She was originally appointed by Governor Edward T. "Ned" Breathitt to fill the seat of her husband, Tom Garrett, who died in office. She was the first woman to hold a leadership post in the Kentucky senate, serving as majority whip. In 1992 she pled guilty to bribery in the "Bop-Trot" scandal.

5. Notably, while the cost of marriage licenses has increased substantially over the years (from $14 in 1982 to $24 in 2012), the portion of funding for the domestic violence programs has remained static at $10.

6. Travis Fritsch, director of the Lexington Spouse Abuse Center, and Kathy (Frederich) Autrey with the Cabinet for Health and Family Services were heavily involved in drafting the legislation with Senator Moloney. I was also present; my career in the violence against women movement had begun just one year earlier in 1983, when I was hired out of graduate school by the Lexington Spouse Abuse Center.

7. As described in later chapters, subsequent sessions of the General Assembly would expand the definition of *violent offender*, increase the required time served before parole to twenty years, and increase the percentage of time served to 85 percent.

8. Testimony on the bill was provided by Representative Bill Brinkley, Logan Calvert, and Bonnie Brown.

9. Representative Burch had become chair of the Health and Welfare Committee in 1986, replacing Gerta Bendl, whose relationship with the house leadership had soured.

8. Legislative Reform: The 1990s

1. Tori Murden McClure currently serves as president of Spalding University in Louisville, Kentucky.

2. BOPTROT refers to the Business, Organizations, and Professions

Committee (BOP) of the legislature (later changed to the Committee on Licensing and Occupations) and the trotting tracks, both of which were involved in a corruption scandal that led to the convictions of multiple individuals both inside and outside the General Assembly.

3. Governor James Garrard served two terms, but his first term in 1796 resulted from his selection by "electors" from various districts in the state; Governor A. B. "Happy" Chandler also served two terms, but they were twenty years apart. Governor Patton's election was also unique in that it was the first following the 1992 constitutional amendment requiring governors and lieutenant governors to run as a slate.

4. I served as the first executive director of this office, with two administrative staff positions and one attorney position.

5. The 1990 legislative session predated the creation of the state coalition of rape crisis centers.

6. Governor Wilkinson had appointed Phyllis Alexander as executive director of the Commission on Women; she previously served as president of the Kentucky Domestic Violence Association.

7. Travis Fritsch went on to serve as staff to the task force, assisted by Marcia Johnson, Barbara Whaley, and other staff members from the attorney general's office.

8. The legislation committee comprised task force lead staff Travis Fritsch, Kathy (Frederich) Autrey, Major Neal Brittain, Sherry Currens, Carol E. Jordan, and Beth Mason.

9. As a result of the partnership between task force staff (particularly Fritsch and Autrey) and the Kentucky State Police, a "domestic violence protective order file" was created in the LINK system, making Kentucky only the second state in the country (after Massachusetts) to establish a special file of this type.

10. Senator Walter Baker would resign from the state senate in 1996 when Governor Paul E. Patton appointed him to serve a partial term on the Kentucky Supreme Court.

11. The compromise made civil and criminal proceedings for the violation of a protective order mutually exclusive and required that, to criminally violate an order, a person had to intentionally violate an order with which he had been served or about which he had knowledge.

12. The task force's work was also aided by a compelling 1992 report released by David Richart and Jackie Town from Kentucky Youth Advocates (KYA) entitled *Beyond the Human Cost: A Preliminary Economic Analysis of the Costs Attributed to Child Sexual Abuse in Kentucky.* Richart was the founding director of KYA and was known statewide as a tenacious and tireless advocate for children and youth. His death from cancer in 2011 was an incredible loss to all those who benefited from his advocacy and to all of us who knew him as a friend.

13. The Jacob Wetterling Act was passed as part of the Violent Crime Control and Law Enforcement Act, H.R. 3355, Pub. L. 103-322.

14. This occurred before all states had fully complied with the Jacob Wetterling Act, so many did not yet have registries.

15. It is not unusual for the same piece of legislation to be introduced in both chambers of the General Assembly, but generally, one passes it and the other does not. In this case, the legislative sponsors were extremely supportive of their bills, and as a result, both SB 107 and HB 115 were passed by both chambers, and each was signed by the governor. This was allowed at the time because the wording in the final versions of both bills was exactly the same. House and senate rules have since addressed this issue.

16. A companion provision in the biennium budget prepared by Governor Paul Patton that session expanded the funding for victim advocate positions to $800,000 annually.

17. The group included Jerry Bowles, Jefferson County Office of the County Attorney; Neal Britton, Kentucky State Police; Sherry Currens, Kentucky Domestic Violence Association; Kathy (Frederich) Autrey, Department for Social Services; Travis Fritsch, Office of the Attorney General; Carol E. Jordan, Department for Mental Health and Mental Retardation Services; Helen Kinton, Sanctuary; Marcia Roth, Jefferson County Office for Women; Matt Veroff, Seven Counties Services Inc.; and Edwina Walker, Women's Crisis Center of Northern Kentucky.

18. As discussed in chapter 5, the leadership of the General Assembly is called the Legislative Research Commission (LRC) and comprises sixteen members from both chambers.

19. The Legislative Task Force on Domestic Violence was staffed by LRC staff Susan Warfield and Scott Varland; Carol E. Jordan, director of the Sexual and Domestic Violence Program in the Kentucky Department for Mental Health and Mental Retardation Services; and Sherry Currens, executive director of the Kentucky Domestic Violence Association.

20. This first version of VAWA originated in the U.S. Senate's Judiciary Committee, which, under the leadership of Senator Joseph Biden, had conducted a multiyear review of the status of violence against women in America. The committee's report was issued in 1993, prompting passage of VAWA in 1994.

21. Those testifying on SB 105 included the bill's sponsor, Senator Jeff Green; Sherry Currens, Kentucky Domestic Violence Association; and Jerry Bowles, Jefferson County Attorney's Office.

22. This same amendment was proposed during the 1998 session and was ultimately incorporated into the governor's crime bill. The significance of that death penalty provision would be raised in a very visible homicide case in the following decade.

23. VINE now serves more than 3,000 crime victims and reportedly tracks more than 85 percent of the nation's offender population.

24. The training mandate for law enforcement officers, while updated in HB 309, originated in SB 17 of the 1984 General Assembly.

25. In the law, *comity* refers to legal reciprocity. In this case, it meant that the court voluntarily accepted responsibility for training court personnel. That is, the judicial branch extended a courtesy to the legislative branch by recognizing the validity and effect of its legislation, even though the legislature's ability to mandate acts by the court is constitutionally limited.

26. The cosponsors of HB 310 were Charles R. Geveden (Democrat from the First District), James P. Callahan (Democrat from the Sixty-Seventh District), Larry Clark (Democrat from the Forty-Sixth District), Drew Graham (Democrat from the Seventy-Third District), Joni L. Jenkins (Democrat from the Forty-Fourth District), Bill Lile (Republican from the Twenty-Eighth District), Mary Lou Marzian (Democrat from the Thirty-Fourth District), Paul Mason (Democrat from the Ninety-First District), Steve Nunn (Republican from the Twenty-Third District), Ruth Ann Palumbo (Democrat from the Seventy-Sixth District), Kenny Rapier (Democrat from the Fiftieth District), Jody Richards (Democrat from the Twentieth District), Dave Stengel (Democrat from the Twenty-Ninth District), and majority floor leader Greg Stumbo (Democrat from the Ninety-Fifth District). I staffed the bill, and testimony was provided by U.S. Attorney Joe Famularo, Attorney General Ben Chandler, and Jerry Bowles of the Jefferson County Attorney's Office.

27. The bill's cosponsors were Mike Bowling (Democrat from the Eighty-Seventh District), Larry Clark (Democrat from the Forty-Sixth District), Bill Lile (Republican from the Twenty-Eighth District), Jesse Crenshaw (Democrat from the Seventy-Seventh District), Joni L. Jenkins (Democrat from the Forty-Fourth District), Mary Lou Marzian (Democrat from the Thirty-Fourth District), Ruth Ann Palumbo (Democrat from the Seventy-Sixth District), and Ernesto Scorsone (Democrat from the Seventy-Fifth District). First Lady Judi Patton and I testified on the bill.

28. The office would not survive after the Patton years; the next administration placed it in the Cabinet for Health and Family Services.

29. The bill was staffed largely by Pam Murphy and Barbara Jones, attorneys in the Justice Cabinet. I played a narrow role, focusing on the sections that advanced the rights of victims.

9. Legislative Reform: 2000 through 2012

1. Before Chapman, Kentucky's last execution had been in 1999. The state currently has approximately forty inmates on death row, including one woman.

2. In federal elections, the state has trended Republican since the 1950s.

3. Stumbo served as attorney general during Governor Beshear's first term and then returned to the Kentucky house of representatives.

4. I staffed the task force, along with Karen Quinn, staff attorney from the Governor's Office of Child Abuse and Domestic Violence Services.

5. As discussed in chapter 8, in 1994 Kentucky passed legislation to create a sex offender registry. That legislation brought the state into compliance with the federal Jacob Wetterling Act passed that same year. The federal law was amended in 1996, through Megan's Law, to require states to pass legislation mandating the public notification of personal information for certain convicted sex offenders.

6. Federal courts have confirmed the federal law's constitutionality. They have also held that due process requires only knowledge of possession of a firearm, not knowledge that possession is illegal. Courts have ruled that no equal protection violation occurs when domestic violence misdemeanants are treated differently from felons or other misdemeanants. With a single exception, courts have rejected the argument that the firearm prohibition violates the Second Amendment right to bear arms (Perry, 2001).

7. HB 263 also amended KRE 608 to allow witnesses to offer personal opinion evidence to show character or truthfulness or untruthfulness; to limit the admissibility of testimony regarding specific conduct for this purpose to cross-examination, unless otherwise admissible under KRE 609; and to clarify that a witness's privilege against self-incrimination is not waived when offering testimony that relates only to credibility.

8. In 1999 the Governor's Council on Domestic Violence was attached administratively to the Governor's Office of Child Abuse and Domestic Violence Services, which Governor Patton had established.

9. As explained in chapter 3, the Jeanne Clery Disclosure of Campus Security Policy and Campus Crime Statistics Act was passed in 1990 and amended in 1998. It requires that all institutions of higher education report annually to students and employees on specific campus crime statistics and security policies and procedures. Campuses must also issue timely warnings to the campus community when serious crimes occur on campus and must file their crime statistics annually with the Department of Education. The law also requires universities to maintain a daily crime log, which must be available to the public.

10. Senator Denise Harper Angel also introduced a version of the dating violence bill in the senate, but it was never heard.

11. Section 1 of the Bill of Rights in the Kentucky Constitution sets out seven essential freedoms related to life, liberty, and the pursuit of happiness; the seventh gives Kentuckians the right to bear arms in defense of themselves and of the state.

10. Violence against Women Legislative Reform: Past and Future

1. The anti-rape and domestic violence movements are broadly defined for purposes of this analysis to include legislative and state government task forces and councils on which advocates (in state coalitions and in government) served and for which they often provided a staffing function.

2. As noted in chapter 8, the hate crimes provision initially included crimes against women in addition to crimes perpetrated because of an individual's race, color, religion, sexual orientation, or national origin. Because many legislators vehemently opposed the inclusion of gender, it was removed before the bill's final passage.

3. In addition to receiving state general funds and federally mandated federal funds, the Kentucky Association of Sexual Assault Programs secures federal funds on its own initiative.

4. In addition to receiving state general funds and federally mandated federal funds, the Kentucky Domestic Violence Association secures federal funds on its own initiative.

5. An additional factor in the decision to discontinue the Rape Coalition was that Kim Allen and I had both assumed state-level positions in the Patton administration and therefore could not staff the coalition as we had before.

6. Unlike prior years, when the bill had robust support from both sides of the aisle, the 2012 effort to pass the Violence Against Women Act failed on party lines and had to be brought back in 2013 to secure extension of its funding and protections.

7. This has also been a productive model at the federal level, where the visible advocacy of President Barack Obama and Vice President Joe Biden, along with the work of national coalitions and women's organizations, helped pass the Violence Against Women Act.

Bibliography

Abrams, M. (2012, November 1). Personal interview.

Adams, R. C. (2004). Wallace Glenn Wilkinson. In L. Harrison (Ed.), *Kentucky's governors* (updated ed., pp. 237–243). Lexington: University Press of Kentucky.

Aderibigbe, Y. A. (1997). Violence in America: A survey of suicide linked to homicides. *Journal of Forensic Science, 42* (4), 662–665.

Administrative Office of the Courts. (2012). *Family courts.* http://courts .ky.gov/courts/familycourt/Pages/default.aspx.

Alessi, R., Estep, B., & Clark, A. (2009, September 20). Nunn saga filled with irony, high drama. *Lexington Herald-Leader.* http://www.kentucky .com/2009/09/20/943159/nunn-saga-filled-with-irony-high.html.

Alessi, R., Estep, B., & Ward, K. (2009, September 15). Ex-state rep. Nunn charged with murder. *Lexington Herald-Leader.* http://www.kentucky .com/2009/09/15/935131/ex-state-rep-nunn-charged-with.html.

Allen, K. (2012, July 26). Personal interview.

Allen, N. E. (2006). An examination of the effectiveness of domestic violence coordinating councils. *Violence Against Women, 12,* 46–67.

Allen, N. E., Larsen, S. E., & Walden, A. L. (2011). An overview of community-based services for battered women. In C. Renzetti, J. Edleson, & R. Bergen (Eds.), *Sourcebook on Violence Against Women* (2nd ed., pp. 245–264). Los Angeles: Sage Publications.

Allen, N. E., Watt, K., & Hess, J. Z. (2008). The outcomes and activities of domestic violence coordinating councils. *American Journal of Community Psychology, 41* (1–2), 63–73.

Alltech FEI World Equestrian Games. (2010). *Alltech FEI World Equestrian Games by the numbers.* Lexington, KY: World Games 2010 Foundation. http://www.alltechfeigames.com/default.

Anonymous. (1982, March 2). Testimony of "Anonymous" of Louisville before the Kentucky House of Representatives Counties and Special Districts Committee. Frankfort, KY: Legislative Research Commission.

Appleton, T. H., Hay, M. P., Klotter, J. C., & Stephens, T. E. (Eds.). (1998). *Kentucky: Land of tomorrow.* Nashville, TN: Publication Management Associates.

Associated Press. (1978, March). ERA supporter vetoes resolution. *Tuscaloosa News.*

Aubrey, E. L., Burton, S. M., Crofts, J. N., Franklin, J. J., Freeman, G. A., Hendrix, L. H., Honaker, J. S., Lawson, N. W., & Taylor, A. E. (2003). *Kentucky government*. Informational Bulletin 137 (Rev.). Frankfort, KY: Legislative Research Commission.

Avery-Leaf, S., Cascardi, M., O'Leary, K. D., & Cano, A. (1997). Efficacy of a dating violence prevention program on attitudes justifying aggression. *Journal of Adolescent Health, 21* (1), 11–17.

Bachar, K., & Koss, M. P. (2001). From prevalence to prevention: Closing the gap between what we know about rape and what we do. In C. M. Renzetti, J. L. Edleson, & R. K. Bergen (Eds.), *Sourcebook on Violence Against Women* (pp. 117–142). Los Angeles: Sage Publications.

Bachman R. (1991). Predicting the reporting of rape victimizations: Have rape reforms made a difference? *Criminal Justice and Behavior, 20* (3), 254–269.

Bachman, R. (1998). The factors related to rape reporting behavior and arrest: New evidence from the National Crime Victimization Survey. *Criminal Justice and Behavior, 25* (1), 8–29.

Bachman, R., & Saltzman, L. (1995). *Violence Against Women: Estimates from the Redesigned Survey*. Washington, DC: Office of Justice Programs, US Department of Justice.

Bailey, J. E., Kellermann, A. L., Somes, G. W., Banton, J. G., Rivara, F. P., & Rushforth, N. P. (1997). Risk factors for violent death of women in the home. *Archives of Internal Medicine, 157* (7), 777–782.

Baker, K., Cahn, N., & Sands, S. J. (1989). *Report on District of Columbia police response to domestic violence*. Washington, DC: DC Coalition against Domestic Violence and the Women's Law and Public Policy Center, Georgetown University Law Centers.

Ballou, M., Tabol, C., Liriano, D., Vazquez-Nuttall, K., Butler, C., & Boorstein, B. W. (2007). Initial development of a psychological model for judicial decision making in continuing restraining orders. *Family Court Review, 45*, 274–286.

Banks, L., Crandall, C., Sklar, D., & Bauer, M. (2008). A comparison of intimate partner homicide to intimate partner homicide-suicide: One hundred and twenty-four New Mexico cases. *Violence Against Women, 14* (9), 1065–1078.

Barner, J. R., & Carney, M. M. (2011). Interventions for intimate partner violence: A historical view. *Journal of Family Violence, 26*, 235–244.

Baum, K., & Klaus, P. (2005). *Violent victimization of college students, 1995–2002* (NCJ 206836). Washington, DC: US Department of Justice, Office of Justice Programs, Bureau of Justice Statistics.

Beatty, D. (2003). Stalking legislation in the United States. In M. P. Brewster (Ed.), *Stalking: Psychology, risk factors, interventions, and law* (pp. 2-2–2-55). Kingston, NJ: Civic Research Institute.

Beauregard, E., & Proulx, J. (2007). A classification of sexual homicide against men. *International Journal of Offender Therapy and Comparative Criminology, 51* (4), 420–432.

Bennice, J., & Resick, P. (2003). Marital rape: History, research, and practice. *Trauma, Violence, & Abuse, 4,* 228–246.

Bergen, R. K. (1996). *Wife rape: Understanding the response of survivors and service providers.* Thousand Oaks, CA: Sage Publications.

Bergen, R. K. (2000). Rape laws and spousal exemptions. In N. H. Rafter (Ed.), *The encyclopedia of women and crime* (pp. 223–225). Phoenix, AZ: Oryx Press.

Bergen, R. K., & Maier, S. L. (2011). Sexual assault serves. In C. Renzetti, J. Edleson, & R. Bergen (Eds.), *Sourcebook on Violence Against Women* (2nd ed., pp. 227–244). Los Angeles: Sage Publications.

Berger, M. C., & Chandra, A. (1999). The gender wage gap in Kentucky, 1968–1997. In M. Smith-Mello, M. T. Childress, J. Sollinger, & B. M. Sebastian (Eds.), *The future well-being of women in Kentucky* (pp. 25–34). Frankfort: Kentucky Long-Term Policy Research Center.

Berger, R. J., Neuman, W. L., & Searles, P. (1994). The impact of rape law reform: An aggregate analysis of police reports and arrests. *Criminal Justice Review, 19* (1), 1–23.

Berger, R. J., Searles, P., & Neuman, W. L. (1988). The dimensions of rape reform legislation. *Law Society Review, 22,* 329–357.

Berk, S., & Loseke, D. (1980). Handling family violence: Situational determinants of police arrest in domestic disturbances. *Law & Society Review, 15* (2), 317–346.

Berry, T. A. (2002). Prior untruthful allegations under Wisconsin's rape shield law: Will those words come back to haunt you? *Wisconsin Law Review,* 1237–1273.

Bill outlawing marital rape wins house approval, goes to senate. (1990, March 2). *Lexington Herald-Leader.*

Black, M. C., Basile, K. C., Breiding, M. J., Smith, S. G., Walters, M. L., Merrick, M. T., Chen, J., & Stevens, M. R. (2011). *The National Intimate Partner and Sexual Violence Survey (NIPSVS): 2010 summary report.* Atlanta, GA: National Center for Injury Prevention and Control, Centers for Disease Control and Prevention.

Blackstone, W. (1966). *Commentaries on the law of England.* Dobbs Ferry, NY: Oceana Publishing. (Original work published in 1765.)

Blanchard, P. (1993). Education reform and executive-legislative relations in Kentucky: HB 940 as the culmination of legislative independence, 1980–1990. *Journal of Kentucky Studies, 10,* http://www.kpsaweb.org/Hughes/Blanchard.Hughes.html#4.

Blanchard, P. (2000). Government and politics. In J. C. Klotter (Ed.), *Our Kentucky: A study of the Bluegrass State* (pp. 38–57). Lexington: University Press of Kentucky.

Blanchard, P. (2004). Paul Edward Patton. In L. Harrison (Ed.), *Kentucky's governors* (updated ed., pp. 251–263). Lexington: University Press of Kentucky.

Block, C. R. (2000). *The Chicago Women's Health Risk Study risk of serious injury or death in intimate violence: A collaborative research project.* Chicago: Illinois Criminal Justice Information Authority.

Block, C. R., & Christakos, A. (1995). Intimate partner homicide in Chicago over 29 years. *Crime and Delinquency, 41,* 496–526.

Bohmer, C. (1991). Acquaintance rape and the law. In A. Parrot & L. Bechhofer (Eds.), *Acquaintance rape: The hidden crime* (pp. 317–333). New York: Wiley.

Bossarte, R. M., Simon, T. R., & Barker, L. (2006). Characteristics of homicide followed by suicide incidents in multiple states, 2003–2004. *Injury Prevention, 12* (2), ii33–ii38.

Bowles, J. (2012, October 29). Personal interview.

Bowling, M. D. (2012, October 19). Personal interview.

Bradley v. State, 1 Miss. (1 Walker) 156, 157 (1824).

Bradshaw v. Ball, 487 S.W.2d 294 (Ky. 1972).

Brady Handgun Violence Prevention Act. (1994). Pub. L. 103-159, 107 Stat. 1536.

Brammer, J. (2008, June 25). Former Rep. Gross Clay Lindsay dies at 77. *Lexington Herald-Leader.* http://bluegrasspolitics.bloginky.com/2008/06/25/former-rep-gross-clay-lindsay-dies-at-77/.

Brammer, J. (2012, June 11). Governor, Kentucky Speedway officials tout improvements at track. *Lexington Herald-Leader.*

Brewster, M. P. (2000). Stalking by former intimates: Verbal threats and other predictors of physical violence. *Violence and Victim, 15,* 41–54.

Brickey, K. F. (1972–1973). An introduction to the Kentucky Penal Code: A critique of pure reason? *Kentucky Law Journal, 61,* 624–640.

Brickey, K. F. (1974). *Kentucky criminal law: A treatise on criminal law under the new Kentucky Penal Code.* Cleveland, OH: Banks-Baldwin Law Publishing Company.

Bridges, A. J., & Jensen, R. (2011). Pornography. In C. Renzetti, J. Edleson, & R. Bergen (Eds.), *Sourcebook on Violence Against Women* (2nd ed., pp. 133–149). Los Angeles: Sage Publications.

Brown, B. (2012, November 1). Personal interview.

Brown, J. Y., Jr. (2013, April 10). Personal interview.

Brown, S. (1984). Police responses to wife beating: Neglect of a crime of violence. *Journal of Criminal Justice, 12,* 277–288.

Brown v. State, 127 Wis. at 201, 106 N.W. at 539 (1906).

Brownmiller, S. (1975). *Against our will: Men, women and rape.* New York: Simon & Schuster.

Bryden, D., & Lengnick, S. (1997). Rape in the criminal justice system. *Journal of Criminal Law & Criminology, 87,* 1194.

Burch, T. J. (2012, October 15). Personal interview.

Bureau of Labor Statistics. (2011). *Women at work*. US Department of Labor. http://www.bls.gov/spotlight/2011/women/.

Burke, A. S. (2007). Domestic violence as a crime of pattern and intent: An alternative reconceptualization. *George Washington Law Review*, 75 (3), 552–612.

Buzawa, E., Hotaling, G., & Klein, A. (1998). The response to domestic violence in a model court: Some initial findings and implications. *Behavioral Sciences and the Law, 16*, 185–206.

Buzawa, E. S., & Buzawa, C. G. (1990). *Domestic violence: The criminal justice response*. Newbury Park, CA: Sage Publications.

Buzawa, E. S., & Buzawa, C. G. (Eds.). (1992). *Domestic violence: The changing criminal justice response*. Westport, CT: Auburn House.

Buzawa, E. S., & Buzawa, C. G. (1996). *Domestic violence: The criminal justice response* (2nd ed.). Newbury Park, CA: Sage Publications.

Byrom, C. E. (2005). The use of the excited utterance hearsay exception in the prosecution of domestic violence cases after *Crawford v. Washington*. *Review of Litigation, 24* (2), 409–429.

Calvert, L. (2012, November 2). Personal interview.

Campanelli, D., & Gilson, T. (2002). Murder-suicide in New Hampshire, 1995–2000. *American Journal of Forensic Medical Pathology, 23*, 248–251.

Campbell, J. C. (1995). Prediction of homicide of and by battered women. In J. C. Campbell (Ed.), *Assessing dangerousness: Violence by sexual offenders, batterers, and child abusers* (pp. 96–113). Thousand Oaks, CA: Sage Publications.

Campbell, J. C. (2004). Helping women understand their risk in situations of intimate partner violence. *Journal of Interpersonal Violence, 19* (12), 1464–1477.

Campbell, J. C., Webster, D., Koziol-McLain, J., Block, C., Campbell, D., Curry, M. A., et al. (2003). Risk factors for femicide in abusive relationships: Results from a multisite case control study. *American Journal of Public Health, 93* (7), 1089–1097.

Campbell, R. (2006). Rape survivors' experiences with the legal and medical systems: Do rape victim advocates make a difference? *Violence Against Women, 12* (1), 30–45.

Campbell, R. (2009). Science, social change, and ending violence against women: Which one of these is not like the others? *Violence Against Women, 15*, 434–439.

Campbell, R., Patterson, D., & Lichty, L. (2005). The effectiveness of sexual assault nurse examiner (SANE) programs: A review of psychological, medical, legal, and community outcomes. *Trauma, Violence, & Abuse, 6* (4), 313–329.

Campbell, R., & Raja, S. (1999). Secondary victimization of rape victims: Insights from mental health professionals who treat survivors of violence. *Violence & Victims, 14* (3), 261–275.

Campbell, R., & Raja, S. (2005). The sexual assault and secondary victimization of female veterans: Help-seeking experiences with military and civilian social systems. *Psychology of Women Quarterly, 29* (1), 97–106.

Campbell, R., Wasco, S. M., Ahrens, C. E., Sefl, T., & Barnes, H. E. (2001). Preventing the "second rape": Rape survivors' experiences with community service providers. *Journal of Interpersonal Violence, 16,* 1239–1259.

Caralis, P. V., & Musialowski, R. (1997). Women's experiences with domestic violence and their attitudes and expectations regarding medical care of abuse victims. *Southern Medical Journal, 90* (11), 1075–1080.

Caringella, S. (2009). *Addressing rape reform in law and practice.* New York: Columbia University Press.

Caringella-McDonald, S. (2000). Rape law reform, In N. H. Rafter (Ed.), *The encyclopedia of women and crime* (pp. 222–223). Phoenix, AZ: Oryx Press.

Carlson, M., Harris, S., & Holden, G. (1999). Protective orders and domestic violence: Risk factors for re-abuse. *Journal of Family Violence, 14* (2), 205–226.

Castle Rock v. Gonzales, 545 U.S. 748 (2005).

Catalano, S. (2006). *Intimate partner violence in the United States.* Washington, DC: US Department of Justice. http://www.ojp.usdoj.gov/bjs/intimate/ipv.htm.

Centers for Disease Control and Prevention. (1991). Current trends in homicide followed by suicide: Kentucky, 1985–1990. *Morbidity and Mortality Weekly Report, 40,* 652–653, 659.

Chan, H-C., & Heide, K. (2009). Sexual homicide: A synthesis of the literature. *Trauma, Violence, & Abuse, 10,* 31–54.

Chellgren, M. (1987, March 11). Spouse abuse centers divide state lawmakers. *Lexington Herald-Leader.*

Chesney-Lind, M. (2002). Criminalizing victimization: The unintended consequences of pro-arrest policies for girls and women. *Criminology and Public Policy, 2,* 81–90.

Clark, T. D. (2000). Education. In J. Klotter (Ed.), *Our Kentucky: A study of the Bluegrass State* (2nd ed., pp. 298–313). Lexington: University Press of Kentucky.

Clay-Warner, J., & Burt, C. H. (2005). Rape reporting after reforms: Have times really changed? *Violence Against Women, 11* (2), 150–176.

Cohen, D., Llorente, M., & Eisdorfer, C. (1998). Homicide-suicide in older persons. *American Journal of Psychiatry, 155,* 390–396.

Coleman, F. L. (1997). Stalking behavior and the cycle of domestic violence. *Journal of Interpersonal Violence, 12,* 420–432.

Collins, M. L. (2013, April 25). Personal interview.

Combs-Lane, A. M., & Smith, D. W. (2002). Risk of sexual victimization in college women: The role of behavioral intentions and risk-taking behaviors. *Journal of Interpersonal Violence, 17*, 165–183.

Commonwealth v. Chretien, 383 Mass. 123, 135 (1981).

Commonwealth v. Fogerty, 8 Gray, 491 (1857).

Commonwealth v. McAfee, 108 Mass. 458 (1871).

Commonwealth v. Wasson, 842 S.W.2d 487 (1992).

Comstock, R. D., Mallonee, S., Kruger, E., Rayno, K., Vance, A., & Jordan, F. (2005). Epidemiology of homicide-suicide events: Oklahoma, 1994–2001. *American Journal of Forensic Medicine and Pathology, 26* (3), 229–235.

Cooper, M., & Eaves, D. (1996). Suicide following homicide in the family. *Violence & Victims, 11* (2), 99–112.

Corbett, C., & Hill, C. (2012). *Graduating to a pay gap: The earnings of women and men one year after college graduation*. Washington, DC: American Association of University Women.

Coulter, M. L., & Chez, R. A. (1997). Domestic violence victims support mandatory reporting: For others. *Journal of Family Violence, 12* (3), 349–356.

Cowan, F. (2012, December 12). Personal interview.

Craven, D. (1997). *Sex differences in violent victimization, 1994: Bureau of Justice Statistics special report* (NCJ 164508). Washington, DC: US Department of Justice, Office of Justice Programs.

Crawford, E., Wright, M. O., & Birchmeier, Z. (2008). Drug facilitated sexual assault: College women's risk perception and behavioral choices. *Journal of American College Health, 57*, 261–272.

Crime in Kentucky: Commonwealth of Kentucky crime report. (2000). Frankfort: Kentucky State Police.

Crime in Kentucky: Commonwealth of Kentucky crime report. (2001). Frankfort: Kentucky State Police.

Crime in Kentucky: Commonwealth of Kentucky crime report. (2002). Frankfort: Kentucky State Police.

Crime in Kentucky: Commonwealth of Kentucky crime report. (2003). Frankfort: Kentucky State Police.

Crime in Kentucky: Commonwealth of Kentucky crime report. (2004). Frankfort: Kentucky State Police.

Crime in Kentucky: Commonwealth of Kentucky crime report. (2005). Frankfort: Kentucky State Police.

Crime in Kentucky: Commonwealth of Kentucky crime report. (2006). Frankfort: Kentucky State Police.

Crime in Kentucky: Commonwealth of Kentucky crime report. (2007). Frankfort: Kentucky State Police.

Crime in Kentucky: Commonwealth of Kentucky crime report. (2008). Frankfort: Kentucky State Police.

Crime in Kentucky: Commonwealth of Kentucky crime report. (2009). Frankfort: Kentucky State Police.

Crime Victim Compensation Board. (2012). *Crime victims compensation program.* Frankfort, KY: Public Protection Cabinet. http://cvcb.ky.gov/Pages/default.aspx.

Cromwell, E. G. (1996). A woman blazes the trail. In D. Taylor (Ed.), *Woman in politics* (pp. 23–54). Frankfort: Kentucky Commission on Women.

Cross, A. (2004). Ernest Lee Fletcher. In L. Harrison (Ed.), *Kentucky's governors* (updated ed., pp. 264–267). Lexington: University Press of Kentucky.

Crowe-Carraco, C. (2000). Women's quest for reform. In J. Klotter (Ed.), *Our Kentucky: A study of the Bluegrass State* (2nd ed., pp. 189–206). Lexington: University Press of Kentucky.

Currens, S. (2002). Kentucky coalition's concerns about mandatory reporting. In J. Zorza (Ed.), *Violence against women: Law, prevention, protection, enforcement, treatment, health* (pp. 24-2–24-4). Kingston, NJ: Civic Research Institute.

Currens, S. (2012, September 26). Personal interview.

Daire, V. (2000). The case against mandatory reporting of domestic violence injuries. *Florida Bar Journal, 74* (1). http://www.floridabar.org/DIVCOM/JN/JNJournal01.nsf.

Davies, L. (2005). *Twenty-five years of saving lives: 1980–2005.* Irving, TX: Mothers against Drunk Drivers. http://www.madd.org/about-us/history/madd25thhistory.pdf.

Davis, R. C., & Smith, B. (1982). Crimes between acquaintances: The response of the criminal courts. *Victimology: An International Journal, 8,* 175–187.

Davis, R. C., Smith B. E., & Davies, H. J. (2001). The effects of no-drop prosecution of domestic violence upon conviction rates (NCJ 193235). *Justice Research and Policy, 3* (2), 1–13.

Davis, R. C., Smith, B. E., & Taylor, B. G. (2003). Increasing the proportion of domestic violence arrests that are prosecuted: A natural experiment in Milwaukee. *Criminology and Public Policy, 2,* 263–282.

Dawson, M. (2005). Intimate femicide followed by suicide: Examining the role of premeditation. *Suicide and Life-Threatening Behavior, 35* (1), 76–90.

DeLeon-Granados, W., Wells, W., & Binsbacher, R. (2006). Arresting developments: Trends in female arrests for domestic violence and proposed explanations. *Violence Against Women, 12* (4), 355–371.

Denno, D. W. (2003). Why the Model Penal Code's sexual offense provisions should be pulled and replaced. *Ohio State Journal of Criminal Law, 1* (207), 207–218.

Dietz, P., Hazelwood, R., & Warren, J. (1990). The sexually sadistic criminal and his offenses. *Bulletin of the American Academy of Psychiatry and the Law, 18,* 163–178.

Division of Protection and Permanency. (2012). *Adult protective services reports: 2002–2011.* Frankfort, KY: Cabinet for Health and Family Services.

Dobash, R. E., & Dobash, R. (1979). *Violence against wives: A case against the patriarchy.* New York: Free Press.

Dobash, R. E., & Dobash, R. (1992). *Women, violence and social change.* London: Routledge.

Doe v. United States, 666 F.2d 43 (4th Cir. 1981).

Douglas, J., Burgess, A., Burgess, A., & Ressler, R. (1992). *Crime classification manual.* New York: Lexington Books.

Dugan, L., Nagin, D., & Rosenfeld, R. (1999). Explaining the decline in intimate partner homicide: The effects of changing domesticity, women's status, and domestic violence resources. *Homicide Studies, 3,* 187–214.

Dunn, H. (2010). The Railroad Killer. *48 Hours Mystery.* CBS Television Network. New York: CBS Corporation.

Dunn, J. L. (2005). Victims and survivors: Emerging vocabularies of motive for battered women who stay. *Sociological Inquiry, 75,* 1–30.

Durborow, N., Lizdas, K. D., O'Flaherty, A., & Marjavi, A. (2010). *Compendium of state statutes and policies on domestic violence and health care.* San Francisco: Family Violence Prevention Fund.

Dutton, D. G. (1988). Profiling of wife assaulters: Preliminary evidence for a trimodal analysis. *Violence & Victims, 3* (1), 5–29.

Dworkin, A. (1986, January 22). Pornography is a civil rights issue. Testimony before the Attorney General's Commission on Pornography, New York.

Eblen, T. (2012, February 14). Mary E. Britton: Physician and trailblazer. *Lexington Herald-Leader,* C1–C3.

Edleson, J. L. (1998, June). Social service agencies have a responsibility to know the difference. *Domestic Abuse Project Newsletter.*

Eigenberg, H., McGuffee, K., Berry, P., & Hall, W. H. (2003). Protective order legislation: Trends in state statutes. *Journal of Criminal Justice, 31,* 411–422.

Eliason, S. (2009). Murder-suicide: A review of the recent literature. *Journal of the American Academy of Psychiatry and the Law, 37,* 371–376.

Ellers, F. (2003). *Progress and paradox: The Patton years, 1995–2003.* Louisville, KY: Butler Book Publishing Services.

Ellis, W. E. (2000). Toward the modern era: 1930 to the present. In

J. Klotter (Ed.), *Our Kentucky: A study of the Bluegrass State* (2nd ed., pp. 286–297). Lexington: University Press of Kentucky.

Ellison, L. (2002). Prosecuting domestic violence without victim participation. *Modern Law Review, 65,* 834–858.

Epstein, D. (1999). Redefining the state's response to domestic violence: Past victories and future challenges. *Georgetown Journal of Gender and the Law,* 127–143.

Estrich, S. (1987). *Real rape.* Cambridge, MA: Harvard University Press.

Evidence Rules Study Committee. (1992). Study committee's prefatory note. *Kentucky Rules of Evidence.* http://www.louisvillelaw.com/kre/index.htm.

Fagan, J. (1989). Cessation from family violence: Deterrence and dissuasion. In L. Ohlin & M. Tonry (Eds.), *Crime and justice: An annual review of research: Vol. 11. Family violence* (pp. 357–426). Chicago: University of Chicago Press.

Fagan, J. (1996). *The criminalization of domestic violence: Promises and limits.* Washington, DC: Office of Justice Programs, US Department of Justice.

Feddock, C. A., Pursley, H. G., O'Brien, K., Griffith, C. H., & Wilson, J. F. (2009). Attitudes of Kentucky women regarding mandatory reporting of intimate partner violence. *Journal of the Kentucky Medical Association, 107* (1), 17–21.

Feder, L., & Henning, K. (2005). A comparison of male and female dually arrested domestic violence offenders. *Violence & Victims, 20* (2), 153–171.

Federal Bureau of Investigation. (1992). *Uniform crime reports.* Washington DC: US Department of Justice.

Federal Bureau of Investigation. (1995). *Uniform crime reports.* Washington DC: US Department of Justice.

Federal Bureau of Investigation. (2008). *Uniform crime reports.* Washington DC: US Department of Justice.

Federal Rules of Evidence. Pub. L. 93-595, 88 Stat. 1926 (1975).

Federal Rules of Evidence (Rape Shield Law, 412). Pub. L. 95-540, 92 Stat. 2046 (1978).

Fenton, Z. E. (2011). State-enabled violence: The story of *Town of Castle Rock v. Gonzales.* In E. M. Schneider & S. M. Wildman (Eds.), *Women and the law stories.* New York: Thomson Reuters/Foundation Press.

Ferraro, K. (1989). Policing woman battering. *Social Problems, 36* (1), 61–74.

Ferraro, K. (1995). *Fear of crime: Interpreting victimization risk.* Albany, NY: SUNY Press.

Ferraro, K. (1996). Women's fear of victimization: Shadow of sexual assault? *Social Forces, 75,* 667–690.

Field, H. S., & Bienen, L. B. (1980). *Jurors and rape: A study in psychology and law.* Lexington, MA: Lexington Books.

Finkelhor, D., & Yllo, K. (1985). *License to rape: Sexual abuse of wives.* New York: Free Press.

Fisher, B. S., & Cullen, F. T. (2000). Measuring the sexual victimization of women: Evolution, current controversies, and future research. In D. Duffee (Ed.), *Criminal justice 2000: Vol. 4. Measurement and analysis of crime and justice* (pp. 317–390). Washington, DC: National Institute of Justice.

Fisher, B. S., Cullen, F. T., & Turner, M. (2000). *The sexual victimization of college women* (NCJ 182369). Washington, DC: US Department of Justice.

Fisher, B. S., Cullen, F. T., & Turner, M. (2002). Being pursued: Stalking victimization in a national study of college women. *Criminology and Public Policy, 1,* 257–308.

Fisher, B. S., Daigle, L. E., & Cullen, F. T. (2010). *Unsafe in the ivory tower: The sexual victimization of college women.* Thousand Oaks, CA: Sage Publications.

Fisher, B. S., Hartman, J. L., Cullen, F. T., & Turner, M. G. (2002). Making campuses safer for students: The "Clery Act" as a symbolic legal reform. *Stetson Law Review, 32,* 61–89.

Fisher, B. S., Sloan, J. J., Cullen, F. T., & Lu, C. (1998). Crime in the ivory tower: The level and sources of student victimization. *Criminology, 36,* 671–710.

Ford, D. A. (2003). Coercing victim participation in domestic violence prosecutions. *Journal of Interpersonal Violence, 18* (6), 669–684.

Ford, D. A., & Regoli, J. (1992). The preventive impact of policies for prosecuting wife batterers. In E. S. Buzawa & C. G. Buzawa (Eds.), *Domestic violence: The changing criminal justice response* (pp. 181–207). Westport, CT: Greenwood.

Foshee, V. A., Linder, F., MacDougall, J. E., & Bangdiwala, S. (2001). Gender differences in the longitudinal predictors of adolescent dating violence. *Preventive Medicine, 32* (2), 128–141.

Fox, J. A., & Zawitz, M. W. (2004). *Homicide trends in the United States: 2002 update.* (Crime brief, NCJ 204885). Washington, DC: Office of Justice Programs, Bureau of Justice Statistics.

Fox, J. A., & Zawitz, M. W. (2007). *Homicide trends in the US.* http://www.ojp.usdoj.gov/bjs/pub/pdf/htius.pdf.

Frantzen, D., San Miguel, C., & Kwak, D. (2011). Predicting case conviction and domestic violence recidivism: Measuring the deterrent effects of conviction and protection order violations. *Violence & Victims, 26* (4), 395–409.

Frazier, P. A., & Haney, B. (1996). Sexual assault cases in the legal system:

Police prosecutor and victim perspectives. *Law and Human Behavior, 20*, 607–628.

Fulgham v. State, 46 Ala. 143, 1871 WL 1013 (Ala. 1871).

Fulkerson, A., & Patterson, S. L. (2006). Victimless prosecution of domestic violence in the wake of *Crawford v. Washington. Forum on Public Policy: A Journal of the Oxford Round Table, 1*, 1–38.

Fuller, P. E. (1992). *Laura Clay and the woman's rights movement.* Lexington: University Press of Kentucky.

Gagne, P. (1998). *Battered women's justice.* New York: Twayne Publishing.

Garkovich, L., & Zimmerman, J. N. (1999). Welfare reform and Kentucky women. In M. Smith-Mello, M. T. Childress, J. Sollinger, & B. M. Sebastian (Eds.), *The future well-being of women in Kentucky* (57–70). Frankfort: Kentucky Long-Term Policy Research Center.

Garner, J., & Maxwell, C. (2008). *Crime control effects of prosecuting intimate partner violence in Hamilton County, Ohio: Reproducing and extending the analyses of Wooldredge and Thistlewaite* (NCJ 222907). Washington, DC: US Department of Justice, National Institute of Justice.

Gartner, R., & Doob, A. (1994). Trends in criminal victimization: 1988–1993. *Juristat 14* (13), 1–20.

Gauthier, D. K., & Bankston, W. B. (1997). Gender equality and the sex ratio of intimate killing. *Criminology, 35* (4), 577–600.

Gelak, D. R. (2008). *Lobbying and advocacy.* Alexandria, VA: TheCapitol. Net.

Gerth, J. (2011, February 27). Need for yearly legislative sessions questionable. *Courier Journal* (McLean, VA).

Gielen, A. C., O'Campo, P. J., Campbell, J. C., Schollenberger, J., Woods, A. B., Jones, A. S., Dienemann, J. A., Kub, J., & Wynne, E. C. (2000). Women's opinions about domestic violence screening and mandatory reporting. *American Journal of Preventive Medicine, 19* (4), 279–285.

Glasgow, J. M. (1980). Marital rape exemption: Legal sanction of spouse abuse. *Journal of Family Law, 18*, 565–586.

Glass, N., & Campbell, J. (1998). Mandatory reporting of intimate partner violence by health care professionals: A policy review. *Nursing Outlook, 46*, 279–283.

Goodman, E. J. (2006, June 30). State removes statute of limitations for rape cases. *New York Gotham Gazette.*

Goodmark, L. (2011). State, national, and international legal initiatives to address violence against women: A survey. In C. Renzetti, J. Edleson, & R. Bergen (Eds.), *Sourcebook on Violence Against Women* (2nd ed., pp. 191–207). Los Angeles: Sage Publications.

Gover, A. R. (2009). Domestic violence courts: A judicial response to intimate partner violence. In P. Higgins & M. B. Mackinem (Eds.),

Problem-solving courts: Justice for the twenty-first century. (pp. 115–138). Santa Barbara, CA: Praeger Publications.

Gover, A. R., MacDonald, J. M., & Alpert, G. P. (2003). Combating domestic violence: Findings from an evaluation of a local domestic violence court. *Criminology and Public Policy, 1,* 109–132.

Grace, F. (2001). *Carry A. Nation: Retelling the life.* Bloomington: Indiana University Press.

Greenfeld, L. A., Rand, M. R., Craven, D., et al. (1998). *Violence by intimates: Analysis of data on crimes by current or former spouses, boyfriends, and girlfriends.* Washington, DC: US Department of Justice.

Greenfeld, L. A., & Snell, T. L. (1999). *Bureau of Justice statistics bulletin: Women offenders* (NCJ 175688). Washington, DC: US Department of Justice.

Gregory, D. E. (2001). Crime on campus: Compliance, liability and safety. *Campus Law Enforcement Journal, 31,* 27–28.

Guyer, R. L. (2003). *Guide to state legislative lobbying.* Gainesville, FL: Engineering the Law.

Hale, Sir Matthew. (1736). *Historia Placitorum Coronæ* (Vol. 1). W. A. Stokes (Ed.). London: Professional Books.

Hall, W. (1997). *Passing for black: The life and careers of Mae Street Kidd.* Lexington: University Press of Kentucky.

Hannah, S. G., Turf, E. E., & Fierro, M. F. (1998). Murder-suicide in central Virginia: A descriptive epidemiologic study and empiric validation of the Hanzlick-Hoponen typology. *American Journal of Forensic Medical Pathology, 15,* 168–173.

Hanzlick, R., & Koponen, M. (1994). Murder-suicide in Fulton County Georgia 1988–1991: Comparison with a recent report and proposed typology. *American Journal of Forensic Medical Pathology, 15,* 168–173.

Hardy, T., & Barrows, M. (2001). Campus rapes: Underreporting by schools boasting safe records. *Investigative Reporters and Editors (IRE) Journal, 24* (4), 16–17.

Harmon, R., Rosner, R., & Owens, H. (1995). Obsessional harassment and erotomania in a criminal court population. *Journal of Forensic Sciences, 40,* 188–196.

Harper, D. W., & Voigt, L. (2007). Homicide followed by suicide: An integrated theoretical perspective. *Homicide Studies, 11* (4), 295–318.

Harrell, A., & Smith, B. E. (1996). Effects of restraining orders on domestic violence victims. In E. S. Buzawa & C. G. Buzawa (Eds.), *Do arrests and restraining orders work?* (pp. 214–242). Thousand Oaks, CA: Sage Publications.

Harris v. State, 71 Miss. 462. 14 South. 266 (1894).

Harrison, L. H. (1993). Collins, Martha Layne. In J. E. Kleber (Ed.), *The Kentucky encyclopedia* (pp. 214–215). Lexington: University Press of Kentucky.

Harrison, L. H., & Klotter, J. C. (1997). *The new history of Kentucky*. Lexington: University Press of Kentucky.

Hartley, C. C. (2003). A therapeutic jurisprudence approach to the trial process in domestic violence felony trials. *Violence Against Women, 9* (4), 410–437.

Haxton, D. (1985). Rape shield statutes: Constitutional despite unconstitutional exclusions of evidence. *Wisconsin Law Review*, 1219–1272.

Hay, M. P. (2009). *Madeline McDowell Breckinridge and the battle for a new South*. Lexington: University Press of Kentucky.

Hayden, S. R., Barton, E. D., & Hayden, M. (1997). Domestic violence in the emergency department: How do women prefer to disclose and discuss the issue? *Journal of Emergency Medicine, 15* (4), 447–451.

Hazel v. State, 157 A. 2d 922, Maryland Court of Appeals (1960).

Hazelwood, R. R., & Burgess, A. W. (2009). *Practical aspects of rape investigations: A multidisciplinary approach* (4th ed.). Boca Raton, FL: CRC Press.

Heleringer, R. L. (2013, April 15). Personal interview.

Hendrix, L. H. (2010). *Constitution of the Commonwealth of Kentucky*. Informational Bulletin 59 (Rev.). Frankfort, KY: Legislative Research Commission.

Henson, M. (1992). To have and to harm: Kentucky's failure to protect women from the men who beat them. *Lexington Herald-Leader* (Special Reprint).

Herbert, P. B. (2002). The duty to warn: A reconsideration and critique. *Journal of the American Academy of Psychiatry Law, 30*, 417–424.

Herbert, P. B., & Young, K. A. (2002). Tarasoff at twenty-five. *Journal of the American Academy of Psychiatry and the Law, 30*, 275–281.

Hirschel, D., Buzawa, E., Pattavina, A., Faggiani, D., & Rueland, M. (2007). *Explaining the prevalence, context, and consequences of dual arrest in intimate partner cases* (NCJ 218355). Washington, DC: US Department of Justice.

Holt, V. L., Kernic, M. A., Lumley, T., & Wolf, M. E. (2002). Civil protective orders and risk of subsequent police-reported violence. *Journal of the American Medical Association, 288* (5), 589–594.

Holt, V. L., Kernic, M. A., Wolf, M. E., & Rivara, F. P. (2003). Do protection orders affect the likelihood of future partner violence and injury? *American Journal of Preventive Medicine, 24* (1), 16–21.

Honeycutt, V. (1992, March 26). Key domestic violence bill may be in trouble. *Lexington Herald-Leader*.

Honeycutt, V., & Warren, J. (2012, March 3). Death toll at 20 in tornado ravaged Kentucky counties. *Lexington Herald-Leader*.

Hotaling, G. T., & Buzawa, E. S. (2003). *Forging criminal justice assistance*. Document No. 195667. http://www.ncjrs.gov/pdffiles1/nij/grants/195667.pdf.

Hudge, M. (2000). The campus security act. *Journal of Security Administration, 23* (2), 25–27.

Hyman, A. (1997). *Mandatory reporting of domestic violence by health care providers: A policy paper.* San Francisco: Futures without Violence.

Hyman, A., Schillinger, D., & Lo, B. (1995). Laws mandating reporting of domestic violence: Do they promote patient well-being? *Journal of the American Medical Association, 273,* 1781–1787.

Ireland, R. M. (1983). Homicide in the nineteenth century Kentucky. *Register of the Kentucky Historical Society, 81* (2), 134–154.

Ireland, R. M. (2000). Violence. In J. Klotter (Ed.), *Our Kentucky: A study of the Bluegrass State* (2nd ed., pp. 156–171). Lexington: University Press of Kentucky.

Irvin, H. D. (2009). *Women in Kentucky.* Lexington: University Press of Kentucky.

Jackson, S. M. (1999). Issues in the dating violence research: A review of the literature. *Aggression and Violent Behavior, 4* (2), 233–247.

Jeanne Clery Disclosure of Campus Security Policy and Campus Crime Statistics Act (2000). 20 USC § 1092(f).

Jenkins, J. (2012, September 20). Personal interview.

Jessica Gonzales v. United States, Petition No. 1490-05, Inter-American Commission on Human Rights, Report No. 52/07, OEA/Ser.L./V/II.128, Doc. 19 (2007).

Jessica Lenahan (Gonzales) et al. v. United States, Case 12.626, Report No. 80/11 (Inter-American Commission on Human Rights, August, 17, 2011).

Johnson, D. (1990, April 29). Kidnapping sows suspicion in trusting town. *New York Times.* http://www.nytimes.com/1990/04/29/us/kidnapping-sows-suspicion-in-trusting-town.html.

Johnson, G. (2012). *Trailblazing governors: Six remarkable women.* North Charleston, SC: CreateSpace.

Johnson, M. P. (2008). *A typology of domestic violence: Intimate terrorism, violence resistance, and situation couple violence.* Boston: Northeastern University Press.

Johnson, M. P. (2011). Gender and types of intimate partner violence: A response to an anti-feminist literature review. *Aggression and Violent Behavior, 16,* 289–296.

Johnson, P. (2013, April 18). Personal interview.

Johnson, R. R. (2008). Assessing the true dangerousness of domestic violence calls. *Law Enforcement Executive Forum, 8* (5), 19–29.

Johnson, R. R. (2011). Predicting officer physical assaults at domestic assault calls. *Journal of Family Violence, 26,* 163–169.

Jones, A. (1996). *Women who kill.* Boston: Beacon.

Jones, J. (1982). Woody Allen lives up to "colorful" reputation. *Daily News* (Bowling Green, KY).

Jones, L. (2004). Wendell Hampton Ford. In L. Harrison (Ed.), *Kentucky's governors* (updated ed., pp. 211–216). Lexington: University Press of Kentucky.

Jordan, C. E. (2004). Intimate partner violence and the justice system: An examination of the interface. *Journal of Interpersonal Violence, 19,* 1412–1434.

Jordan, C. E. (2009a). Advancing the study of violence against women: Evolving research agendas into science. *Violence Against Women, 15,* 393–419.

Jordan, C. E. (2009b). Advancing the study of violence against women: Response to commentaries and next steps. *Violence Against Women, 15,* 440–442.

Jordan, C. E., Campbell, R., & Follingstad, D. (2010). Violence and women's mental health: The impact of physical, sexual and psychological aggression. *Annual Review of Clinical Psychology, 6,* 607–628.

Jordan, C. E., Clark, J. J., Pritchard, A. J., & Charnigo, R. (2012). Lethal and other serious assaults: Disentangling gender and context. *Crime and Delinquency, 58,* 425–455.

Jordan, C. E., Hughes, E. S., & Gleason, M. J. (2005). Criminal prosecution and civil remedies for victims of sexual offenses: Amendment of the rape shield law. *Bench and Bar, 69* (2), 11–16.

Jordan, C. E, Logan, T. K., Walker, R., & Nigoff, A. (2003). Stalking: An examination of the criminal justice response. *Journal of Interpersonal Violence, 18* (2) 148–165.

Jordan, C. E., Nietzel, M. T., Walker, R., & Logan, T. K. (2004). *Intimate partner violence: A clinical training guide for mental health professionals.* New York: Springer Publishing Company.

Jordan, C. E., Pritchard, A., Duckett, D., & Charnigo, R. (2010). Criminal offending among respondents to protective orders: Crime types and patterns that predict victim risk. *Violence Against Women, 16* (12), 1396–1411.

Jordan, C. E., Pritchard, A., Wilcox, P., & Duckett-Pritchard, D. (2008). The denial of emergency protection: Factors associated with court decision-making. *Violence & Victims, 23* (5), 603–616.

Jordan, C. E., Quinn, K., Jordan, B., & Daileader, C. R. (2000). Stalking: Cultural, clinical and legal considerations. *Brandeis Journal of Family Law, 38* (3), 513–579.

Jordan, C. E., Wilcox, P., & Pritchard, A. (2007). Stalking acknowledgement and reporting among college women experiencing intrusive behaviors: Implications for the emergence of a "classic stalking case." *Journal of Criminal Justice, 35,* 556–569.

Jordan, C. E., & Wilson, S. A. (2002). *Proposed amendments to the Kentucky Rules of Evidence.* Frankfort, KY: Governor's Office of Child Abuse and Domestic Violence Services.

Jurik, N. C., & Winn, R. (1990). Gender and homicide: A comparison of men and women who kill. *Violence & Victims, 5*, 227–242.

Kaci, J. H. (1994). Aftermath of seeking domestic violence protective orders: The victim's perspective. *Journal of Contemporary Criminal Justice, 10*, 201–219.

Kane, R. (2000). Police responses to restraining orders in domestic violence incidents: Identifying the custody-threshold thesis. *Criminal Justice & Behavior, 27*, 561–580.

Karch, D. L., Lubell, K. M., Friday, J., Patel, N., & Williams, D. (2008). Surveillance for violence deaths: National Violent Death Reporting System, 16 states, 2005. *Morbidity and Mortality Weekly Report (MMWR)*. http://www.cdc.gov/mmwr/preview/mmwrhtml/ss5703a1.htm.

Karem, D. (2012, September 21). Personal interview.

Karjane, H. K., Fisher, B. S., & Cullen, F. T. (2002). *Campus sexual assault: How America's institutions of higher education respond* (NIJ, 1999-WA-VX-0008). Newton, MA: Education Development Center.

Kee, H. C., Frost, J. W., Albu, E., Lindberg, C., & Robert, D. L. (1998). *Christianity: A social and cultural history* (2nd ed.). Upper Saddle River, NJ: Prentice Hall.

Keilitz, S. (2000). *Specialization of domestic violence case management in the courts: A national survey.* Williamsburg, VA: National Center for State Courts.

Keilitz, S., Hannaford, P., & Efkeman, H. (1997). *Civil protection orders: The benefits and limitations for victims of domestic violence* (Research Report No. R-201). Williamsburg, VA: National Center for State Courts.

Kellermann, A., & Heron, S. (1999). Firearms and family violence. *Emergency Medicine Statistics Reports, 47*, 28–37.

Kellermann, A. L., & Mercy, J. A. (1992). Men, women and murder: Gender-specific differences in rates of fatal violence and victimization. *Journal of Trauma, 33*, 1–5.

Kellermann, A. L., Rivara, F. P., Rushforth, N. B., Banton, J. G., Rey, D. T., Francisco, J. T., et al. (1993). Gun ownership as a risk factor for homicide in the home. *New England Journal of Medicine, 339*, 1084–1091.

Kelly, H. A. (1994). Rule of thumb and the folklaw of the husband's stick. *Journal of Legal Education 44* (3), 341–365.

Kelly, K. A. (2003). *Domestic violence and the politics of privacy.* New York: Cambridge Books.

Kentucky Crime Victim Compensation Board. (2012). *Crime victim compensation program.* Frankfort, KY: Public Protection Cabinet. http://cvcb.ky.gov/Pages/default.aspx.

Kentucky Domestic Violence Association. (2012). *Statistics.* Frankfort, KY: Author. http://www.kdva.org/resources/statistics.html.

Kentucky Hospital Association. (2012). *KHA hospitals*. Louisville, KY: Author. http://info.kyha.com/KHADBS/hospitals.asp.

Kentucky State Board of Elections. (2012a). *Constitutional amendment, 1975*. http://elect.ky.gov/SiteCollectionDocuments/Election%20Results/1973-1979/75const.pdf.

Kentucky State Board of Elections. (2012b). *Turnout statistics: Primary May 22, 2012*. http://elect.ky.gov/statistics/Pages/turnoutstatistics.aspx.

Kethineni, S., & Beichner, D. (2009). A comparison of civil and criminal orders of protection as remedies for domestic violence victims in a midwestern county. *Journal of Family Violence, 24*, 311–321.

Kethineni, S., & Falcone, D. N. (2001). Protective orders in domestic violence cases in a mid-western county. *Justice Professional, 14*, 323–344.

Kidwell v. U.S., 38 App.D.C. 566 (1912).

Kilpatrick, D. G., Edmunds, C. N., & Seymour, A. E. (1992). *Rape in America: A report to the nation*. Arlington, VA: National Crime Victims Center.

Kilpatrick, D. G., & Ruggiero, K. J. (2003). *Rape in Kentucky: A report to the Commonwealth*. Frankfort, KY: Office of the Governor.

Kleber, J. (Ed.). (1992). *The Kentucky encyclopedia*. Lexington: University Press of Kentucky.

Klein, A. (1996). Re-abuse in a population of court-restrained male batterers: Why restraining orders don't work. In E. S. Buzawa & C. G. Buzawa (Eds.), *Do arrests and restraining orders work?* (pp. 192–213). Thousand Oaks, CA: Sage.

Klein, E., Campbell, J. C., Soler, E., & Ghez, M. (1997). *Ending domestic violence: Changing public perceptions/halting the epidemic*. Thousand Oaks, CA: Sage Publications.

Klotter, J. C. (2000). *Our Kentucky: A study of the Bluegrass State*. Lexington: University Press of Kentucky.

Klotter, J. C. (2003). *Kentucky justice, southern honor, and American manhood: Understanding the life and death of Richard Reid*. Baton Rouge: Louisiana State University Press.

Koss, M. P. (1992). The under detection of rape: Methodological choice influences incidence estimates. *Journal of Social Issues, 48*, 61–75.

Koss, M. P., Dinero, T. E., Seibel, C. A., & Cox, S. L. (1988). Stranger and acquaintance rape: Are there differences in the victim's experience? *Psychology of Women Quarterly, 12*, 1–24.

Koss, M. P., & Gidycz, C. A. (1985). Sexual Experiences Survey: Reliability and validity. *Journal of Consulting and Clinical Psychology, 53*, 422–423.

Koss, M. P., Gidycz, C. A., & Wisniewski, N. (1987). The scope of rape: Incidence and prevalence of sexual aggression and victimization in a national sample of higher education students. *Journal of Counseling and Clinical Psychology, 55* (2), 162–170.

Koss, M. P., Goodman, L. A., Browne, A., Fitzgerald, L. F., Keita, G. P., & Russo, N. F. (1999). *No safe haven: Male violence against women at home, at work, and in the community.* Washington, DC: American Psychological Association.

Koss, M. P., & Oros, C. J. (1982). Sexual Experiences Survey: A research instrument investigating sexual aggression and victimization. *Journal of Consulting and Clinical Psychology, 50,* 455–457.

Koziol-McLain, J., & Campbell, J. C. (2001). Universal screening and mandatory reporting: An update on two important issues for victims/survivors of intimate partner violence. *Journal of Emergency Nursing, 27,* 602–606.

Kratochvil, R. (2010). Intimate partner violence during pregnancy: Exploring the efficacy of a mandatory reporting statute. *Houston Journal of Health Law & Policy, 10,* 63–113.

Labriola, M., Bradley, S., O'Sullivan, C. S., Rempel, M., & Moore, S. (2009). *A national portrait of domestic violence courts* (2006-WG-BX-0001). Washington, DC: National Institute of Justice.

Lancaster, N. (1985). Judicial reform in Kentucky: Dedication, desire for excellence led to 1975 passage of judicial article. *Accent on the Courts, 7* (4), 1–3, 24–28.

Lane, F. S. (2000). *Obscene profits: The entrepreneurs of pornography in the cyber age.* New York: Routledge.

Langan, P. A., & Levin, D. J. (2002). *Recidivism of prisoners released in 1994.* Bureau of Justice Statistics (NCJ 193427). Washington, DC: US Department of Justice.

Langford, L., Isaac, N. E., & Kabat, S. (1998). Homicides related to intimate partner violence in Massachusetts. *Homicide Studies, 2,* 353–377.

Lawless, D. G. (2012, September 12). Personal interview.

Lawson, R. G. (1969–1970). Criminal law revision in Kentucky: Part 1—Homicide and assault. *Kentucky Law Journal, 58,* 242–274.

Lawson, R. G. (1998–1999). Interpretation of the Kentucky Rules of Evidence: What happened to the common law? *Kentucky Law Journal, 87* (3), 517–582.

Lawson, R. G. (1999–2000). Modifying the Kentucky Rules of Evidence: A separation of powers issue. *Kentucky Law Journal, 88* (3), 525–589.

Lawson, R. G. (2005). Difficult times in Kentucky corrections: Aftershocks of a "tough on crime" philosophy. *Kentucky Law Journal, 93* (2), 305–376.

Lawson, R. G. (2012, September 14). Personal interview.

Legislative Ethics Commission. (2011). *Annual report: 2010–2011.* Frankfort, KY: Author.

Legislative Research Commission. (1970). *General Assembly action: 1970 regular session* (Informational Bulletin 84). Frankfort, KY: Author.

Legislative Research Commission. (1972). *General Assembly action: 1972 regular session* (Informational Bulletin 98). Frankfort, KY: Author.

Legislative Research Commission. (1974). *General Assembly action: 1974 regular session* (Informational Bulletin 107). Frankfort, KY: Author.

Legislative Research Commission. (1976). *General Assembly action: 1976 regular session* (Informational Bulletin 113). Frankfort, KY: Author.

Legislative Research Commission. (1978). *General Assembly action: 1978 regular session* (Informational Bulletin 128). Frankfort, KY: Author.

Legislative Research Commission. (1980). *General Assembly action: 1980 regular session* (Informational Bulletin 135). Frankfort, KY: Author.

Legislative Research Commission. (1982). *General Assembly action: 1982 regular session* (Informational Bulletin 143). Frankfort, KY: Author.

Legislative Research Commission. (1984). *General Assembly action: 1984 regular session* (Informational Bulletin 147). Frankfort, KY: Author.

Legislative Research Commission. (1986). *General Assembly action: 1986 regular session* (Informational Bulletin 154). Frankfort, KY: Author.

Legislative Research Commission. (1988). *General Assembly action: 1988 regular session* (Informational Bulletin 162). Frankfort, KY: Author.

Legislative Research Commission. (1990). *General Assembly action: 1990 regular session* (Informational Bulletin 170). Frankfort, KY: Author.

Legislative Research Commission. (1992). *General Assembly action: 1992 regular session* (Informational Bulletin 182). Frankfort, KY: Author.

Legislative Research Commission. (1994). *General Assembly action: 1994 regular session* (Informational Bulletin 190). Frankfort, KY: Author.

Legislative Research Commission. (1996). *General Assembly action: 1996 regular session* (Informational Bulletin 197). Frankfort, KY: Author.

Legislative Research Commission. (1998). *General Assembly action: 1998 regular session* (Informational Bulletin 200). Frankfort, KY: Author.

Legislative Research Commission. (2000). *General Assembly action: 2000 regular session* (Informational Bulletin 203). Frankfort, KY: Author.

Legislative Research Commission. (2001). *General Assembly action: 2001 regular session* (Informational Bulletin 204). Frankfort, KY: Author.

Legislative Research Commission. (2002). *General Assembly action: 2002 regular session* (Informational Bulletin 207). Frankfort, KY: Author.

Legislative Research Commission. (2003). *General Assembly action: 2003 regular session* (Informational Bulletin 211). Frankfort, KY: Author.

Legislative Research Commission. (2004). *General Assembly action: 2004 regular session* (Informational Bulletin 214). Frankfort, KY: Author.

Legislative Research Commission. (2005). *General Assembly action: 2005 regular session* (Informational Bulletin 217). Frankfort, KY: Author.

Legislative Research Commission. (2006). *General Assembly action: 2006 regular session* (Informational Bulletin 220). Frankfort, KY: Author.

Legislative Research Commission. (2007). *General Assembly action: 2007 regular session* (Informational Bulletin 223). Frankfort, KY: Author.

Legislative Research Commission. (2008). *General Assembly action: 2008 regular session* (Informational Bulletin 229). Frankfort, KY: Author.

Legislative Research Commission. (2009). *General Assembly action: 2009 regular session* (Informational Bulletin 229). Frankfort, KY: Author.

Legislative Research Commission. (2010). *General Assembly action: 2010 regular session* (Informational Bulletin 232). Frankfort, KY: Author.

Legislative Research Commission. (2011). *General Assembly action: 2011 regular session* (Informational Bulletin 235). Frankfort, KY: Author.

Legislative Research Commission. (2012). *General Assembly action: 2012 regular session* (Informational Bulletin 238). Frankfort, KY: Author.

Legislative Research Commission. (2013). *The Constitution of the Commonwealth of Kentucky* (Informational Bulletin 59). Frankfort, KY: Author.

Legrave, R. (1998). A supervised emancipation. In F. Thébauld (Ed.), *A history of women in the west: Toward a cultural identity in the twentieth century* (p. 474). Cambridge, MA: Harvard University Press.

Lemon, N. (2009). *Domestic violence law* (3rd ed.). St Paul, MN: West Group.

Lemon, N. K. D. (2001). *Domestic violence law.* St. Paul, MN: West Group.

Leonard, K. E., Quigley, B. M., & Collins, R. L. (2002). Physical aggression in the lives of young adults: Prevalence, location and severity among college and community samples. *Journal of Interpersonal Violence, 17* (5), 533–550.

Levitt, M. J., Silver, M. E., & Franco, N. (1996). Troublesome relationships: A part of human experience. *Journal of Social and Personal Relationships, 13* (4), 523–536.

Lewis, J. J. (2011). *About women's history.* http://womenshistory.about.com/od/quotes/a/andrea_dworkin_2.htm.

Lewis, S. F., & Fremouw, W. (2001). Dating violence: A critical review of the literature. *Clinical Psychology Review, 21* (1), 105–127.

Lisak, D., Gardinier, L., Nicksa, S., & Cote, A. (2010). False allegations of sexual assault: An analysis of ten years of reported cases. *Violence Against Women, 16* (2), 1318–1334.

Loftus, T. (1995, September 14). Plan would alert crime victims all over the state. *Louisville Courier-Journal.*

Logan, J., Hill, H. A., Black, M. L., Crosby, A. E., Karch, D. L., Barnes, J. D., & Lubell, K. M. (2008). Characteristics of perpetrators in homicide-followed-by-suicide incidents: National Violent Death Reporting System: 17 U.S. states, 2003–2005. *American Journal of Epidemiology, 168* (9), 1056–1064.

Logan, T. K., Leukefeld, C., & Walker, R. (2000). Stalking as a variant of intimate violence: Implications from a young adult sample. *Violence & Victims, 15* (1), 91–111.

Logan, T. K., Shannon, L., Walker, R., & Faragher, T. (2006). Protective orders: Questions and conundrums. *Trauma, Violence & Abuse, 7,* 175–205.

Logan, T. K., & Walker, R. (2009). Civil protective order outcomes: Violations and perceptions of effectiveness. *Journal of Interpersonal Violence, 24* (4), 332–348.

Logan, T. K., & Walker, R. (2010a). Civil protective order effectiveness: Justice or just a piece of paper? *Violence & Victims, 25,* 332–348.

Logan, T. K., & Walker, R. (2010b). Toward a deeper understanding of the harms caused by partner stalking. *Violence & Victims, 25* (4), 440–455.

Logan, T. K., Walker, R., Jordan, C. E., & Leukefeld, C. (2006). *Women and victimization: Contributing factors, interventions, and implications.* Washington, DC: American Psychological Association.

Long, M. (2012, September 20). Personal interview.

Loseke, D. (2000). Ethos, pathos, and social problems: Reflections on formula narratives. *Perspectives on Social Problems, 12,* 41–54.

Loving, J. (2013, April 18). Personal interview.

MacDonald, J. M., Manz, P. W., Alpert, G. P., & Dunham, R. G. (2003). Use of force: Examining the relationship between calls for service and the balance of police force and suspect resistance. *Journal of Criminal Justice, 31,* 119–127.

MacKinnon, C. A. (1984). Commentaries: Not a moral issue. *Yale Law & Policy Review, 2* (2), 321–345.

Maguigan, H. (1991). Battered women and self-defense: Myths and misconceptions in current reform proposals. *University of Pennsylvania Law Review, 140,* 379–486.

Maguire, K., & Pastore, A. L. (Eds.). (1999). *Sourcebook of criminal justice statistics* (NCJ 176356). Washington, DC: Bureau of Justice Statistics, US Department of Justice.

Mahoney, P. (1999). High rape chronicity and low rates of help-seeking among wife rape survivors in a nonclinical sample: Implications for research and practice. *Violence Against Women, 5* (9), 993–1016.

Maiuro, R. D. (2001). Sticks and stones may break my bones, but names will also hurt me: Psychological abuse in domestically violent relationships. In K. D. O'Leary & R. D. Maiuro (Eds.), *Psychological abuse in violent domestic relations* (pp. ix–xx). New York: Springer.

Malecha, A. T., Lemmey, D., McFarlane, J., Willson, P., Fredland, N., Gist, J., & Schultz, P. (2000). Mandatory reporting of intimate partner violence: Safety or retaliatory abuse for women? *Journal of Women's Health and Gender-Based Medicine, 9* (1), 75–78.

Malphurs, J. E., & Cohen, D. (2002). A newspaper surveillance study of homicide-suicide in the United States. *American Journal of Forensic Medical Pathology, 19,* 275–283.

Mann, C. R. (1998). Black female homicides in the United States. *Journal of Interpersonal Violence, 5,* 176–201.

Marital-rape bill gets approval of house panel. (1990, February 16). *Lexington Herald-Leader.*

Marital rape permissible under state law. (1989, October 25). *Paintsville (KY) Herald.*

Marsh, J. C., Geist, A., & Caplan, N. (1982). *Rape and the limits of reform.* Boston: Auburn House.

Marx, B. P., Calhoun, K. S., Wilson, A. E., & Meyerson, L. (2001). Sexual revictimization prevention: An outcome evaluation. *Journal of Consulting and Clinical Psychology, 69,* 25–32.

Marzian, M. L. (2013, April 11). Personal interview.

Marzuk, P., Tardiff, K., & Hirsch, C. (1992). The epidemiology of murder-suicide. *Journal of the American Medical Association, 267,* 3179–3183.

Maxwell, C. D., Garner, J. H., & Fagan, J. A. (2001). *The effects of arrest on intimate partner violence: New evidence from the Spouse Assault Replication Program.* Washington, DC: US Department of Justice, National Institute of Justice.

May, D. C. (2001). The effect of fear of sexual victimization on adolescent fear of crime. *Sociological Spectrum, 21,* 141–174.

McConnell, S. (2004, Spring). Advocacy in organizations: The elements of success. *Generations: A Journal of the American Society on Aging,* 25–30.

McCreedy, K., & Dennis, B. (1996). Sex related offenses and the fear of crime on campus. *Journal of Counseling and Development, 66,* 414–418.

McCullough, D. (1992). *Brave companions: Portraits in history.* Chicago: Simon & Schuster.

McFarlane, J., Campbell, J. C., Wilt, S., Sachs, C. J., Ulrich, Y., & Xu, X. (1999). Stalking and intimate partner femicide. *Homicide Studies, 3* (4), 300–316.

McFarlane, J., Malecha, A., Gist, J., Watson, K., Batten, E., Hall, I., et al. (2004). Protection orders and intimate partner violence: An 18-month study of 150 black, Hispanic, and white women. *American Journal of Public Health, 94* (4), 613–618.

McFarlane, J., Willson, P., Lemmey, D., & Malecha, A. (2000). Women filing assault charges on an intimate partner: Criminal justice outcome and future violence experienced. *Violence Against Women, 6* (4), 396–408.

McLaren, J. A., Henson, V., & Stone, W. E. (2009). The sexual assault nurse examiner and the successful sexual assault prosecution. *Women & Criminal Justice, 19,* 137–152.

Meloy, J. R. (1989). Unrequited love and the wish to kill: Diagnosis and treatment of borderline erotomania. *Bulletin of the Menninger Clinic, 53,* 477–492.

Meloy, J. R. (2000). The nature and dynamics of sexual homicide: An integrative review. *Aggression and Violent Behavior, 5* (1), 1–22.

Mercy, J. A., & Saltzman, L. E. (1989). Fatal violence among spouses in the United States: 1976–85. *American Journal of Public Health, 79,* 595–599.

Metzmeier, K. X. (2006). United at last: The judicial article and the struggle to reform Kentucky's courts. In *History of the courts of Kentucky* (Legal Studies Research Paper No. 2007-14). Louisville, KY: University of Louisville Law School.

Miller, N. (2004). *Domestic violence: A review of state legislation defining police and prosecution duties and powers.* Alexandria, VA: Institute for Law and Justice. http://www.ilj.org/publication/DV_Legislation-3.pdf.

Miller, P. M. (2004). Brereton C. Jones. In L. Harrison (Ed.), *Kentucky's governors* (updated ed., pp. 244–250). Lexington: University Press of Kentucky.

Miller, S. L. (2005). *Victims as offenders: The paradox of women's violence in relationships.* New Brunswick, NJ: Rutgers University Press.

Miller, S. L., Iovanni, L., & Kelly, K. D. (2011). Violence against women and the criminal justice system. In C. Renzetti, J. L. Edleson, & R. K. Bergen (Eds.), *Sourcebook on Violence Against Women* (2nd ed., pp. 267–287). Los Angeles: Sage Publications.

Milroy, C. M. (1995). The epidemiology of homicide-suicide (dyadic death). *Forensic Science International, 71,* 117–122.

Minton, J. (2010). *In re: Order amending Rules of Criminal Procedure (RCr); Rules of Civil Procedure (CR); and Family Court Rules of Procedure and Practice (FCRPP).* Frankfort: Supreme Court of Kentucky.

Mohandie, K., Meloy, J. R., McGowan, M. G., & Williams, J. (2006). The RECON typology of stalking: Reliability and validity based upon a large sample of North American stalkers. *Journal of Forensic Sciences, 51* (1), 147–155.

Moloney, M. R. (2012, August 13). Personal interview.

Monhollen v. Commonwealth, 947 S.W.2nd 61 (Ky. Ct. App. 1997).

Moracco, K. E., Andersen, K., Buchanan, R. M., Espersen, J. M., & Duffy, C. (2011). Who are the defendants in domestic violence protection order cases? *Violence Against Women, 16* (11), 1201–1223.

Morgan, D. T. (2003). *Southern Baptist sisters: In search of status 1845–2000.* Macon, GA: University of Mercer Press.

Mrs. Sawyer to head commission of women. (1970, September 17). *Jefferson Reporter* (Buechel, KY).

Muftic, L. R., Bouffard, J. A., & Bouffard, L. A. (2007). An explanatory study of women arrested for intimate partner violence: Violent women or violent resistance? *Journal of Interpersonal Violence, 22* (6), 753–774.

Mullen, P. E., & Pathé, M. (1994). The pathological extensions of love. *British Journal of Psychiatry, 165,* 614–623.

Murphy, C. M., & Cascardi, M. (1993). Psychological aggression and abuse in marriage. In R. L. Hampton, T. P. Gullotta, G. R. Adams, E. H. Potter, & R. P. Weissberg (Eds.), *Family violence: Prevention and treatment* (Vol. 1, pp. 86–112). Newbury Park, CA: Sage Publications.

Mustaine, E. E., & Tewksbury, R. (1999). A routine activity theory explanation for women's stalking victimizations. *Violence Against Women, 5* (1), 43–62.

Myers, W., & Blashfield, R. (1997). Psychopathology and personality in juvenile sexual homicide offenders. *Journal of the American Academy of Psychiatry and the Law, 25,* 497–508.

Nation, C. A. (1909). *The use and need of the life of Carry A. Nation* (Rev. ed.). Topeka, KS: F. M. Steves & Sons. (Kansas Historical Society call no. K B N19 1909)

National Association of Crime Victim Compensation Boards. (2012). *Crime victim compensation: An overview.* Alexandria, VA: Author. http://www.nacvcb.org/index.asp?bid=14.

National Center for Victims of Crime. (2005–2006). *Report to Congress on stalking and domestic violence, 2005 through 2006* (NCJ 186157). Washington, DC: US Department of Justice, Office of Violence Against Women.

National Council of State Legislatures. (2012a). Annual versus biennial legislative sessions. http://www.ncsl.org/legislatures-elections/legislatures/annual-versus-biennial-legislative-sessions.aspx.

National Council of State Legislatures. (2012b). Term limited states. http://www.ncsl.org/legislatures-elections/legisdata/chart-of-term-limits-states.aspx.

National Council of State Legislatures. (2012c). Women in state legislatures: 2012 legislative session. http://www.ncsl.org/legislatures-elections/wln/women-in-state-legislatures-2012.aspx.

National Criminal Justice Association. (1993). *Project to develop a model anti-stalking code for states* (NCJ 144477). Washington, DC: US Department of Justice, National Institute of Justice.

National Organization for Women. (2011). Gonzales *ruling endangers women and children.* http://www.now.org/nnt/summerfall-2005/gonzalesvcastlerock.html.

National Organization for Women Legal Defense and Education Fund. (1987). *A state-by-state guide to women's legal rights.* New York: National Organization for Women.

National Weather Service. (2012, March 2). *East Kentucky tornadoes.* Jackson, KY: National Oceanic and Atmospheric Administration. www.crh.noaa.gov.

Negrey, C. (1999). Life in the balance: Integrating employment and family. In M. Smith-Mello, M. T. Childress, J. Sollinger, & B. M. Sebastian (Eds.), *The future well-being of women in Kentucky* (pp. 13–24). Frankfort: Kentucky Long-Term Policy Research Center.

Nicklin, J. E. (1999). Colleges differ widely on how they tally incidents under crime reporting law. *Chronicle of Higher Education, 45* (38), A41.

Nicklin, J. E. (2000). Shift in crime-reporting law fails to end debate over accuracy of statistics. *Chronicle of Higher Education, 46* (40), A50.

Niedermeier, L. E. (2007). *Eliza Calvert Hall: Kentucky author and suffragist.* Lexington: University Press of Kentucky.

Nobles, M. R., Fox, K. A., Piquero, N., & Piquero, A. R. (2009). Career dimensions of stalking victimization and perpetration. *Justice Quarterly, 26,* 476–503.

Notable Kentucky African Americans Database. (2011). University of Kentucky Libraries. http://www.uky.edu/Libraries/NKAA/subject .php?sub_id=4.

Nourse, V. (1997). Passion's progress: Modern law reform and the provocation defense. *Yale Law Review, 106* (5), 1331–1448.

Office for Victims of Crime. (2011). *SART toolkit: Resources for sexual assault response teams.* Washington, DC: Office of Justice Programs, US Department of Justice.

Office for Victims of Crime. (2012). *Crime victims fund.* Washington, DC: Office of Justice Programs, US Department of Justice. http://www.ovc .gov/pubs/crimevictimsfundfs/intro.html.

Office of the Kentucky Attorney General. (1991). *Attorney General's Task Force on Domestic Violence Crime: General findings and comprehensive recommendations.* Frankfort, KY: Author.

Office of the Kentucky Attorney General. (1995). *Attorney General's Task Force on Child Sexual Abuse: Final report.* Frankfort, KY: Author.

Painter, N. I. (1996). *Sojourner Truth: A life, a symbol.* New York: W. W. Norton.

Patton, J. (2012, February 11). WEG ended 2010 with financial loss despite aid from Lyons, Princess Haya. *Lexington Herald-Leader.*

Perry, A. L. (2001). Federal domestic violence firearms prohibitions continue to withstand constitutional scrutiny. *Domestic Violence Report, 6,* 89–90.

Pleck, E. (1987). *Domestic tyranny: The making of American social policy against family violence from colonial times to present.* New York: Oxford University Press.

Polletta, F. (2006). *It was like a fever: Storytelling in protest and politics.* Chicago: University of Chicago Press.

Porter, J. W. (1911). Woman's suffrage. *Western Recorder,* 3.

Porter, J. W. (1916). National Suffrage Association. *Western Recorder,* 8.

Potter, G. (Ed.). (1997). *Kentucky women: Two centuries of indomitable spirit and vision.* Louisville, KY: Big Tree Press.

Powell, R. A. (2001). *Kentucky governors.* Tampa, FL: Silverhawke Publications.

Powers, G. D. (1995). *I shared the dream: The pride, passion, and politics of the first black woman senator from Kentucky.* Forest Hills, NJ: New Horizon Press.

Rape, Abuse, & Incest National Network. (2009). Stranger rape: Major categories. http://www.rainn.org/get-information/types-of-sexual-assault/stranger-rape.

Rebovich, D. (1996). Prosecution response to domestic violence: Results of a survey of large jurisdictions. In E. Buzawa & C. Buzawa (Eds.), *Do arrests and restraining orders work?* (pp. 176–191). Thousand Oaks, CA: Sage Publications.

Recktenwald, E. (2012, September 26). Personal interview.

Renkey, L. E. (1971). *Kentucky Penal Code.* Frankfort: Kentucky Crime Commission and Legislative Research Commission.

Rennison, C. M., & Welchans, S. (2000). *Intimate partner violence* (Crime Data Brief, NCJ 178247). Washington, DC: US Department of Justice, Bureau of Justice Statistics.

Rep. Gross Clay Lindsay dies at age seventy-seven. (2008). *West Kentucky Journal.* http://www.westkyjournal.com/news.php?viewStory=432.

Resnick, H. S., Holmes, M. M., Kilpatrick, D. G., Clum, G., Acierno, R., Best, C. L., & Saunders, B. E. (2000). Predictors of post-rape medical care in a national sample of women. *American Journal of Preventive Medicine, 19* (4), 214–219.

Richart, D., & Town, J. (1992). *Beyond the human cost: A preliminary economic analysis of the costs attributed to child sexual abuse in Kentucky.* Louisville: Kentucky Youth Advocates.

Richie, B. (2000). A black feminist reflection on the antiviolence movement. *Signs: Journal of Women in Culture and Society, 25* (4), 1133–1137.

Robinson, P. H., & Dubber, M. D. (1999). *An introduction to the Model Penal Code.* https://www.law.upenn.edu/fac/phrobins/intromodpencode.pdf.

Rodriguez, M. A., McLoughlin, E., Nah, G., & Campbell, J. C. (2001). Mandatory reporting of domestic violence injuries to the police: What do emergency departments think? *Journal of the American Medical Association, 286* (5), 580–583.

Rodriguez, S. S., Quiroga, H., & Bauer, M. (1996). Breaking the silence: Battered women's perspectives on medical care. *Archives of Family Medicine, 5,* 153–158.

Rose v. Council for Better Education, 790 S.W.2d 186, 60 Ed.Law Rep. 1289 (1989).

Roth, M. (2012, November 1). Personal interview.

Rusk v. State., 43 Md. App. 476, 406 A.2d 624 (Md. Ct. Spec. App. 1979).

Russell, D. E. H. (1990). *Rape in marriage* (2nd ed.). Bloomington: Indiana University Press.

Ryan, E., & Fraas, E. D. (2004). Martha Layne Collins. In L. Harrison (Ed.), *Kentucky's governors* (updated ed., pp. 229–236). Lexington: University Press of Kentucky.

Salazar, L. F., Baker, C. K., Price, A. W., & Carlin, K. (2003). Moving beyond the individual: Examining the effects of domestic violence policies on social norms. *American Journal of Community Psychology, 32* (3/4), 253–264.

Saxe, J. G. (1869, March 27). Impeachment trial. *University Chronicle* (University of Michigan–Ann Arbor), 3 (23), 4.

Schaefer, J., Caetano, R., & Clark, C. (1998). Rates of intimate partner violence in the United States. *American Journal of Public Health, 88* (11), 1702–1704.

Schafran, L. (1993) Women in the criminal justice system: Writing and reading about rape: A primer. *St John's Law Review, 66,* 979–1045.

Schaum, M., & Parrish, K. (1995). *Stalked: Breaking the silence on the crime of stalking in America.* New York: Pocket Books.

Schechter, S. (1982). *Women and male violence: The visions and struggles of the battered women's movement.* Boston: South End.

Schneider, B. (2012, December 24). Tornadoes, drought team up for top spot. *Lexington Herald-Leader.*

Schneider, E. M. (2000). *Battered women & feminist lawmaking.* New Haven, CT: Yale University Press.

Schneider, E. M., & Wildman, S. M. (2011). *Women and the law stories.* New York: Thomson Reuters/Foundation Press.

Schulhofer, S. (2001). Society needs better laws against rape. In M. E. Williams (Ed.), *Rape* (pp. 143–152). San Diego, CA: Greenhaven Press.

Schulman, M. (1979). *A survey of spousal violence against women in Kentucky* (Study No. 792701, conducted for Kentucky Commission on Women, sponsored by the US Department of Justice, Law Enforcement Assistance Administration). Washington, DC: Government Printing Office.

Searles, P., & Berger, R. J. (1987). The current status of rape reform legislation: An examination of state statutes. *Women's Rights Law Reporter, 10,* 25–43.

Seidman, I., & Vickers, S. (2005). The second wave: An agenda for the next thirty years of rape law reform. *Suffolk University Law Review, 38,* 468–491.

Sexton, R. F., & Cross, A. (2004). Louie B. Nunn. In L. Harrison (Ed.), *Kentucky's governors* (updated ed., pp. 206–210). Lexington: University Press of Kentucky.

Sharps, P. W., Koziol-McCain, J., Campbell, J., McFarlane, J., Sachs, C., & Xiao, X. (2001). Health care providers' missed opportunities for preventing femicide. *Preventive Medicine, 33* (5), 373–380.

Shepard, M. F., & Pence, E. L. (Eds.). (1999). *Community responses to domestic violence: Lessons from Duluth and beyond.* Thousand Oaks, CA: Sage Publications.

Sherman, L. (1992). The influence of criminology on criminal law: Evaluating for misdemeanor domestic violence. *Journal of Criminal Law & Criminology, 85* (1), 901–945.

Sherman, L. W., & Berk, R. A. (1984). The specific deterrence effects of arrest for domestic violence. *American Sociological Review, 49,* 261–272.

Sherman, L. W., Schmidt, J. D., Rogan, D. P., Smith, D. A., Gartin, P. R., Cohn, E. G., Collins, D., & Bacich, R. (1992). The variable effects of arrest on criminal careers: The Milwaukee domestic violence experiment. *Journal of Criminal Law & Criminology, 83,* 137–169.

Sherr, L. (1995). *Failure is impossible: Susan B. Anthony in her own words.* New York: Random House.

Shiels, M. (2000). Civil causes of action for stalking victims. *Victim Advocate: The Journal of the National Crime Victim Bar Association, 2* (2), 13–16.

Siegel, R. V. (1996). The rule of love: Wife beating as prerogative and privacy. *Yale Law Journal, 106,* 2116–2208.

Smith, A. (2001). Domestic violence laws: The voices of battered women. *Violence & Victims, 16* (1), 91–110.

Smith, C. W. (1988). "The rule of thumb": A historic perspective? *Focus, 1* (7), 1.

Smith, G. L. (2002). *Black America series: Lexington, Kentucky.* Lexington: University Press of Kentucky.

Smith v. Commonwealth, KyApp., 566 S.W.2d 181, 183 (1978).

Smith-Mello, M., Childress, M. T., Sollinger, J., & Sebastian, B. M. (1999). *The future well-being of women in Kentucky.* Frankfort: Kentucky Long-Term Policy Research Center.

Snyder, H., Finnegan, T., & Kang, W. (2007). *Easy access to the FBI's supplementary homicide reports: 1980–2005.* http://ojjdp.ncjrs.gov/ojstatbb/ezashr/.

Sonkin, D. J. (Ed.). (1987). *Domestic violence on trial: Psychological and legal dimensions of family violence.* New York: Springer Publishing.

Special sessions persist despite annual law-making sessions in Kentucky. (2012, April 16). *Lexington Herald-Leader.* http://www.kentucky.com/2012/04/16/2153476/special-sessions-persist-despite.html.

Spitzberg, B. (2002). The tactical topography of stalking victimization and management. *Trauma, Violence, & Abuse, 3* (4), 261–288.

Spitzberg, B., Nicastro, A., & Cousins, A. (1998). Exploring the interactional phenomenon of stalking and obsessive relational intrusion. *Communication Reports, 11* (1), 33–48.

Spitzberg, B. H., & Rhea, J. (1999). Obsessive relational intrusion and sexual coercion victimization. *Journal of Interpersonal Violence, 14,* 3–20.

Spohn, C., & Horney, J. (1992). *Rape law reform: A grassroots revolution and its impact.* New York: Plenum Press.

Sponsor: Marital rape bill could win OK this session. (1990, February 19). *Lexington Herald-Leader.*

Spousal rape bill clears Senate. (1990, March 28). *Lexington Herald-Leader.*

Sprague, S. S. (2004). Julian Morton Carroll. In L. Harrison (Ed.), *Kentucky's governors* (updated ed., pp. 217–220). Lexington: University Press of Kentucky.

Stacy, M. (2012, May 19). Marissa Alexander gets 20 years for firing warning shot. *Huffington Post.* http://www.huffingtonpost.com/2012/05/19/marissa-alexander-gets-20_n_1530035.html.

Stanko, E. A. (1985). *Intimate intrusions: Women's experience of male violence.* London: Unwin Hyman Publishers.

Stanton, E. C. (1887). Declaration of sentiments. In E. C. Stanton, S. B. Anthony, & M. J. Gage (Eds.), *History of woman suffrage* (Vol. 1, p. 70). Memphis TN: General Books.

Stark, E. (2007). *Coercive control: How men entrap women in personal life.* New York: Oxford University Press.

Starr, K., Hobart, M., & Fawcett, J. (2004). *Findings and recommendations from the Washington State Domestic Violence Fatality Review.* Seattle: Washington Coalition against Domestic Violence.

State v. Frazier, 48 Tex. Crim. 142, 86 S.W. 754 (1945).

State v. Oliver, 70 N.C. 60, 61–62 (1873).

State v. Rhodes, 61 N.C. 4 (1868).

State v. Rusk, 424 A. 2d 720, 289 Md. 230 (1981).

Steffensmeier, D. J., & Allan, E. (1996). Gender and crime: Toward a gendered paradigm of female offending. *Annual Review of Sociology, 22,* 459–487.

Stein, K. (2013, April 10). Personal interview.

Stets, J. E., & Straus, M. A. (1990). Gender differences in reporting of marital violence and its medical and psychological consequences. In M. A. Straus & R. J. Gelles (Eds.), *Physical violence in American families: Risk factors and adaptation to violence in 8,145 families* (pp. 151–166). New Brunswick, NJ: Transaction.

Stewart, H. R. (1991). *Women in Kentucky: A documented profile.* Frankfort: Cabinet for Workforce Development, Commonwealth of Kentucky.

Stivers, R. (2012, December 5). Personal interview.

Straus, M. A. (1977). Wife-beating: How common and why? *Victimology, 2,* 443–458.

Straus, M. A. (1979). Measuring intrafamily conflict and violence: The Conflict Tactics (CT) Scales. *Journal of Marriage and Family, 41* (1), 75–88.

Straus, M. A. (2011). Gender symmetry and mutuality in perpetration of clinical-level partner violence: Empirical evidence and implications for prevention and treatment. *Aggression and Violent Behavior, 16,* 279–288.

Straus, M. A., & Gelles, R. (1986). Societal change and change in family violence from 1975 to 1985 as revealed by two national surveys. *Journal of Marriage and the Family, 48,* 465–479.

Straus, M. A., & Gelles, R. (1990). *Physical violence in American families: Risk factors and adaptation to violence in 8,145 families.* New Brunswick, NJ: Transaction.

Straus, M. A., Gelles, R., & Steinmetz, S. (1980). *Behind closed doors: Violence in the American family.* Garden City, NY: Anchor Press.

Stumbo, G. D. (2012, September 18). Personal interview.

Sugarman, R. (1999). *The status of Kentucky women in higher education.* Frankfort: Kentucky Long-Term Policy Research Center.

Tachau, M. K., & McClure, B. L. (2004). John Y. Brown, Jr. In L. Harrison (Ed.), *Kentucky's governors* (updated ed., pp. 221–228). Lexington: University Press of Kentucky.

Tangonan, S. (2001, October 17). Officer was involved in '93 domestic case: Detective now is charged in another dispute. *Louisville Courier-Journal.*

Tarasoff v. Regents of the University of California, 17 Cal. 3d 425, 551 P.2d 334, 131 Cal. Rptr. 14 (Cal. 1976).

Thébaud, F. (1997).The Great War and the triumph of sexual division. In F. Thébaud (Ed.), *A history of women in the West: Toward a cultural identity in the twentieth century* (pp. 21–75). Cambridge, MA: Harvard University Press.

Thurman v. City of Torrington, 595 F.Supp. 1521 (1984).

Tice, K. (1997). Madeline McDowell Breckinridge: 1872–1920. In G. Potter (Ed.), *Kentucky women: Two centuries of indomitable spirit and vision* (pp. 26–27). Louisville, KY: Big Tree Press.

Tjaden, P. (2003). Prevalence and characteristics of stalking. In M. P. Brewster (Ed.), *Stalking: Psychology, risk factors, interventions, and law* (pp. 1-1-1-19). Kingston, NJ: Civic Research Institute.

Tjaden, P., & Thoennes, N. (1998). *Stalking in America: Findings from the National Violence Against Women Survey.* Washington, DC: National Institute of Justice, Centers for Disease Control and Prevention.

Tjaden, P., & Thoennes, N. (2000a). *Extent, nature and consequences of intimate partner violence* (NCJ 181867). Washington, DC: National Institute of Justice.

Tjaden, P., & Thoennes, N. (2000b). The role of stalking in domestic violence crime reports generated by the Colorado Springs Police Department. *Violence & Victims, 15* (4), 427–441.

Touraine, A. (1981). *The voice and the eye: An analysis of social movements.* Cambridge: Cambridge University Press.

Travis, A., Johnson, L., & Milroy, C. (2007). Homicide-suicide (dyadic death), homicide and firearms use in England and Wales. *American Journal of Forensic Medical Pathology, 28,* 314–318.

Tuerkheimer, D. (2004). Recognizing and remedying the harm of battering: A call to criminalize domestic violence. *Journal of Criminal Law & Criminology, 94* (4), 959–1032.

United States v. Commonwealth, 563 F.2d 307 (6th Cir. 1977).

United States v. Morrison, 529 U.S. 598, 120 S.Ct. 1740 (2000).

University of Kentucky, Special Collections and Digital Programs Division. (2010). *A chronology of UK.* http://web.archive.org/web/20071028003431/www.uky.edu/Libraries/libpage.php?lweb_id=311&llib_id=13.

US Department of Commerce. (2012). *Law enforcement, courts, and prisons: Crimes and crime rates.* Washington DC: US Census Bureau, US Department of Commerce.

US Department of Justice. (2000). *Violence by intimates.* Washington, DC: Bureau of Justice Statistics.

US Department of Justice. (2001). *Stalking and domestic violence: Report to Congress* (NCJ 186157). Washington, DC: Office of Justice Programs.

US Department of Justice. (2002). *Enforcement of protective orders* (NCJ 189190). Washington, DC: Author.

Van Houten, M. (Holcomb). (2013, April 11). Personal interview.

Violence Against Women Act (1994). 42 U.S.C. § 3796gg-4.

Violent Crime Control and Law Enforcement [Violence Against Women] Act (1994). HR 3355, Pub. L. 103-322.

Walker, E. (2012, October 9). Personal interview.

Wall, M. J. (2010). *How Kentucky became southern.* Lexington: University Press of Kentucky.

Walsh, S., & Hemenway, D. (2005). Intimate partner violence: Homicides followed by suicides in Kentucky. *Journal of the Kentucky Medical Association, 103,* 589–600.

Ward, D., & Mann, J. L. (2011). *The handbook for campus safety and security reporting* (ED-04-CO-0059/0004). Washington, DC: US Department of Education, Office of Postsecondary Education.

Warr, M. (1984). Fear of victimization: Why are women and the elderly more afraid? *Social Science Quarterly, 65,* 681–702.

Warr, M. (1985). Fear of rape among urban women. *Social Problems, 32,* 238–250.

Wechsler, H. (1968). Codification of criminal law in the United States: The Model Penal Code. *Columbia Law Review, 68* (8), 1425–1456.

White, J. W., & Koss, M. P. (1991). Courtship violence: Incidence and prevalence in a national sample of higher education students. *Violence & Victims, 6,* 247–256.

Wilcox, P., Jordan, C. E., & Pritchard, A. J. (2006). Fear of acquaintance versus stranger rape as a "master status": Towards refinement of the "shadow of sexual assault." *Violence & Victims, 21* (3), 357–373.

Wilcox, P., Jordan, C. E., & Pritchard, A. J. (2007). A multidimensional examination of campus safety: Victimization, perceptions of danger, worry about crime, and precautionary behavior among college women in the post-Clery era. *Crime & Delinquency, 53* (2), 219–254.

Wilkinson, D. E. (2000). Mary E. Britton. In J. E. Kleber (Ed.), *The Kentucky encyclopedia* (p. 125). Lexington: University Press of Kentucky. http://www.kyenc.org.

Williams, S. N. (1984). Rape reform legislation and evidentiary concerns: The law in Pennsylvania. *University of Pittsburgh Law Review, 44,* 955–975.

Wilson, E. (1982). Interview with Andrea Dworkin. *Feminist Review, 11,* 23–29.

Wilson, M., Daly, M., & Daniele, A. (1995). Familicide: The killing of spouse and children. *Aggressive Behavior, 21,* 275–291.

Wistrom, D. B. (2013, March 9). Kansas house approves bill eliminating statute of limitations in rape cases. *Wichita Eagle.*

Wolfson, A. (1982, March 13). Legislators' letter attacks spouse abuse bill. *Louisville (KY) Times.*

Wooldredge, J. (2007). Convicting and incarcerating felony offenders of intimate assault and the odds of new assault charges. *Journal of Criminal Justice, 35* (4), 379–389.

Worden, P. (2000). The changing boundaries of the criminal justice system: Redefining the problem and the response in domestic violence. In C. Friel (Ed.), *Criminal justice 2000: Vol. 2. Boundary changes in criminal justice organizations* (pp. 215–266).Washington, DC: National Institute of Justice.

Wright, G. C. (1990). *Racial violence in Kentucky, 1865–1940: Lynchings, mob rule, and "legal lynchings."* Baton Rouge: Louisiana State University Press.

X, Laura. (1999). Accomplishing the impossible: An advocate's notes from the successful campaign to make marital and date rape a crime in all 50 U.S. states and other countries. *Violence Against Women, 5* (9), 1064–1081.

Zorza, J. (1992). The criminal law of misdemeanor domestic violence, 1970–1990. *Journal of Criminal Law & Criminology, 83,* 240–279.

Zorza, J. (Ed.). (2002). *Violence against women: Law, prevention, protection, enforcement, treatment, health.* Kingston, NJ: Civic Research Institute.

Index

Kentucky domestic violence and rape laws from pages 1–181 are referred to as "in Kentucky." From page 183 to the end of the book, all laws are Kentucky statutes unless otherwise specified. Chapter numbers for pages referring to endnotes are provided in parentheses as needed.

About the Author

Carol E. Jordan presently serves as executive director of the Institute for Policy Studies on Violence Against Women at the University of Kentucky and holds faculty appointments in the Departments of Psychology and Psychiatry. Jordan has a career spanning more than thirty years in public policy, legislative advocacy, research, and the development of programs concentrating on violence against women. She has authored three books, eight book chapters, and more than three dozen peer-reviewed journal articles on violence against women, particularly focusing on civil and criminal justice issues,

Carol E. Jordan, 2011. (Courtesy of the University of Kentucky)

the mental health effects of violence, the victimization of college women, and the legislative history of addressing gendered violence.

Jordan received her bachelor of science degree from Texas A&M University in 1980 and a master of science in clinical psychology from Eastern Kentucky University in 1983. Following graduate school, she held her first position in a domestic violence shelter and went on to serve as the first director of a statewide sexual and domestic violence program in the Department for Mental Health. In 1996 she was recruited by Governor Paul E. Patton to serve as the founding executive director for the Governor's Office of Child Abuse and Domestic Violence Services, a position she held for eight years. Ms. Jordan then helped create the University of Kentucky

Center for Research on Violence Against Women, serving as the first director of that program from 2003 until 2014.

Jordan has been recognized nationally by the U.S. Department of Justice, the U.S. Department of Health and Human Services, the National Foundation for the Improvement of Justice, and the National Sexual Violence Resource Center. She has also received awards from the Kentucky Domestic Violence Association, the Kentucky Association of Sexual Assault Programs, the Kentucky Mental Health Coalition, the Kentucky Psychological Association, and the Kentucky General Assembly for her work. In 2005 she was honored by the University of Kentucky with the Sarah Bennett Holmes Award for Outstanding Contributions on Behalf of Women, and in 2012 she received the William E. Lyons Award for Outstanding Service from the university. In 2010 she was awarded a Presidential Proclamation from Texas A&M University.

CPSIA information can be obtained at www.ICGtesting.com
Printed in the USA
BVOW01*0315240414

351543BV00002B/4/P